ANCIENT JAFFNA

Paráķrama Báhu the Great
carved on a rock at Polonnaruwa

[Photo by Plate Ltd.

ANCIENT JAFFNA

BEING

A RESEARCH INTO THE HISTORY OF JAFFNA

FROM

VERY EARLY TIMES

TO

THE PORTUGUESE PERIOD

MUDALIYAR C. RASANAYAGAM

FOREWORD BY

S. KRISHNASWAMI AIYANGAR

Published by

Facsimile Publisher
12 Pragati Market
Ashok Vihar, Ph-2
Delhi-110052
facsimilepublisher.com

Distribution Network
gyanbooks.com
India, USA, Canada, UK, Australia, France

ISBN : 978-93-5324-565-8 (HB)
First Published, 1926

2nd Impression 2020

Printed at: Gyan Press, Delhi.

Ancient Jaffna

Author: Mudaliyar C. Rasanayagam

RESPECTFULLY DEDICATED TO

His Excellency

SIR HUGH CLIFFORD, G.C.M.G., G.B.E.,

GOVERNOR OF CEYLON.

CONTENTS

PREFACE

THIS little volume is the unexpected result of an attempt to compile a School History of Jaffna. Almost unperceived my reading took me far afield, and led me to conclusions often directly opposed to the views hitherto generally accepted. I have thought it proper therefore to publish some of my studies, in order to have them criticised and corrected before they become parts of a more elaborate work. The 3rd and 5th Chapters were, for the same purpose of inviting discussion, read before the Ceylon Branch of the Royal Asiatic Society under the titles "The Tamil Kingdom of Jaffna and the Early Greek Writers" and "The Identification of the Port of Kalah." They are reprinted here with the Society's permission.

The book ought really to be dated 1923, for it was ready for the printers then. Illness and press of work that compelled me to put off the publication of it have also prevented me from consulting recent books and periodicals and trying to obtain further light on some of the obscure points. But I hope that other students, and particularly the young leisured members of our learned circles will take up these questions and go into them thoroughly.

For it is to the younger men we must look for the best work in this field. The older generation of students in Ceylon to-day is mostly composed of mere "Pandits" with whom prejudices and pleasing theories pass for canons of criticism and tests of accuracy; and it must be regretfully admitted that racial and personal vanity are only too often permitted to warp the judgment of those who, as seekers of knowledge, should above all things be disinterested and sincere. It may be that in some cases these influences act only on the subconscious mind; but the point that matters is that in nearly all cases the effects are plainly to be seen where they should not be at all. It is easier for the young to avoid these pitfalls; and with a University in our midst, I trust the study of our own History will soon be taken up in the proper spirit, simply and solely to find out the truth so far as we can know it.

My thanks are due to Dr. P. E. Pieris, M A., D. Litt: (Cantab); C.C.S. and Mr. H. W. Codrington, B.A. (Oxon), C.C.S. for the elucidation of several knotty points which arose from time to time, to Messrs. P. C. Villavarayan, B A. (Oxon), Bar.-at-Law and R. R. Crossette Thambiah, Advocates, who were kind enough to look through the proofs, to Mr. S. W. Coomaraswamy of Tellippalai for the translation of most of the Tamil quotations found in the notes and to Mr. D. Jayaratne of the Office of the C. B. R. A. S. for the elaborate Index. The assistance rendered by several of my other friends in many other directions is also hereby acknowledged.

I am deeply indebted to Dr. S. Krishnaswamy Aiyangar, M.A., Ph. D., whose activities in Historical Research are so well known not only in India but also in Ceylon, for the Foreword he has been kind enough to contribute.

C. RASANAYAGAM.

JAFFNA,

9th September 1926.

FOREWORD

WHEN my friend, the Hon'ble Mr. Justice V. V. Srinivasa Aiyangar, suggested that I might contribute a foreword to a work on the history of Jaffna by a friend of his, I agreed to do so on trust with hardly any conception either of the character or compass of the work to which I was asked to contribute the foreword. When subsequently I heard it was a work by Mr. Rasanayagam Mudaliar of the Ceylon Civil Service. I had but little doubt that I had not promised to sponsor the work of an unknown or inexperienced author in the field of research. I have had occasion to know some specimens at least of Mr. Rasanayagam's work before, and I was almost certain that I would be helping forward the work of a scholar whose learning and critical acumen were well worthy of my support and sympathy whether I found it possible to agree with him in all his conclusions or no. After reading the book through, though with unfortunate interruptions, I have no hesitation in putting on record here my feeling that the work embodies a great amount of labour and extensive research resulting in the bringing together of a volume of material much of which is hardly known outside of Jaffna and a considerable part of which would completely disappear if not put on record and utilised for purposes of history. This vast material is marshalled and presented in a form to make the chequered history of Jaffna, extending over much more than 1600 years, read something like a connected narrative. Mr. Rasanayagam exhibits, in this laudable work of his, much critical acumen and judgment, so that the whole account does not appear as the mere *disjecta membra* of history strung together as a tribute of patriotism of the scholar to his motherland. The result is, on the whole, a fairly reliable and readable history of Jaffna, which had remained a desideratum for long, though histories of Jaffna were not altogether wanting.

If on occasions Mr. Rasanayagam let his patriotism get the better of his judgment, it is excusable having regard to the fact that on the whole he allowed his patriotism to remain under the control of his critical judgment. If we take occasion to point out, even in a foreword, certain places where he has let his patriotism get the better of his judgment, it is certainly with a view to drawing the author's attention to what may not be quite obvious to him, and not with any view to finding fault with him. In the course of his investigations, there are passages in the work, which to the casual reader, would show that the author is attempting to appropriate to his native land what really belongs to others. As one instance, we may point to his effort to identify the Mávilangai of Siṛupáṇáṛṛupaḍai with Jaffna. The text has it that the Mávilangai under description has 'the name as well as the characteristic products of the old great Lanka', which would indicate that one has to look for this Mávilangai elsewhere than in the Lanka of old. There are several Mávilangais in India described as Kíḻ-Mávilangai, meaning east or lower Mávilangai and Naḍu-Náṭṭu Mávilangai, from which an inference as to the existence of another Mávilangai would be warranted. The attempt to identify the Mándai of the Tamil classics with Mantoṭa otherwise Mahátiṭṭa in Ceylon may be provable; but Mr. Rasanayagam himself notes the fact that to some at least of the authors of the classical period it was known as Kuṭṭuvan Mánḍai. It was up to Mr.

Rasanayagam to prove the Kuṭṭuvan conquest of the West coast of Ceylon, which again may be possible, but will not be accepted without some proof. Almost the same remark may be made of several of the identifications that he attempts of the places referred to in the Classical Geographers, but we would draw attention only to the larger attempt at the identification of the Sabaj of the Muhammadan historians. Mr. Rasnayagam lets his faith take command of his criticism in attempting to identify this with localities round Jaffna. The Sabaj of the Muhammadan historians and the Maharaja of India in that connection alike refer to the empire of Srí Bhoja in Sumatra. Srí Bhoja and Srí Vijaya were alternative names of the capital of the important kingdom developing into an imperial power in Sumatra, which played a great part in the period extending from the seventh to the thirteenth century A. D., as the researches of the French School at Hanoi and of Col. Gerini amply show. These are merely instances where further research by the author would be welcome.

The attempt of the author to derive the name Íḻam does not appeal to us as quite successful; Íḻam to us seems to be directly derived from the Pali word Sihaḷam, which in Tamil would be Singaḷam or even Singaṇam, but a strict Tamilising would make it Íḻam, much as the Jajnagar of Kosala becomes Sadinagar and then Adinagar in Tamil inscriptions. The transformation of the S into I and the la into ḻa is not so difficult of achievement philologically. The question whether the Pali word has a Tamil original must be left open for the present.

Before closing, we invite attention to a statement that occurs on pages 152 and 153 that the Aryan Brahmans who emigrated into the Tamil Country imitated the habits of the Tamils and elevated themselves in public estimation, and hence came to be called *Andanar*. It may be so, but we want some evidence in support of the statement, as the Puṛanánúṛu poem on Párpana Váhai by a Non-Brahman author, Ávúr Múlám Kiḻár gives the contrary impression, not to mention other references to the high esteem in which the Brahman was held in his own right. On page 33 occurs a statement that the Mahábhárata now contains twenty four thousand slokas, (after additions, amplifications and interpolations). It is well-known that the Mahábhárata at present is supposed to contain "*sapada laksha grantha,*" one lac and twenty-five thousand *slokas*. The Southern version actually contains certainly more than a lac of *slokas*.

Notwithstanding these blemishes, tho work deserves well of all those who may be interested in the study of the history of this ancient land of India, not merely of Jaffna, as it embodies undoubtedly a vast volume of honest and earnest work in the collection and collation and continuous presentation of a vast amount of historical material. We may point out before closing what is more creditable to the author, the exhaustive references to Tamil literature in regard to the various points taken up for discussion. It must have taken years of work to elaborate the thesis into its present form, and we can only wish the author a good reception for the work. In literary efforts work is its own reward, and it is more so in work of this character. Let me conclude with the hope that the author will, in addition to this reward, have also a measure of appreciation from those who could appreciate good work of this kind.

Madras University,
29th August 1926. S. KRISHNASWAMI AIYANGAR.

LIST OF ILLUSTRATIONS

LIST OF REFERENCES

Accounts.	The Accounts of India and China, by Suleyman and Abu Zaid.
Aelian.	Ancient India as described by Megasthenes and Arrian ; translated by J. W. Mc. Crindle.
Aiṅguru :	Aiṅguru Núru ; V. Sáminàta Aiyar's edition. (Tamil).
Akam :	Akam Nánúru (Tamil).
Akapporuḷ :	Akapporuḷ Viḷakkam, by Naṛkavirása Nampi : A. Kumarasamy Piḷḷay's Edition (Tamil)
Almanac.	Ceylon Almanac for 1833.
Anc : Geo :	The Ancient Geography of India, by Sir A. Cunningham.
Anc : Ind :	Ancient India, by Vincent Smith ; 1908 edition.
Aṅgá :	Aṅgádipáṭam ; A Tamil work on Anatomy, a part of the medical work "Segarájasékaram", (Tamil, unpublished).
Arab : Nts.	The Arabian Nights Entertainments.
Arch : S. R.	Archaeological Survey Report, (South Indian).
Arch : S. S. I.	The Archaeological Survey of South India.
A. R. S. I. E.	Annual Report of South Indian Epigraphy.
Artha :	The Artha Sástra, by Cháṇakya, translated by Sáma Sástry.
Atana :	The. Atanagaluvansa (Pali), translated into Sinhalese by J. de Alwis.
Baldeus.	A Description of the great and most famous Isle of Ceylon, by Philip Baldeus.
Barros.	The Portuguese work "Da Asia ", by Joao de Barros.

Batuta.	The Travels of Ibn Batuta, translated by Rev. S. Lee.
Bell.	Archaeological Report of the Kegalle District, by H. C. P. Bell.
Bertol :	A view of the Agricultural, Commercial, and Financial Interests of Ceylon, by Anthony Bertolacci ; 1817 edition.
Bible. D :	The Holy Bible-Douay version.
Bible. R :	The Holy Bible-Revised Version.
Casie :	The History of Jaffna, by Simon Casie Chetty.
Cathay.	Cathay and the Way Thither, by Col. H. Yule.
Ceylon Ant :	The Ceylon Antiquary.
Ch. Mand. S :	The Chōḷa Maṇḍala Sadagam (Tamil).
Chris :	Christianity in Ceylon, by Sir Emerson Tennent.
Cilap :	Cilappadikāram, V. Sāminātа Aiyar's edition (Tamil).
Cintāmaṇi.	Jīvaka Cintāmaṇi, by Tiru-takka-tēvar, V. Sāminàta Aiyar's edition (Tamil).
Cirupāṇ :	Cirupāṇārṛrupadai, V. Sāminàta Aiyar's edition of Pattuppāṭṭu (Tamil).
C. L. R.	The Ceylon Literary Register.
Coins :	The Coins of Ancient India, by Sir A. Cunningham.
Contributions.	Some Contributions of South India to Indian Culture, by Dr. S. Krishnaswami Aiyangar, M.A., Ph. D.
Couto.	A Portuguese History of Ceylon, by Diogu de Couto, translated by J. Ferguson and published in J. (C. B.) R. A. S. Vol. XX.
Dak : K. P.	Dakshina Kailāsa Purāṇam by Paṇḍita Rāja, edited by P. P. Vaitiyalinga Dēsigar (Tamil).
Damba :	Dambadeniya Asna (Sinhalese).

Deccan.	History of the Deccan, by Professor G. Jouveau Dubreuil.
Deg.	Notes on the History of the District of Hughli or the Ancient Rada, by Nandolal Deg.
Dévâram :	Dévâram : Hymns composed by the three Saiva Saints, Sambanda Múrty, Tirunávukarasu and Sundara Múrty (Tamil).
Dévai Ulá.	Dévai Ulá, by Palapaṭṭaḍai Chokkanáta Pulavar (Tamil).
Dipa :	Dípavaṁsa ; Upham's translation of the Sacred and Historical Books of Ceylon.
Dipa : & Mah :	Dípavaṁsa and Mahávaṁsa, by Wilhelm Geiger, translated by Ethel. M. Coomaraswamy.
Ep. In.	Epigraphia Indica.
Fa. Hien.	Travels of Fa Hien, the Chinese Traveller, translated by Professor Legge.
Farrar.	Old Ceylon, by Reginald Farrar.
Forgot. Coin.	The forgotten Coinage of the Jaffna Kings, by Revd. S. Gnánapragásar.
Gar. Nam.	Garshasp Namah, a Persian poem written by Asedi ; quoted in Travels in the East.
Gaz.	The Ceylon Gazetteer, by Simon Casie Chetty.
Haffner.	Travels on Foot through the Island of Ceylon, by J. Haffner.
Hiouen.	History of the Travels of Hiouen Thsang, translated by S. Beal.
H. O.	The Hindu Organ, a Newspaper published in Jaffna.
Ind. Ant.	The Indian Antiquary.
Ind. Ship.	The History of Indian Shipping, by Rhadakumad Mookerjie.
Ira, Akap.	Iṛayanár Akapporuḷ, C. W. Thamotharam Pillai's Edition (Tamil).

Jaff. Hist.	History of Jaffna, by A. Mootootamby Pillai, Second Edition (Tamil).
Jaff. Kings.	The Kings of Jaffna during the Portuguese period, by Revd. S. Gnánapragásar. O. M. I.
J. Beng. B.R.A.S.	The Journal of the Bengal Branch of the Royal Asiatic Society.
J. Bom. B.R.A.S.	The Journal of the Bombay Branch of the Royal Asiatic Society.
J. B. O. R. S.	The Journal of the Bihar and Orissa Research Society.
J. C. B. R. A. S.	The Journal of the Ceylon Branch of the Royal Asiatic Society.
J. H. J.	History of Jaffna, by S. John (Tamil).
J. R. A. S.	The Journal of the Royal Asiatic Society.
Kali :	Kalitogai ; C. W. Thamotharam Pillai's Edition (Tamil).
Kaliṅ :	Kaliṅgattup-Paraṇi, by Jayaṅkoṇḍán (Tamil).
Kambaṅ.	Rámáyaṇam, by Kamban (Tamil)
Kavya :	Kavyasékaraya, by Totagamuwa Sri Rahula (Siṅhalese).
Kiḷḷai. V. T.	Kiḷḷai Viḍu Tútu, by Varada Paṇḍitar of Chunnágam (Tamil).
K. M.	Kailáya Málai, by Mutturása Kavirásar, edited by T. Kailasa Pillai (Tamil.)
Kok. San.	Kókila Sandésaya, by the Principal of Irugalkula Pirivena, Mulgirigala ; W. F. Gunawardhana Mudaliyar's edition (Siṅhalese).
K. P.	Kanda Puráṇam, by Kachiyappa Sivácháriyar, Árumuga Návalar's edition (Tamil).
Kuraḷ.	Tirukuraḷ, by Tiruvaḷḷuvar (Tamil).
Kuriñchi.	Kuriñchipáṭṭu ; V. Sáminâta Aiyar's edition of Pattupáṭṭu (Tamil).
Kurun :	Kuruntogai ; Tirumaḷigai Sauri Perumáḷ Araṅgan's edition (Tamil).

Kurun. V.	Kurunègala Vistaraya (Siṅhalese-unpublished)
Mack. Coll :	The Mackenzie Collections.
Mad. Kan.	Madurai Kañchi, V. Sáminatá Aiyar's edition of Pattupáṭṭu (Tamil).
Mad. Man.	Madurai Mánmiyam (Tamil).
Mah :	The Mahávaṅsa; Mudlr. Wijesinghe's translation.
Maha :	The Mahávaṅsa ; Geiger's translation.
Mah. P.	do Sri Sumangala's edition (Pali).
Mah. Pali	do English Transliteration of Pali-Geiger's edition.
Mahab : M.	The Mahábhárata ; Manmatha Nath Dutt's translation.
Mahab : P.	The Mahábhárata ; Protap Chandra Roy's translation.
Mahab : R.	The Mahábhárata ; V. Ramanuja Chariar's edition (Tamil).
Malai ; K.	Malaipaḍu Kaḍám ; V. Sáminàta Aiyar's edition of Pattupáṭṭu (Tamil).
Maṇi.	Maṇimékalai; V. Sáminàta Aiyar's edition (Tamil)
Mannar.	A Monograph of Mannar, by W. J. S. Boake.
Mántai.	Mántaippaḷ, by Sidampara Táṇḍava Madura Kavirάyar of Karuvai Nallúr (Tamil).
Marco :	The Travels of Marco Polo; Translated by Col. H. Yule.
Meadows.	Meadows of Gold, by Mas''udi.
Med : Sinh : Art.	Mediaeval Siṅhalese Art, by Ananda K. Coomaraswamy, D. Sc.
M. E. R.	Annual Report of the Madras Government Epigraphist.
M. L. R.	The Monthly Literary Register.
Mullai :	Mullaipáṭṭu, V. Sáminàta Aiyar's edition of Pattupáṭṭu (Tamil.)

Muller: Ancient Inscriptions in Ceylon, by Dr. E. Muller.

Muttol: Muttoḷḷáyiram (Tamil), published in Sen Tamil.

Muzum: Hindu History, by A. K. Muzumdar.

Nágadípa: Nágadípa and Buddhist Remains in Jaffna, by P. E. Peiris, D. Litt.

Nampota: Nampota (Siṅhalese).

Nánmaṇi: Nánmaṇikkaḍikai—One of the Poetical collection பதினெண்கீழ்க்கணக்கு (Tamil)

Nannúl: Nannúl—Tamil Grammar, by Pavaṇandi.

Naṟṟiṇai. Naṟṟinai—A. Náráyanasámy Aiyar's edition (Tamil).

Ned: Vad: Neḍunalváḍai; V. Sáminátа Aiyar's edition of Pattupáṭṭu (Tamil).

New Dates. Some new dates of Páṇḍyan Kings, by Swamikannu Pillai.

Nights. Thousand and one Nights—translated and annotated by Lane.

Nik: San: Nikaya Sangrahava by Dharmakirti Saṅgharája—translated by C. M. Fernando.

Ousley. Travels in the East, by Sir William Ousley-Edition of 1819.

Padir: Padiṟṟupattu, V. Sáminátа Aiyar's Edition (Tamil).

Paḷa Moḻi: Paḷa Moḻi—one of the Poetical collection. பதினெண் கீழ்க்கணக்கு (Tamil)

Pallavas. The Pallavas, by Professor G. Jouveau Dubreuil.

Para. San: Paravi Sandésaya, by Totagamua Sri Rahula; Fonseka's edition (Siṅhalese).

Parker. Ancient Ceylon, by H. Parker.

Patt. Pálai. Paṭṭina Pálai; V. Sáminátа Aiyar's edition of Pattupáṭṭu (Tamil).

Paul. The Overlordship of Ceylon, by Dr. S.C. Paul, M.D.

Perak. S.	Perakumba Sirita, by Toṭagamua Sri Rahula; D. B. Jayatileka's edition (Siṅhalese).
Perigrinations.	Perigrinations of Indian Buddhists in Burma and in the Sunda Islands, by Professor Q. Muller Hess.
Periplus.	Periplus of the Erythraean Sea; Translations by Vincent, Mc. Crindle and W. H. Schoff.
Periya:	Periya Puráṇam, by Sékkiḷār, Ārumuga Návalar's Edition (Tamil.)
Perumpán:	Perumpáṇáṟṟupaḍai; V. Sáminàta Aiyar's edition of Pattupáṭṭu (Tamil).
Philalethes.	The History of Ceylon, from the earlier period to the year 1815, by Philalethes, A. M. (Oxon)
Pieris.	Ceylon: Portuguese Era, by P. E. Pieris, M. A., D. Litt: Cantab.
Place Names.	Place Names of Jaffna (Iḍappeyar Varaláṟu), by S. W. Coomaraswamy (Tamil).
Pliny.	Natural History, by Pliny; Mc. Crindle's translation.
Port. India.	The Portuguese in India, by Danvers.
Port: Mss.	Portuguese Manuscripts found at the Hague, by Mr. E. R. Reimers, Government Archivist.
Porunar:	Porunaráṟṟupaḍai; V. Sáminàta Aiyar's edition of Pattupáṭṭu (Tamil).
Pridham:	An Historical, Political and Statistical Account of Ceylon and its Dependencies, by Charles Pridham, Two Vols. 1849.
P. R. U.	Pararájasékaran Ulá (Tamil—unpublished) not extant.
Ptolemy.	Geography of the World, by Ptolemy; Mc. Crindle's Translation.
Puja:	Pujavalia; Translated by Gunasekara Mudaliar.
Puṟam.	Puṟa Nánúṟu; V. Sáminàta Aiyar's edition (Tamil)

Queiroz.	Conquista Temporal e Espiritual de Ceylao, by Padre Fernao de Queiroz, written in 1687, published at Colombo, 1916.
Raghu :	Raghuvamsam by Arasakésari of Nallúr, Jaffna : S. Ponnampalam Pillai's edition (Tamil).
Raghunath. R.	Raghunath Abyudáyam, by Rámabadrambá (Telugu)
Raghunath. V.	Raghunath Abyudáyam by Vijayaraghava Nayaka (Telugu).
Rajarat.	Rajaratnacari ; Upham's translation of the Sacred and Historical Books of Ceylon.
Rajavali.	Rajavali ; Upham's translation of the Sacred and Historical Books of Ceylon.
Rámáyaṇa. D.	Rámáyaṇa ; Translation by Manmatha Náth Dutt.
Rámáyaṇa. G.	do Metrical translation, by Griffith.
Reb. Ceilao.	Rebeiro's Ceilao, by P. E. Pieris, D. Litt.
Ribeyro.	A Portuguese work on Ceylon, by Ribeyro.
Rifles.	"Ceylon", by an Officer late of the Ceylon Rifles.
R. M.	Rájamuṛai ; A. Tamil work on the Kings of Jaffna (not extant-unpublished).
Sah : Rat :	Sáhitya Ratnakara, by Yañna Náráyaṇa Dikshita (Telugu).
Sah : Sudha :	Sáhitya Sudha by Góvinda Dikshita (Telugu).
Sara : M.	Sarajóti Malai, by Bhója Rája Paṇḍitá ; Kokkuvil Edition (Tamil)
Sarpa : S.	Sarpa Sástram—A Tamil work on Snake bite and its cure ; a part of the medical work Segarája-sékaram (Tamil-unpublished).
S. Ch. Ula.	Saṅgara Chóḷan Ulá (Tamil).
Sega. A.	Segarájasékaram—Astrological work (Tamil).

Sega. M.	Segarájasékaram-Medical work (Tamil—unpublished).
Seru. V.	Séruvávilla Vistara (Sinhalese-unpublished).
Sess. PP.	The Sessional papers of Ceylon.
Shrines.	South Indian Shrines, by Jagatisa Aiyer.
S. I. I.	South Indian Inscriptions; Edited by Prof. E. Hultzsch, Rai Bahadur V. Venkayya and Rao Sahib Krishna Sastri.
Slater.	The Dravidian element in Indian Culture, by Gilbert Slater.
Sources:	The Sources of Vijayanagar History, by Dr. S. Krishnaswami Aiyangar.
S. Tamil.	Sen Tamil; A Monthly Magazine published at Madura (Tamil).
Sud. Sam.	Sudha Samhita (Sanskrit),
Tamils.	Tamils Eighteen Hundred Years Ago, by Kanagasabai Pillai.
Tam. Nav. S.	Tamil Návalar Saridai, edited by Kanagasuriam Pillai (Tamil).
Tam. Vara.	Tamil Varalaru, by S. S. Srinivasa Pillai (Tamil).
Tani Pádal.	Tanipádal-tirattu (Tamil Anthology)
Tanj. Gaz.	The Tanjore Gazetteer,
Tap.	The Taprobanian.
Tennent.	Ceylon, by Sir Emerson Tennent.
Thombo.	The Kingdom of Jaffna Patam—1645, First Thombo of Beligame; by P. E. Pieris, D. Litt.
Tiru. K.	Tirukóvaiyar, by Saint Manikkavásagar (Tamil)
Tiru K. K.	Tirukónamalai Kónésar Kalvettu, by Kavi Raja, published with Dakshina Kailása Puránam, (Tamil).
Tiru. K. P.	Tirukónésala Puranam (Tamil).
Tirumu.	Tirumurukarrupadai, V. Sáminàta Aiyer's edition of Pattupáttu (Tamil).

Tirup.	Tiruppugal, by Arunagiri Nátar (Tamil).
Tiru. V.	Tiruvásagam, by Saint Mánikkavásagar. translated by Dr. G. U. Pope.
Tiru. V. A. P.	Tiruvátavúr Adigal Puránam (Tamil)
Tiru. V. P.	Tiruvilayádal Puránam, by Perumbarra Puliyúr Nambi ; V. Sáminatá Aiyar's edition (Tamil).
Tiru. V. P. P.	Tiruvilayádal Puránam (Prose), by Arumuga Návalar (Tamil).
Tiva.	Tivákaram. A Dictionary of Synonyms in verse (Tamil).
Ton. M. S.	Tondai Mandala Sadagam (Tamil).
Trav. A. S.	The Travancore Archaeological Series, by Gopinath Row.
Vaiyá Pádal.	Vaiyá Pádal, edited by J.W.Arudpragasam (Tamil)
Valen.	Ceylon, by Valentyn.
Velupillai.	Yalpána Vaipava Kaumudi, by K. Velupillai (Tamil).
Vijaya. D. N.	Vijaya Dharma Nádagam, A dramatic work composed by Rama Sundaran, son of Sidambara Udaiyar of Vannarponne (Tamil-unpublished).
Vishnu. P.	Vishnu Puránam, translated by Wilson, 4th Edition.
Visva. P.	Visva Puránam, by Sidampara Kavirayar of Kilivanúr (Tamil—unpublished.)
Wanni.	A Historical Sketch of the Wanni, by J. P. Lewis
Wheeler.	History of India, by Talbhoys Wheeler.
Winslow.	Tamil-English Lexicon, by Rev. W. Winslow.
Y. V. M.	Yálpána Vaipava Málai by Mailvágana Pulavar translated by C. Brito.

INTRODUCTION

TO the Jaffna Tamil the study of the ancient history of his mother-country ought to be of paramount interest. His attachment to his birthplace is indeed proverbial. Go where he may in search of wealth and live where he may for the time being, even in the fairest and the most favoured of lands he feels himself but a sojourner; and sooner or later he follows his heart back to home, to spend his last days in those well-remembered spots and among the friends of his earliest love. Jaffna in distress has never appealed to him in vain; his response has always been ready and whole-hearted. The history of a country reflects, and bears witness to, the national character. What feelings of just pride and patriotism would swell in the heart of every true son of Jaffna, if he could but have a peep into the glories of her past!

At times like the present when many are endeavouring to lift the thick veil of obscurity that envelopes the ancient history of Ceylon, it may seem presumptious on our part to undertake such a colossal task. Some of the statements made in the book may appear incorrect or capable of different interpretation. But this attempt at research has been performed with the sole object of arriving at the truth, and in the fervent hope that more competent students will soon be able to present a more satisfactory treatment of a subject which is very necessary for the education and the enlightenment of the youth of Jaffna.

In the year 1736 A.D., at the request of Jan Maccara, the then Dutch Governor of Jaffna, one Mailvágana Pulavar of Mádagal compiled in Tamil prose the Yaḻpáṇa Vaipava Málai, the earliest history of Jaffna. His authorities were certain earlier writings such as the Kailáya Málai, Vaiyá Páḍal, Pararájasékaraṉ Ulá and Rája Muṟai (Royal Chronicles),* the oldest of which was certainly not earlier than the 14th or the 15th century A.D. Whatever might have been the source of the earlier writers, whether they drew their material from authentic records or from mere tradition, it cannot be denied that the Vaipava Málai was a faithful account of all that was available at the time. Today, except the Kailáya Málai which has been printed †, and a few manuscript copies of Vaiyá Páḍal ‡, the other works are very rare and hardly

---

* The metrical preface of the Yáḻpána Vaipava Málai contains the following verse :—

உரராசர் தொழுகழன்மேக்கறூ னென்றோது
  முலாந்தேசுமன்னனுரைத் தமிழாற்கேட்க
வரராச கைலாயமாலை தொன்னூல்
  வரம்புகண்ட கவிஞர்பிரான் வையாபாடல்
பரராசசேகரன்றன் னுலாவுங்காலப்
  படிவழுவாதுற்றசம்பவங்கடீட்டுந்
திரராசமுறைகளுந் தேர்ந்தி யாழ்ப்பாணத்தின்
  செய்தி மயில்வாகன வேள் செப்பினனே.

At the request of the Dutch Governor named Maccarra at whose feet powerful chiefs bow down, Mailvaganam, after consulting Kailáya Málai, Vaiyá Pádal composed by the poet Vaiyá learned in ancient lore, Pararájasékaraṉ Ulá and Rája Muṟai (Royal chronicles) which correctly delineated the events at different periods, wrote the history of Yaḻpáṇam in Tamil.

† Published by Mr. T. Kailásapiḷḷai of Nallore, Jaffna.

‡ Since published by Mr. J. W. Arudpragasam, Central College, Jaffna.

procurable. It is lucky that the Vaipava Málai was printed several years ago and translated into English by the late Mr. C. Brito, for at the present day it is impossible to procure any of the older manuscripts for the purpose of testing the correctness of the printed version. The fact that all the statements made in the Kailáya Málai including those that will be proved hereafter to be misconceptions, were bodily taken and introduced into the Vaipava Málai, stamps it with the impress of an honest attempt at history on the part of that 'well-meaning villager', Mailvágana Pulavar.

Some of the historians of Jaffna that have from time to time appeared within the last 35 years,* have so well succeeded in mutilating, altering and amending the Vaipava Málai according to their whims and fancies, that there are now but few who acknowledge its historical value. On the contrary, the belief seems to be gaining ground that it is only a compendium of ancient folklore, old women's tales and mythical anecdotes.

It would certainly not be reasonable to dismiss this work as altogether untrustworthy, merely because some of the events recorded there have been declared to be inaccurate in the matter of chronology. Research in this branch ought to follow the far safer method of modern European scholars; and ancient inscriptions, coins, carved stones and contemporaneous literature, should be carefully studied to see if they refute or confirm the traditional history of the land.

* Tamil Histories of Jaffna have been written and published by Messrs. S. John of Uduvil, A. Mootootamby Pillai of Vannarpanne and K. Vélupillai of Vasávilán.

Indeed, in those far-off ages history was written under very different circumstances. There is no doubt that our earliest works were based on mere tradition. Tradition, as we all know, was handed down by word of mouth from generation to generation, and, moulded and shaped into different forms in the process, it grows in the course of a few centuries into something not quite the same as the original. However, by careful sifting and analysis the truth can be ascertained. The Mahávaṅsa for instance, although composed in the 5th century A.D., speaks of events of a thousand years earlier, known to the compiler only by tradition and hearsay. But with care, it can be, and has been used as material for the early history of Ceylon. We have only to follow the methods used by the critics and historians who made use of the Mahávaṅsa.

In order to reconstruct the history of Jaffna from its earliest times, it becomes necessary to examine critically our ancient traditions in the light of contemporary documents, and, in the absence of any local literature and inscriptions, to search for further information in the literature and chronicles of other countries. In this respect the Mahávaṅsa is most useful. It is a Court chronicle containing the annals of the Ceylon kings, and its writers who most probably regarded the Tamils as a horde of cruel marauders pass over both them and their efforts in silence, except when they made themselves too unpleasant to go unnoticed.

Had the monastic annalists of the Siṅhalese chronicle with the instinct of true historians depicted impartially the events that took place in the North from time to time, the task of the Jaffna historian of today would have been rendered much lighter.

Considering how little we know of the political history of the country, and even of the dynasty of kings who ruled over Jaffna from the eleventh to the seventeenth centuries, it is not surprising that we should know still less about the allied branches of archaeology and epigraphy. But how long are we to remain in this listless if not disgraceful state of ignorance? To a true son of Jaffna, is it not galling to have to wait till some foreign scholar finds time and leisure to make investigations and enlighten him on the history of his motherland. And although he may be willing to wait, the sources of information appear not to be endowed with eternal patience. The literature of the land unfortunately committed to such a fragile material as the palm leaf is fast disappearing. The archaeological remains have been almost fully depleted of their carved and inscribed stones which have, in the march of civilization, either been turned to metal for the roads or hidden safely away in the foundations of new houses. The rapidity with which the devastating tide of progress is washing away old landmarks is clearly apparent in every direction. Traditional beliefs, old legends, local folklore and manners and customs peculiar to the people of the country are fast vanishing. Every caste is giving up its own for the sake of the dress and ornaments, the speech and conventions of some other which is considered superior. National games and amusements are giving place to Western innovations, and in another generation their very names will be forgotten. There is little left of our ancient literature and even less of ruins and archaeological remains. These scanty sources of information should be made use of as early as possible; else our only links with the past will be gone for ever. If we therefore venture to interpret some of the dark problems of historical antiquity with the help of evidence now hidden away in obscure nooks and corners, and try to awaken a general interest in the history of our country, the certainty that in a few more years, these matters will cease to be heard of altogether, is our sole and sufficient excuse.

CHAPTER I.

The Nágas.

WHEN and by whom Ceylon was first populated are matters enveloped in obscurity. Whether the earliest inhabitants were a people indigenous to the island, as some of the hill tribes to India, or whether they were immigrants from outside must perhaps remain undecided. The Maháváṅsa says that about the sixth century B. C., there were the Yakkhas confined to the centre of the Island, and the Nágas dominating the western and the northern parts.* North Ceylon was therefore called Nágadípa and was for centuries so referred to in the old histories.

The late Mr. Kanagasabai, the author of 'Tamils 1800 Years Ago', thought that the Yakkhas were the ancient 'Yuh chi' a yellow race that emigrated from the central table-land of Asia into India through the Himalayan passes long before the arrival of the Áryan settlers, and that they "eventually spread over the whole of Bengal and emigrated thence by sea to Southern India and Ceylon"† This is in a way confirmed by Mr. Parker's description of the Veddahs of Ceylon—the survivors of the ancient Yakkhas. He says that their "cheek bones are

---

* Mah. i.

† Tamils. p : 45.

somewhat prominent", that "their eyes are deep set" and that "some faces are practically hairless below the eyes, and there is rarely more than a very sparing growth of hair on the face, a very thin short moustache and a little short hair on the chin being all that is present".* But Professor R. Virchow, quoted by Mr. Parker, thinks that "no elaborate proof is needed that neither Sinhalese nor Veddahs, at least in the form of their skulls, present the slightest indication of any relationship to the Mongols. Such a remarkably dolichocephalous tribe has never yet been found among the Mongols".† "On the other hand, among the remnants of the old Dravidian or perhaps pre-dravidian tribes of Hindustan we find even today evidence of analogies with the Veddahs".‡ It is, however, clear from ancient writers, both Sanskritic and Tamil,¶ that the Yakkhas were the enemies of the Áryans and for a long time resisted the progress of the white-skinned race into India. They were contemptuously called 'Asuras' (tee-totallers),§ Rakshasas (giants and monsters) and 'Yakkhas' (devils), and on account of their strength, courage and valour, supernatural powers were ascribed to them by the early Áryans. During the pre-epic period they had established a powerful kingdom at Laṅkápura in Ceylon and asserted their authority in the Dekkan and

---

* Parker, p: 42.

† ibid p: 43.

‡ ibid p: 34.

¶ The Védas, the Epics and the Puráṇas,

§ The Āryans called themselves *Suras* (those who drink); and the teetotallers of the East are still held in contempt by some of the Western Āryans! *Suras* became synonymous with *Devas* when the Āryans called themselves by the latter name.

other parts of India. Readers of the Rámáyaṇa may be aware how powerful was Rávaṇa, the Yakkha king of Ceylon, and how far advanced the Yakkhas were in the art of warfare. These Yakkhas were, within a few centuries of the arrival of Vijaya, absorbed into the Nágas, the Kaliṅgas from the Gangetic valley in North India and the Tamils and other Dravidian tribes from South India, who flowed into Ceylon from time to time, either as conquerors or as immigrants. The result of this gradual process of fusion was a new race called the 'Siṅhala' or the 'Siṅhalese'.

Fa Hien, the Chinese traveller, who visited Ceylon between 400 and 414 A. D., while describing the Island, says: "The country originally had no human habitations, but was occupied only by spirits and Nágas, with which the merchants of various countries carried on a trade. When the trafficking was taking place, the spirits did not show themselves. They simply set forth their precious commodities, with indications of the price attached to them, while the merchants made their purchases according to price and took the things away".* The word which the translator has rendered as 'spirits' was no doubt 'Yakkhas', and their system of barter described above can still be seen among the Veddahs, the remnants of the ancient Yakkhas, who did not get absorbed into the permanent population.

The Nágas were supposed by the ancients to be serpents living underground ("páta̤la") obviously because

---

* Fa Hien; C. L. R., vol: ii, p: 216.

in Sanskrit the word 'nága' means 'serpent'. They were also supposed to be endowed with supernatural powers by which they could metamorphose themselves into human beings at will.* There have been various conjectures made as to the origin of the true Nágas. Some have thought that they were so called because they were serpent-worshippers;† and others have surmised that the name was derived from the fact that their headcovering was in the shape of the hood of a hydra-headed cobra. The sculptures and paintings found in the ancient Buddhistic ruins of India and Ceylon, representing the Nágas as 'dvarapalayas' etc, perhaps led to the second idea. The origin of their name cannot certainly be traced to serpents or serpent-worship, for they were so named long before the advent of the Áryans in whose language alone the word signified 'serpents'.

The Nágas, according to Mr. A. K. Muzumdar, were Thibeto-Burmans and were, about 4000 B. C., driven by some political disturbance from Central Asia into India through the North-Eastern gate. "Their muscular frame, yellow complexion, flat nose, small eyes, high cheek bones and scanty beard show that they originally belonged to the Mongoloid stock".‡ Jambulus, a captive of Ethiopia who was sent out to sea, appears to have

* Mr. Talboys Wheeler speaking of the Scythic Nágas in his History of India (vol : i, p : 147) says "In process of time these Nágas became identified with serpents, and the result has been a strange confusion between serpents, and human beings."

† Casie., C. B. R. A. S. vol ; i ; Tennent, vol : i, p: 331.

‡ Muzum. Bk : i, chap: v:

reached Ceylon before the beginning of the Christian era. He probably touched a port on the northern or north-western coast of Ceylon, for, in his writings he has referred to the islands on that coast. He says that the people there "had no hair other than that on their heads, eyebrows and chins",* thereby affording clear proof of the Mongolian descent of the Nágas. Whatever may be the time fixed by learned historians for the influx of the Áryans into India, it is now generally admitted that the Nágas preceeded the Áryans. The latter found them already settled down in the northern parts of India, and it was perhaps due to these Áryan invasions that the Nágas were forced to seek fresh homes in the Dekkan, in South India and in Ceylon.

The Rámáyaṇa, which contains the earliest references to Ceylon, mentions them. Ráma, while despatching Hanumán in search of Síta, describes the Nága capital, in addition to other South Indian towns, as one of the places which ought to be included in his search.†

In the Mahábhárata, the Nágas are frequently mentioned as living in various parts of India and Ceylon in a highly civilized state under their own kings and under well established laws.

The Nágas were therefore a prominent non-Áryan race in India and their names are preserved in various parts of the country, viz, Nagpur (Nágapuram), Nágarjuna

---

* Pridham, Appendix, i, pp 777-778.

† Rámáyaṇa. D, Kishkinda Kándam, p: 815. The Nágas are here represented as snakes.

Hills, Nágarcóil, Nágarcot, Nágapaṭṭinam, etc. Nága kings are constantly mentioned in historical records. The Buddhist records speak of Nága rulers in Kampilya and elsewhere. Nágadatta and Nágaséna are among the names of kings mentioned in the Allahabad pillar-inscription of Samudra Gupta. There is a Nágarjuna in the dynastic lists of the Silaharas of Nepaul and of Kashmir. Nágavardhana was a nephew of the Chalukya king Pulakésin ii, and Nágabhatta was a king of the Gurzaras about 800A. D. Powerful Nága kings were ruling round Nagpur about the second and third centuries A.D. and intermarried among the Sátavá-hanas and the Pallavas. Kings of Nágavamsa, with the tiger crest and the snake banner, were ruling at Chakrakuṭa and at Boghavati of the Bastur State in the Central Provinces even after the eleventh century A. D. Several of their inscriptions have been found and published.*

Not only did the Nága princes intermarry with the royal families of the Dravidians but they were also readily admitted into the Áryan fold. Sisu Nága a prince of Nága extraction, was the founder of one of the early ruling dynasties of Magadha, and the princes of this dynasty are called in the Purāṇas "Kshatriya bandavah" or "Kshatri-yadamah," epithets which carry the meanings 'kings with Kshatriya connections' and 'Kshatriyas of low order.'†

According to the Mahávaṅsa, the Nága strongholds in the sixth century B.C. were at Nagádipa in the North and at Kalyáṇi on the west coast of Ceylon. We are told

---

* Ep : Ind : vol; x, p: 25.

† Ind : Ant : vol, xlv. p : 10.

in graphic words that when Mahódara was reigning at Nágadípa, his nephew Cúlódara at Kannavaddhamána mountain (Kandamádanam near Rámésvaram) and his uncle Maṇiakkhika at Kalyáṇi, a conflict arose between Mahódara and Cúlódara for a gem-set throne then in Nágadípa. While these two Nága kings, with their vast armies, were fighting for the possession of the throne, Buddha appeared on the scene, settled their dispute, claimed the throne, and, seating himself on it, he preached to them a sermon on reconciliation. As a result of this preaching eighty "kóṭis" of Nágas are said to have been converted to Buddhism.* This was during the second visit of Buddha to Ceylon. From that time the gemset throne became an object of worship and for several centuries attracted thousands of Buddhist pilgrims to Nágadípa.

The story of the conflict between the Nága kings and the intervention of Buddha as peacemaker is corroborated in every detail by Maṇimékalai a Tamil epic, composed about the middle of the second century A.D.† But what-

---

* Mah : i.

† "இருங்கடல்
வாங்குதிரை யுடுத்த மணி பல்லவத்திடைத்
தையாவோ வென்றழுவாண் முன்னர்
விரிந்திலங் கவிரொளி சிறந்து கதிர்பரப்பி
யுரைபெறு மும்முழ நிலமிசை யோங்கித்
திசைதொறு மொன்பான் முழநிலமகன்று
விதிமாணுடியின் வட்டங்குயின்று
பதும சதுரமீமிசை விளங்கி
யறவோற் கமைந்த வாசன மென்றே
மறு மலரல்லது பிறமரஞ் சொரியாது
பறவையு முதிர் சிறைபாங்குசென்றதிராது
தேவர் கோனிட்ட மாமணிப் பீடிகை
பிறப்பு விளங்கவிரொளி.யறத்தகை யாசனங்
கீன்நிலமருங்கி நாக நாடாளு
மிருவர் மன்னவ ரொரு வழித்தோன்றி [Contd.]

ever the historical value of the story itself, we are concerned only with its scene and its setting; and it is very probable that Maṇi-pallavam, where the event is placed by the Tamil author, is identical with the Nágadípa of the Mahávaṁsa.*

The statement that 80 crores of Nágas were converted by Buddha † goes to prove the extensive settlements of these people in the North and West of Ceylon.

யெமதீதென்றே யெடுக்க லாற்றார்
தம்பெரும் பற்று நீங்கலு நீங்கார்
செங்கண் சிவந்து நெஞ்சு புகையுயிர்த்து
தம்பெருஞ் சேனையொடு வெஞ்சினம் புரிநா
ளிருஞ்செரு வொழிமினெம தீதென்றே
பெருந்தவமுனி வனிருந் தறமுரைக்கும்
பொருவறு சிறப்பிற் புரையோரேத்துந்
தரும பீடிகை."

Maṇi: viii, 1-2, 43-63.

In the sea-girt land of Maṇi-pallavam, before the eyes of her thus wandering alone, there appeared the great gem set seat, placed there by (Indra) the king of the Celestials—a seat of becoming splendour, spreading effulgent rays of light. Rising from the ground to the standard height of three cubits and extending towards all directions into a width of nine cubits, set all round with crystal glass cut to different forms and shape, and exhibiting a square with *padma* (lotus) design, stood the seat of Buddha. Here the trees dare not shed any but fragrant flowers, nor the birds dare make noise even with their fluttering plumes. Now for this seat of Dharma of splendour effulgent, endowed with the virtue of enlightening its beholders of their previous birth, there appeared in contest two Nága kings from the Southern regions, each claiming the seat for himself. Unable were they to remove it nor could they rid themselves of their strong desire to possess it. There, while with mighty armies they waged a fierce strife with bloodshot eyes and hearts aflame with rage, the austere *Muni* (Buddha) bade them cease their strife and rivalry. Being seated thereon he preached to them his *Dharma*. So worthy of reverence even by the devotees of matchless excellence is that seat of *Dharma*.

* Nágadípa; J. C. B. R. A. S. vol : xxvi.

† But according to Rájaratnacari, the number was 100,000. Rajarat : p : 21.

In the third century B.C., during the reign of one Tissa Raja of Kalyáṇi (Kelaniya), according to the Rajavali,† 'the sea was seven leagues distant from Calany;' but on account of what had been done to a Terunnánse ‡ "the gods who presided over the destinies of Ceylon became enraged and caused the sea to deluge the land. Once before during the epoch called 'Duvapara yuga,' on account of the wickedness of Ravana, the whole space from Mannar to Tutucorin in which were the fortress of Ravana with 25 palaces and 400,000 streets was swallowed by the sea. So now, in this time of Tissa Raja, king of Calany, 100,000 large towns of the description called Pattunagam (paṭṭanam), 970 fishers' villages and 400 villages inhabited by pearl fishers making altogether eleven-twelfths of the territory which belonged to Calany were swallowed up by the sea. Many, however, escaped and of the large towns Catupity Madampe escaped". It was perhaps at this period too that the submersion of 49 Tamil lands including the hill and the river Kumari mentioned in certain Tamil works took place.¶ After the destruction of his kingdom and of his capital at Kaváḍa-

---

† Rájavali; pp: 190-191; vide infra, p. 25.

‡ *Terunnanse* was a Buddhist High Priest. The king, suspecting him of having been in terms of intimacy with the queen, had him boiled in a cauldron of oil. The priest was innocent. Rájavali; p: 190. Mah. chap: xxii.

¶ (a) "வடிவே லெறிந்த வன்பகை பொறாது
பஃறுளி யாற்றுடன் பன்மலை யடுக்கத்துக்
குமரிக் கோடுங் கொடுங் கடல் கொள்ள"

Cilap: Canto xi, 11: 18–20. [Contd.]

puram, the Páṇḍyan appears to have gone northwards with his people and established a new kingdom in Southern India with his captial at Madura.* The submer-

---

Unable to bear the enmity engendered by the throw of the sharp javelin, the cruel ocean engulfed the Kumari Hill together with several adjacent hills and the river Pahruli.

[For the legend of the Páṇḍyan throwing the javelin to dry up the ocean, see Sport No : 21 out of the Sacred Sports of Siva in Tiruviḷayáḍal Puráṇam.]

(b) "அக்காலத்து அவர் நாட்டுத் தென்பாலி முகத்திற்கு வடவெல்லை யாகிய பஃறுளி யென்னு மாற்றிற்கும் குமரி யென்னு மாற்றிற்கு மிடையே எழு நூற்றுக் காவத வாறும் இவற்றின் நீர் மலிவானென மலிந்த எழ்தெங்க நாடும், எழ்மதுரை நாடும், எழ்முன் பாலை நாடும், எழ்பின் பாலை நாடும், எழ்குன்ற நாடும் எழ்குணகரை நாடும், எழ்குறும்பனை நாடு மென்னும இந்த நாற்பத்தொன்பது நாடும், குமரி கொல்லமுதலிய பன்மலை நாடும், காடும், நதியும், பதியும், தடநீர்க் குமரிவடபெருங்கோட் டின் காறும் கடல் கொண்டொழி" ந்தது.

Cilap: canto viii, 11 : 1-2, note by Adiyáṛkunallár.

In those days tha sea engulfed land to the extent of 700 *kavatams* between the river Pahruli the northern boundary of his (Páṇḍyan) Southern States and the Kumari river, together with the following fertile countries situated therein, viz, seven Theṅgu (cocoanut) States, seven Madura States, seven Muṇpálai States, seven Kuṉṟa (hilly) States, seven Kuṇakarai (Eastern Coast) States and seven Kurumpaṉai (dwarf palmyrah) States in all 49 States, and several hill countries like Kumari and Kollam, villages, forests, rivers and cities as far as the Kumari Hill to the north, with the river Kumari of broad waters.

(c) Nakkirar's commentary to *Irayanar Ahapporul* and the preface to Iḻampúraṇar's commentary to *Tolkappiyam* contain similar descriptions of the cataclysm.

* "மலிதிரை யூர்ந்துதன் மண் கடல் வௌவலின்
மெலிவின்றி மேற்சென்று மேவார் நாடிடம் படப்
புலியொடு வின்னீக்கிப் புகழ்பொறித்த கிளர் கெண்டை
வலியினான் வணக்கிய வாடாச் சீர்த்தென்னவன்."

Kali. 104.

As the sea with its creeping billows had engulfed his country, the Southern Lord of undying fame and strength proceeded higher up, and, having elbowed the tiger and the bow, planted his famous fish on strange territory.

[The tiger was the flag of the Chóḻas, the bow that of the Céras and the fish that of the Páṇḍyas.]

sion of the 49 Tamil lands which extended to the South of Cape Comorin would probably have synchronised with the destruction of that portion of Ceylon. The notation used in the island of Minicoy is purely Siṅhalese, containing a duo-decimal system up to a hundred, thus showing that Minicoy was a part of Ceylon at a certain period, and that it became separated at a time before the adoption of the decimal system by the Siṅhalese. The cardinal numbers used at Minicoy are as follows :—

1. ekké. 2. dé, 3. tiné 4. hattaré, 5. pahé, 6. háyé 7. hatté, 8. areg 9. nuvé, lo, dihé, 11. egára eklus, 12. dolóss, 13. dolóss ekke, 14. dolóss dé, 23. dolóss eklus 24. phasihi and so on, * which are similar to the Siṅhalese cardinals.

The retention of ekkolahé for 11 and dolohé for 12 in the Siṅhalese notation, terms which are quite different to dahátuné, dahá hattaré etc, which actually represent numerals of a decimal notation, clearly proves the ancient connection of Minicoy with Ceylon, and that the Siṅhalese had a duo-decimal notation before Minicoy was separated from Ceylon. There is a clear indication that the Siṅhalese borrowed the decimal system from the Tamils, and it is reasonable to suppose that this must have been after the third century B. C. What is the origin of the duo-decimal system among the ancient Siṅhalese and the people of Minicoy? Was it Sumerian or Chaldean, as surmised by Slater, † or one of indigenous evolution among the Nágas and the Yakkhas? And how was Minicoy which,

---

* Slater. p. 73.

† „ p. 74.

is situated to the West of the South Indian Peninsula connected with Ceylon?

Megasthenes, who was the Grecian ambassador at the Court of Chandra Gupta, wrote about 300 B.C., that Taprobane (Ceylon)was separated from the mainland (of India) by a river, * and his statement indicates that, during his time, the Indian Peninsula extended further southwards, and that the sea which divided it from Ceylon was so narrow as to be called a river. Megasthenes having lived and written before the deluge described in the Rájavali, it can be safely surmised that Kavádapuram and the 49 Tamil lands were engulfed at the same time as the western Nága kingdom of Ceylon—viz., during the reign of Kelani Tissa (about 250 B.C). The third Tamil Sangam must have been formed at Madura sometime afterwards.

Bhaskaracharya furnishes an astronomical datum to the effect that the Equator passed through the ancient Lanká, and some scholars therefore think that the Lanká of Rávana was the present Sumatra!†

A large slice of the Nága kingdom in Ceylon was thus submerged, leaving only a small portion of Nágadípa—including the Jaffna Peninsula and a few adjoining islands—perhaps, under a Nága king. This kingdom, however, was not confined to the Jaffna Peninsula alone, but extended also over the greater part of the Vannis, including the Púnakari and Mannar dis-

---

* Ind : Ant : Vol, vi, p; 129.

† Lanká of Rávana by N. S. Adhikari; J. Bom: B. R. A. S Vol : xxv, No. 2.

tricts, which appear to have been in a flourishing condition in those early days.

In Ciṟupáṇáṟṟupaḍai, one of the ten idylls of the Saṅga period, which describes certain conditions prevailing in the first or the second century A. D., a king called Nalliyakóḍan is panegyrised by a poet named Nattattanár. Nalliyakóḍan was one of several kings who ruled over Laṅká * (Ceylon), with his royal residence at Ámúr. † On his way to this city, the poet had to pass through two of the other towns in his kingdom, namely, a fortified

---

* " நறுவீநாகமு மகிலு மாரமுந்
துறையாடு மகளிர்க்குத் தோட்புணையாகிய
பொருபுனறரூஉம் போக்கருமரபிற்
றொன்மா விலங்கைக் கருவொடு பெயரிய
நன்மாவிலங்கை மன்னருள்ளு
மறுவின்றி விளங்கிய வடுவில்வாய்வா
ளுறுபுலித்துப்பி னோவியர் பெருமகன்."

Cirupaṇ, 11: 161.221:—

The Lord of the *Oviyar* of spotless fame, endued with the strength of a tiger, intrepid of body and limbs and possessed of a sword of faultless blade, one out of the (several) kings of great and and ancient Laṅká, whose shores are constantly beaten by rolling billows, where *punnai*, *aghil* and *sandalwood* are washed against the shoulders of bathing women—Laṅká ineffable on account of its strength begotten of auspicious inception,

[The *Oviyar* were a tribe of Nágas inhabiting the sea coast. Aghil and sandalwood being washed against the bodies of bathing women shows that the place was a port and that those articles had dropped out of the ships]

† " அந்தணரருகா வருங்கடி வியனகர்
அந்தண் கிடங்கின் அவன் ஆமூர் "

Ibid—11 : 187-188,

His Āmụr guarded by invincible guards, surrounded by a beautiful and cool moat and containing broad mansions.

town * on the sea coast which the commentator calls Eyilpaṭṭinam, and another town called Vélúr.† From the fact that Nalliyakóḍan is mentioned as one of the kings of Laṅká (Ceylon), and as a chief of the Óviyar,‡ one of the Nága tribes of North Ceylon, and from the description of the towns themselves, one is led to surmise that the fortified town of Eyilpaṭṭinam was Mantai (Mátoṭa); that Ámur was the Aakote of Ptolemy in Jaffna, and that Vélúr which was between these two towns, was in all probability a village in the Púnakari or the Viḍattaltívu district, now known by some other name or covered by jungle.

According to tradition which finds full expression in Tamil works like Visva Puráṇam, Mántaippaḷ and Vijaya Dharma Náḍagam,¶ Mántai was a town of remote

---

* "பாடல்சான்ற நெய்த நெடுவழி
மணிநீர்வைப்பு மதிலொடு பெயரிய
பனிநீர்ப் படுவிற் பட்டினம்"

Ibid—11 : 151—153.

On the long way along the sea coast stands the famous city prase d by the poets, the city surrounded by a wall and a moat of crystal waters and containing many a cool tank.

† "திறல்வேலுநுதியிற் பூத்த கேணி
விறல்வேல் வென்றி வேலூர்"

Ibid—11 : 172-173.

The victorius Vélúr, where the lotus buds in the tanks appear like the heads of javelins belonging to the valourous Vélan.

‡ Ciṟupaṇ: 1 : 122, vide supra, note p:13

¶ Visva Puránam has not yet been printed. It was composed by one Sidambara Kaviráyar of Kiḷiyanúr in South Arcot about 200 years ago

Mántaippaḷ was composed by one Sidambara Táṇḍava Madura Kaviráyar of Karuvai Nallúr about 400 years ago and was published by Mr. Sangaralinga Páradi in 1922.

Vijaya Dharma Nádagam is an unpublished dramatic work composed about the early part of the 19th century, by one Ráma Sundaran son of Sidambara Udayár of Vaṇṇarpaṇṇe, Jaffna.

antiquity and the place of origin of the five classes of artisans* and of their chief, Visvakarma, the architect of the gods. These artisans did, in all probability, belong to the Nága tribe of Óviyar, who ruled at Mántai in ancient times. The power and greatness of these artisan rulers can be gauged when it is known that the earliest Yakkha kings of Ceylon found their wives among them. Padma Kómaḷai, the queen of Súra Panma, the great Asura king of Ceylon, who fought against and was defeated and killed by Kanda Kumára, was the daughter of a Dévakanmi† (artisan). Manḍódari, the chaste wife of Rávaṇa, the hero of the Rámáyaṇa, was the daughter of Maya, who not only presented his son-in-law with an invincible weapon but also built for him the beautiful city

---

* The five classes of artizans are :—

1. Manu	Kollar (கொல்லர்)	...Black-smiths.
2. Maya	Tachchar (தச்சர்)	...Carpenters.
3. Tuvashta	Kannár (கன்னார்)	.. Brass-founders.
4. Silpa	Sirpi (சிற்பி)	...Masons, Stone cutters, Sculptors, Architects, Image makers and Painters.
5. Visvaññia	(தட்டார்)	...Gold-smiths.

[These five artisans were born out of the five faces of Visvakarma.]

Mántai, p. 4.

மாந்தை நகருறைவோருள் லோகத்தின் வாணிபமே புரிவோர்
காந்த மலைக்குரியோர் பஞ்சாளரிற் கண்ணுவர் தோற்றினரே."

Vijaya. D. N.

Of those who dwell in the city of Mántai, who carry on the trade of the inner country and of those who belong to the magnetic mountain, there appeared the artificers called Kaṇṇuvar out of the five classes of artisans.

† K. P. Arasusey Paḍalam, v: 11.

of Laṅkápura.* Kubéra, the uncle of Ráváṇa, married Chitraréka, a daughter of another Dévakanmi. These kings, among whose families the Yakkha kings of Ceylon found their queens, were supposed to have been the descendants of Visvakarma, the progenitor of the artisan tribe. The proximity of the kingdom of Mántai to Laṅkápura, the capital of the Yakkhas, made the royal connections between the rulers of the two kingdoms feasible. This is an instance of the historical truths that may be found concealed in the exaggerated traditional stories contained in the ancient Puráṇas. It is said that he (Visvakarma) built an iron fort at Mántai.† This iron fort is referred to by Hiouen Thsang as one which had a high tower on the top of which some attractive women

---

*(a) Kamban, Canto: vii (Uttara Káṇḍam, Rávaṇan Pirappu Paḍalam), vv: 63 and 64.

(b) Ibid, Canto vi (Yutta Káṇḍam, Mantira Paḍalam) v: 1.

(c) " இருபது கையுடையான் றனக்கு மண்டோதரியை
ஈந்தருண் மயனார் பண்ணைப் பள்ளிகளாண்டே "

(d) " சூரபன்மன் மனைவி பதுமகோமளை தந்தை
சுரர்புனைவற் பணிந்து கூவாய்குயிலே

(e) " சித்திரரேகையென் னுந் தனதன் மகிழ் தேவியே
தெய்வ கம்மியன் பெண்ணென்றே கூவாய்குயிலே."

Mántai: pp. 8 and 24.

† " சொல்லருமடைகடோறுந் துலங்கிய மாந்தையெய்தி "
" சித்திரமேடைசூழ்ந்த டில்லிநன் னகரடுத்த
உத்தரதிக்கின்மிக்க வூசிக்காந்தத்தினாலே
சுற்றிலுமகலநாலைந் தோசனை தூரமுள்ள
முத்திறை மிருந்தகோட்டை சிருட்டித்தார் முத்தினத்தில்."

Visva, Panchakritiya Káṇḍam,
vv: 3 and 4. Mántai, p. ix.

Having reached Mántai of feitile fields, they built to the north of Delhi surrounded by beautiful plains, a fort of about 4 or 5 yojanas in circumference with magnetic iron in 3 days.

[The statement that Mántai was to the north of Delhi was due to the erroneous impression of the author.]

were kept to inveigle mariners into the harbour and to entertain them, while the Rákshasa (Nága) men attacked and plundered the ships.* With the growth of the Indian sea-borne trade, a proportionate number of merchant vessels began to sail over the Indian seas. The Nágas of Mántai (Mátoṭa), whose stronghold was on the great highway of the merchant vessels which had to cross over to the Bay of Bengal from the Arabian Sea and vice versa, developed into sea-pirates and lived by plundering and robbing unwary merchants. Kshemendra, a Cashmerian poet of the tenth century, relates that, in the day, when the Emperor Asóka was reigning at Pataliputra, certain Indian merchants, who traded with the distant islands, came to his Court and "informed him of their losses and complete ruin brought about by the depredation of sea-faring pirates called Nágas, who destroyed all their ships and plundered their treasure." Asóka issued "an edict inscribed on a copper plate, which was, however contemptuously set at nought by those for whom it was meant." It was only after he became a devout Buddhist that he was able to make the Nágas respect his edict.†

---

* "The records of the Buddhist religion say :—In the middle of a great iron city of this Ratnadvipa (Pao-chu) was the dwelling of the Rakshasi women (Lo-l'sa). On the towers of this city they erected two high flagstaffs with lucky or unlucky signals, which they exhibited (to allure mariners), according to circumstances when merchants came to the Island (Ratnadvipa). Then they changed themselves into beautiful women, holding flowers and scents, and with the sound of music they went forth to meet them, and caressingly invited them to enter the iron city; then having shared with them all sorts of pleasure, they shut them up in an iron prison and devoured them at their leisure."

Hiouen: M.L.R, vol : i, p: 148,

† Ind: Ship: p: 114.

The Nágas, referred to in the above story, were evidently those about Mántai (Mátoṭa,) and the early period of their piratical profession can also be seen from the same.

The iron fort, which is euphemistically called a magnetic mountain in Tamil works,* was perhaps the source of the belief among the medieval Muhammedan writers that there was a magnetic mountain which drew towards it all the iron-clad ships in its neighbourhood and wrecked them, a belief which is graphically described in the Arabian Nights.† The belief in the existence of an iron fort at Mántai is enhanced by the knowledge that

---

* a. "செங்கமல மாலையணிதேவனே மாந்தைநகர்
புங்கவனே காந்தமலைப் பூரணகெம் பீரமன்ணு."

Vijaya. D. N.

Oh! the ruler of the city of Mántai, the valourous lord of the magnetic mountain, the god who wears the wreath of pink lotus flowers.

b. "காந்தமா மலைக்கோட்டை மேவிய
காவலன் புகழ்கூறவே"

Vijaya. D. N.

To sing the praises of the lord of the magnetic mountain fort

c. "காந்தமுறுந்தடமதிலுங் கமழுமலர்ப் பொழிலுமுற்ற
மாந்தை நகர்."

Mántai, p : 20.

The city of Mántai guarded by broad magnetic walls and abounding in fragrant flowery groves.

† a. The Arab. Nts., The Story of the Third Calender.

b. Even so early as the beginning of the fourth century, the legend of a loadstone attracting iron-bound ships is mentioned by a writer quoted by Sir. Emerson Tennent:—

"A thousand other islands lie adjacent to Ceylon, and in a group of these called Maniolae (Maṇalúr, and the dependent islands of the Jaffna sea ?), is found the loadstone which attracts iron, so that a vessel coming within its influence, is seized and forcibly detained, and for this reason the ships which navigate these seas are fastened with pegs of wood instead of bolts of iron."

Tennent, vol :i, p: 563, note.

about the same period (first century A.D.) there was a brass fort at Dwáraka, a town in the ancient Yádava country and to the north of Bombay.*

The iron fort, which continued to be a great menace to the sea-faring trade of Ceylon, was destroyed, says the Chinese traveller Hiouen Thsang, by Vijaya.† In all probability, however, it was destroyed by Karikála Chóḻa the greatest of the early Chóḻa kings, who in the first century A.D.‡ conquered Ceylon and carried away a large number of captives to work on the banks of the Kávéri. It was perhaps after the destruction of this iron fort that he earned the sobriquet of "destroyer of the hanging fort," from several Saṅga poets.¶ It was also perhaps after the

---

* "செம்பு புனைந்தியற்றிய சேணெடும் புரிசை
உவராவீகைத் துவரை"

Puṛam. v. 201

Dwáraka, the delightful, containing the beautiful large fortress made of brass.

† Hiouen : M. L. R. vol. i, p : 148.

‡ Rajavali : p : 231.

¶ (a) "ஒன்னருட்குந் துன்னருங்கடுந்திறற்
றூங்கெயிலெறிந்த நின்னூங்கணோர்."

Puṛam. v. 39

Your great ancestor, who destroyed the strong and evil doing hanging fort feared by foreigners.

(b) "வீங்குதோட் செம்பியன் சீற்றம்விறல் விசும்பிற்
றூங்குமெயிலுந் தொலைத்தலால்."

Paḻamoḻi v: 49

The wrath of the broad shouldered Chembiyan (Chóḻa) who destoryed the fort hanging in mid air.

(c.) "தூங்கெயின் மூன்றெறிந்த சோழன்காணம்மானை"

Cilap. Vaḷtukádai, Ammánáivari.

The Chóḻa who destroyed three hanging forts

(d.) "தூங்கெயிலெறிந்த் செம்பியன்."

Ciṛupáṇ. 1 : 81-82'

[Contd.]

conqnest of Ceylon that the Chóḻa king received the title of Chembiyan. The north-western porition of Ceylon was first called 'Támraparṇi,' a name which was later applied to the whole of Ceylon by the Greeks. As the word 'támra' is equivalent to 'chembu' in Tamil, the conqueror of Támraparṇi was in all likelihood, entitled to be called Chembiyan. This surmise receives some confirmation from the fact that no king earlier than Karikála appears to have been called by that name.

The tradition connecting Mántai with Visvakarma and with artisans must have reached the ears of Pridham when he wrote that a colony of goldsmiths had settled down at Mántai in olden times.* Mántai is referred to as a kingdom in ancient Tamil classics,† and it appears

---

The Chembiyan (Chóla) who destroyed the hanging fort

(e) "தேங்குதூங்கெயி லெறிந்தவவன்."

Kalin., Rájapáramparium, v : 17,

He who destroyed the hanging fort which caused fear.

* Pridham, vol. ii, p. 496.

† (1) வரைபொரு நீண்மார்பின் வட்கார்வணக்கு
நிறைபொருவேன் மாந்தைக்கோவே-நிரைவளையார்
தங்கோலம் வவ்வுதலாமோ வவர்தாய்மார்
செங்கோல னல்லனென.

(2) புன்னைச்சோலை புனற்றெங்கு சூழ்மாந்தை
நன்னகநின் றலரு நன்னாட-னென்னைகங்
கங்குலொருநாட் கனவினுட்டைவந்தா
னென்கொலிவ ரறிந்தவாறு

Muttol : vv. 52 & 82
S. Tamil, vol. iii, pt. iii.

(3) "பொங்குதிரை பொருதவார் மணலடைகரை
புன்காநாவற் பொதிப்புற விருங்கனி
கிளைசெத்து மொய்த்ததும்பி பழஞ்செத்துப்
பல்காலலவன் கொண்டகோட்கூர்ந்து
கொள்ளாநரம்பினி மிரும்பூச
விரைதேர் நாரையெய்திய விடுக்குந்
துறைகெழு மாந்தையன்ன."

Naṛ, v. 35.

[Contd]

that the ruler there was an artisan in the first or second century A.D.*

The idea of some of the South Indian Tamil scholars that Mántai was a port, as well as the seat of a kingdom ruled over by Céra princes† on the West Coast of Travancore, which formed a port of the Céra dominion, is obviously incorrect. This idea arose from the fact that Mántai was referred to in a Kuṛuntogai verse as Kuṭṭuvan Mántai.‡ The name Kuṭṭuvan represented the Céra king Seṇ-Kuṭṭuvan of Cilappadikàra fame. He is alleged to have led a naval expedition by sea and to have conquered

---

(4) " தண்கடற் படுதிரைபெயர்த்தலின் வெண்பறை
நாரை நிரைபெயர்ந் தயிரையாரு
மூரோ நன்றுநன் மாந்தை
யொருதனிவைகிற் புலம்பாகின்றே."

Kuṛun : v. 166

(5) Naṛ : 395.

* " மாந்தையிலே வாழுமகு டத்தியாகியுனக்
கேந்துதழும்போ விரண்டுண்டு-வேந்தர்
முடித்தழும்புன் காலிலே முத்தமிழோர்க்கீயும்
படித்தழும்புன் கையிலே பார்."

Oh ! crowned Tiyági of Mántai ! you have two marks of injuries (on your body) ,one on your foot made by the crowns of kings (who bow down to you), and the other on your palm caused by handling benefactions given to those who are versed in the three kinds of Tamil (literature).

† See Ainguru : p. 16.

‡ See Kuṛun : p. 48. note. to v. 34.

" முழுஅதியானை யிண்குருகின் கானலம்
பெருந்தோட்ட மள்ளரார் ப்பிசைவருஉம்
குட்டுவன் மாந்தை யன்ன."

Kuṛun : v. 34.

Like unto the city of Mántai belonging to Kuttuvan, where the elephants feeding in the groves on the sea-coast are frightened by the noise made by the cultivators of Peruntóṭam (Mátóṭa.)

an unnamed enemy kingdom,* which was probably that of Mántai, as at that time the Nágas of Mántai had become notorious sea-pirates and there infesting the seas even on the west coast of Travancore. These pirates had perhaps their base for open sea-piracy at Mántai and, after this conquest, the town must have been known as Kuṭṭuvan Mántai. Seṅ-Kuṭṭuvan's father, Nedun Céralátan, known as the Red-Céra, also led an expedition against a colony of pirates and is said to have destroyed their tree-totem, a mighty Kaḍamba.† The fact that the

---

* "காலுளைக் கடும்பிசி ருடையவாலுளைக்
கடும்பரிப்புரவி யூர்ந்தநின்
படுந்திரைப் பனிக்கடலுழந்ததாளே. Padir : v. 41. ll : 25-27

You, who had ridden swift footed and white maned horses, your feet have now touched the waters of the cold inhospitable seas.

"கோடுநரல் பௌவங்கலங்கவேலிட்
டுடைதிரைப் பரப்பிற் படுகடலோட்டிய
வேல் புகழ்குட்டுவன்." Padir : v. 46. ll : 11—13.

Kuṭṭuvan of conquering fame, whose throw of the lance made the sea with the bending billows, in which the chanks resound, to tremble and recede.

"பொங்கிடும் பரப்பிற் கடல் பிறக்கோட்டிக்
கங்கைப்பேர் யாற்றுக்கரைபோகிய-செங்குட்டுவன்
Cilap: xxx. Kaṭṭurai, ll: 12—14.

Senguṭṭuvan, who first overcame the waters of the surging sea and then marched towards the banks of the Ganges.

† "கடம்பு முறடிந்த கடுஞ்சினவேந்தே!"
Padir; v. 12, ll: 3.

O! King of great ire! Who first destroyed the Kaḍamba tree.

"துளங்கு பிசிருடைய மாக்கடனீக்கிக்
கடம்பறுத்தியற்றிய வளம்படுவியன்மனை
Padir: v. 17, 1: 4-5.

The awe inspiring drum made out of the Kaḍamba tree cut down after passing over the great sea where the rain falls in shimmering sheets

"கடம்புமுதறடிந்த காவலனைப்பாடி"
Cilap; xxix. Náḻtukáḍai.

Singing the praises of him (Cera King) who first destroyed the Kaḍamba tree.

noise made by the cultivators of Peruntoṭam(which appears to be a translation of Mátóṭa), frightened the elephants on the sea coast of Mántai, as stated in the Kuṛuntogai verse referred to in the notes. clearly proves the identity of Mántai.

Mr. Kanakasabai Pillai, the author of 'Tamils 1800 Year Ago', thought that the country mentioned in Cirupáṇáṛṛupaḍai referred to Mavilaṅgai, near the eastern coast of India and to the North of the river Kávèri.* Professor S. Krissnaswamy Aiyangar, however, was of opinion that, as far as he was able to make out, there was no authority for taking 'Mavilaṅgai's to mean a country, as Mr. Kanagasabai had done the passage in Cirupáuṇáṛṛupaḍai not lending itself to that interpretation.† Mavilaṅgai in India, was not a country but a town or village, and is refered to as 'Malaṅge' by Ptolemy.‡ From the fact that several kings were said to have been ruling over the country called Má-Laṅká, and from the interpretation given by the well known commentator, Nachchinárkiniyár, there is not the slightest doubt that Ceylon was the place referred to as Má-Laṅkai, or Mahá Laṅká (the great Laṅka). Cirupáṅaṛṛupaḍai.

In further confirmation of the above, I quote two verses from Puṛanánúṛu, an anthology made by the third Tamil Saṅgam, of classical poems ranging from 200 B. C. to 200 A. D. Both verses are attributed to a poet named Nannáganár, who as his name indicates, was

* Tamils. p. 27.

† I. A.. vol. xlvi, p. 72.

‡ Ptolemy.

a Nága, perhaps of North Ceylon. The first* is in praise of Nalliyakóḍan, who is referred to as the ruler of Má-Laṅká and the other† of his son Villi Átan who is termed the ruler of Laṇká, (the prefix 'mà' being omitted) These passages, of accepted antiquity and genuineness, may well be allowed to settle the point that the kingdom of Nalliyakóḍan, referred to in Cirupáṅáṟṟupaḍai, was in North Ceylon.

Nága kings were reigning at Kudirai Malai too on

---

* "ஓரையாயத் தொண்டொடி மகளிர்
கேழலு ழுதவிருஞ்சேறு கிளைப்பின்
யாமையீன் புலவுநாறு முட்டையைத்
தேனாரும்பற் கிழங்கொடு பெறூஉ
மிழுமென வொலிக்கும் புனலம்புதவிற்
பெருமாவிலங்கைத் தலைவன்சீறியா
ழில்லோர் சொன்மலை நல்லியக்கோடனை
யுடைய வாழி"

Puṛam. v: 176.

Oh ! my heart that owns Nalliyakòḍan whe wears the garland of songs sung by minstrels with the lyre—the Lord of great Laṅkà of resounding waters, where one receives (for food) fresh smelling tortoise eggs, found by young women with shining bracelets, while at play, in the black soil turned up by the boar, with honey smelling *ambal* yams. May you ever flourish !

† "யானேபெறுகவன் றாணிழல் வாழ்க்கை
யவனேபெறுகவென் னாவிசைநுவா
னெல்லரிதொழுவர் கூர்வாண் மழுங்கிற்
பின்னைமறத்தோ டரியக்கல்செத்
தள்ளல்யாமைக் கூன்புறத்துரிஞ்சு
நெல்லமல் புறவி னிலங்கை கிழவோன்
வில்வி யாதன்."

Puṛam. v : 379.

May I obtain the protection of the shadow of his feet ! and may he receive my praises in verses of musical cadence! Such, is Villi Ātan, the Lord of Laṅká of fertile paddy fields where the reapers, mistaking the tortoises, lying half buried in the mud, for stones, hasten to sharpen their blunted sickles on their curved backs.

the west coast of Ceylon. It was perhaps Kudira Malai which was referred to as Aca Nagaram (Aswa Nagar) in some of the Cave inscriptions.* Kudira Malai is mentioned in ancient Tamil classics as a kingdom ruled over by two very munificent chieftains, Eḻiṇi and Koṟṟan.† The hill, Mudiram, of another munificent king, Kumaṇan, was also supposed to be Kudirai Malai.‡ Bertolacci and Pridham refer to the existence of several ruins at the foot of the hill Kudirai Malai and in the adjoining island of Káraitívu. The ancient poets, who sang the praises of Eḻiṇi, Koṟṟaṇ and Kumaṇan, did not sufficiently indicate the position of Kudirai Malai, their residence, so that it may be identified without the

---

* Muller.

† (1) "ஊராதேந்திய குதிரைக் கூர்வேற்
கூவிளங் கண்ணிக் கொடும்பூணெழினி"

Puṛam : v, 158, ll : 8—9.

Eḻiṇi of the high Kudirai (hill) which cannot be ridden, carrying a sharp lance and wearing flowers and wreaths.

(2) "ஊராக்குதிரைக் கிழவ"
"கைவள்ளீகைக்கடுமான் கொற்ற"

Puṛam : v. 168 ll : 14 and 16.

Oh ! Chieftain of Kudirai that cannot be ridden
Oh ! Koṟṟa who posseses a fleet horse and a hand which gives unstintingly.

‡ (1) "அதிராயாணர் முதிரத்துக்கிழவ
இவண்விளங்குசிறப்பினியறேர்க்குமண"

Puṛam : v. 158, ll : 25 and 26.

Oh ! Chieftain of the hill Mudiram, Oh ! Kumaṇa of the greatness above described and of artificial car.

(2) "பழந்தூங்குமுதிரத்துக்கிழவன்
திருந்துவேற்குமணனல்கியவளனே"

Puṛam : v. 163, ll : 8 and 9.

The wealth granted by Kumaṇan of the sharp lance, the chieftain of the hill Mudiram in which (Jak) fruits hang abundantly.

suspicion of a doubt. But for the presence of the ruins, and the mention of it under the name of Hippuros by the Greek travellers, the surmise of some of the Indian Tamil scholars that it was somewhere in the Western Ghats might have materialised into a fact.

As late as the second century A.D., there is a reference to this Nága kingdom in the story of the Chóḻa-King Kiḻḻi Vaḻavaṉ and his love match with Píli Vaḻai the beautiful daughter of Vaḻai Vaṉaṉ the Nága king of Maṇi-Pallavam (Jaffna.)* The loss of their son, on his way from Maṇi-Pallavan to the Chóḻa country, so grieved the king that he neglected to celebrate the annual festival in honour of Indra at his capital, the city of Káverippúmpaṭṭinam. The indignant god punished him for this neglect by causing the Chóḻa capital to be destroyed by an inundation.† According to the Tanjore

---

* "நாகநாடு நடுக்கின்றாள்பவன்
வாகைவேலோன் வளைவணன்றேவி
வாசைமயிலை வயிற்றுட் டோன்றிய
பீலிவளை."

Maṇi. canto, xxiv, ll; 54-5.

Pili Vaḷai born of the womb of Vásamayilai, the wife of Vaḷai Vaṇaṇ of the victorious javelin, who rules over the Nága country without fear.

† "நாகநன்னா டாள்வோன் றன்மகள்
பீலிவளையென்பாள் பெண்டிரின் மிக்கோள்
பனிப்பகைவானவன் வழியிற் றோன்றிய
புனிற்றிளங் குளவியொடு பூங்கொடி பொருந்தித்
தீவகம் வலஞ்செய்து தேவர்கோனிட்ட
மாபெரும் பீடிகை வலங்கொண் டேத்துழிக்
கம்பளச்செட்டி கலம்வந்திறுப்ப
வங்கவன்பாற் சென்றவன் றிறமறிந்து
கொற்றவன் மகனிவன் கொள்கெனக் கொடுத்தலும்
பெற்றவுவகையான் பெருமகிழ்வெய்திப்
பழுதில்காட்சிப் பைந்தொடி புதல்வனைத்
தொழுதனன் வாங்கித் துறைபிறக் கொழியக்

[Contd.]

கலங்கொண்டு பெயர்ந்தவன்றே காரிரு
ளிதங்குநீ ரடைகரை யக்கலங்கெட்டது
கெடுகலமாக்கள் புதல்வனைக்கெடுத்தது
வடிவேற்கிள்ளி மன்னனுக்குரைப்ப
மன்னவன் மகனுக்குற்றது பொறாஅ
னண்மணியிழந்த நாகம்போன்று
கானலுங் கடலுங் கரையுந்தேர்வழி
வானவன் விழாக்கோண் மாநகரொழிந்தது
மணிமேகலாதெய்வ மற்றது பொறாஅ
ளணிநகர்தன்னை யலைகடல் கொள்கென
விட்டனள்சாபம் பட்டதிதுவால்
விரிதிரைவந்து வியனகர் விழுங்க"

Ibid—Canto xxv, ll : 178—203.

When Pílivaḷai, the pre-eminent among women, the daughter of the ruler of Náganádu with her young child born of the dynasty of the Sun, went round and worshipped the Great Seat (of Buddha) placed in this Island (Maṇipallavam), by the God of the Celestials (Indra), Kambaḷa Chetty's ship came there. She having ascertained from him whither he was bound, entrusted to him her child to be taken and delivered to his father, the (Chóḷa) king. He (the Chetty) who was pleased at being selected for the purpose, received with due reverence the son of the woman of faultless beauty. But on the very day the harbour was left behind, the vessel was wrecked in a storm, and the ship-wrecked sailors carried the news of the loss of his son to the king Kiḷḷi of the sharp javelin. The king unable to bear the loss, wandered over, shore and sea, like unto a cobra that lost its gem, so that the city neglected to celebrate the festival (in honour) of Indra. Maṇimékalai, (the goddess of the sea), incensed at this (negligence), uttered a malediction that the sea should engulf the city, and accordingly the broad waves of the sea swallowed the great city.

(b) "வென்வேற்கிள்ளிக்கு நாக நாடாள்வோன்
றன்மகள்பீலிவளை தான்பயந்த
புனிற்றிளங்குழவியைத் தீவகம் பொருந்தித்
தனிக்கலக் கம்பளச் செட்டிகைத்தாலும்
வணங்கிக்கொண்டவன் வங்கமேற்றிக்
கொணர்ந் திடுமன்னுட் கூரி ருளியாமத்
தடைகரைக்கணித்தா வம்பிகெடுதலு
மரக்கலங் கெடுத்தோன் மைந்தனைக்காணா
தரசர்க்குணர்த்தலு மவனயர்வுற்று
விரைவனன்றேடி விழாக்கோண்மறப்ப"

Mani. canto xxix, ll: 3—13.

[Contd.]

Gazetteer,* this Kiḷḷi Vaḻavaṉ, who married the Ceylon Princess, came to the throne in 105 A.D., and his brother, Perunaṟkiḷḷi, succeeded him and reigned till 150 A.D. A king called Kókiḷḷi is also said to have married a Nága princess (perhaps of north Ceylon too) and to have had by her a son named Toṇḍaimáṉ Iḻantirayaṉ, to whom Toṇḍai Maṇḍalam country was afterwards granted by the Chóḻa king

The lost child of Kiḷḷi Vaḻavaṉ, it is alleged, was afterwards found washed ashore and was named Toṇḍaimáṉ Iḻantirayaṉ.† Whether Iḻantirayaṉ was the son of Kiḷḷi Vaḻavaṉ or of Kókiḷḷi, one thing is clear—that he was the son of a Kiḷḷi (a Chóḻa king) by a Nága princess of Maṇi-pallavam. Toṇḍai Maṇḍalam was separated from Chóḻa Maṇḍalam by his father and named after him, and he was made the first king of this district, with his capital at Kañchi or Kañchipuram (modern Conjee-

---

When Pílivaḷai, the daughter of the ruler of Nágánáḍu handed over her son born to Kiḷḷi of the victorious javelin to Kambaḷa Chetty the owner of the single ship, at the island (of Mani-pallavam), and when he with reverence carried him (the prince) embarking on his vessel, it was wrecked near a coast at midnight. He whose vessel, was wrecked informed the king of the loss of his son, and the latter through grief, hastened in search of his son and thus forgot about the festival.

* Tanj. Gaz. p. 17.

† அந்நீர்த்
திரைதருமரபின் * * *
* * * * *
பல்வேற்றிரையன் "

Perumpan. ll : 30. 31 and 37.

Tirayaṉ possessing different kinds of weapons, so called as he was washed ashore by the waves of the sea.

varam).* Kiḻḻi in whose reign the catastrophe befell Puhár or Káveripúmpaṭṭinam, removed his capital to Uṛaiyúr and was present at the consecration of the temple built for the worship of Pattinikaḍavuḷ by Seṅguṭṭuva Céra with Gaja Báhu of Laṅká, as described in the Epic of the Anklet (Cilappadikáram).† Gaja Báhu reigned in Ceylon from 113 to 135 A.D.‡ and, therefore, the destruction of Puhár must have been before this event. This transfer to the new capital is confirmed by Ptolemy who, writing about 150 A.D., calls Orthora (Uṛaiyúr or

---

* "அவள் யான் பெற்ற புதல்வனை என்செய்வே னென்றபொழுது தொண்டையை அடையாளமாகக்கட்டிக் கடலிலேவிட அவன் வந்து கரையேறின் அவற்கு யான் அரசுரிமையை எய்வித்து நாடாட்சி கொடுப்பலென்று அவன் கூற, அவளும் புதல்வனை அங்ஙனம் வரவிடத்திரைதருதலின், திரையனென்று பெயர் பெற்றான்.

Perumpan. Nachinarkiniyar's note to ll : 31 & 37.

When she (the Nága princess) asked what she should do with the son born to her, he (the Chóḷa king) said that if she placed her child on the sea with a *tondai* creeper tied as a mark, and if he reached the shore safe, he would give him the rights of a king, and make him the ruler of a country. She did so with her son, and as he was carried by the waves, he received the name Tirayan.

[That his capital was at Káñchipuram is known from line 420 of the same work.]

† (a) See Infra. Chap. ii; Cilap. Canto xxx, ll : 157—160.

(b) 'அதுகேட்டுச் சோழன் பெருங்கிள்ளி கோழியகத்து எத்திறத்தானும் வரந்தருமிவளோர் பத்தினிக்கடவுளாகுமென நங்கைக்குப் பத்தினிக் கோட்டமுஞ் சமைத்து நித்தல் விழாவணி நிகழ்வித்தோனே.'

Cilap. Uraiperukaṭṭurai. 4.

Hearing of the (prosperity of other countries by the inauguration of the worship of Kaṇṇakai) the Chóla king Perum Kiḻḻi, thinking that she (Kaṇṇakai), being a goddess of chastity, would grant all prayers, built at Uṛaiyúr" a temple for her worship and offered daily offerings and carried on festivals in her honour.

‡ Mah;, The Editor's List of Kings, part : i ; but Geiger in his edition of the Mahávaṇsa gives 171-193 A.D. for ja Gaja Báhu.

Uṛantai) the capital of the Chóḷas. During the time of Kiḷḷi, who is known by several honorific names his brother Iḷaṅkó, or Iḷaṅkiḷḷi, was the viceroy at Káñchi. Kiḷḷi erected a Buddhist chaitya at Káñchi and also caused a grove and a tank to be made in imitation of those at the Island of Maṇi-pallavam.† Thoṇḍai Maṇḍalam, as a separate kingdom under the sovereignity of Toṇḍaimáṉ Iḷantirayaṉ must have come into existence about 150 or 175 A.D. He was the progenitor of the powerful dynasty of the Pallavas who reigned over an extensive kingdom on the eastern coast of India for several centuries. This Nága origin of the Pallavas is confirmed by the description given in the Vélúr-páḷayam plates ‡ that the first member of the family of the Pallavas acquired all the emblems

---

* Ptolemy.

De Couto who had heard from the people about the inundation that devastated a great portion of Ceylon during the time of Kelani Tissa, co founds it with the present one as he says "And already in the time of the same Ptolemy who lived in the year of our Lord 143, it appears that the sea had begun to cause this devastation : because (Ptolemy) says that around Taprobana there were one thousand three hundred and seventy-eight islands".

J.C.B.R.A.S. Vol : xx. p. 83.

† ' பாரக வீதியிற் பண்டையோரிழைத்த
கோமுகையென்னுங் கொழுநீரிலஞ்சியொடு
மாமணிப்பல்லவம் வந்ததீங்கெனப்
பொய்கையும் பொழிலும் புனைமினென்றறைந்தத்
தெய்வதம்போயபிற் செய்தியா மமைத்த
இவ்விடம் "

Maṇi. Canto, xxviii. ll ; 201-6.

After the deity directed me to make an ornamental grove and pond, as if the great Maṇi-pallavam itself has been bodily transferred to this place, by the side of the tank of cool waters called Kómuki made by my fore-fathers in the Páraka (curtain ?) Street, and went away, these are (the pond and grove) that I made.

‡ M.E.R., 1910-1911.

of royalty on marrying the daughter of the Lord of Serpents. The ruling dynasty of Toṇḍaimaṇḍalam did in all probability, derive the name 'Pallava' from Maṇi-Pallavam, the native place of Iḷantirayaṉ's mother. Pallavam means in Tamil 'a sprout' or 'the end of a bough' and, to observers sailing from India, the Peninsula would have appeared just like a sprout or growth on the mainland of Laṅká. Some of the later Pallavas were called by surnames ending in 'ankura', a Sanskrit word signifying 'a sprout', as will be seen in such names as Buddhyankura Nayankura, Taranankura and Lalitankura*. In the Rayakóṭṭa plates,† however, a Pallava king called Skanda Sishya, whose reign is supposed to have been earlier than that of Vishnu Gopa, who was a contemporary of Samudra Gupta (300 A. D.), claims descent from Asvaddhámaṉ, (a Brahman warrior mentioned in Mahábháratá), through a Nága princess. The origin of Iḷantirayaṉ was perhaps so far forgotten by this time that the puranic story, manufactured under Brahmanical influence, began to be believed. Hence the later Pallavas claim to belong to the "Bharadvaja Gótra"

In the second century A. D. the Nágas of North Ceylon grew powerful enough to become sovereigns of all Ceylon, as will be seen from the names in the following list of Ceylon kings‡ taken from the Mahávaṅsa.

1.	Mahallaka Nága or Mahalla Ná	135 A.D.
2.	Bhatika Tissa (son)	141 A.D.

* Ep. Ind., vol. viii, p. 145.

† Ibid , vol. v, insc.no. 8.
Ibid , vol.lii, pp. 77—80.

‡ Mah., Editors' list of kings, part i, and chap. xxxvi

3.	Kanittha Tissa (brother)	165 A. D.
4.	Cula Nága or Sulu Ná (son)	193 A. D.
5.	Kuḍḍa Nága (brother)	195 A.D.
6.	Siri Nága I (brother-in-law)	196 A.D.
7.	Woharaka Tissa (son)	215 A.D.
8.	Abhaya Nága (brother)	237 A.D.
9.	Siri Naga II (nephew)	245 A.D.
10.	Vijaya (son)	247 A.D.

It is also curious that about this time (200 A D.), the Nágas of Central India also became very powerful, and one of their royal families, called the Chuṭu Nágas, took the place of the Sátaváhanas. The elder Pallava kings were contemporaries of the Chuṭus. They intermarried among them and eventually succeeded to the throne of the Chuṭus of the Nága race.*

It seems clear, therefore, that a Nága kingdom existed in north Ceylon continuously from the sixth century B. C. to the middle of the third century A.D. Its capital must have been either Kadiramalai (Kantaróḍai) in Jaffna or Mátoṭa. In these places there are piles of ruins yet to be excavated; and at Kantaróḍai in particular, where a number of Indian and Roman coins have been picked up even on the surface of the soil.†

Bertolacci, a historian of the early nineteenth century says that, "Mantota was the capital of a Kingdom founded by the Brahmins who had almost all the northern part

* Deccan.

‡ J. C. B. R. A. S., vol. xxvi, Nágadípa.

of Ceylon including Jaffna Patam".* But, judging from the events described in the Mahávaṁsa and the Maṇimékalai it is more probable that the capital was at Kadiramalai and that Mátota was only the chief port and seat of commerce, perhaps ruled by a chieftain under the paramount power of the king of Kadiramalai.

How long before the sixth century B C. did this kingdom of the Nágas come into existence? There is a tradition in Jaffna that Arjuna, one of the Páṇḍava princes, visited Jaffna in the course of his pilgrimage to the various shrines and sacred waters of his time, which were scattered all over India. The late Mr. John mentions it in his history of Jaffna. Let us here test the correctness of this tradition in the light of the Mahábhárata.

The Mahábhárata contained in its original form only a few thousand slókas; but, in course of time, it was so added to and amplified by interpolations that it now contains no less than 24,000 slókas. It is not probable that the northern version would contain any interpolations regarding the southern countries; but the southern translations are so full of interpolations regarding the Tamil countries that they cannot be relied on for the purpose of this investigation. But the Sanskrit version is relatively uncorrupted and we can safely base our deductions and conclusions on it, preferring it to the most widely-accepted oral traditions. In the Sanskrit Mahábhárata,† it is said that Arjuna, after crossing the country of the Kalingas and "seeing on his way many countries, holy places and charming mansions, proceeded slowly along the sea shores

---

* Bertol, p. 12.

† Mahab, M. Arjuna Vana Varsha Parva, chaps, ccxvii, 12—27: ccxix, 23—24; ccxx, i.

and reached Maṇipuram." There he met and married a (Nága) princess called Chitrángadai, the daughter of Chitraváhaṉ, the king of Maṇipuram, stayed there three years and left it, after the birth of a son, to visit other holy 'thírthas.' After visiting these 'thírthas,' he returned to Maṇipuram, to see his wife and son. From Maṇipuram he "proceeded towards Gokarna and saw one after the other all the sacred waters and other holy places that were on the shores of the Western Ocean."

The belief that it was a Páṇḍyan princess that Arjuna married is well rooted in the minds of our people and has been fostered for several centuries. Poets have sung of it and legendmakers have woven their tales on this assumption, with the result that an attempt to demolish an established belief may now prove unsuccessful. Even the stage has infused into the minds of our younger folk the belief that Arjuna married Alli, the amazonian queen of Madura. His burning love for her, his earlier unsuccessful attempts to marry her and his final triumph are graphically described in the plays which follow the 'Alli Arasáni Málai' of Pughaléndi Pulavar, written about the 12th century A.D. The South Indian writers were so sure that Maṇipuram was the capital of the Páṇḍyans, and Chitraváhaṉ a Páṇḍyan, that the later kings of Madura went so far as to include his name in their dynastic lists.* It is therefore necessary to approach the subject with an unprejudiced mind.

* The ancestor of the Páṇḍyas is described in the larger Sinnamanūr plates as (1) Pañchavan. (2) One who overcame the Lord of the Kurus and (3) One who absolved Vijaya from the curse of Vasu. Arjuna is the ancestor referred to in (1) and (2) and his son Vavraváhan in the third, as the defeat of Arjuna by his son in the contest for the sacrificial horse was the result of a curse by Vasu in a former birth.

M. E. R. 1907.

From the description given in the Mahábhárata it is very clear that Maṇipuram was so situated as to make it convenient to Arjuna to return to this place after visiting the 'thirhas' on the shores of the Southern Sea, and from there to proceed to Gokarna on the western coast of India. The 'shores of the Southern sea' meant either Kumari (Cape Comorin, which was then the mouth of a river) or Sétu (Adam's Bridge).

Only some holy shrine or sacred waters in or near Maṇipuram would have taken Arjuna there. Now, Kírimalai on the north coast of the Peninsula, one of the most important 'thírthas', was well known to the ancient Indians under the name of Nákulam and later Nakulésvaram.* It is, therefore, more than probable that Maṇipur (or Maṇipuram) was near Kírimalai. Its close proximity to the South Sea, and the facility it afforded to Arjuna to proceed to the west coast of India, gave him the opportunity to see his wife and child again. No other place in these regions could have given him this chance.

In one of the Tamil versions of the Mahábháratat† the first portion of his adventures is given as follows: "The

---

* "Nákulam náma samsuddha asti stánam mahitalé."
Súdha Sam: p. 325.

On the earth there is a very holy place defined by the name *Nakula.*

[The name, which perhaps had its origin from the people called Nágas, was later corrupted to Nakulam and then translated into the Tamil name Kirimalai as *nakulam* நகுலம் and *kiri* கிரி are synonymous.

† Mahab: R. p. 836.

hero (Arjuna) after passing the country of the Kaliṅgas proceeded on his way, seeing beautiful temples and places He, who is of great might, saw the Mount Mahéndra, praised by the Rishis. There he bathed in the Godávari, passed on to the Káveri and reached the celebrated sacred spot at the confluence of its waters with the sea. Here he bathed and also performed the ceremonies in honour of the Gods, Rishis and the Manes. Then he duly proceeded to Maṇalúr on the sea shore." The references to Mahéndra and the Godávari and to the confluence of the Kávéri with the sea, which came to prominence as a sacred spot only about the first century A.D. after the establishment of the Chóḷa capital of Káverippúmpaṭṭinam are obviously interpolations; and Maṇipuram seems to have been altered to Maṇalúr by the translators.

And according to the Tiru Viḷaiyáḍal Puráṇam Manalúr or Manalpuram,* a place slightly to the east of the present town of Madura and not on the sea coast, was the capital of the Páṇḍyan kings before the establishment

---

* (1) "பொருளினு மொழுக்கத்தானும் பொருவரும் போதத்தானு
மருளினுஞ்சிறந்த நீடோருங்குல வணிகன் பொங்கர்
மருமலிமலர்த்தடஞ்சூழ் மாமணலூரிலினின்றங்
கருதிய பொருள்களை மேலுந் தேடுவான் கருதிப்போனான்."

(2) "துயில்கொழுந்தனி வணிகனுஞ் செறிதொலைவிலா விருடொலையவே
வெயில்விரிந்த பினனுகரும் பெருவனமதாக வெருண்டெழுந்
தெயிலிலங்கிய கோயில்கண்டு திகைத்திதென் கொலெனாத்தெருண்
டயிலிலங்கு மணற்புரத்தரசற்குவந்தறிவித்தனன்."

Tiru, V. P. Sport, 53, vv. 6 and 10.

of Madura, and, according to 'Madura Mánmiyam *' this town was also known as Maṇalúr, Manavúr and Maṇavai.

What is quite certain is that a town known as Maṇalúr, Maṇalpuram, Maṇalúrpuram, Maṇavúr and Maṇavai, called also Maṇipuram in the Mahábhárata, was once situated somewhere on either coast of the Southern Ocean. It is equally certain that all these names were given at various times to Jaffna. But the authors of 'Tiruviḷaiyáḍal Puráṇam' and 'Madura Mánmiyam', who lived later than the thirteenth or the fourteenth century A.D., being unable to get over the allusions made to this place in older writings, located it as the ancient capital of the Páṇḍyan kingdom, in order to suit the popular belief that Chitraváhaṉ was a Páṇḍyan.

Now it is rather significant that Maṇaṟṟiḍal was a name given to Jaffna in the 'Yáḻpáṇá Vaipava Málai', † and that the name Veligama (sandy district), a Siṅhalese name with the same meaning, was given to a portion of Jaffna by the Siṅhalese. And it is no doubt the echo of the names Maṇalúr and Maṇavúr that is heard in the expression 'Maṇavai Árya Varótaiyaṉ' (மணவையாரிய வரோதயன்) and Maṇavaiyarkóṉ (மணவையர்கோன்) in a Tamil work

---

* " கருப்பணிதார்க்குல சேகரமாறன் றொடுத்தபடித்
திருப்பணிபூசை மதுரேசருக்குச் சிறக்கச்செய்து
மருப்பணிசோலை மணலூருந்தனன் வாய்த்தசெம்பொற்
பருப்பதமொத்தபுயன் மலயத்வச பாண்டியனே."

Mad; Man:

† Y. V. M. p. 5.

composed in Jaffna in the fourteenth century A.D.* Maṇavai seems to be a contracted poetical form of Maṇavúr or Maṇipuram, just as Anurai is of Anuradhapura and Singai † of Sińhapura. The name Maṇaṟṟi, as that of a country conquered by a Páṇḍyan, is found in a verse quoted in the commentary of Iṛaiyaṉár Ahapporul‡ It refers, no doubt, to Jaffna.

Even so late as in the twelfth and thirteenth centuries, European and Arab travellers who came to the East have called this kingdom of Jaffna by a name which is unmistakably reminiscent of its ancient names Maṇipuram and Maṇipallavam. Odoric, a Francis-

---

* a. மன்னர்மன்னு செகராசசேகரன் மணவையாரியவரோதயன் "

Sega A. Palavinaippaḍalam, v. 10.

Segarajasékaran, the Ārya king of Manavai, served by enemy kings.

b. " செடுந்தரங்க மிரங்குகூலத்

தெண்டிரைசூழ் மணவையர்கோன் செகராசசேகரமன் செவ்

வேல்வென்றி

கண்டுதிறை புரிந்தவர்போல் "

Ibid,—Yatirai Padalam, v. 31.

Like those who, on the sight of the bloody and victorious javelin of Segarajasékaran, the king of sea girt Maṇavai, the shores of which are washed by resounding billows, paid their tributes.

† (1) Tenkasi inscription of Parakrama Pāṇḍya Arikesaridéva.

Trav : A. S. part vi.

(2) Tiru : K. P.

(3) Kotagama Tamil inscription : Bell.

‡ " மின்னேரொளிமுத்தவெண் மணன்மேல் விரைநாறுபுன்னைப்

பொன்னேர்புது மலர்த்தாய்ப் பொறிவண்டு முரன்றுபுல்லா

மன்னோரழிய மணற்றிவென்றான் கன்னிவார் துறைவாய்த்

தன்னேரி லாததகைத்தின்றியான் கண்டதாழ் பொழிலே."

Ira : Ahap ; p. 52.

can friar who came to the East about 1322 A. D., speaks of three kingdoms called 'Malabar', 'Minibar and 'Mobar' in Southern India. He says that from the realm of 'Minibar' it is a journey of ten days to another realm which is called 'Mobar', and this ('Mobar') is very great and has under it many cities and towns, and in this realm is laid the body of the Blessed Thomas the apostle,* Further down, Odoric, calls this place ('Minibar') an island and adds, "the king of this island or province is passing rich in gold and silver and precious stones. And in this island are found a great store of good pearls as in any part of the world,"†

This description affords ample testimony to the identification of the island as the kingdom of Jaffna. as, at the time Odoric went on his travels, the Jaffna kings had become so powerful that they had the monopoly of the pearl fisheries, and hence the 'the great store of good pearls' mentioned by Odoric. It is, therefore, plain that it was the kingdom of Jaffna that was called 'Minibar' by him and it was Coromandel that was called 'Mobar.'

Edirisi, an Arab traveller of the tenth century, called this island 'Manibar', and so does Abulfeda; and a Turkish work, translated by Von Hammer for the Bengal Journal, has the word 'Monibar'.‡

In 1348 or 1349 A. D., John de Marignolli, Papal Legate to the court of the great Khan, on his return from China landed at columbam and from there he went to

---

* Cathay , p. 82.

† ibid , p. 84.

‡ ibid , p. 74.

the famous queen of Saba, by whom he was honourably treated. From there he went to Seyllan (Ceylon).* In another place he says that, wishing to go from Columbam on a visit to the shrine of St. Thomas, he embarked on board certain junks from lower India, (which he called 'Minibar') and being caught in a storm, he was driven to a harbour of Seyllan called Pervellis, over against Paradise."† If Columbam was in 'Minibar', and if 'Minibar' was another name for 'Malabar', as is supposed by Col. Yule, Marignolli would not have specially mentioned 'Minibar' as the place of embarkation. From the above passage, it is plain that 'Minibar' was outside Columbum. He must have gone to 'Minibar' on his way to Ceylon or to the shrine of St. Thomas. 'Minibar was undoubtedly the kingdom of Jaffna. In another place, Marignolli says that the second kingdom of India is called 'Mynibar.'‡ The king of Jaffna had at the time attained such eminence as to have become the overlord of the whole Island of Ceylon, and Marignolli was not far wrong in calling it the second kingdom in India.

During the Rámáyaṇa period, the capital of the Páṇdyans was at Kaváḍapuram and there is nothing to show that at the time of Arjuna's visit, which was not much later, ¶ the capital had been removed to Madura or to Maṇalúr.

A Céra king called Céramán Peruñcóṟṟu Utiyaṉ

* Cathay, p. 346.
† ibid, p. 356.
‡ ibid, p. 374.
¶ Muzumdar pp. 453-454.

Céralátan̤, who lived at the time of the Mahábhárata war, was praised in verse by his poet-friend, one Mudi Nága Ráyár of Muriñciyúr, for his munificence in feeding both the armies that took part in the battle of Kurukshétra.* That this tradition about the Céra king feeding the armies in the greater war of the Kauravas was current during the early part of the Christian era, is proved by an allusion made to it by the author of Cilappadikáram.† Tne poet, Mudi Nága Ráyar, is said to have flourished about the time of the first Tamil Saṅgam and to have been a member of it. ‡ But, if the Rámáyaṇa is correct in saying that the capital of the Páṇḍyan kingdom—at the time of the Ráma-Rávaṇa war—was at Kavádapuram, it ought to have been some time after the great deluge in which southern

---

* " நீயோ பெரும்
வலங்குளைப்புரவி ஐவரொடுசினைஇ
நிலந்தலைக்கொண்ட பொலம்பூர்தும்பை
ஈரைம்பதின்மரும்பொருது களத்தொழியப்
பெறுஞ்சோறு மிகுபதம் வரையாதுகொடுத்தோய்."

Puram, v. 2.

When the five (Pándavas), possessing horses with the right whorl (on foreheads), fell out with the twice fifty (Kurús) crowned with wreaths of *tumbai* flower, who had dispossessed (the former) of their country, and waged war until the latter were killed, you the great one fed them (both armies) without the expectation of any remuneration.

† " ஓரைவர் ஈரைம்பதின் மருடன்றெழுந்த
போரிற்பெருஞ்சோறு போற்றாது தானளித்த
சேரன்பொறையன் மலையன்."

Cilap, canto, xxix, Usalvari.

Céra, the king of the Malaya country, who supplied food without request at the war which arose between the five (Pàndavas) and the twice fifty (Kurus)

‡ Iṛa : Ahap : p. 4.

Madura, with its first Saṅgam, was engulfed. We can, therefore, surmise that the time of the destruction of southern Madura synchronised with the destruction of a great portion of Rávaṇa's kingdom, which took place somewhere about 2347 B C. as stated in the Rajavali.* If the Kurukshétra war, as is now believed, was later than the Ráma-Rávaṇa war, we can safely take Muḍi Nága Ráyar as a member of the second Tamil Saṅgam, which was at Kaváḍapuram. If the deluge that destroyed Kaváḍapuram and the forty nine Tamil countries be taken as the one which occurred during the time of Kelani Tissa in the third century B.C., † then the error of locating the Páṇḍyan capital at Maṇalùr near Madura during the Mahábhárata period becomes clearly apparent.

The Mahábbárata, which mentions the Paṇḍyans as ruling kings, does not call Chitraváhaṉ a Paṇḍyan. On the other hand, he is referred to as a Nága king and his daughther as a Nága princess. It is said that when the Páṇḍavas celebrated their horse sacrifice, the sacrificial horse, " wandering at its leisure, at last arrived within the dominions of the ruler of Maṇipura," who was Vavraváhan the son of Chitráṅgadai by Arjuna, and was seized and detained by him. When Arjuna offered battle, he was mortally wounded by his son and was only saved from death by the interference of Ulipi, another of his Nága wives, who is referred to as an aunt of the prince and a cousin of Chitráṅgadai.‡ Ulipi was admittedly

* See supra, p. 9

† Rajavali. p. 191.

‡ Mahab : P. Aswamédha Parva, sec. lxxix, p. 192-200.

a Nága princess, and it is therefore wrong to suggest that Chitraváhaṉ was a Páṇḍyan.

It is also said that Vavraváhaṉ, while fighting against Arjuna, "raised his standard which was decorated most beautifully, and which bore the device of a lion in gold" and that "his flag decked with gold and resembling a golden palmyrah on the King's car was cut off" by Arjuna.* This standard displaying a lion appears, therefore, to have been the one used by the Nága kings of North Ceylon long before the advent of Vijaya, and the fact that a flag representing a palmyrah tree was used on the car of Vavraváhaṉ shows that he was a king of North Ceylon. The flag of the Páṇḍyas, during the period of the third Saṅgam (from 200 B.C. to 300 A.D.), and even before, as is proved by several allusions in the literature of the period, was the fish,† and there is no reason to suppose that their flag was at any earlier period either the lion or the palmyrah tree. On the contrary, the Standard of the Lion, which appears to have been the emblem of the Nágas of North Ceylon, continued to be the flag of the Ceylon king till the Island was ceded to the British in 1815 A.D.

It would also appear that the portion of the Indian Peninsula which is now the southern extremity of it was then under the sway of the Nága kings of Maṇipuram and that the poet Viyása was quite accurate in stating that the sacrifical horse strayed into the dominions of Vavraváhaṉ and not into his capital. These Nágas who, in all proba-

* Mahab : P. Aswamédha Parva, see Lxxix, pp. 192—290.

† See supra, p. 10. note*

bility, emigrated from the regions of Bengal and Assam, following the custom of ancient emigrants, called the capital of their new dominion in north Ceylon, Maṇipuram, which is still the name of an important town in Assam, where the ruins of an ancient city of that name are still found.

The Sinnamanúr copper plates, inscribed long after the Tamil Mahábhárata and at a time when the people of India believed that Arjuna had married a Páṇḍyan princess, could not be expected to contain any other account.

If, therefore, it is admitted that Maṇipuram was a town in the Jaffna Peninsula, it is not difficult to identify it with Kantaróḍai, as recent excavations have led to the discovery of very ancient Indian coins called Puranás in that locality.* These coins were in use at a period anterior to 500 B.C., and they clearly prove the intercourse, commercial and otherwise, that existed between North India and Ceylon in that remote period.

A Nága kingdom was, therefore, existing in Jaffna in the fifteenth century B. C., the period generally allotted to the events described in the Mahábhárata. And the daughter of of the Nága king reigning there was handsome and accomplished enough to attract a proud Áryan like Arjuna, gay Lothario though he was.

* J.C.B.R.A.S. vol. xxvi ; Nágadípa.

CHAPTER II

The Kalingas

THE earliest historical records of foreign colonization in Ceylon begin with the advent of Vijaya and his followers, which according to the Mahávaṅsa*, was in the sixth century B. C. but, according to the Yálpáṇá Vaipava Málai, † in the eighth century B. C. It is also stated in the Mahávaṅsa that Vijaya 'landed in the division Tamba-paṇṇi of this land of Laṅká' ‡. Although there have been scholars who have held that Tambapaṇṇi was on the southern coast of Ceylon—near the mouth of the river Kirindi Oya¶ and others who have thought that it was at a place called Periaturẹ, on the east coast—between Mullaitive and Trincomalie § the consensus of opinion among the Siṅhalese scholars of the present day is that it was on the west coast of Ceylon, near the present town of Puttalam. The identification of this landing place has been a matter of controversy for a very long time, and it is now found necessary to renew the discussion for the sake of research into the ancient history of Jaffna. A

---

* Mah. chap. vi.

† Y. V. M. p. I.

‡ Mah. chap. vi.

¶ Parker, p. 245.

§ De Couto, Dec. v. Bk. i, chap. v; Journal, C. B.R.A.S. vol. xx, p. 63. See Ceylon by Sir E. Tennent, xol. i, p. 330, note 2.

place on the western coast was fixed on the assumption that the town of Tammanná, or Tambapaṇṇi Nuvara, naturally would have been built by Vijaya close to his landing place; and the site of this ancient city afterwards called 'Tammanná Aḍaviya,' was placed by one of the Siṅhalese poets of the 15th century, the author of Kókila Sandésaya, to the north of Muṇṇessaram in his description of the route from Matara to Jaffna.* The late Mr. H. Neville has given a description of the ruins found in 'Tammanná Aḍaviya' about twelve miles north-east of Puttalam and has identified the place as the site of the ancient Tammanná Nuvara,† but Mr. Parker was equally certain that the site of Ruhuna Mágama, near Tissamaharáma Tank, was that of Tammanná Nuvara.‡ Wherever the town of Tammanná Nuvara might have been, there are no certain grounds to

---

* " Pempenná kata kuvéni Vijayinduṭa
bimdunná laka himikara sepatakoṭa
um denná sahá visu nuvara idikoṭa
Tammanná aḍaviya déka yan nosita "

Kók. v. 186.

Tammanná adaviya—the place where Kuvéni saw, and fell in love with Vijaya, and where they built a town and resided after she gave to Vijaya the sovereignty of the land (Laṅká) look at it and fly away.

" Lobaḍa vadá rá bi mat kattalama
Sábada paturuvá dena ranga attalama
Sabanda bálà siṭá tuṭu kara nettalama
nubada pama nova véda yan Puttalama "

Kók. v. 187.

At Puttalam-please your eyes by looking at the women drunk with toddy, please your ears by listening to their songs and go on your journey without delay.

† Tap. vol. i, pp. 42-49

‡ Parker, pp. 17-19.

suppose that it was built in or near the place where Vijaya landed. Both Mr. Neville and Mr. Parker, as well as the others who were in search of Tambapaṇṇi, relying on the description of the landing of Vijaya given in the Mahávaṅsa,* were misled by that impression. The Dípavaṅsa, which is supposed to be an earlier work than the Mahávaṅsa, does not say that Tambapaṇṇi Nuvara was built by Vijaya at or near the place where he first landed in Ceylon.† The theory that Tambapaṇṇi was somewhere near Puttalam finds such favour nowadays, that, in order to meet its needs, it has even been suggested that Vijaya must have come not from Lála in Bengal but from Láḍa. Láḍa was a district on the western coast of India extending from Guzerat and the Peninsula of Kathiawar to Bombay, seized and populated in Epic times by an áryanised tribe called the Yádavas, in the course of their migrations from the banks of the Jumna, their home in the Vedic period. The imagination of Mr. Neville, led by his usual philological extravagances, soared so high, that he went hunting for this country of Lála or Láḍa to the banks of the Indus ‡

---

* Mah. chap vii.

† "That crowd of men having gone on board their ship sailing on the sea, were driven away by the violence of the wind, and lost their bearings. They came to Lankadípa, where they disembarked and went on shore . . . . , The red coloured dust of the ground covered their arms and hands; hence the name of the place was called Tambapanni (copper coloured). Tambapanni was the first town in the most excellent Lankadípa; there Vijaya resided and governed his kingdom."

‡ Tap, vol: i, pp: 51-54.

On the contrary, we have the authority of the Mahávaṅsa itself that the grandmother of Vijaya was the daughter of a Vaṅga (Bengal) prince by a Kaliṅga princess. The story runs that she eloped with, or was forcibly carried away by, one Siṅha, probably a robber chief of Lála and that she lived with him in that country until she gave birth to a son and daughter. Then, unaccustomed as she was to the life of a robber, she found an opportunity to escape from this Siṅha and sought refuge in the Vaṅga country with her children. The enraged husband went thither and destroyed the crops, laid waste the country and harassed the people for having given refuge to his wife and children.* Whether Siṅha was a man or even the lion of the traditional belief, if he was from Láḍa the present Guzerat, the distance of 700 miles would have been too great for him to traverse. And it would have been more than impossible for a weak woman and her children to have undertaken and to have safely accomplished on foot the long and perilous journey to Vaṅga through trackless forests infested with wild beasts and robbers.

The story goes on to say that, after giving up the kingdom of Vaṅga to his step-father Siṅha Báhu, the father of Vijaya returned to his own land Lála and there founded a city called Siṅhapura † That this Siṅhapura was not in Láda but in the Kaliṅga country can be easily seen from the numerous later references in the Mahávaṅsa.

To take the flimsy hypothesis that Vijaya, on his way

---

* Mah. chap. vii.

† Mah. chap. vi.

to Ceylon, touched at Suppáraka* and Bhárukachcha† (identified as Supara and Baroach on the west coast of India to the north of Bombay), and to argue that he must have embarked from the Yádava country of Láḍa, will go more to prove the ignorance of the authors of the Mahávaṅsa and the Dípavaṅsa as regards the ancient geography of India, than to prove that he (Vijaya) actually sailed from the west coast. Supara and Baroach were such well known ports at the time the Mahávaṅsa and the Dípavaṅsa were written that the authors probably thought of lending some colour to their account of the voyage of Vijaya by stating that he touched at those ports on his way.

In the Tamil Epic Cilappadikáram, composed about three centuries earlier than the Mahávaṅsa, Siṅhapura is mentioned twice.‡ In the same poem, discussing line 47 of the preface, Aḍiyárku Nallár, the commentator who lived in the 14th or the 15th century A.D., describes Siṅhapura as a town in the Kaliṅga country, taking as his authority a later reference in the same poem. In the Maṇimékalai too, Siṅhapura is mentioned as a town situated in the Kaliṅga country.¶

---

* Mah. Chap. vi, v. 46.

† Dīpa. Chap. ix, v. 26.

‡ (1) "சிங்காவண்புகழ்ச் சிங்கபுரத்து"

Cilap. Preface, l, 47

Siṇhapura of Sinha fame.

(2) "கடிபொழிலுடுத்த கலிங்க நன்னாட்டு
தீம்புனற்பழனச் சிங்கபுரத்தினும்"

Cilap. Canto xxiii, ll. 138 and 140.

In Siṅhapura of beautiful arable lands with cool water, situated in the Kaliṅga country surrounded by fragrant groves.

¶ "காசில்பூம்பொழிற் கலிங்கநன்னாட்டுச்
சிங்கபுரம்"

Mani. Canto xxvi, ll. 15 and 17.

Siṅhapura, in the good and faultless country of Kaliṅga of flowering groves.

Kaliṅga was one of the earliest kingdoms established in the Dekkan by Dravidian tribes and long before the Áryan push. According to the Vishnu Puráṇa, it was founded, by Kaliṅga, one of the putative sons ofBali,* on being driven out by Indra and Vishnu from his kingdom on the Upper Indus about 2800 B.C. Originally, it covered Orissa and a part of Bengal. It is mentioned in the Rámáyaṇá and the Mahábhárata as one of the flourishing States of the Dekkan. Aṅga, Vaṅga and Kaliṅga are referred to in the later Epic as mlechcha† (Dravidian) kingdoms. In the great war between the Páṇḍavas and the Kurús, the Kaliṅga king, Srutáyu, fought with his two sons against the Páṇḍavas and the three were killed by Bhíma. Its ancient capital was Sri Kakola, corrupted to the present Chicacole. Kaliṅga is also repeatedly mentioned in the Buddhist legends. The remote antiquity of Kaliṅga and its non-áryan origin in now admitted by all historians.

It is a fact well known to all students of the history of Ancient India that the Kaliṅgas were a people who were almost the first among Indian races to cross the seas, not only for commercial enterprise but also for the sake of conquest and colonization. They founded colonies in Ceylon, in far off Java and in the Straits Settlements. It was they who established the town of Siṅgapura—now called Singapore—in the Straits Settlements, and Indians, from whatever country they may hail, are still known among the Malays as 'klings,' a corruption of the term 'Kaliṅgas'.

---

* Vishṇu. P., p. 444.

† Mahab. M.

An insignificant town, by name Siṅhapura, still exists in the Chicacole district of Ganjam Zilla in Orissa, and in all probability it is the site of the city built by the father of Vijaya, bereft now of all its ancient glory and importance. General Cunningham supposes that Siṅhapura, the capital of Siṅhabáhu the father of Vijaya, is the town of that name, situated 115 miles to the west of Gaṅjam, and at one time the capital of Kaliṅga*

There are others who think that Siṅhapura is the present village of Siṅgúr which is a station in the Tarakésvar branch of the East Indian Railway, ten miles from Tarakéswara in the district of Hughli. This village is in the district of Rada which is the same as Lála or Láḍa.† This identification may be correct, for ancient Siṅgúr appears to have been of considerable size and importance and a flourishing commercial town on the old bank of the river Sarasvati. The followers of Vijaya were also called Gangetic settlers, and the descendants of those who settled in North Ceylon called themselves afterwards as of the Gaṅgakula or Gaṅgavamsa.

No further proof is necessary to establish the fact that Siṅhapura, founded by Vijaya's father, was a town in the ancient Kaliṅga, and not one in the far off Láḍa, the country of the Yádavas.

The utter improbability of placing Siṅhapura, the capital of Siṅhabáhu, on the banks of the Indus, as sup-

---

* Anc. Geo. p. 519.

† Deg. J. Beng. B.R.A.S. New Series, vol. vi, p. 624.

posed by Mr. Neville, is so obvious that it need not be discussed here.

It is of course not surprising that prince Vijaya, the most adventurous of an adventure-loving nation, should have embarked with 700 followers, and with an equal number of women and children, in search of fresh woods and pastures new. If he had sailed from the shores of Kaliṅga, where else could he have landed except somewhere in the northern or eastern coast of Ceylon? On the other hand, those who are aware of the direction of the monsoons that blow over the Indian Ocean will not be slow to arrive at the conclusion that a vessel drifting, as stated in the Mahávaṅsa from the coast of Guzerat, can never be driven to the coast of Ceylon, but must go either to a place on the western coast of India, much closer to the place of embarkation, or far to the west in the Arabian Sea. The suggestion of De Couto that Vijaya landed at Periyatuṛe, between Mullaitive and Trincomalie, or that of Parker that the mouth of the Kirindi Oya was the spot, would be much nearer the truth than the popular impression that it was at or near Puttalam.

But, according to a local tradition which still exists, and which has been embodied in the Yáḻpáṇa Vaipava Málai, Vijaya landed on the northern coast of Jaffna and took up his residence at Kadiramalai.* If, indeed, copper coloured earth had anything in common with the name Tambapaṇṇi, as stated in the Mahávaṅsa, there is no place in Ceylon where copper coloured earth can be

---

* Y. V. M., p.2.

found so close to the shore as the north coast of Jaffna. It is said that Vijaya, who was undoubtedly a Hindu, built the temple called Tirutambalésvaram in the north of Ceylon.* This temple must have been built near the present Kírimalai, as there are lands in the vicinity still going under the name of 'Tirutampálai.' Tamba is the Sanskrit word for copper; and the Tambapaṇṇi of the Siṅhalese chronicler can therefore quite conceivably be the 'Tirutambalésvaram' mentioned in the Yáḻpáṇa Vaipava Málai.

This conclusion finds additional proof in the Mahávaṅsa; for it is mentioned there that the boats which conveyed the women and children among the followers of Vijaya touched at Mahinda dípa and at Nagga dípa respectively, where they settled.† Naggadípa, where the children are alleged to have landed, is certainly Nicobars, the Nakkávaram of the Tamils, which was so called as it was populated by naked cannibals.‡ But there is a difference in the reading of the name of the island where the women are said to have landed. Geiger thought that it was Mahiladípa; Mudlr: Wijesinghe and Sri Sumaṅgala read it as Mahindadípa.¶ If the correct reading is Mahisadípa, which is more probable, the place can be identified. In ancient times, the eastern portion of the Jaffna Peninsula was a separate island and was known as Erumaimullaitívu, from the name of a plant 'erumaimullai' (prenna serratifolia) which grew abun-

* Y. V. M. p. 3.

† Mah. chap. vi.

‡ Sanskrit, 'Nagga,' = Tamil, 'Nakka'=Naked. cf. "நக்கசாரணர் நாகர் வாழ்மலை" Maṇi. Canto, xvi, l. 15

¶ Mah.; Maha.; Mah. P.; Mah. Pali. chap. vii.

dantly there. The name appears to have been later applied to the whole of the Jaffna Peninsula*, in the same manner as Nágadípa, which was the name of the principal island and which was applied not only to the whole peninsula but also to a portion of the Vannis. The name Erumai-mullai-tívu might have been shortened to Erumai-tívu (erumai=buffalo) and translated to Mahisa dípa in Pali. These identifications confirm the fact that all the three vessels in which the Kaliṅga emigrants embarked navigated down the Bay of Bengal and touched at places to which they would naturally have been driven.

The statement in the Mahávaṅsa that all the men travelled in one boat, all the women in another, and all the children in a third† cannot for a moment be considered as correct. It is more than probable that Vijaya and his party landed at the abovementioned place (Tiru-tampálai), and that another party landed at Erumai-mullai-tívu. In all probability, it was these colonists who built a city on the north-eastern corner of Jaffna and called it Siṅhapura, which, in later times, was to become famous in the history of Jaffna as Siṅgai Nagar. The ruins of this city, covered over with sand, can still be seen at Vallipuram.

The suggestion that the Periature of De Couto referred to Mátoṭa (great harbour)‡, coupled with the fact that the district in which Mátoṭa is situate was in

---

* Winslow. See under எருமைமுல்லைத்தீவு.

† Mah. chap. vi.

‡ J. C. B. R. A. S., vol. xx, p. 63, note 4.

very early times known as Támravarṇi,* lends credence to the theory that the probable landing place of Vijaya was Mátoṭa and that Tambapaṇṇi is only another form of Támravarṇi.

According to the Vaipava Málai, Vijaya had his permanent residence at Kadiramalai for some time, though he was engaged in building and restoring temples in different parts of the Island.† His town of Tambapaṇṇi was built much later, after his marriage with Kuvéni and after the conquest of the Yakkhas;‡ and it is not unreasonable to conjecture that he named his town, wherever he might have built it, after the name of the place where he first landed. It is idle to suppose that he met and married Kuvéni on the day and at the place he first disembarked, or that he defeated the Yakkhas, whose stronghold was either at Maiyaṅgana or at Laggala, within a few days of his landing. The Jaffna tradition that he landed at some port on the north coast, stayed at Kadiramalai, built the temple of Tirutambalésvaram, perhaps as a thank-offering for his safe arrival, and then went round Ceylon building new temples and repairing those that were in ruins,¶ is the more probable one. In the course of these travels he must have met and married Kuvéni, the Yakkha princess, and after his marriage with her the idea of overcoming the Yakkhas and possessing the kingdom would naturally have occurred to him.

---

* See infra, chap. iii, p.

† Y. V. M., p. 3.

‡ Ibid p. 4: Mah. chap. vii.

¶ Ibid p. 3.

The description of Vijaya's arrival in Ceylon,—in the Rajavali—that "while sailing towards the country of Runa Rata, in the midst of the sea, they perceived the large rock called Sumanakúṭa Parvata or Adam's Peak, and they concluded among themselves that it was a good country for them to reside in, and so they landed at the place called Tammannátoṭa in Ceylon"* seems to be a confused reference to his travels in South Ceylon for the purpose of building the temple of 'Santhira-Sékaran-koyil at Matthurai '.†

It may well be that Mr. Parker's identification of the site of Tambapaṇṇi Nuvara is correct. For, in the circumstances, it would have been only natural for Vijaya to found his kingdom in the extreme South, as remote as possible from the place which gave him refuge when he first landed in Ceylon.

It is also matter for grave doubt whether the proud Páṇḍyan of South India would have readily consented to give his daughter in marriage to an unknown adventurer. Vijaya had just come to a kingdom over a people who were then supposed to be devils and demons. "From Kanyá-Kumari to the Himalaya mountains," all Indians despised "the country of the Rákshasas," as they termed Laṅká in contempt.‡ On the other hand, his royal lineage too was a matter of doubt and would not have been known. The present town of Madura could not have then come into existence, and the 'Southern

* Rajavali., p. 168.

† Y. V. M., p. 3.

‡ Ibid p. 2.

Madura,' if the Rajavali is to be believed, had been engulfed by the ocean. At that time the Páṇḍyan capital must have been Kaváḍapuram, which was destroyed about the third century B. C.* If the chronicles had stated that an alliance of the nature did take place between a Páṇḍyan princess and a scion of a royal family that had ruled over Laṅká for several centuries or even generations, it would have been more credible. Besides, there has not been one single instance of a similar alliance after Vijaya. It appears that the earliest author of the Maháva̐ṅsa had a motive in dividing the men, women and children who accompanied Vijaya into three separate boats. It was with the purpose of effecting, later, a wholesale marriage alliance in the Páṇḍyan country. He, however, forgot to mention that the 700 male companions of Vijaya refrained from marriage until Vijaya abandoned his Yakkha wife and children, or that, if they had contracted marriages among the Yakkhas and the Nágas among whom they settled, they too as his true followers abandoned their wives and children in imitation of Vijaya.

Notwithstanding the assertions to the contrary in the Siṅhalese and the Jaffna chronicles, we are therefore led to suggest that the princess who supplanted Kuvéni in the heart of Vijaya was a Nága princess, either from the north or from the west of Ceylon. Similar alliances became only too common among the successors of Vijaya. We read that about two centuries after his death, the capital of the Southern kingdom came under the sway of

---

* Vide supra, chap. i, pp. 9 & 10.

Mahá Nága, the brother of Dévánampiya Tissa, a prince of Nága parentage, and that it remained under the Nága princes for several centuries.

If this tradition of Vijaya's landing and sojourn in the North be true, where was Kadira malai? It would appear that, at the time the 'Kailáya málai' was composed, the bare tradition that Vijaya had landed at Jaffna and stayed at 'Kadiramalai' remained, but that the position of 'Kadiramalai' was altogether forgotten. So the pious author had no other alternative but to jump to the conclusion that the 'Kadiramalai' referred to in the tradition was no other place than Kataragama, the scene of the heroic deeds of his god 'Kanda Kumára' alias 'Kártikéya'.* Kataragama is also known in Tamil as 'Kadiramalai'. The fact that this 'Kadiramalai,' which was not only the residence of Vijaya for a time, but also the capital of many kings before and after him, was so close to the place where the author composed his poem

---

" வரிந்தசிலை

வேடர்குலமாதுபுணர் வேலாயுதகரன்செங்
காடன்புதல்வன் கதிர்காமன்-ஏடவிழுந்
தார்க்கடம்பன் பேர்முருகன் ருமோதரன் மருகன்
சீர்குரவன்றேவர் திரட்கொருவன்-சூர்ப்பகையை
மாற்றுங்குகன் குழகன்வாய்ந்த வடியார்துயரை
யாற்றுங்கும ரனருளாலே-போற்றுதவர்
வாய்ந்த கதிரைமலை

K. M.

Kadirai malai sacred to the carrier of the lance, the husband of bow armed veddah maid, the son of Seṅkáḍan (Sivan), Kadirgáman, the wearer of the wreath of kaḍamba flowers, Murugan, the nephew of Dámódaran (Vishnu), the able chief, the leader of the celestial forces, the destroyer of the Asura enemies, Kugan, Kuḷagan, Kumaran who removes the troubles of his devotees—Kadiraimalai where he dispenses his grace and where he is worshipped.

was evidently unknown to him. And it would have continued to remain obscure for generations to come had it not been for the excavations and discoveries of Dr. P. E. Pieris at Kantāróḍai. This little known village has proved to be a second Anurhádhapura, in the matter of its ruins of historical interest.

Now, it is a commonplace of history that, when waves of conquest or colonization come upon a country, the old names of places are translated into the tongue of the invaders or settlers. Most of the old names of places are thus lost to posterity. So this place which had enjoyed the name of 'Kadiramalai' for several centuries was transformed into a Siṅhalese village and renamed 'Kadiragoḍa', when the Siṅhalese people settled down there ages later. ('malai' in Tamil and 'goḍa' in Siṅhalese are synonymous.) The village which was, in the 15th century, known as 'Kadiragoḍa' when the Siṅhalese 'Nampota' was written,* went through such changes of name as 'Kandergoda' and 'Kandercudde' during the time of the Portuguese†, and was known as 'Kantaróḍai' and 'Óḍaikurichchi' by the time the Dutch became supreme in Jaffna.‡ It follows, therefore, that the present Kantaróḍai was the ancient Kadiramalai. It had, no doubt, been the capital of the Nágas for several centuries before the advent of Vijaya, and it continued for several centuries after to be the seat of government of Chiefs, sometimes under the suzerainty of some of Vijaya's successors and sometimes independent-

---

* Nampota, p. 3.

† Thómbo, p. 47.

‡ Y. V. M. p. 34.

ly of such suzerainty. The discovery of extensive Buddhistic archaeological remains and of large quantities of Indian and Roman coins affords ample testimony of its ancient greatness.*

Seeing that Vijaya was a pious Hindu and an enthusiastic builder of temples, it is quite possible that, after building the town of Tammanná nuvara, he inaugurated the worship of Kanda Kumâra (otherwise known as Vélaṉ or Murugaṉ the heroic god of the Tamils,) at Kataragama or Kajaragama, close to his capital. The earliest name of this holy shrine which was on the top of a hill and which became an object of worship long before the advent of Vijaya, must have certainly been the Tamil name Kadiramalai. The village, which was below the hill and on the banks of the Menik Ganga, was, in Siṅhalese times, called Kataragama, the Pali form of which was Kajaragama. Its derivation from Kartigéya gráma, as some scholars have attempted to derive it, has neither phonetic similarity nor linguistic authority. The other Tamil name—Katirkámam—is the literal transformation of the Siṅhalese name Kataragama and has no connection with the Tamil components 'katir' (divine glory) and 'kámam' (love), a resemblance seen through religious fervour only. The tradition mentioned in the Yáḻpáṇa Vaipava Málai that Vijaya built a temple for 'Kadirai Áṇḍavar'† might possibly have referred to the temple at Kataragama.

The question then arises—why has no mention of this portion of the life of Vijaya been made in the

* Nágadipa, J. C. B. R. A. S., vol. xxvi.

† Y. V. M. p. 3.

Maháváṅsa, if there was any truth in the tradition above referred to? But the omission is not at all surprising. At the time the Siṅhalese monk began to write down the great history, such supernatural stories had grown round the legend of Vijaya's advent that his sojourn at Kadiramalai was altogether forgotten at Anurádhapura, the capital of Vijaya's successors. It certainly existed in and around Kadiramalai itself; but, as the people then living in Jaffna were not on quite the friendliest terms with their southern neighbours, there was no opportunity for the story to reach the ears of the chroniclers.

The fact that Vijaya was the guest of the Nága king of Kadiramalai accounts for the peaceful relations which existed between those kings and Vijaya and his early successors. Although the latter removed their capital to Anurádhapura, their sway over the whole of Laṅká was not always complete and uninterrupted. Several principalities arose, a little later, in different parts of the Island, and became, at certain times, independent of the central power. The kingdom of Jaffna too must have become independent or feudatory, according to the power wielded by the king at Anurádhapura. The Nága kings, however, continued to rule at Kadiramalai, for in the second century A.D. we find that a Chóḻa king, Kiḷḷi Vaḷavaṉ, married the daughter of the Nága king of Jaffna.*

There appears to have been constant communication and intercourse between Jaffna and the centre of the

* Vide supra, chap. i, p. 26; Maṇi. Canto xxiv. ll: 27-61.

Island. Jambukóḷa (now Sambu tuṛai) was the port of disembarkation of the Buddhist emigrants from Magadha during the time of Dévánampiya Tissa and his successors.* A great trunk road seems to have been in existence, leading from Jambukóḷa and passing through Kantaróḍai and running parallel to the present central road to the northern gate of Anurádhapura.† The remains of two stone bridges, one over the Malvatu Oya, and the other over the waste weir of Pávaṛkuḷam lying to the north of Anurádhapura, and two others at Olukkuḷam and over Kalláṛu, point to the direction taken by this ancient trunk road from Anurádhapura to Jambukóḷa. The road which passed over these stone bridges is still known by the name of 'Máwata' (the high road) to the people of the Vanni, although no traces of the road itself now exist.‡ The following references to Jaffna, as related in the Mahávaṅsa, show in what periods the kings of Anurádhapura exercised authority enough to enable them to pass unchallenged through that district.

The ambassadors sent by Dévánampiya Tissa to king Asóka of Magadha embarked at Jambukóḷa and reached Páṭaliputra in 14 days; and Asóka's ambassadors, sent to Ceylon, landed at Jambukóḷa and reached Anurádhapura in 12 days.¶ The minister, Ariṭṭha, sent by Dévánampiya Tissa to the Court of Asóka to escort the théri Saṅghamittá, and a branch of the great Bo tree

* Mah. chap. xix.

† Ibid.

‡ Sess. pp. 1886, p. 114.

¶ Mah. Chap. xi.

under which Buddha attained Buddhahood, embarked at Jambukóḷa Paṭṭana*. Saṅghamittá and the Bo tree landed at Jambukóḷa, where Dévánampiya Tissa had repaired earlier for the purpose of receiving them. He also built a superb hall called 'Samuddhásanna Sálá' near the beach for the reception of the Bo tree. The high road from the northern gate of Anurádhapura to Jambukóḷa "was sprinkled with white sand, decorated with every variety of flowers and lined with banners and garlands of flowers." "On the tenth day of the month of Maggasira, elevating and placing the Bo branch in a superb car, this sovereign, who had by enquiry ascertained the consecrated places, escorting the monarch of the forest, deposited it at the site of the Pácína vihára and entertained the priesthood as well as the people with their morning meal. There (at the spot visited at Buddha's second advent) the chief théra Mahinda narrated, without the slightest omission, to this monarch the triumph obtained over the Nágas by the deity gifted with the ten powers."† The site of Pácína vihára and the spot visited during Buddha's second visit ought to have been Kantaróḍai, which was reached by the procession at the hour of refection,‡ as Kantaróḍai is only about four or five miles from the port of Jambukóḷa. It is said that the procession reached Anurádhapura on the 14th day.¶

Of the first eight plants (Bo) raised out of the seed

* Mah, Chap. xviii.

† Ibid xix.

‡ Ibid

¶ Ibid

of the tree planted at Anurádhapura, one was planted at Jambukóḷa paṭṭana on the spot where the Bo tree was deposited on its disembarkation*. The very old Bo tree standing by the side of the Paraḷáy Kandaswámy temple at Chuḷipuram, about half a mile from the port, was perhaps the plant here referred to.

Dévánampiya Tissa "erected a vihára at the port of Jambukóḷa in Nágadípa; likewise the Tissamahá vihára and the Pácína vihára."† The ruins of a dágoba and vihára can still be seen close to the port; and the place called Tissa maḷuva, about a hundred yards opposite to the Kandaswámy temple above mentioned, perhaps marks the site of Tissamahá vihára. The ancient broad road from Jambukóḷa to Tissamahá vihára (the present Tissa maḷuva) is still in existence, but serves no useful purpose.

Pácína vihára was built at Kadiramalai, at the spot where the Bo tree procession halted. Mr. Parker, relying on the following ancient inscriptions found at Náva Nírávi Malai, Puliaṅkuḷam Malai and Érupotána kanda, argues that Pácína vihára was built by Dévánampiya Tissa somewhere near those hills and that that was the spot made sacred by the second visit of Buddha to Nágadípa. The inscriptions are :—

1. Rájá nága jita rájá uti jaya abi anuridhi ca rájá uti ca karapitase una lena catu disasa sagaya agatagata na pasu viharaye aparam (i) ta loke ditu yasa tena.

Abhi Anuridhi the wife (of) king Uttiya (and)

---

* Mah. chap. xix.

† Ibid xx.

daughter (of) king Nága, and king Uttiya have caused this cave to be made for the community of the four quarters, present or future at the Pásu vihára, an illustrious famous place in the boundless world.

2, Gapati tapasa sumana kulasa leṇe sagasa dine agata anagata catu disa sagasa pasu visaraya.

The cave of the family (of) the ascetic Sumana, the householder: given to the community of the four quarters, present or furture at the Pásu tank.*

From the above inscriptions, it appears that Uttiya the brother and successor of Dévánampiya Tissa married Abhi Anuridhi, the daughter of his brother Mahá Nága, that husband and wife had a cave made at Pásu vihára, and that an ascetic named Sumana also made a cave near Pásu tank. Mr. Parker identifies this Pásu vihára as Pácína vihára built by Dévánampiya Tissa, but he was unable to make this identification agree with the statement in the Mahávaṅsa that the site of the Pácína vihára was within half a day's journey from Jambukóḷa, the port at which the Bo tree was landed.†

From the time of Dévánampiya Tissa to the reign of Mahallaka Nága, a period of about 400 years, no mention of Nágadípa is made in the Mahávaṅsa. Not even the Tamil conqueror Elára or Elála whose beneficent rule of 44 years evoked the admiration of such

* Parker, pp. 423 and 425; J.C.B R.A.S. vol: xiii, pp; 166, 167.
In most of these early Cave inscriptions appears a word *perumaka* which is purely the Tamil word *perumakan* (பெருமகன்) meaning 'a Chief," a Lord' or 'a King.' Cf Cirupáṇ: 1, 22.

† Parker, pp. 423 aud 425.

a hostile author as that of the Mahávaṅsa, appears to have taken any special interest as regards the northern principality. The presumption, therefore, is that in those years the northern principality was quite independent and quiet. It is said that Elára belonged to the noble dynasty of the Chóḷas, and some of the mythical legends of justice and liberality connected with the ancient Chóḷa kings are also attributed to him. His royal connection is, however, doubtful as tradition connects him with voyages on the sea. The traditional belief among the Tamil sea-men that the mention of his name in times of distress would bring relief, and songs containing his name sung while rowing or tacking confirm the tradition.*

There had been several Tamil invasions and Tamil kings had ruled at Anurádhapura; and a large number of Tamils who migrated into the island as traders, colonists and conquerers would have remained in Ceylon. In the meantime therefore, the fusion of the several races composed of the Nágas, Yakkhas, Kaliṅgas and Tamils was taking place in the Island. The Yakkhas who were given positions of power and trust during the early days of the Kaliṅga kings,† were gradually relegated to the lower grades of society, as Nága connections began to increase and the high grades of society were composed of the Nágas, Kaliṅgas and Tamils, who by fusion became the ruling and the cultivating classes of Ceylon. Vijaya himself set the example of marrying a Yakkha prin-

* The chorus of the songs sung by Tamil sea-men ends with the words ēlēlō. ēlēlō, ēlavali, ēlēlō. ஏலேலோ யேலேலோ யேலவலி யேலேலோ.

† Mah, chap, x., p: 43.

cess and then a Tamil or Nága princess and others, followers and descendents, would not have been slow to make local alliances. It will not therefore be out of place to note here some of the royal alliances mentioned in the Maháva̎ṅsa and other chronicles during the early centuries of the Christian era.

The first person in the line of Ceylon kings who went under the name of Nága was Mahá Nága the brother of Dévánampiya Tissa. He would not have been called a Nága if his parents or his ancestors had not had any Nága connections. His genealogy was as follows:—

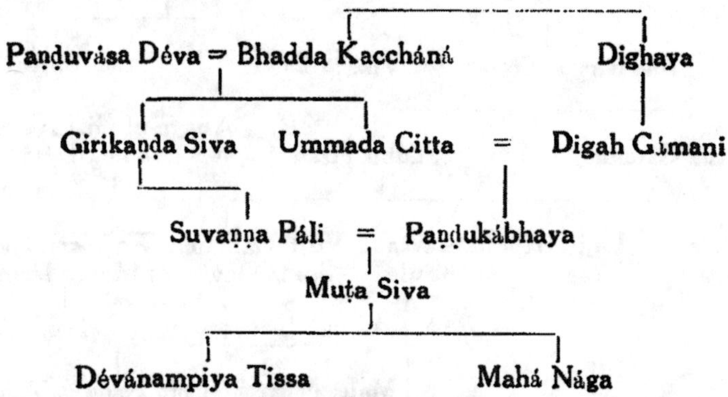

As the name of Muṭa Siva's queen is not mentioned, it is more than likely that he was the first to marry a Nága princess, and as Kelaniya Tissa, the grandson of her son Mahá Nága, later became the King of Kaḷyáṇi, she must have been a princess of that district. From that time Nága connections became rather common until they culminated in the marriage of Gajabáhu whose successors on the throne became altogether Nágas. How the Nága strain in the blood of the Ceylon kings began to appear in Mahá Nága and continued to grow stronger from time to time until the dynasty became altogether Nága can be seen from the following table:—

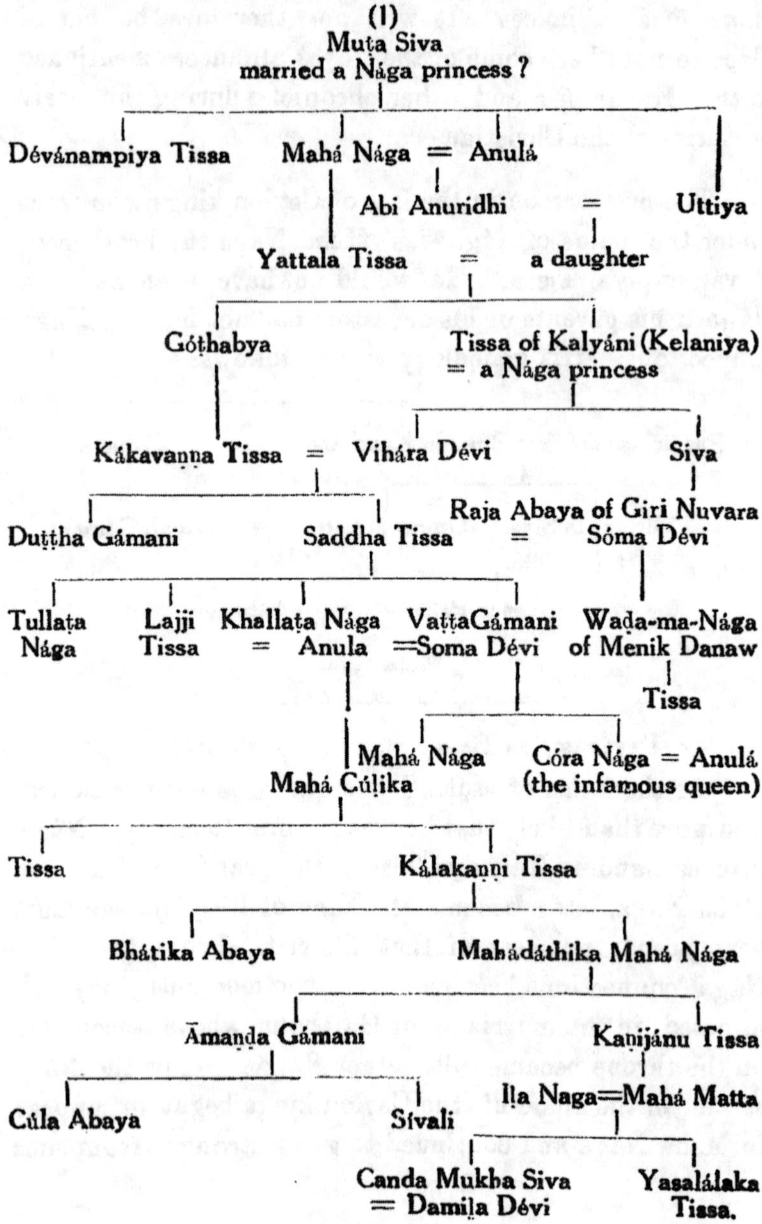

2

Lambakanna Vasabha
= Mettá Subha
Porter king Mahallaka Nága

Vaṅkanásika Tissa = Mahámatta Bháṭika Tissa Kaniṭha Tissa

Gajabáhu I = a daughter

Cúḷa Nága Kuḍḍa Nága = female Siri Nága

Subha Déva

Abhaya Nága Vohárakа Tissa = daughter

Siri Nága

Vijaya.

(3)

Lamba Kaṇṇas

Saṅgha Tissa Siri Saṅgha Bódhi Góṭhábaya

Jeṭṭha Tissa Mahá Séna

Siri Mághavaṇṇa Jeṭṭha Tissa

Buddha Dása

Upatissa II Mahá Náma = a Tamil

Sothi Séna Saṇgha = Jantu.

Mahá Nága's great grandson Kákavaṇṇa Tissa married Vihára Dévi the daughter of Tissa, the Nága king of Kályaṇi * She was the mother of Duṭṭha Gámani one

* Maha. chap. xxii.

of Ceylon's greatest kings. We are told on the authority of Séruvávilla Vistara that Siva Maharája of Kalyáṇi, supposed to be the son of Tissa who was with his kingdom engulfed by the sea, and a brother of Vihára Dévi who was married to Kákavaṇṇa Tissa of Mágama, had a nephew called Rája Abhaya. Kákavaṇṇa Tissa married him to his niece Sóma Dévi and established him in the principality of Giri Nuvara near Trincomalie. She had a son called Vaḍa-má-Nága, a sure indication of the Nága origin of his parents (Northern Branch). The latter is supposed to have reigned at Manik Danaw or Má-Nága Danaw near Lénadora. From his son Tissa sprang the Mayúra Vamsa of later times.*

The late Mr. H. Neville thought that the chaṇḍáḷa woman with whom Sáli Kumaraya, the son of Duṭṭha gámani, contracted his morganatic marriage, as related in the Maháváṇsa,† was really not a chaṇḍáḷa but a daughter of Vaḍa-má.Nága, and that the mesalliance was not of caste but only of class or rank.‡ If it was true, it is rather surprising that Duṭṭha gámani who married a goiváṇsa lady, the mother of Sáli Kumaraya, should have considered the marriage of his son to a lady of higher rank than his own mother, a mesalliance.

Duṭṭha gámani's younger brother Saddha Tissa had

---

* Tap., vol. i, p. 40.

The names of Abhaya Rájá, Vaḍa-má-Nága and Tissa appear in Muller's inscriptions Nos. 30, 34 and 94 found at Galgomua, Embulamba and Galkuḷam respectively.

† Mah. chap. xxxiii.

‡ Tap., vol. i, p. 40.

a son called Kallāṭa Nága,* and his brother Vaṭṭa gámani had a son called Mahá Nága who afterwards earned the name of Córa Nága, on account of the life of a marauder he led before he came to the throne.† By the opposition he displayed towards Buddhism, in destroying several Buddhist temples, he proved himself to be a Hindu and therefore connected with the northern Nágas.

Bhátika Abhaya had a brother called Mahádáṭhiya Mahá Nága who ascended the throne in 9 A. D.‡ These names ending in Nága clearly testify to the fact that one of their parents was a Nága or that in any case they were descendants of Nágas. Any doubt that may exist regarding the truth of the Nága connections of these kings will be dispelled by a view of the statue of Vaṭṭa gámani in the rock temple at Dambulla. The holes in his ear lobes and the ornaments, similar to the hood of a cobra, worn in them, are sure signs of his Nága birth. Gold ornaments resembling the hood of a cobra called 'Nága-paḍam' were till very recent times worn by the women of Jaffna on their ears. Similar ornaments are still worn by the Tamil and Chetty women on the west coast of Ceylon.

Amaṇḍa gámani (21-30 A. D) had a nephew called Iḷa Nága who, when deposed by the Lambakaṇṇas (so called on account of the heavy ear ornaments they wore)

---

* Mah., chap. xxxiii.

† Ibid xxxiv.

‡ Ibid

who were his attendants, fled to the Tamil country by the way of Mahátittha for the purpose of obtaining the help of the Tamils.* It is also said that Vasabha who succeeded Subha, the king who was once a gate porter, was a Lambakaṇṇa youth resident in the North.† It is therefore evident that the Lambakaṇṇas who were the attendants of Iḷa Nága and who deposed him were either Nágas or mixed Tamils and Nágas from Nágadípa and became his attendants on account of his Nága connections. So we need not be surprised to read that the wife of Canda Mukha Siva (42-52 A.D.) the son of Iḷa Nága (38-44 A.D) was a Tamil lady named Damiḷa dévi,‡ and that Vasabha's son Vaṅkanásika Tissa (110-113 A.D.) married Mahamatta the daughter of the porter king Subha.¶ Vasabha was a Lambakaṇṇa youth resident in the north of the Island (Jaffna) before he took up service under his maternal uncle who was the chief of the troops at Anurádhapura § The term Lambakaṇṇa applied to him designates that the Nága princes of Jaffna had already mixed with the Tamils.

Vaṅka-násika Tissa's son Gajabáhaka Gámani or Gajabáhu (113- 35 A.D) who was invited by the Céra king Seṅguṭṭuvan to be present at the inauguration of

---

* Mah. chap, xxxv.

† Ibid

‡ Ibid

¶ Ibid

§ Ibid

the temple built by him for the worship of Kannakai,* and who introduced her worship into Ceylon under the name of Pattini Deviyo, married a Nága princess from Jaffna. From the fact that Vijaya discarded his first wife Kuvéni and the absence of any marriage of the Kalinga kings with the royal house of the Yakkhas, it is apparent that they preferred the Nágas of the North for the perpetuation of their royal lineage.

When Gajabáhu went to conquer the Chóḷas, he is said to have marched to Jaffna and thence proceeded to 'Soḷi Raṭa.' He brought back double the number of captives taken in his father's time, "the foot ornaments of Pattiny Déwey, the arms of the four gods and the

---

* "கடல்சூழிலங்கைக் கயவாகு வேந்தனும்
அன்னாட்செய்த நாளணிவேள்வியுள்
வந்தீகென்றே வணங்கினர் வேண்டத்
தந்தேன் வரமென் றெழுந்ததோர்குரல்."

Cilap., canto xxx, ll. 160, 162—164.

When king Gajabàhu of Lankà, surrounded by the sea, worsihpped (Kannakai.) and prayed to her to appear and grant his prayer at the sacrifice performed on that day, there rose a voice saying that his prayer was granted.

"அதுகேட்டுக் கடல்சூழிலங்கைக் கயவாகுவென்பான் நங்கைக்கு நாட்பலி பீடிகை கோட்டமுந் துறந்தாங்கு அரந்தை கெடுத்துவரந்தரு மிவளென ஆடித்திங்களகவையினாங்கோர் பாடிவிழாக்கோள் பன்முறையெடுப்ப மழைவீற்றிருந்து வளம்பலபெருகிப் பிழையாவிளையுணாடாயிற்று."

Cilap., Uraiperukaṭṭurai, 3.

Hearing of this, (i.e., prosperity of other countries by the inauguration of the worship of Kannakai) Gajabàhu, the king of sea-girt Lankà first erected altars for the performance of daily sacrifice to the goddess and then built temples and carried on festivals in her honour, with processions along the streets of his city, on Mondays in the month of Ādi (July-August), under the belief that she would dispel all ills and grant all prayers. Consequently seasonable rains fell, and the land became prosperous by unfailing and abundant harvest.

patra Dawtoo of Budhu which had been taken away during the time of the former king"* This account of the Rajavali confirms the statement in the Cilappadikáram that Gajabáhu introduced the worship of Kaṇṇakai or Pattini dévi to Ceylon.† The arms of the gods and the 'patra Dawtoo" were no doubt spoils of victory, but the foot ornaments of Pattini dévi were brought for the first time, for the purpose of worship, after his friendly visit to the Court of the Céra king who invited him on the occasion of the inauguration of the temple to Kaṇṇakai. There is no ground to suppose that the foot ornaments of Pattini dévi were taken away by the Chóḻa king, during the time of Gajabáhu's father, as there is no evidence of the introduction of the worship during the time of any of the earlier kings. The anklet and not an image is still the only emblem which is worshipped in many a Kaṇṇakai temple in the Island.

A colossal statue of a king is said to have been standing opposite to the temple of Kaṇṇakai at Aṅgaṇámaikaḍavai (aṅgaṇá=a goddess) near Kantaróḍai and broken by an elephant about a century ago. The feet and head of such a statue were found by Dr. P. E Pieris in the premises of the temple and are now placed in the Jaffna museum. This statue was perhaps that of Gajabáhu who after consecrating the temple for the worship of Kaṇṇakai placed his statue in front of it. The reign of Gajabáhu is dealt with very shortly in the Mahávaṅsa, a fact which is surprising with regard to the great number of inscriptions he has left.

---

* Rajavali, p. 231.

† Vide supra p. 73, note : p. 29, notes.

On the death of Gajabáhu, he was succeeded by his father-in-law Mahállaká Nága (135-141 A.D.). By this time the kings of Anurádhapura had by alliances with the Nágas, Tamils and others become mixed and so degenerate, that the Nágas of the North became powerful and began to assert their authority. Mahállaká Nága, unlike his predecessors, took some interest in the land of his birth and built the vihára callled Sálipabbata in the isle of Nágadípa in addition to those he built in other parts of Ceylon.*

According to the Rajavali, Gajabáhu's son Bhátri Tissa Rája (141-165 A.D.), the next king, caused the Palupala dágoba to be built at the root of the tree Kiripalugaha and made offering to the same.† Kiripalugaha is the same as the rájáyatana tree which Indra held as a parasol over Buddha when he made his visit to Nágadípa, and which he planted there.‡ This dágoba was therefore built at Nágadípa by Bhátri Tissa. The Nága kings who succeeded Mahállaka Nága took similar interest in Jaffna thereby showing their connection with that land.

Kaṇiṭṭa Tissa, (165-193 A.D) the second son of Mahállaka Nága, who succeeded Bhátika Tissa repaired the edifice constructed over the cetiya at Nágadípa ¶ His son Cúla Nága, after him his brother Kuḍḍa Nága, and after him his brother-in-law Siri Nága and then the

* Mah., chap. xxxv.

† Rajavali, p. 232

‡ Mah chap. I.

¶ Ibid. chap. xxxvi.

latter's son Vohâraka Tissa reigned in succession. During the reign of Vohâraka Tissa, his minister Muka Nága built a well round Tissa vihára in Nágadípa,† and the king himself gave "constant maintenance to the temple of Model Patiny and caused walls to be built round the temples called Nagadiva Tuna and Tissamaha vihára."‡

Vohâraka Tissa's brother Abhaya Nága (237-245 A. D.), on his criminal intimacy with the brother's queen being detected, dreading his brother's resentment, fled with his confidential attendants to Bhallatittha and there embarked on board a vessel for the opposite coast. ¶ This Bhallatittha may perhaps be identified as the present Valveṭṭituṛai on the northern coast of Jaffna. He returned with a large force of Tamils, defeated his brother and reigned for eight years. He was succeeded by his brother's son Sri Nága (245-247 A. D.) after whom his son Vijaya reigned for one year'

Vijaya was killed by three men of the Lambakaṇṇa race named Saṅghatissa, Saṅghabodhi and Góthâbhaya § who, though described in the Mahávaṅsa, as residents of Mahiyaṅgana, were evidently persons connected with the people of the Northern kingdom. They reigned one after the other.

---

* Mah. chap. xxxvi.

† Ibid

‡ Rajarat. p. 60.

¶ Mah. chap. xxxvi.

§ Ibid

Saṅghatissa I (248—252 A. D.) was in the habit " of visiting the island of Pácína attended by the women of the palace and his ministers for the purpose of eating jambus. The inhabitants of that island unable to bear the burden of these royal progresses, infused poison into the jambus intended for the Rájá, (and placed them) among the rest of the fruit. Having eaten those jambus, he died at that very place."* The isle of Pácína must have been Nágadípa where the Pácína vihára was built by Dévánampiya Tissa.†

Góthakâbaya the minister of Siri Saṅghabódhi who succeeded Saṅghatissa I, turned traitor, fled to the 'North' and marched back, with an army from there, against the city. Saṅghabódhi fled on his approach and he seized the kingdom and reigned for 13 years (254—267 A. D.)‡

There is a story connected with the flight of Siri Saṅgha Bódhi which exactly resembles that of the Tamil Chief Kumaṇan of Mudiram or Kudirai Malai described in poems 158—165 of Puranánúru.§ The liberal and munificent nature of either in offering to take off his head, on which a prize was placed, for the purpose of rewarding a friend, seldom finds a parallel in history. On account of the greatness exhibited by this selfles spirit, the later kings of Ceylon took 'Siri Saṅgha Bódhi' as one of their alternate throne names. As the poet Perum Citranár who sang the praises of Kumaṇan lived during the time of Atiyamáṉ Neḍumáṉ Añji of Takaḍúr who was praised

---

* Mah. Chap. xxxvi.

† Ibid. chap. xx.

‡ Idid. chap. xxxvi.

§ See supra. Chap : i. p. 25.

by Ouvaiyár and Paraṇar,* as Ouvaiyár was sent on an embassy by Neḍumáṇ Añji to the Court of Toṇḍaimáṉ Iḷam Tirayaṉ of Káñcipuram,† and as Paraṇar sang the praises of Céraṉ Seṅguṭṭuvaṉ‡ who invited Gaja Báhu of Ceylon to his Court,¶ Kumaṇan must have lived about the middle of the second century A. D., at least a century earlier than Siri Saṅgha Bódhi. Kumaṇan and Siri Saṅgha Bódhi, therfore, could not have been one and the same person; and it is clear that Siri Sangha Bódhi emulated the conduct of the Chieftain of Kudiraimalai.

The King Máha Séna who was the younger son of Góthâbhaya of the Lambakaṇṇa dynasty, was a follower of the Wytulya heresy § which was but an introduction of the worship of the Hindu gods and of Hindu rites into Buddhism, and became very popular after the 12th century A. D. That these Lambakaṇṇas were also Nágas can be seen from an inscription found at Karambagala near Koggala, nine miles from the Ambalantoṭa Rest House near Hambántoṭa, in which Máha Séna is called Nága Máha Séna Mahárájá. ||

The Nágas had so successfully established themselves on the South and East by founding principalities at Mahágama, Giri Nuvara (Koṭṭiyár) and Lénadora, that at the

* Puram, 99

† Ibid. 95

‡ Padir: 5th pattu

¶ Cilap. canto xxx, l. 160

§ Mah. chap xxxvii

|| Muller, 21a, p. 31

time Ptolemy wrote his geography (about 150 A.D.) the people of South Ceylon were called Nageiroi (Nágas) and those of the East Nagadiboi (Nágas). He also mentioned two towns, one Nakadouba to the north of Hambántoṭa and the other Nagadiba near Trincomalie. The existence of a village called Naimana (nai=nága), two miles to the north of Matara, with the tradition that there was an ancient Nága temple at the locality, and of a royal city called Mápápaṭuna (now called Mákáviṭṭa) in the vicinity, clearly shows that the Nágas once occupied even the extreme South of the Island. Naimana was perhaps the town called Mahánágakula mentioned, in the Mahávaṅsa, as the place where the Siṅhalese princes sought refuge during the Chóḷa invasion.

To sum up, therefore, the Kaliṅga dynasty of Vijaya and the mixed Kaliṅga—Nága line that followed it disappeared with Yasalálaka Tissa in 60 A.D. Several sons of this family, however, though bereft of royal power, lived in different parts of the island, and, if the Mahávaṅsa is to be believed, some of their descendants were from time to time called upon to assume the reins of Government like "Cincinnatus," straight from the plough. A purely Nága dynasty started with Mahállaka Nága in 135 A.D., and continued till the murder of Vijaya in 248 A.D. Then the Lambakaṇṇas, a mixed Tamil and Nága dynasty began with Saṅga Tissa in 248 A.D., and continued till the murder of Sotthi S'na by his sister in 434 A.D. Dhatus'na, a scion of the old Kaliṅga dynasty came to power in 643 A.D.

Thus in spite of the reticence of the Mahávaṅsa, very

probably intentional, it will be clearly seen that for a thousand years after the advent of Vijaya, the principality in the North existed undisturbed, while the central power at Anurádhapura passed through several changes of dynasties and several storms of conquest. First by mere alliance, and then by acquiring control over their neighbours, the kings of the North saw to it that they had no serious difficulties to contend with, and hence their continual reign for such a long period.

CHAPTER III

Foreign Trade and Intercourse

THE proverbial wealth of 'Ormus and of Īnd' and that of the 'utmost Indian isle Taprobane' had, from the remote past, so excited the cupidity of merchants and mariners, that they braved the dangers of the deep, even in their little vessels, and sailed to the 'gorgeous East' in search of her 'barbaric pearl and gold.' In the shallow waters of North Ceylon, they found safe anchorage and protection from the winds and storms of the Arabian Sea, and of the Bay of Bengal, during the monsoons; and this meeting place developed, in course of time, into the emporium of the East. From its central position in the Indian Ocean, and its contiguity to the Indian Peninsula, Ceylon possessed advantages as an emporium of trade unequalled by any other country in the East. While Indian ports offered their own produce and received the goods of other countries, the marts in North Ceylon not only supplied their own goods and received foreign merchandise, but also served as a centre for the distribution of trade between the far East and the far West. In the words of Cosmas Indico-pleustes, an Egyptian monk who lived in the early part of the sixth century A.D., "Sieledeba (Ceylon) being thus placed in the middle as it were of India, received goods from all nations and again distributed them, thus becoming a great emporium."*

* Tennent, vol. i, p. 570 (quotation from Cosmas).

Tho location of this ancient emporium has been discussed by eminent scholars, on several occasions, with no satisfactory result. Bertolacci and Pridham thought that it was somewhere in the North-western coast. Sir Emerson Tennent located it at Pt. de Galle; Valentyn and Col. Yule, though not satisfied with previous identifications, were yet unable to suggest anything new. Mr. H. Neville, of more recent years, surmised that it was close to Kalpitiya. An attempt therefore, made with some degree of certainty, will not be without justification.

In remote antiquity, the coasting trade from one half of Asia to the other half must have passed by the deep passages across the Adam's Bridge or by the Straits of Mannar, and consequently, a great port must have risen on the North-west coast of Ceylon. Bertolacci, an officer of the Ceylon Civil Service, who served in the island for about 16 years, in his book on Ceylon written in the early part of the nineteenth century, was of opinion that the entrepôt of the early Ceylon trade, Western as well as Eastern, was confined to the Northern extremity of the Gulf of Mannar * The existence of the extensive ruins at Mátoṭa and of the celebrated Giant's Tank close to it, are indubitable signs of an immense population well advanced in agriculture. This tank is apparently the most ancient work extant in Ceylon, so ancient that it is not mentioned as having been built by any of the kings who reigned in Ceylon after Vijaya. The Giant's Tank must, therefore, have been the work of the remotest times, constructed probably by the ancient Nágas, who were the people

---

Bertol. Intro. p. 11.

then living in that part of Ceylon.* It was the earliest attraction to the traders of Phoenicia, Egypt and Arabia, and an index of the early civilization and the prosperity of these people.

The proof of this prosperity is the existence of a large number of ruins along the western coast, commencing from Munnéssaram in Chilaw, a temple mentioned in the Rámáyaṇa as one, at which Ráma worshipped during his invasion of Laṅká, and extending northward through the districts of Puttalam, Ponparipu (golden plains), Nánáṭṭáṉ, Musali, Mátoṭa, V.ḍattaltívu, Pallavaráayaṉkaṭṭu, Púnakari, Kalmuṉai, and Jaffna. The dilapidated temples at Munnéssaram, Uḍappu, Karatívu, Kallár, Mátoṭa and Arasapuram clearly prove that the people were Hindus. The temple at Kallár, 7½ miles from Marichchikaṭṭi whose tottering ruins were being guarded by a solitary brahman priest, even so late as the time when J. Haffner, the Dutchman, travelled on foot from Jaffna to Colombo,† says Pridham, though dilapidated was once so famous, that the priests who officiated in it were allowed

* See Infra. chap : i. pp : 15-24.

† A fable regarding this temple, heard from the lips of the officiating brahman and related by J. Haffner in his "Travels on foot through the island of Ceylon," clearly illustrates the Nága origin of this temple. He says that a chieftain was attacked on this spot by a royal serpent of dreadful size, when he prayed to a goddess who immediately appeared in the form of a beautiful woman, and plucking a hair from her flowing locks and transforming it into a sword cut off the head of the serpent and vanished. In gratitude, the, Chieftain caused this temple to be erected on the spot, which was even then annually visited by pilgrims from all parts of the Island.

many important privileges, including a moiety of the pearl oysters fished on the banks of Kondáchchi.* Near Kudirai Malai (Horse mountain), one of the most interesting places regarding the antiquities of Ceylon, stands tne site of a Royal residence, once occupied by an Amazon princess called Alli Arasány, whose amour with Arjuna, one of the heroes of the Mahabhárata, forms the subject of a popular drama in the Tamil districts.

The ancient names of some of this chain of ruined towns are Tammanna Nagaram, Tavirikia Nagaram, Acá Nagaram, Kudirai Malai, Mántai, (Mátoṭa), Arasapuram and Kadira malai. In addition to stone pillars, carved and uncarved, bricks and tiles, large quantities of beads, bangles and other ornaments of vari-coloured glass are found mixed with the soil, in almost all these ruins. Of these, Mántai and Kadiramalai (Kantaróḍai) are the most important. Mántai is a hill of piled up ruins. This interesting spot which would probably have yielded sufficient evidence of the trade relations that existed in ancient times between the East and the West, was altogether neglected by the Archaeological Department. Instead of being conserved for careful investigation, it was sold by Government to the Náṭṭucoṭṭai Chetties who in their search for the site of the ancient temple of Tirukétísvaram have committed such acts of vandalism, that the possibilities of a scientific investigation hereafter are reduced to a minimum. As for Kadiramalai, archaeological research is no longer possible as the entire area, which contains the ruins, has passed into the hands of private

* Pridham. vol: ii. chap: i.

proprietors. Large quantities of beads of various kinds, and fragments of necklaces of different shapes and sizes, made of glass and coral, cornelian and agate, jade and alumina, with holes perforated for stringing together, had been found here.* Ancient coins, both Roman and Indian, have also been picked up. These finds have almost all been confined to the Western portion of the village, which should represent the residential quarters of royalty while temples and sacred buildings seem to have been placed more towards the East. The coins and beads picked up in such large quantities, point to the length of time the city must have served, as the capital of a kingdom, and as the centre of a large population, floating and permanent, attracted to the place by foreign trade.

Before the use of the compass was known, when mariners could not safely venture far out to sea, but were forced to hug the coast, the ships sailing from the Malabar to the Coromandel Coast had no other alternative but to pass via Danushkóṭi or through the Straits of Mannar, as it was impracticable to go round the South of the Island of Ceylon, without undue precariousness and delay, caused by the annual monsoons. Even now, when navigation is much improved, the Jaffna vessels, which ply between Ceylon and the Coromandel Coast, effect only one voyage in the year and wait for the other monsoon for their return home. If, therefore, in former times, the navigators found it difficult to go round Ceylon, without

* The beads etc. were inspected by Professor Flinders Petrie at Dr. A. Nell's request. The professor, is certain that they are Egyptian of the Ptolemaic period and came by way of trade between Egypt and Ceylon.

wasting the greater part of the year in the needless venture, it is but right to suppose that they would have resorted to the Straits of Mannar and the Jaffna Lagoon. At first, when the vessels were small and extremely light, and the Straits, which later became gradually silted up, were navigable for such vessels, mariners would have passed through these seas to the Coast of Coromandel; but afterwards, when larger vessels of heavier tonnage came into use, the emporium en route at Mátoṭa and Jaffna would have become a necessity. The merchants too, who hailed from Arabia, Persia and the Malabar Coast, would have preferred to dispose of their goods at these depôts, and to return home laden with the produce of Ceylon and of the Coromandel, at the change of the monsoon. Numberless establishments would have, therefore, arisen at Mátoṭa and Jaffna, to serve the requirements of this active cosmopolitan commerce. It must have been this flourishing trade, which made a powerful and popular State grow and expand in so unproductive and uncongenial a part of the Island as Mátoṭa, as it must have been the decline of that trade which made them abandon the town to its present state of barrenness and desolation.

The Phoenicians, the Arabs, the Ethiopians, the Persians, the Greeks and the Romans from the West, the Chinese, the Javanese and the Burmese from the East, not to speak of the nations of India, vied with each other at various times to monopolise the trade of North Ceylon.

Casie Chetty, in his 'History of Jaffna,' says "There can be no doubt, the commercial intercourse of the Greeks and the Romans with Ceylon was confined to the Northern and North Western parts."* The people of the Coromandel Coast had, from time immemorial, intimate commercial intercourse with the parts of North Ceylon. Many came and settled down at these ports, carrying on a brisk trade, and forming connections with families of the same caste as themselves, as is still the case at point Pedro and Valveṭṭyturai.

It is on record that about a thousand years before the Christian era, the fleets of King Solomon, piloted by the adventurous and experienced seamen of Phoenicia, called at the sea-ports of South India and Ceylon, in search of materials for the building of the great temple of Jerusalem, and carried away gold, algum trees and precious stones from Ophir. The King's ships also went to Tarshish and "every three years once came the ships of Tarshish bringing gold and silver, ivory, apes and peacocks."†

Ophir has been supposed to be identical with Tarshish, and it has been conjectured, not without reason, that Ophir was the country of which Tarshish was the sea-port.‡ The site of Tarshish has been identified by Sir Emerson Tennent as Point De Galle in the South of Ceylon,¶ and Ophir, by Cunningham, as Sauvira in the Western coast of

---

* Casie; J. C. B. R, A. S vol; i. 1847-1848 p: 77. note.

† Bible R. I Kings, chap; x, v: 22; II Chronicles, chap: xx, v: 21.

‡ Tap: vol; ii, p: 10.

¶ Tennent, vol: i, p: 554, note-I: vol. ii. p: 102.

India.* If the port of Tarshish was in Ceylon, and not on the Western Coast of India, it was certainly not Galle, but a place on the North-Western coast of Ceylon. Ophir, it was suggested, is derived from the Greek word "Ophis"—meaning a serpent—and the word for serpent in Hebrew, was also supposed to be the same † It was therefore thought that Ophir designated the country of the Nágas, but the latter was not located at all. If the derivation was correct, Ophir was certainly no other than the northern part of Ceylon, which was, several centuries before historical times, populated by the Nágas, but the derivation is not correct. Although the Greek word "Ophis" means a serpent, yet the Hebrew words for serpent "Nâchâsh" or "Sârâph" have no phonetic similarity to Ophir. As it was the Hebrews and not the Greeks who called the place Ophir, to resort to the Greek term "Ophis" for elucidation would be an error.

We venture to suggest, however, that Ophir was the country of the "Óviyar," a tribe of Nágas who lived in and around Mántai (Mátoṭa), as will be seen from Ciṛupáṇáṟṟupaḍai, a Tamil Saṅga work referred to earlier.‡ The phonetic similarity between Ophir and Óviyar is certainly striking; and Ophir must have been borrowed in the same manner, as the Hebrew words for ivory, apes, aghil and peacocks—ibha, kapi, ahalim and tukeyim respectively, which are identical with their Tamil names

* Coins. p: 4.

† Tap: vol: ii, p: 10.

‡ See infra, chap: i, p: 13, note: Ciṛupáṇ. 1: 122.

ipam, kapi, aghil and tókai. * The Hebrew mariners, no doubt, borrowed the names from the Tamil inhabitants of the port from which they obtained them. In the same manner, the Greeks carried away rice, ginger and cinnamon with their names oryza, gingiber, and karpion which are identical with their Tamil names arisi, inchivér and karuva,† perhaps from the same port. These Tamil names could have been obtained only from the ports in South India or North Ceylon as Tamil was spoken neither in Galle nor in Sauvira.

If Ophir was really the country of the Óviyar, and there s no reasnn why it should not be, the port can be identified as Mántai (Mátoṭa) which was also known as Tirukétísvaram whence, perhaps the corrupted form Tarshish. Tirukétísvaram means the holy shrine of Ísvara (Siva) worshipped by Kétu, the noble serpent (cauda draconis) of mythology, thus proving that the shrine was built and worshipped by the Nágas from very early times. Ivory, apes, aghil and peacocks could have been easily obtained on the coast of Mátoṭa, and peacocks were abundant in the islands of the Jaffna Sea, even so late as the time of Baldeus, ‡ and were exterminated by the Dutch who found them a table delicacy,

The Phoenician History of Sanchoniathon¶ is the earli-

* Tamils. chap : iii, p: 31.

† Ibid.

‡ a. Baldeus, chap : xlvi.

b. "In Pungardiva, there was an abundance ot deer, does, buffaloes and pea-fowl". Ribeyro, chap : xxv.

¶ Tennent, vol : i, p : 571.

est record regarding a kingdom in the north of Ceylon. He is alleged to have lived before the Trojan war, and is said to have been a contemporary of Semiramis. Acccording to him, "four Kings govern the Island (Ceylon) all subordinate to the paramount sovereign, to whom they pay as tribute cassia, ivory, gems and pearls, for the king has gold in greatest abundance." After describing the kings ruling in the South, he continues, "the third rules the region towards the north which produces pearls. He has made a great rampart on the isthmus to control the passage of the barbarians from the opposite coast for they used to make incursions in great numbers." This account confirms the fact that the North of Ceylon was under its own king and that the fortified town "on the isthmus to control the passage of the barbarians" was Máṭoṭa. This Phoenician history, however, is supposed to be a spurious one as the description of Ceylon is more like the conditions that prevailed during the fourth or fifth century A. D. than about the 5th Century B. C.*

The trade along the coast of India and Ceylon, several centuries before the Christian era, remained in the hands of the Arabs and was long and jealously guarded by them against the encroachments of other nations, by the sedulous dissemination of fabulous and blood-curdling stories of the dangers of navigation. The baobab trees which form a special feature in the landscape of Mannar and Mántai, perhaps the tree-totems of these early Arabs, testify to the truth not only of their ancient settlements in those parts but also of their animistic worship.

* Tennent, vol : i, p: 71

One Hippalus, a seaman in the reign of the Emperor Claudius, observing the steady prevalence of the monsoons, discovered the shorter route across the Indian ocean to the shores of India and Ceylon. Since then the trade with the West attained extensive proportions, and the knowledge of Ceylon which, in the times of the earlier writers like Megasthenes and Strabo was very meagre, increased to such an extent as to produce the comparatively full descriptions of Pliny, written within 50 years of the discovery of Hippalus.*

About 50 A.D., when Claudius was Emperor of Rome, a ship in which the freedman of Annius Plocamus was sent to collect the revenues of Arabia, was caught by the monsoon and carried to Hippuros, a point which is still known by its Tamil equivalent Kudiraimalai, and which was at the time a land mark of Ceylon for those who navigated the Arabian seas. Here, the mariners were kindly received by the people and taken before their King, who treated them hospitably, and, on hearing from them of the greatness and magnificence of Rome, wished to make an alliance with the Roman Emperor. He sent an embassy consisting of four persons, the chief of whom was one named Rachia, to the Court of Cladius.† That the mariners easily found their bearings and knew their way back home is a fair indication of the previous intercourse which existed between that port and the Red Sea. Although the ship touched a point near Kudiraimalai, it would have been easy thence to reach the then

* Tennent, vol: i, p: 555.

† Pliny, lib: vi, chap: xxiv.

chief port of Mántai (Mátoṭa) or Jaffna. The sailors would not have taken an embassy, nor would the members of the embassy have entrusted themselves to the ship, unless they were assured of the way home. From these envoys Pliny learnt that, " There were five hundred towns in the island, of which the chief was Palaesimunda the residence of the King with a population of two hundred thousand souls." They also spoke of "a lake called Megisba of vast magnitude giving rise to two rivers, one flowing by the capital and the other northwards towards the continent of India." They also described the coral which abounds in the Gulf of Mannar.* Casie Chetty in his early history of Jaffna, conjectured that Palaesimunda was Jaffna Patam and that Rachia, the ambassador who went to the Court of Claudius, was a Tamil "Áráchchiár" sent by the king of Jaffna, similar to the one (Sellappoo Aratchy) sent later by Bhuvan ka Báhu vi, to the Court of Lisbon,† and not a Rájah as fancied by Sir Emerson Tennent,‡ quite apart from the inherent improbability of a King embarking on an embassy to so distant a country.

The anonymous author of the Periplus of the Erythrean Sea seems to have gone on his travels within a

---

* Pliny, lib : vi, Chap. xxvi.

† a. Casie : J. C. B. R. A. S., vol. i, 1847-1848, p. 78, note.

b. It is stated that the King of Cotta caused a figure of his grandson, who was later known as Don Juan Dharmapala, to be made of gold, and sent the same by one Sellappo Arachchi to be delivered to the king of Portugal. The golden image was with great pomp crowned by the King at Lisbon. Rájavali, p. 286.

c, Almanac, p. 261.

‡ Tennent, vol. i, p. 556.

few years of Pliny's death,* for his knowledge of Ceylon, except that of the Northern portion appears to have been very faint, but when Ptolemy compiled his great work about 150 A.D., the correct and minute details of Ceylon, as given by him, are clear indications of the extensive information that have been gained by the traders of his period To understand clearly the meaning of the statements made by Ptolemy, it will be better to quote in full the several passages, as given in the translation of his work, so far as it relates to the northern portion of Ceylon, with which alone we are, at present, concerned.

He says :—

Bk. vii, Chap. iv.

"Sect. 1, Opposite Cape Cory which is in India is the projecting point of the island of Taprobane which was called formerly Simoundou, and now Salike. The inhabitants are commonly called Salai. Their heads are quite encircled with luxuriant locks like those of women. The country produces rice, honey, ginger, beryl, hyacinth and has mines of every sort, of gold and silver and other metals. It breeds at the same time elephants and tigers."

"2. The point already referred to as lying opposite to Cory is called North Cape (Boreion Akron) and lies lon. : 126° and lat.: 12° 30'

---

* The date of the Periplus has been determined recently by J. Kennedy.

J. R. A. S. 1918. p: 106.

3. The descriptive outline of the rest of the island is as follows:—

Cape Galiba	....	lon. 124°	lat. 11° 30'
Margana, a town	....	123° 30'	10° 20'
Iogana, a town	....	123° 20'	8° 50'
Anarismoundou, a cape	....	122°	7° 45'
....			
Mouth of the river Ganges	....	129°	7° 20'
The source of the river	....	127°	7° 15'
Spatana Haven	....	129°	8°
Nagadiba or Nagadiva, a town	....	129°	0° 30'
Pati Bay	....	128° 30'	9° 30'
Anoubingara, a town.		128° 20'	9° 40'
Modouttou, a mart	....	128°	11° 20'
Mouth of the river Phasis	....	127°	11° 20'
The sources of the river	....	126°	8°
Talacory (or Aakote), a mart	....	126° 20'	11° 20'

after which the North cape."

Then follows a description of the mountains, the rivers, the people, the inland towns and the islands. Of the people are mentioned the Nagadiboi as living in the East and the Nageiroi on the South.

Of the inland towns, Poudouke at	124°	3° 40'
and Nakadouba	128° 30'	on the line
and of the islands, Nagadiba	135°	8° 30'

are mentioned.

Again he says in Book: I, Chap: 13:—

"Beyond the cape called Cory where the Kolkhic Gulf terminates, the Argaric Gulf begins and the distance thence to the city of Kouroula which is situate to the north-east of Cory is 3400 Stadia. The distance right across, may, therefore, be estimated at about 2030 stadia since we have to deduct a third because of the navigation having followed the curvature of the Gulf, and have also to make allowance for irregularities in the length of the courses run. If now we further reduce this amount by a third, because the sailing, though subject to interruption was taken as continuous there remain 850 stadia determining the position of Kouroula as situated north-east from Cory."

In Bk: vii, Chap., I, are described the towns in Damurike.

'Sect. 11. **Land of Pandion.**

In the Orgalic Gulf, Cape Cory called also Kalligikon

Argeirou, a town.

Salour, a mart.

12. **Country of the Batoi.**

Nikama, the metropolis

Thelkeir.

Kouroula, a town.

13 **In Paralia specially so called: the country of Toringoi.**

Mouth of the river Khaberos.

Khaberis, an emporium,

Sabouras, an emporium."

Before discussing the identification of the places mentioned by Ptolemy, it will be advantageous here to quote the description found in the Periplus of the Erythrean sea, as it will be of great assistance in such identification.

After giving a description of the roadsteads on the western coast of India, it proceeds as follows:

> "After Bakari occurs the mountain called Pyrrhos (or the Red) towards the South near another district of the country called Paralia (where the pearl fisheries are which belong to King Pandion) and a city of the name of Kolkhoi. In this tract the first place met with is called Balita, which has a good harbour and a village on its shore. Next to this is another place called Komar, where is the cape of the same name and a haven................From Komari (towards the South) the country extends as far as Kolkhoi, where the fishing for pearls is carried on........Condemned criminals are employed in this service. King Pandion is the owner of the fishery. To Kolkhoi succeeds another coast lying along a gulf having a district in the

interior bearing the name Argalou. In this single place are obtained the pearls collected near the island of Epiodorus. From it are exported the muslins called Ebargareitides."

"Among the marts and anchorages along this shore to which merchants from Damurike and the north resort, the most conspicuous are Kamara and Podouke and Sopatma which occur in the order in which we have named them. In these marts are found those native vessels for coasting voyages which trade as far as Damurike, and another kind called "sangara" made by fastening together large vessels formed each of single timber and also others called "Kolondiophonta" which are of great bulk and employed for voyages to Khruse and the Ganges. These marts import all the commodities which reach Damurike for commercial purposes, absorbing likewise nearly every species of goods brought from Egypt, and most descriptions of all the goods exported from Damurike and disposed of on this coast of India. Near the region which succeeds, where the course of the voyage now leads to the East there lies out in the open sea and stretching towards the West the island now called Palaisimoundon, but by the ancients Taprobane. To cross over to the Northern side of it takes a day. In the south part it gradually stretches towards the west till it nearly reaches the opposite coast of Azania. It produces pearl, precious (transparent) stones, muslins, and tortoise shell."

As Ptolemy was not a traveller and as he never visited this Island nor the other places mentioned in his work, but obtained all his information from merchants, strict accuracy of details, in the modern sense, could not be expected in his description of the sea-coast, not only of India but also of Ceylon, the latter of which would have presented to him great difficulties of comprehension, on account of the several islands between which navigation had to be accomplished, and of the many turns and twists due to the sinuous nature of the coast. As his ambition was to give a geographical description of the places in terms of longitudes and latitudes, he possibly constructed a map in accordance with the fragmentary hearsay material in his possession, marked the places on it, and then proceeded to draw the latitudes and longitudes before giving a description of the places themselves in his book. Although his latitudes and longitudes are not quite correct, yet to have drawn a map comparatively so free from errors as he did, borders on the marvellous. Even the Portuguese in the sixteenth century did not give as correct a map of Ceylon, as Ptolemy did in the second century A. D.

A map of the coast lines of South India and of North Ceylon reconstructed from geographical information supplied by Ptolemy is appended. From it a very fair knowledge of the conception of Ptolemy can be obtained. According to him, the Jaffna Peninsula which was then an Island, was considered to be on the coast of India and the Island of Nágadípa by which name it was then known was placed very far to the east in the Bay of Bengal. The Elephant Pass Lagoon was made into a broad sea,

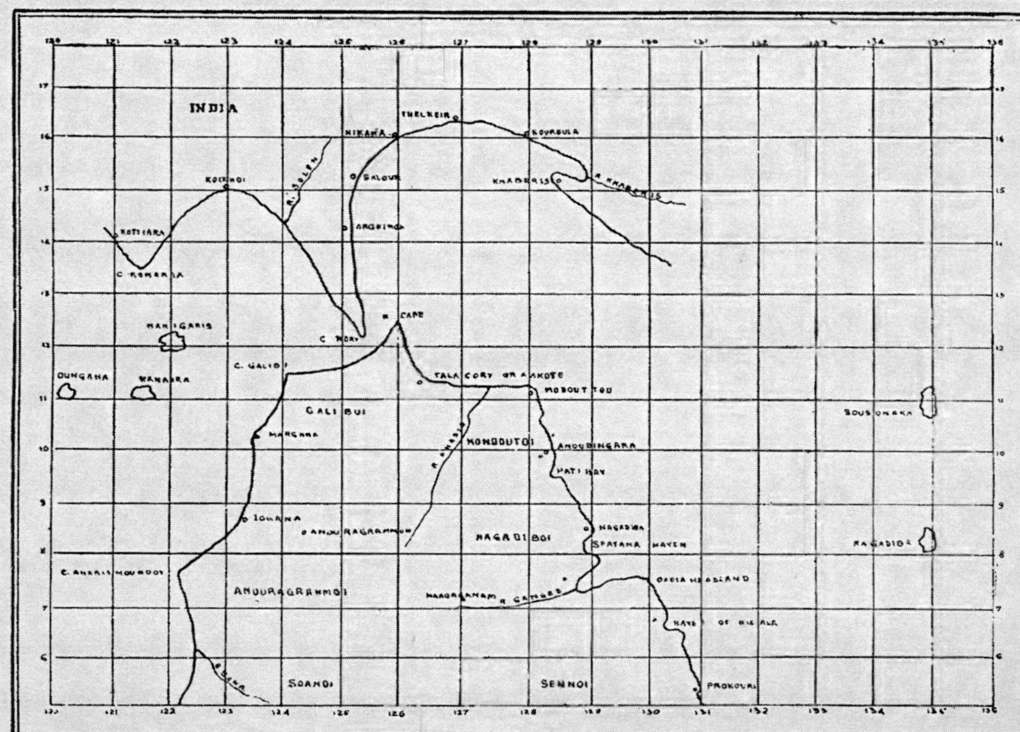
INDIA
THELKEIR
NIKAÑA
KOURGULA
KOTTIARA
C. KOMARIA
MANIGARIS
WANARA
DUNGANA
C. GALIOI
CAPE
C. MORY
KOKKHOI
SALOUR
ARGEIROS
KHABERIS
TALACORY OR AAKOTE
MOBOUT TOU
GALIBUI
MARGANA
MONGOUTOI
ANOUBINGARA
PATI HAY
IOUANA
ANOURAGRAMMON
NAGADIBOI
NAGADIBA
SPATANA HAVEN
C. ANARISMOUNDOY
ANOURAGRAMMOI
R. GANGES
ORETA HEADLAND
SOANOI
SENNOI
PROKOURI
SOUSOUKA
NAGADIOA

thus proving that the mariners from the west never visited the ports on the northern coast of the peninsula, but used the lagoon as the great roadway to enter the Bay of Bengal. Ptolemy's mistakes are certainly excusable. The names of places, though not their positions, may be taken as correct, and they should be identified with reference to the course of navigation or by comparison with the description given in the Periplus.

The several writers,* who attempted to identify and locate the places mentioned by the Greek authors, were not sure of the course taken by the early western navigators, and had the advantage neither of local knowledge, nor of the assistance afforded by recent archaeological discoveries. They have, therefore, identified some of the towns situated in North Ceylon as towns in South India, under the supposition that, when those early navigators passed Cape Comorin, they hugged the Indian coast till they reached Coromandel; whereas the mariners actually crossed over to Ceylon and sailed through the Elephant Pass Lagoon to the Bay of Bengal, and then northward to the Coromandel Coast. That is how the existence of the river Phasis, as they called 'Kaṉagaráyaṉ-Aru' the only river in Ceylon which flows northwards, could have come to their knowledge.

What the unknown author of the Periplus knew of Ceylon was even more limited. After making a passing mention of Ceylon he goes on to say that "it (Ceylon) gradually stretches towards the west till it nearly reaches

---

* Vincent, Bishop Caldwell, Mc Crindle, Tennent and others.

the opposite coast of Azania," which is Africa, thereby showing that he had at no time circum-navigated Ceylon. Mr. Casie Chetty was therefore not far wrong when he said that the commercial intercourse of the Greeks and of the Romans was confined to the Northern kingdom.*

Komar, Kolkhoi and Salour have been correctly identified; Komar, as Cape Comorin, and the other two as Koṛkai and Sáliyúr,† the celebrated towns in South

---

* See Supra, p: 87 note.*

† (a) "தத்து நீர்வரைப்பிற் கொற்கைக் கோமான்"

Cirupáṇ·, 1: 62

The King of Koṛkai, which is bounded by the waves of the sea.

(b) " பேருல்கத்து மேஎன் தோன்றிச்
சீருடைய விழுச்சிறப்பின்
விளைந்து முதிர்ந்த விழு முத்தி
னிலங்குவளை யிருஞ்சேரிக்
கட்கொண்டிக் குடிபாக்கத்து
நற்கொற்கை.

Mad:. Káñ: ll : 133-138

The good (town of) Koṛkai deserving of praise in being considered by the great as a place of pre-eminence, in which are the coast hamlets of toddy drinking people who fish shining chanks and pearls of ripe age. (As Koṛkai is said to have been bounded by the sea, and to have contained the residences of pearl and chank fishers, it must have been in the second century A. D. a sea-coast town, although it is now several miles inland.)

(c) " கொடும் புணரிவிலங்கு போழக்
கடுங்காலொடு கரைசேர
நெடுங்கொடி மிசையிதையெடுத்
தின்னிசையமுரச முழங்கப்
பொன்மலிந்தவிழுப்பண்ட
நாடார நன்கிழிதரு
மாடியற் பெரு நாவாய்
மழைமுற்றிய மலைபுரையத்
துறைமுற்றிய துளங்கிருக்கைத்
தெண்கடற் குண்டகழிச்
சீர்சான்றவுயர் நெல்லி
னூர்"

Mad:, Káñ:, ll : 77-88

India referred to in Tamil poems of the third Saṅgam. Koṛkai was the headquarters of the Páṇḍyan to carry on the pearl fisheries belonging to his kingdom, and the Periplus offers the interesting piece of information "that they are worked by condemned criminals." Koṛkai was also the residence of the Páṇḍyan sub-king.

The Cape Cory of Ptolemy has also been properly identified as Kóṭi or Dhanushkóṭi in the Island of Ramésvaram, but his north Cape "Boreion Akron" lying opposite to it cannot be the one on the North Coast of the Jaffna Peninsula. It must have been at Talaimannár, where the railway line now ends.* The author actually took that as the northern point of Ceylon, and thought that the coasts proceeding South and North from Mannar did really project westward and eastward respectively.

Ptolemy appears to have thought that Simondou was the old name of Ceylon, but according to the Periplus, Ceylon was then known as Palaisimoundon, whereas, according to the informants of Pliny, it was the name of the chief town and royal residence "with a population of two hundred thousand souls." Many a learned writer has attempted to elucidate this name, some taking it as a

Sáliyúr, into whose deep harbour of cool waters, come merchant vessels, ploughing through the rolling billows, with sails unfurled, drums sounding and flags flying from the masts, and full of success reach the shore for the country to enjoy the profitable merchandise laden therein that the town, surrounded by the crowd of ships unloading goods, appears like a mountain top covered with dark clouds.

* Mr. H. W. Codrington C. C. S. was the first to make this identification.

Pali or Sanskrit word* and others holding that at one time Ceylon was really called Simondou. The word obviously represented the Tamil name "Palaisīḻamaṇḍalam." Ceylon was known to the ancient Tamils as Īḻam and 'Īḻamaṇḍalam;' and it has continued to be so known to the present day. From Īḻam' came 'Sīḻam,' 'Sihaḻam,' and 'Siṅhaḻam,'† and from Sīḻam came 'Zeilon' of the Portuguese, 'Ceilan' and 'Seilan' of the Dutch and 'Ceylon' of the English. The island was also known as 'Heladiva' or 'Heludiva' as Elu was the language of the inhabitants,

---

* a. Vincent, the translator of the Periplus, quoting from another writer, says that Palaisimoundon represented Parashri Mandalam, Parashri being the Indian Bacchus whom the king worshipped!

b. On Palaesimondou, Pridham has the following note—"the Palaesimundi oppidum of the ancients is thought by some to have been situate in the Jaffna peninsula, but its precise situation remains to be determined. It is described by the Rachia (the ambassador to the Court of Claudius) as being the principal city, and having a capacious harbour, which would almost induce one to look for it on the north-west coast of Ceylon. The theory of Forbes who traces its etymology to the Siṅhalese words *palacia*—lower, and *mandhala*—province (in which case it may be freely rendered 'lowlands,) in allusion to the general division of the Kandyan districts into *Udacia* and *Palacia*, upper and lower, is very ingenious and even suggestive but can it legitimately be made to extend to a Malabar Province?"

Pridham, vol. ii. p. 511.

c. "Palai-Simundu, Lassen conjectures to be derived from the Sanskrit Pali-Simanta, 'the head of the sacred law,' from Ceylon having become the great centre of Buddhist faith."

Tennent, vol. i, p, 549. note.

d. A contributor to the Indian Antiquary thinks that the original of Palaesimundou was *Parasamudra* which was the island of Siṅhala (Ceylon), according to the commentator of the Artha Sastra of Kautilya, as the gems from Ceylon were called *parasamudra.*

Ind. Ant., vol. xlviii, pp. 195—196.

† Y.V.M., App. p. xlvii.

and it probably received the name Íḻam from the same source. From 'Heladiva' came 'Sihaladiva,' perhaps shortened from 'Sri Heladiva' and hence 'Sielediba' and 'Cielediba' of the medieval writers. From 'Síḻam dípa' came 'Serendib' of the Arabs. The name 'Salike' for the island and 'Salai' for the people, as stated by Ptolemy, must have been corruptions of Síḻam.

When the Greek traders came to Ceylon, they heard, perhaps, from the lips of the Tamils who preponderated at the sea-ports, that the Island which was formerly called 'Íḻa Maṇḍalam' or 'Siḻa Maṇḍalam' or Paḻaya Siḻa Maṇḍalam (paḻaya in Tamil means old) was also called 'Támṛaparṇi,' and therefore they wrote that the Island's former name was Palai Si mondou dropping the syllable 'ḻa" in síḻa and that the name then in use was Taprobane. The name Taprobane was mentioned by the Greek writers and in one of the Asóka edicts. Onesicrates who lived about 400 years before Ptolemy was the first to mention it. Two centuries only had then passed after the advent of Vijaya and his followers, and the Pali name Tambapaṇṇí, if its derivation as stated in the Mahávaṅsa be true, would not have then come into use, and even if it did, it could not have possibly become so current, considering the fixity of Indian habits and grooves of thought, as to have been in common use at the ports where the Tamils were predominant. It is more probable therefore that the name was borrowed by the Greeks from the Tamil Támraparṇi. Támraparṇi of which the Pali form was Tambapaṇṇí had nothing to do with the copper coloured sand and the palms of the original Kaliṅga Immigrants—a fanciful derivation of the author of the

Maháyańsa*—but was a name given to Ceylon by the Tamil immigrants from the Tinnevelly district, through which runs the river called to this day Támraparṇi. The North-western coast of Ceylon being opposite to the mouth of that river, the name would have readily suggested itself to those early immigrants.

If we take the earlier statement in the Maháyańsa that Vijaya "landed in the division of Tambapaṇṇí of the land of Lańká,"† as a proof that that part of Ceylon where he landed was then known as Támraparṇi.‡ and that the earlier Greek traders used to call at a port there and applied that name to the whole island of Ceylon, then the correctness of the statement made in the Periplus, that Ceylon was then called ' Palaisimoundon, but by the ancients Taprobane," will become apparent. As Pliny was the first to make mention of the name Palaisimunda, Taprobane was certainly the more ancient name. Chanakya, the author of the Arthasastra written in the 4th century B.C., mentions two varieties of pearls called 'Páṇḍya Kavádaka' and 'Támravarnika.'¶ The former must have been pearls fished on the Indian coast, when Kavádapuram was the capital of the Páṇḍyan country, and the latter those fished off the coast of Ceylon. This confirms the theory that one of Ceylon's earliest names was Támraparṇi—so early that it was even so known

---

* Mah. chap : vii.

† Ibid vi.

‡ Támraparni being originally a South Indian name, it is quite possible that this appellation was bestowed on the country long previous to Vijaya's landing.

¶ Artha. p. 86.

before Kavádapuram was destroyed by an inundation of the sea. As the name Támraparni or Taprobane is now lost and the name Ílamandalam still exists, the correct rendering would be as stated in the Periplus and not as stated by Ptolemy, the prefix 'palai' being wrongly applied. It is, however, curious that the wrong prefix 'palai' should have been applied to Simoundou instead of to Taprobane by the two persons Pliny and the unknown author of the Periplus. Is it in imitation of Megasthenes who called the people of Ceylon Palaigonoi* which is undoubtedly a corruption of Palai Nagoi (palaya Nágar-ancient Nágas, or Íla Nágar—Nágas of Ílam)?

The derivations given by the Sinhalese chronicler to Tambapanni and Sinhalam † are fanciful, and not probable. The people of Ceylon came to be called Sinhalese not because they were the descendants of the lion, but because they populated the land called Ílam, Sílam, Sihalam or Sinhalam. The story of a lion living with a princess was too wild a piece of romance even for the sixth or the seventh century B. C. Legends of this nature belong to a much earlier age, and the fact that Vijaya's grandfather was known as Sinha made it easy for the author of the Mahávansa to make up a fanciful derivation for the word Sinhalam. As for Tambapanni *tamba* is copper and *panni* may also mean the palm of the hand, and imagination supplied the connection between the two.

The phonetic similarity tempts one to conjecture that Palaisi moundou was a corruption of *Pisasu mundal*

* Ind. Ant. vol. vi. p. 122.

† Mah., chap. vii.

(devil's point), which is a promontory in Pallaváráyankaṭṭu. This promontory would have been prominently brought to the notice of the early mariners. and they would not have been slow to apply that name to the chief town, to the river on which it was situate, and lastly to the island itself. There are several promontories on the west coast called by the Tamil name *Mundal*, and Ptolemy himself mentions one of the name of Anarismoundou.

The lake Megisba of vast magnitude referred to by Pliny must have been the Giant's tank (Tamil-Mahá vávi) and the two rivers rising from it, one flowing by the capital and the other towards the continent of India, must have been the Pálávi, the waste weir of Giant's tank which flowed by the side of Mátoṭa, and the Kanagaráyaṉ Áṛu which is still flowing northward. The Greeks called the latter "the river Phasis" perhaps finding certain points of similarity with the river of that name flowing through the district of Colchis and falling into the Black Sea. The envoys who went to the Court of Claudius must have been under the impression that the river had its source in the Giant's tank.

The island of Epiodorus is probably the island of Mannar as there is no other island near which pearl oysters are fished in this region. The extensive trade in pearls, which existed in the first century A.D., can be easily seen from a quotation from Pliny. He says "Our ladies glory in having pearls suspended from their fingers, or two or three of them dangling from their ears, delighted even with the rattling of the pearls as they knock against each other; and now at the present day the poor classes are even affecting them as people are in the habit of saying that a pearl worn by a woman in public is as good as a lictor walking before her. Nay even more than this they put them on their feet and that not only on the laces of their sandals but all over the shoes; it is not enough to wear pearls but they must tread upon them and walk with under foot as well."*

The district of Paralia is wrongly located by both Ptolemy and the author of the Periplus. The former calls it the country of the Toringoi (Teluṅgar or Chóḻaṅgar—Chóḻas) and places it about the mouth of the river Kávéri, and the towns mentioned by him as being situate in that district are also Chóḻa towns. The latter locates it at the southern most portion of the Indian Peninsula, although somewhat more correctly he places it near the pearl fisheries.

"Árkali" is a Tamil word meaning 'the resounding Sea' and therefore applied to 'the Ocean.'† 'Parakali or paraṅkali from the root 'para' meaning 'to spread', 'to extend' or 'to be diffused', representing 'the broad sea,' is the opposite term of 'árkali,' and therefore applied to 'the shallow sea.' These names appear to have been applied to the lands adjoining these seas also. Ptolemy calls the sea to the north of Ramésvaram 'Orgalic Gulf'

---

* Pliny, chap. ix, 54.

† a. "ஆர்கலிசூழ் தென்னிலங்கை"

Tiruv., Kuyilpattu. v: 2.

Ceylon surrounded by the resounding sea.

b. "ஆர்கலிமுழவினதிகர் கோமான்,'

Puram. v: 91, by Ouvaiyár.

The (Céra) king Adikan whose drum is the resounding sea.

undoubtedly the Tamil word 'árkali', and also the country on the Indian coast adjoining it, whereas the country on the opposite coast is called 'Argalou' by the author of the Periplus.

The portion of the mainland of Ceylon extending from Aripu to Púnakari was in ancient times called 'Parankali' and afterwards corrupted to 'Perunkaḷi.' The district of Viḍattaltívu was called Pringally during the early years of the British rule, * the district of Máto-ṭa was called Peringally by Baldeus†, and that portion of the mainland lying opposite to the Island of Mannar is still called Peruṅkaḷipaṭṭu. Pringally, Peringaly and Peruṅkaḷi are but variations of Paraṅkali or Parakali and Paralia mentioned by Ptolemy and in the Periplus must therefore represent this district.

Sect: 12, Chap: 1 of Bk: vii of Ptolemy should therefore read:—

12. **In Paralia, specially so called—the country of the Batoi**

---

* "In 1810 the district of Pringally or as it is commonly called the district of Werteltivu and the port of Werteltivu were separated from the Mannar Collectorate and attached to that of the Wanni."

Wanni, M.L.R., vol. i, p. 28.

† "Mantote begins to the north of the Salt river, near the village of Pringally extending to the south along the sea shore as far as the river Aripouture."

Baldeus, chap. xliv, p. 709.

[There is evidently a mistake in this sentence, as the words Mantote' and 'Pringally' should be transposed.]

Nikama—the metropolis
Thelkeir
Kouroula—a town,

and in sec: 13, the words 'Paralia specially so called' ought to be deleted, and it should read:—

13. **In the country of Toringoi**
Mouth of the river Kaberos
Kaberis, an emporium
Sabouras, an emporium.

Batoï is the Greek term for Véḍar (huntsmen) who must have resided in the interior. The Moudouttoi and the Nagadiboi would have been in fact the people residing in this district, but Ptolemy locates them elsewhere and calls the people living in this locality Galiboi.

It was this district of Paralia, which contained the marts and anchorages along the shore, to which the merchants from Damurike and the north resorted. It is wrong to conclude that the words 'this shore', in the sentence 'among the marts and anchorages along this shore to which the merchants from Damurike and the north resort,' found in the Periplus are intended to mean the Indian coast. Damurike represents Tamiḻakam (தமிழகம்), the Tamil country in South India, and if the marts were in the Indian coast, Damurike need not be separately mentioned. By 'north' is meant the country near the mouth of the Ganges. The term 'Chryse' is the equivalent of gold in Greek and appears to refer to Suvarṇa Bhúmi in Sanskrit. It has been identified with the Malay Peninsula. 'This shore' is further described as 'another coast lying along a gulf having a district' in which pearls are to be collected near the island of Epiodorus. W. H. Schoff the latest translator of the Periplus renders the passage which refers to this district as follows:—

"Beyond Colchi there follows another district called the Coast Country, which lies on a bay, and has a region inland called Argaru. At this place, and nowhere else are bought the pearls gathered on the coast thereabouts; and from there are exported muslins, those called Argaritic," and identifies Argaru with Uṛaiyúr the ancient capital of Chóḻamaṇḍalam. The improbability of Schoff's identification of Argaru with Uṛaiyúr will be clear, when it is known that Uṛaiyúr was not a district but a town, and the Chóḻa capital, about the second half of the first century A.D., was Káveripúmpaṭṭinam and not Uṛaiyúr. To the north of Koṛkai, there were no towns on the Indian coast connected with the pearl fisheries, whereas there were some on the Ceylon coast. If the language of the above passage is construed to mean the coast opposite to that of India, the location of the district of Argalou or Argaru from which pearls were collected and muslins exported will be apparent. The word which Schoff translated to 'Argaritic' was perhaps neither 'ARGARITIDES' as read by him, nor 'EBARGARITIDES' as taken by Mac Crindle, but MARGARITIDES as supposed by Vincent.* For the trade along this shore, the most inportant ports were Kamara, Podouke and Sopatma which must be sought for on the coast of Ceylon and not of India. It would be

* Vincent one of the translators of the Periplus says in a note that the reading of this passage by Salmasius was sindones margaritides—muslins sprinkled with pearls.

more correct to say that they were in the district of Paralia or Peruṅkaḷi.

Sopatma is no doubt Sópaṭṭinam which in Tamil means 'a fortified town.* Therefore the Eyil paṭṭinam of Cirupáṇáṟṟupaḍai and the Sopatma or Sópaṭṭinam of the Periplus stand identified with Mántai or Mátoṭa, which was a fortified town on the North-western coast of Ceylon. Sites of Roman buildings, once the residences of Roman merchants, in addition to Roman coins and articles of foreign trade have been found here.† Mámúlanár,

* The Tamil word có (சோ) means a fortification.

cf: சோவின் அருமை யழித்தமகன்

Nánmaṇi, v: 2.

The man who destroyed the strength of the fortification.

† De Couto in his History of Ceylon says:—" And in addition to all these proofs we find today in Ceilao vestiges of Roman buildings, which shows that they formerly had communication with that island. And we may even say more, that in it were found the same coins that this freedman (Annius Plocamus) took, when Joao de Mello de Sao Payo was Captain of Manar in Ceilao, in the year our Lord 1574 or 1575 (mistake for 1585), in excavating some buildings that stand on the other side in the territories that they call Mantota, where even today there appear here and there very large ruins of Roman masonry work; and whilst some workmen were engaged in taking out stone, they came upon the lowest part of a piece of foundation, and on turning it over they found an iron chain of such strange fashion that there was not in the whole of India a craftsman who would undertake to make another like it."

Couto, Dec. v, Bk. i, chap. vii.

J.C.B.R.A.S., vol. xx, p. 83.

Pridham commenting on the above passage says;—"I confess I do not see why we should limit ourselves to such a course (that the coins found were brought there by Annius Plocamus) when we know that both Roman and Greek coins must have been in part the circulating media employed in oriental commerce, one of whose emporia was doubtless in this very district."

Pridham, vol. ii, p. 497.

one of the Tamil poets of the third Saṅgam, who flourished about the latter part of the first century A. D. refers to the importance of the port of Mántai and speaks about the wealth brought over the seas by the ships of foreigners.* If this important emporium is not the Sopatma of the Periplus, the alternative left is that it was omitted altogether by the author for some unknown reason, while localities far less important receive mention.

Kamara can be easily identified with Ámúr of Ciṟupáṇáṟṟupaḍai and Aakote of Ptolemy. This same place Ptolemy calls Kouroula in Book I, chap : 13, as lying at a distance of 1350 stadia to the North east of cape Cory. The irregularities of the route deplored by him and on which he based his computation of the distance can be easily appreciated when the town is identified with the

---

b. 'The whole district of Mantota (Maha totam—Great garden) is surrounded with a halo of interest for the antiquary, and it is far from improbable that the measures that cannot fail to be taken, sooner or later, to restore its former fertility to this neglected but very capable district may evoke some relic of the past to elucidate what is now shrouded in mystery."

Pridham, vol : ii, p: 499.

* "நன்னகர் மாந்தை முற்றத் தொன்னார்
பணிதிறைகொணர்ந்த பாடுசேர் நன்கலம்
பொன்செய் பாவைவயிர மொடாம்ப
லொண்ணுவால் நிறையக் குவைஇயன்றவ
ணிலத்தினத்துறந்த நிதியத்தன்ன "

Akam. v: 127. by Mámúlanár.

Like unto the treasure left behind in this country (in exchange) for heaps of pepper, by the fair ships of foreigners, which braving dangers have brought over the bending billows, images of gold, diamond and amber, to the harbour of the good city of Mántai.

ancient Kadiramalai, * the capital of the Nága kings, which has now dwindled into the insignificant village of Kantaróḍai, though possessing untold archaeological wealth. If Kouroula was on the Indian coast, there was no necessity on the part of the informants of Ptolemy to speak of the irregular course of navigation. The distance of 1350 stadia or 155 English miles, as stated by Ptolemy, between cape Cory and Kouroula, will be found not to agree with the actual distance between Danushkóṭi and Kadiramalai. But too much reliance should not be placed on the computation of distances by sea voyages made at this early period, when mariners had no reliable contrivances to register the speed of vessels. If the route, however, ran from Danushkóṭi to Mátoṭa, and from Mátoṭa to Kalmuṇai and thence to Kadiramalai, the distance as stated by Ptolemy would be almost correct. As illustrating what little reliance could be placed on the distances mentioned by the Greek authors, we need only refer to the distance between Tyndis and Muziris on the western coast of India, identified as the present Thoṇḍi and Koḍungalúr respectively, which is stated in the Periplus as 800 stadia, but which in fact is only about 500 stadia.

It is rather doubtful if Talacory and Aakote represented the same place. Talacory was the ancient Talmuṇai (Cory and Muṇai being synonymous) now corrupted to Kalmuṇai, situated on the narrow arm of the mainland projecting into the Jaffna lagoon towards Colombuturai. It was no doubt an ancient mart, as old

Kadiramalai in the mouth of the illiterate became Kadrahai and Karalai, which was written Karoula as heard by the writer.

ruins can be seen about the place, and as Roman coins have been picked up there of late. Sir Emerson Tennent believing Talacory and Aakote to be the same, indentified them with Toṇḍaimáṉ Áru. This cannot be correct, as Toṇḍaimáṉ Áṛu came into existence only in the early part of the twelfth century A. D., after Karuṇákara Toṇḍaimáṉ, the famous General of the Chóḷa king Kulótuṇga I, and was neither a place of importance before that nor a cape. This error of Sir Emerson Tennent has presumably led the writers on Ceylon geography to call the most north-easterly cape of Jaffna, Palmyra Point.

If Kamara be Kadiramalai and Sopatma is Mátoṭa, Poudouke should, according to the description given in the Periplus, be midway between the two and can be safely identified with Púnakari. Púnakari, being the first station in the mainland on the line of the great trunk road which led from Jambukóḷa to the northern gate of Anurádhapura, would have been specially selected for the erection of triumphal arches and for "being decorated with every variety of flowers and lined with banners and garlands of flowers," on great festive occasions such as the procession of the Bo plant during the time of Dévánampiya Tissa, * or during royal visits. Hence, the place would have been most appropriately called Púdúki (பூதுக்கி-place hung with flowers) and its later transformation to Púnakari (city of flowers) is quite natural.

Of the three towns mentioned by Ptolemy as being in the country of the Batoi or, more correctly, Paralia

* Mah. chap: xix.

(sect. 12, chap. 1, Bk. vii), Kouroula has been thus identified as Kadiramalai or the present Kantaróḍai. Thelkeir is no doubt another form of Talacory. It therefore follows that the metropolis Nikama (Nigama or Niyaṅgama) should be Mátoṭa. It is not at all surprising to see that Ptolemy should have given two sets of names to the important marts on this coast,

Kouroula and Aakote	for Kadiramalai
Talacory and Thelkeir	for Kalmuṉai
Moudouttou and Nikama	for Mátoṭa.

When we consider that these names were mentioned to him at different times, by different merchants possibly speaking different tongues and that he modified those foreign names according to the predilections of his own tongue, some measure of confusion would have been inevitable.

It is also clear that Poudouke or Púnakari which was a port when the Periplus was written, had ceased to be one during the time of Ptolemy, and Talacory or Thelkeir, identified as Kalmuṉai, had come into prominence. Incidentally, it may be said, that this is a further circumstance in support of the view that Periplus was anterior in date to Ptolemy. Ptolemy who had, however, heard of the name 'Poudouke' assigned to it a place in the interior of the Island, and another further north than Madras.

Larger vessels probably rounded the promontory and found safe anchorage in the inner coast of Talacory or Kalmuṉai. From this spot, smaller boats called 'sangara' or *Sangadam* mentioned in the

Periplus, which could ply in shallow water, carried the goods through Vaḷukkai Áṛu to Kadira malai. Vaḷukkai Áru which is now a narrow dry channel except during the rainy season, was a salt creek navigated by small boats engaged in the removal of salt stored at Kantaróḍai even so recently as the Dutch times, and Baldeus calls it a salt river.*

Ptolemy mentions a town and an island, bearing the name of Nagadiva, situated on the same latitude, and an inland town Nakadouba, which he locates on the Equator. He also places the Nagadiboi on the East and the Nageiroi on the South, thus showing that the districts of Trincomalie, Mátara and Hambantoṭa were also peopled by the Nágas. It is difficult for one to believe now that the Nágas were ever living in the South and the East, but a critical study of the history of the period will disclose the truth of the statement. From the third century B. C., when Mahá Nága, the brother of Dévánampiya Tissa and a prince of Nága extraction, established his kingdom at Mágama in the South, his descendants, his Nága connections and a large concourse of Nága followers appear to have gradually settled in and about the districts. Nága princes had also successfully established themselves at Giri nuvara near Koṭṭiár and at Lénadora to the North of Matale. About the time of Ptolemy, a Nága dynasty of kings ruled at Anurádhapura.

It is therefore not surprising that, having heard from the merchants that the Nageiroi and the Nagadiboi were living on the South and the East, Ptolemy should have fixed the towns of Nakadouba and Nagadiba in those

---

* Baldeus, chap: xix.

districts respectively. The present Naimana might have been the ancient Nakadouba. Nagadiba the island should be Nágadípa of the Maháváṅsa, which has been identified beyond all doubt as the present peninsula of Jaffna, * and Nagadiba the town should have been its capital Kouroula or Kadiramalai.

Anoubingara, a town, and Modouttou, the mart, were also incorrectly identified as Katchia Veli and Kokalay respectively. In spite of the unmistakable phonetic resemblance, if not identity, between Modouttou and Mátoṭa, the veneration for Ptolemy's infallibility in the location of these places led to the somewhat violent transfer of this mart to the eastern coast. Anoubingara can be traced to Siṅgai Nagara or Siṅha pura,† a town built and occupied by the Kaliṅga colonists who accompanied Vijaya, and who are said to have landed at Mahisadípa. It came into prominence and fame during the time of the later Jaffna kings called Árya Chakravartís, and its extensive ruins can still be seen at Vallipuram near Point Pedro.

Close to these extensive ruins is Kuḍákarai which was in ancient times the actual harbour. It lies between Verugumuṇai and Koṭṭóḍai. After the settlement of the Kaliṅga colonists at this spot, the commercial intercourse between Ceylon and the Coromandel Coast became extensive, for, we hear of elephants having been exported from Ceylon to Kaliṅga as early as 300 B. C. Aelian on the

* Nágadípa; J. C. B. R. A. S., vol. xxvi.

† Siṅgai Nagara was transformed to Ana Siṅgara and then to Anoubingara by the foreign merchants.

authority of Megasthenes writing about the elephants of Taprobane says:—

"These island elephants are more powerful than those of the mainland, and in appearance larger, and may be pronounced to be in every possible way more intelligent. The islanders export them to the mainland opposite in boats, which they construct expressly for this traffic from wood supplied by the thickets of the island, and they dispose of their cargoes to the king of the Kalingai". *

As the information of Aelian was obtained from Megasthenes, it would be clear, that there had been a sea-borne trade between Ceylon and Kaliṅga earlier than 300 B. C. From the position of Siṅhapura or Siṅgai Nagar on the north-eastern corner of the Jaffna Peninsula, and from the fact that, till the early part of the 19th century, elephants from Ceylon were shipped from the port of Kalah or Kayts of which the site of the elephant quay is still shown, it is easy to surmise that the elephants were in those early days exported from Siṅgai Nagar. That the elephants were shipped on specially constructed crafts is known from the fact, that, 'elephant ships' are mentioned as part of the trophies of Kháravela, the King of Kaliṅga in his Hathigumpha inscription of 160 B. C. †

The necessity for a slight readjustment in the order of places in this region as given by Ptolemy, is not surprising when we consider the sinuous nature of the coast on the north of Ceylon. If Nágadípa be taken to repre-

* Ælian, p; 170.

† J.B.O.R.S. vol. iii p. 465.

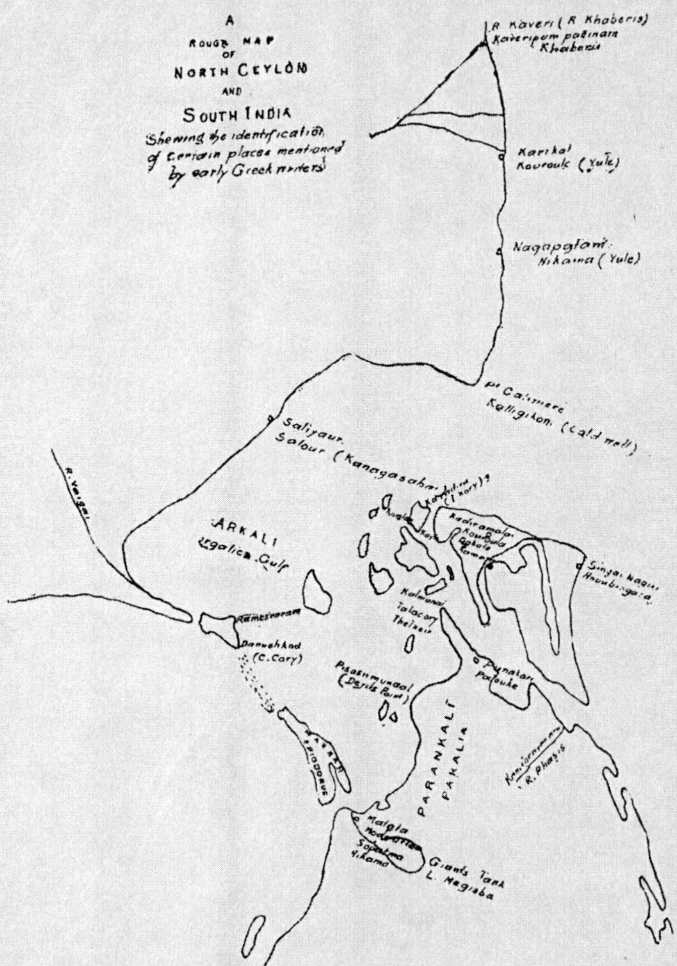

To face page 119.]

sent the larger country of the Jaffna Peninsula, the correct order of the places would be

Anoubingara	Siṅgai Nagara or Siṅhapura
River Phasis	Kanagaráyaṉ Áru
Talacory } Thelkeir }	Talmuṉai or Kalmuṉai
Kouroula } Aakote }	Kadiramalai or Kantaròḍai
Madouttou	Mátoṭa,

as shown in the annexed map.

In describing these places, the Periplus furnishes important information regarding the art of navigation among the Tamils. There were small boats called 'sangara' or 'saṅgaḍam' to ply between the ports in the shallow inland seas, and larger vessels called 'kolondiophonta' built in some of these ports 'for voyages to Khruse and the Ganges'. To this day these larger vessels are built at Valveṭṭyturai and Kayts, ports which came into prominence subsequent to the decline of commerce with Rome.

The Jaffna lagoon appears to have been the great roadway for foreign vessels, for after visiting Sopatma and Kamara "the course of the voyage bends to the east", and through it the Bay of Bengal was reached. Then the narrow sand bank, now forming the isthmus between the peninsula and the mainland, was not in existence, and the sea which is now silted up was navigable for larger vessels. The fact that dead chanks are now being fished in the bed of the Jaffna lagoon at a depth of 15 to 20 feet is a clear indication that the sea was then deep enough even for these larger craft.

According to the Periplus, the three ports mentioned above imported all the goods which should reach Damurike (Tamilakam or the Tamil country in South India), absorbing all that was brought from Egypt, and all species of goods that came from Damurike to be exported to other countries.

Cosmas Indicopleustes, a later Greek writer of the sixth century A. D. while describing Ceylon and its people, says:—"There are two kings ruling at opposite ends of the Island, one of whom possesses the hyacinth and the other the district in which are the port and emporium, for the emporium in that place is the greatest in those parts". * Of the two kings mentioned here, the one who possessed the hyacinth was the king of Anurádhapura, as the gem has been described by several travellers to Ceylon as one of extraordinary size and brilliance, † and the other was no doubt the king of Jaffna, in whose dominion was the great port and emporium. If the word hyacinth be taken to represent gems generally and not a special gem, even then the king possessing the country of gems would be the king of Anurádhapura. Sir Emerson Tennent, while referring to this statement of Cosmas, in one passage says that the king in whose dominion was the great port and emporium 'was, of course, the Rajah of Jaffna', ‡

* Tennent, vol: i, p: 567. (quotation from Cosmas)

† Hiouen Thsang, Marco Polo, Friar Odoric and Ibn Batuta refer to this gem in their writings.

‡ Chris : p: 4.

and at another argues that this 'singular kingdom, of which little was known', was somewhere in the south of Ceylon, about Pt: de Galle.* It was not probable that Galle had attained its eminence as a port and emporium by the early part of the sixth century A. D., when Cosmas wrote, whereas Sundara Múrty, one of the four Tamil Saiva saints, who flourished about the seventh century A. D., while singing the praises of the Lord of Tirukétísvaram, describes the harbour of Mátoṭa as one crowded with ships.†

When we consider the fact that the course adopted by the ancient navigators, in order to reach Mátoṭa, was along the several deep channels found between Danushkoṭi and the island of Mannar, that the sea near Mannar was then not so shallow as at present, and that the Jaffna lagoon was the roadstead for the larger vessels like the Chinese junks, the denial of Sir E. Tennent of 'the expediency and the practicability of the navigation' along this route would be found to have no justification. The rapidity with which the sea in those parts became silted up can be readily understood, when one knows that no vessel of any size can now approach within miles of Mátoṭa, that the ancient Páláví which perhaps served as a safe anchorage is now entirely blocked up, that the land between the Páláví and the sea is more than a quarter mile in width and covered with heavy jungle and that it is now impossible even for a small boat to navigate the

---

* Tennent, vol: i, p: 589.

† " வங்கம்மலிகின்ற கடன்மாதோட்ட நன்னகர் "
Sundara Múrty's Dévāram, Tirukétísvarapatikam, vv: 3 & 5.
The good city of Mátoṭa by the sea abounding with ships.

Elephant Pass lagoon with ease. The era of large ships among the nations of the world so synchronised with the silting up of the lagoon, which gradually became unfit for navigation, that such vessels had, perforce, to seek the protection of other ports. There is reason to suppose that the northern seas were not so shallow formerly as they are at present. If they were becoming shallower on being filled up with sand blown over by the South-West monsoon at the rate of two feet in a hundred years, the water would have been deep enough 1500 years ago, for the largest sized junks to pass through.

It is not necessary to show here that the Tamils and the Nágas took any active part in the commerce and navigation of the period; the country inhabited by them, or in their power, happened by a physical accident to be on the highway of the trade between the East and the West, where the parties to the trade could effect a mutual exchange and save on either side a protracted navigation. The vestiges of great antiquity, which still remain in these districts, combined with the statements of the ancient writers, Roman as well as Tamil, testify to the practicability of the navigation of these seas by the ancients.

When foreign commerce increased and when Arab, Roman and Indian ships began to call more frequently, the Nágas of Mátoṭa and another Tamil tribe, called the Kaḍambas,* evolved into sea pirates. The Nágas con-

* "துடியன் பாணன் பறையன் கடம்பனென்
றின் நான் கல்லது குடியுமில்லை" Puram. 335.

Tuḍiyan, Páṇan, Paṛayan and Kaḍamban,
Except these four there are no other Tamil tribes.

fined themselves to the Straits between India and Ceylon and to the Bay of Bengal, but the activities of the Kaḍambas were more extensive and productive of better results. They had their head-quarters at the mouth of the Aripo river, which was then known as the Kaḍamba river, and infested the Arabian Sea as far north as Cochin in the Malabar Coast. Their predatory acts were so much feared by the Roman merchants that their vessels loaded with merchandise had to be protected by Roman cohorts carried on board. Pliny had therefore to remark "at the present day voyages are made to India every year, and companies of archers are carried on board because the Indian seas are infested with pirates." The great Chóḻa king Karikála subdued the Nágas and destroyed their 'hanging fort' at Mátoṭa, about the middle of the first century A.D., and the Céra king Seṅguṭṭuvaṉ, and his father before him, exterminated the power of the Kaḍambas, by storming their stronghold and cutting down their *totem* the kaḍamba tree,* about the middle of the second century A.D. Some of these Kaḍamba pirates, who were scattered by Seṅguṭṭuvaṉ, remained on the west coast of India, and two centuries later became a powerful ruling dynasty with their capital at Banavási.

Till about the fifth century A.D., most of the trade with China was done overland through India. The ambassadors, who went to Rome in the reign of Claudius, stated that their ancestors had, in the course of their commercial pursuits, reached China by traversing India and the Himalayan mountains, long before sea voyages were attempted, and in the fifth century, the Ceylon king,

---

* See supra, chap. i, p. 22 and notes.

in an address delivered by his envoy to the Emperor of China, said that both routes were then in use. The first embassy from Ceylon to the Court of China reached its destination in 405 A.D., having gone apparently overland, as it was ten years upon the road.* The sea route to China came into prominence later than the fifth century A.D., when the present ports on the Northern coast of Jaffna became popular. All the sea-borne trade was in the hands of the Nágas, the Tamils and the Arabs; and large numbers of the latter remained in Ceylon for the purpose and earned the name of *Marakkalayas* (people of the ships; Tamil *marakkalam* means a ship) from the Siṅhalese.

The earliest Chinese writers like Fa Hian and Hiouen Thsang do not refer to North Ceylon in their writings. However, there is a very short passage in the History of the Travels of Hiouen Thsang which may be taken to refer to a place in the North. The passage is :—"Going from this mountain, i. e., Mount Malaya, in a north-eastern direction there is a town at the sea dividing; this is the place from which they start for the Southern Sea and the country of Sang-kialo (Ceylon)."†

This town Che-li-ta-lo, (supposed by some to be Charitapura and equated with Nágapaṭṭinam), which is so situate as to divide the sea, and from which voyage to Ceylon was continued, was not Kavéripúmpaṭṭinam as surmised by Dr. Burnell,‡ but Siṅhapura or Siṅgai

---

* Cathay, Prelim. Eassy, p: lxvii

† Hiouen. p; 233,

‡ Ind. Ant., vol. vii, p: 40.

Nagar on the north eastern coast of Jaffna. Hiouen Thsang describes two important kingdoms in South India, one Dravida with Kañchipura as the capital, and the other Malakuṭa. Dravida has been identified as the Pallava country from the name of its capital, but Malakuṭa, Dr. Burnell cojectured, to be the Chóḻa country, from the name of a village near Tanjore called Malaikúṭa Chúḍamaṇi Chadurvédamaṅgaḷam found in an inscription.* The Chóḻamaṇḍalam was neither called Malaikúṭa nor Malaináḍu; and the Malaikúṭa (Mount Malaya) referred to by the Chinese traveller was really the Céra Country, as at that time the Chóḻa and the Páṇḍya powers had perhaps dwindled into insignificance, and the Pallava and the Céra were the only powers to speak of in South India. Therefore going from Malaikúṭa or the Malabar Coast, one had to pass the Cape of Comorin, and from there sail in a north-eastern direction to reach the Bay of Bengal. The town on this passage which sounds very much like Che-li-ta-lo is Siṅhapura. It was from this place, the voyage to Ceylon which was then more confined to the east coast than to the west, was continued.

In the fifth and sixth centuries, Chinese ships appear rarely to have sailed further west than Ceylon. Thither, they came with their silks and other commodities, those destined for Europe being chiefly paid for in silver, and those intended for barter in India were transhipped into smaller craft adapted to the Indian seas, by which they were distributed at the various ports east and west of Cape Comorin.†

---

* Ind: ant: vol. vii, p. 40.

† Tennent vol. i, p. 565.

The description of the Indian trade by Cosmas* is so corroborative of the earlier account given by the author of the Periplus, that the existence and the importance of the marts at Mátoṭa and Kadiramalai are beyond all doubt. The ships of Arabia, Persia and the Malabar Coast called at Mátoṭa and Talacory, and despatched their goods to Kadiramalai in smaller boats, called *sangadam*. Náván-tuṛai, lying to the west of the Jaffna Fort, which is still known by the name of Sangaḍa Návántuṛai, was perhaps the port which gave protection to these smaller craft. As long as the Elephant Pass lagoon was navigable, the Chinese ships too anchored off Talacory, but later they, as well as the ships from Coromandel and the Ganges, touched at the several ports on the northern coast of the Jaffna Peninsula, and despatched their merchandise either by land or by sea, according to the ports they touched at, to Kadiramali which was certainly the great emporium of exchange.

In the second century A. D., the ships sailing from the Páṇḍyan country in South India to Java and Sumatra,

---

* " As its position is central, the island is the resort of ships from all parts of India, Persia and Ethiopia, and, in like manner many are despatched from it. From the inner countries, I mean China and other emporiums, it receives silk, aloes, cloves, clove wood, chandana and whatever else they produce. These it again transmits to the outer ports, I mean to Male (Malabar)· whence the pepper comes, to Kalliyana, where there is brass and sesamine wood, and materials for dress (for it is also a place of great trade) and to Sindon where they get musk, castor and androstachum, to Persia, the Homeric coasts and Adule. Receiving in return the exports of these emporiums, Taprobane exchanges them in the inner ports (to the east of Cape Comorin) sending her own produce along with them to each."

Tennent, vol: i, p: 569.
(quotation from Cosmas).

invariably touched at a port in the Jaffna Peninsula, as will be seen from allusions in the Maṇimékalai.*

About the seventh or the eighth century A.D., Mátoṭa, perhaps by reason of the difficulty of navigation, was abandoned, the eastern entrance to the Elephant Pass lagoon was blocked up, and Kayts under the name of Kalah (the identification of which is treated in a later c̲hapter) became the centre of trade, and ships from the East as well as the West found safe anchorage at this place. This was the port visited by European and Muhammedan travellers until the 16th century when the Portuguese appeared on the scene.

In Chapter I as well as in this chapter, the great coin finds at Kantaróḍai have been touched upon. Coins of a period extending from 500 B. C., or even earlier, to about the fourth or the fifth century A. D., have been picked up.

---

* a. " வங்கமாக்களொடுமகிழ்வுடனேறிக்
காலவிசை கடுக்கக் கடல்கலக் குறுதலின்
மாலிதை மணிபல்லவத்திடை வீழ்த்துத்
தங்கியதொரு நாள் "

Maṇi, Canto, xiv, ll: 75–82.

He (one Āputṛan on his way to Jává) gladly embarked with the merchants, and as the sea became rough on account of storms, the captain put in at Maṇi-pallavam, and stayed there a day.

b. " கலஞ்செய் கம்மியர் வருகெனக்கூஉ
யிலங்குநீர்ப் புணரியெறிகரையெய்தி
வங்கமேறினன் மணிபல்லவத்திடைத்
தங்காதக்கலஞ் சென்று சார்ந்திறுத்தலும் "

Maṇi., canto, xxv, ll : 124—127.

(Puṇya Rájá, the king of Nágapuram in Jává) calling the ship-builders, repaired to the coast and embarked from there. The ship proceeded calling at no intermediate port and anchored at Maṇi-pallavam.

The fact that such a large quantity of Roman coins, not to speak of the many varieties of Indian coins, have been found in one place (Kantaródai) testifies to its ancient commercial importance. The Roman coins found have not yet been studied, but Mr. Sewell who has made an elaborate study of the Roman coins found in India considers that a careful examination of the coin-finds leads to the following conclusions :—*

1. There was barely any commerce between Rome and India during the Consulate.

2. With Augustus began an intercóurse which, enabling the Romans to obtain oriental luxuries during the early days of the Roman Empire, culminated about the time of Nero who died about 68 A. D.

3. From this time forward the trade declined till the date of Caracala in A. D. 217.

4. From the date of Caracala it almost entirely ceased.

5. It revived again though slightly, under the Byzantine Emperors.

We may therefore estimate 300 years, extending from 50 B. C to 250 A.D, as the glorious period of prosperity of this country which synchronises with the Augustan age of Tamil lierature under the patronage of the third Sangam of Madura.

---

* J.R.A.S. 1904, p. 591.

CHAPTER IV

Ancient Civilization

THE Nágas living in North Ceylon, being the race nearest to India, would naturally have been akin to the South Indians—with whom they were in constant communication—in their religion, manners, customs, language, as also in their modes of thinking. There is an ample literature in South India from which we can gain an insight into the habits and manners and into the state of civilization of the people of South India between 200 B.C. and 300 A.D. It is a reasonable presumption that the people in North Ceylon would in all likelihood have evolved for themselves a civilization similar to that prevailing in South India. An attempt, therefore, to describe the civilization of North Ceylon about the beginning of the Christian era will accordingly be by analogy alone, which may find proof and corroboration in future years when Ceylon's untold wealth of archæological remains comes to be explored.

In addition to the indigenous civilization of the Nágas of North Ceylon, which appears to have been admitted by the Greek writers*, the large volume of commercial intercourse which they had with foreign nations would have given them facilities to improve in the arts and sciences, in industries and in their modes of life. If, as has been already shown in a previous chapter, there were so many thriving ports sought for by foreign

---

* Vincent, in his translation of the Periplus, says that there is a reading of the original Greek, which can be rendered into "Formerly Taprobane, lies out in the open sea to the West. The northern part is civilized and frequented by vessels equipped with masts and sails."

merchants, and if there was a great deal of enterprise in seafaring among the people themselves, the conclusion is irresistible that there was a prosperous industry in the land; a flourishing trade invariably presupposes a volume of industry. Among the ancient Hindus, agriculture and commerce were considered to be of the highest importance; handicrafts and the fine arts received the greatest patronage.

Long before some of those remarkable, and even stupendous engineering works, in the shape of tanks and irrigation channels, were conceived and constructed, agriculture was the most prominent industry of the people, even before the advent of Vijaya, and it certainly had reached such a state of importance as to constitute the chief source of the wealth of the people. Rice was the staple food of prince and peasant alike. It is incorrect to suppose that the people of Ceylon—the Nágas as well as the Yakkhas,—led such a precarious existence as to procure their sustenance from the produce of the jungle or the chase,* for we can trace several passages in the Mahávaṅsa, in which rice is mentioned as the chief food of the people within a few years of Vijaya's arrival. The pastoral scene in which Girikaṇḍa Síva, one of the Governors of Páṇḍuk Abaya, the successor of Vijaya, superintends the reaping of his paddy fields, and his daughter Suvaṇṇa Páli takes to him and to his reapers, their repast of rice, as graphically recorded in the MaháTvaṅsa,† is an interesting episode which confirms the theory that agriculture was the important industry of the people. The mention of this ancient practice by which it became

* Tennent, vol. i, p. 420.
† Mah. chap. x.

the duty of the daughter to carry the mid-day meal to her father, although he was rich enough to command a hundred servants, and although one of her palanquin bearers could easily have performed that service, makes one to long for a return of those ancient and happy times.

It was this cultivation of rice which brought in a large revenue to the State and which gave to the country that material affluence which was reflected in the immense tanks and dágobas, the ruins of some of which yet remain to attest the truth. If agriculture was the chief pursuit of the people after Vijaya's advent, according to the ample testimony of the Mahávaṅsa, it must be presumed to have been so even before that event, for there is not the slightest evidence of his having wrought any change in that direction. When we consider the fact that the last 2000 years have produced no change either in the system of cultivation adopted by the people or in their implements of husbandry, although the country has passed through the sway of some of the most civilized nations of the world, it requires no very prolonged flight of imagination to conjecture how many thousand years should have passed before the people reached that standard of cultivation. All the circumstances therefore show that agriculture was an honourable pursuit; and that it was carried on in an extensive scale by prince and peasant alike. It is, therefore, no wonder that the dignity of agriculture was the subject of praise by the poets of the ancient Tamil-land. *

---

* "உழுதுண்டு வாழ்வாரே வாழ்வார் மற்றெல்லாம்
தொழுதுண்டு பின்செல்பவர்."

Kuṛaḷ, 1033.

Who ploughing eat their food, they truly live;
The rest to others subservient eating what they give.

The uncertainty of rainfall led to the storing and husbanding of local showers; and certain years of famine, caused by the failure of rain, must have suggested the idea of conceiving and carrying out the building of those stupendous tanks which are still the wonder and admiration of the world. The larger tanks, which were connected with the smaller ones by a net-work of canals, supplied the requisite amount of water that was needed for cultivation all the year round.

In the Tamil work Ciṟupáṇáṟṟupaḍai, Mátoṭa is referred to as a town surrounded by many tanks of cool waters. The lake Megisba, mentioned by Pliny, was in all probability the Giants' tank which served as a reservoir for feeding the hundreds of smaller tanks scattered over the district. The vast extent of land irrigated by this tank can be imagined from the report made by Captain Schneider, the Colonial Engineer to the Ceylon Government in 1807, that this tank could feed land sufficient for the production of one million parrahs of paddy.† In view of the fact that a number of other similar tanks had been built in Ceylon before the third century A.D., the paddy output must have been considerable and large quantities of paddy would consequently have been exported to India and other countries. It is no matter for surprise, therefore, that one of the Tamil poets while describing the different articles of merchandise stored in the warehouses of Kávérippúmpaṭṭinam—about the first quarter of the second century A.D.—should have mentioned 'food stuffs

---

* See supra, chap. i, p. 14, note *

† Bertol : Introduction.

from Ceylon.'* This very Ceylon that, out of her plenty, gave, two thousand years ago. to India and other countries such abundant food, has now so fallen upon evil days that she is obliged to obtain two-thirds of her staple food from outside!

Weaving was another important industry carried on in the northern part of Ceylon. Cotton seems to have been the material that was wrought into cloths. Cotton must have been cultivated to such a large extent in the Jaffna Peninsula and in the Vannis that it exceeded the requirements of the country, for the name of Parutti Tuṛai (cotton port), given to a port in the north, still remains to testify to the export of that material to other countries. Even after the British occupation of the maritime provinces of Ceylon, cotton was so extensively cultivated in the Mannar District, that a European Superintendent was appointed by Government to superintend the cultivation of Government plantations.† The Nágas were so skilled in the art of weaving that the cotton stuffs manufactured by them have been compared to the 'sloughs of serpents,' to

---

* "நீரின்வந்த நிமிர்பரிப்புரவியுங்
காலின்வந்த கருங்கறிமூடையும்
வடமலைப்பிறந்த மணியும் பொன்னுங்
குடமலைப்பிறந்த வாரமுமகிலுங்
தென்கடன் முத்துங்குணகடன் றுகிருங்
கங்கைவாரியுங் காவிரிப்பயனு
மீழத்துணவுங் காழகத்தாக்கமும்."

Paṭṭina : ll. 185—191.

High-mettled steeds from over the seas,
Bags of black pepper brought in ships propelled by sails,
Gems and gold of the northern mountains,
Sandalwood and aghil of the western ghats.
Pearls of the southern seas and coral of the eastern seas
Goods procurable in (the regions of) the Ganges, the
Produce of (countries watered by) the Kávéri,
Foodstuffs from Ceylon and precious goods from Burma.

† Mannar, p. 41.

'woven wind,' and to 'vapour of milk';* and they are generally described as of such fine texture that the eye could not make out its warp and woof. * It is said that a Chieftain named Áay offered to the image of a god under the banyan tree (Siva) one of these priceless muslins which had been given to him by one Níla Nága.†

---

* a. "நோக்குநுழைகல்லா நுண்மையபூக்கனிந்
தரவுரியன்னவறுவை."

Porunar. ll : 82-83.

Flowered cloth, like unto the slough of the serpent, and of such fine texture that the eye cannot make out its warp and woof.

b. "காம்பு சொலித்தன்ன அறுவை."

Ciṛupán : l, 236.

Cloth resembling the fine sheath torn off the bamboo shoot.

c. "ஆவியன்ன அவிர்நூற்கலிங்கம்."

Perumpán : l. 469.

Cloth made of shining thread, like unto the vapour (of milk).

d. "புகைவிரிந்தன்ன பொங்குதுகிலுடீஇ."

Puṛam., v. 398, l : 19.

Clad in cloth resembling expanded smoke.

e. "கண்ணுழைகல்லா நுண்ணூற்கைவினை
வண்ண அறுவையர்."

Maṇi : Canto, xxviii, ll : 52-53.

Maidens clad in cloth of excellent quality, woven by hand and too fine to be distinguished by the eye.

f. "பாம்புபயந்தன்ன வடிவின்காம்பின்
கழைபடுசொலியின் இழைமணிவாரா
ஒண்பூங்கலிங்கம்."

Puṛam. v. 383, ll : 10—12.

Bright flowered cloth resembling the slough of the serpent and the sheath torn off the bamboo shoot, with gems along the warp.

† "   நிழறிகழ்
நீலநாகனல்கிய கலிங்க
மாலமர் செல்வர்க்கமர்ந்தனன் கொடுத்த
..........................ஆய்."

Ciṛupáṇ : ll : 95—97.

(The chieftain) Āay devotedly offered to the deity under the banyan the brilliant cloth presented to him by Níla Nága.

According to the Periplus, a kind of muslin sprinkled with pearls, called *ebargareitides*—evidently a mistake for *margaritides*—was exported from the island of Epiodorus (Mannar).* These muslins, which by reason of their fineness and transparency, were specially sought after by fashionable Roman ladies, who apparently preferred effect to modesty, fetched fabulous prices in foreign markets. Pliny, therefore, exclaimed "so has toil to be multiplied, so have the ends of the earth to be traversed, and all that a Roman dame may exhibit her charms in transparent gauze."† In a later passage Pliny goes on to say that "India drained the Roman Empire annually to the extent of 55,000,000 sesterces," (equal to about £487,000) and "this is the price we pay for our luxuries and our women."

These transparent fabrics and gauzy stuffs were as coveted by the fair Persian maidens in the harems of Susa and Ecbatana and also by the royal maidens in the Courts of India and Ceylon as they were by the wealthy ladies of Rome. This strange desire on the part of high born dames of India and Ceylon to clothe themselves in ultra diaphanous garments is amply supported by the fresco paintings found at Ajanta and Sígiriya, in which the royal maidens are so depicted as to appear semi-nude in spite of their garments, while their more dusky handmaidens are modestly clothed in cheaper stuff. Whether weaving was an industry also carried on by the Yakkhas, or whether they purchased their raimant from the Nágas is not known; but one thing is clear;—that the Yakkhas were dressed in fine linen and were aware of the use of such luxuries as the adorning of their beds with curtains.

* See supra, chap. iii, p. 110, note*

† Pliny, vi, 20.

This can be gathered from the account of the entertainment accorded to Vijaya by Kuvéni.*

The important industry of pearl-fishing was a Government monopoly even from the earliest times. There were two fisheries, one on the Indian coast and the other on the Ceylon coast. † The Ceylon fishery was the more important one ; and Megasthenes, the Grecian Ambassador to the court of Chandra Gupta, writing in the third century B. C., said that Ceylon was more productive of gold and large pearls than India. ‡ The population along the sea coast was mostly composed of pearl fishers; and in the deluge which took place in the time of Kelani Tissa, 400 villages of pearl fishers were destroyed. ¶ The author of the Periplus says that the Páṇḍyaṉ worked the fisheries with condemned criminals and Ptolemy calls the people on the sea coast Galiboi, perhaps the Tamil word Kaḷḷar (thieves). The pearl fishery attracted a large number of western merchants to the coast of north Ceylon and several temples, to which a moiety of the revenue was assigned by the kings, flourished in the land.

Chank fishing, which was carried on in the sea between Mannar and Jaffna from time immemorial, must have given work to a very large number of chank fishers and chank cutters. If, according to Madurai Káñci, one of the Tamil ten idylls, there was a colony of chank cutters at Koṟkai in the second century A.D.,§ there must

---

* Mah. chap. vii.
† Sea supra, chap. iii, p. 104.
‡ Ælian, p. 62.
¶ Rajavali, pp. 190-191.
§ See supra, chap. iii, p. 100, note. † (b)

have been a larger number of these artificers in Jaffna; and this theory is confirmed by the discovery of cut chank cores in the small excavation made by Dr. P, E. Pieris at Kantaróḍai. * Mr. W. Muttuvélupiḷḷai, an old and influential resident of this village turned up cartloads of these cores a few years ago and had them burnt for lime. This is a sure indication that, during the period Kadiramalai was the capital, there was a colony of artificers engaged in cutting chanks and turning them into rings, bangles and other personal ornments as is done at Dacca in Bengal to the present day. Although chank ornaments have now gone out of fashion among the women of Jaffna, millions of chanks are annually exported to North India where they are fashioned into different kinds of ornaments.

Iron implements and brass utensils appear to have been in general use, but excavations up to date have not brought up many brass articles. Iron appears to have been smelted out of ore found in Ceylon, and many iron smelting forges have been unearthed. The iron output, obtained even in this crude manner, must have been large as it enabled the rulers of Mántai (Mátoṭa) to erect an iron fort. Axes and spears, javelins and arrow heads were made of iron. Even the use of scissors was not unknown. † Poṭtery of different shapes and sizes, glazed and unglazed were in use. This is evidenced by the large quantities of broken pieces found near and around ancient ruins, and in fact indicating, as a sure sign, the existence of

* Nágadipa ; J.C.B.R.A.S., vol. xxvi.

† "மயிர்குறைகருவி மாண்கடையன்ன."

Porunar : 1; 29.

Like unto the beautiful loops in the shanks of the hair-trimming instrument, i.e., scissors.

these ruins. The lamps used by the poor classes were made of burnt clay, but brass lamps were used in opulent houses. A lamp, shaped according to the figure of a swan, and the figure of a female, with a raised hand holding a lamp—evidently an introduction of the Roman merchants,—are mentioned in the Tamil Classics.* Ceylon was at one time famous for the production of gold, although it is not now found in sufficient quantities to be profitably collected. The name Poṉparipo still survives to indicate at least one place where gold was found. Īḻam, one of the names for Ceylon, has, on account of such production, become a synonym in Tamil for gold. At a time when *rajakaria* was rampant, time and labour were matters of no count. Hundreds, if not thousands, must have been employed to collect gold, even in the smallest quantities, by winnowing the sand on the banks of certain Ceylon rivers.

The Nága and the Yakkha kingdoms were the seats of well-ordered and well-organised monarchical governments

---

* a. "யவனரோதிமவிளக்கு".

Perumpáṇ : II : 316-317.

Swan shaped lamp of the Yavanas (Greeks).

b "யவனரியற்றிய வினைமாண்பாவை
கையேந்தைய கனிறையநெய் சொரிந்து
பருஉத்திரிகொளீஇய குரூஉத்தலை நிமிரெரி."

Neḍ : Váḍ : II: 101—103.

Lights with flames rising with red-coloured heads from thick wicks set in an admirable bowl held in the hand of a maiden figure artistically made by the Yavanas (Greeks), and filled with oil.

c. "பாவைவிளக்கிற் பருஉச்சுடர் அழல".

Mullai : I: 85.

A large flame burning in the bowl of a lamp held in the hand of a maiden figure (of gold).

d. "கையமைவிளக்கம்."

Mullai : I : 49.

Lamp held in hand (of a maiden figure).

dating as far back as, or even earlier than, the period of the Rámáyaṇa. The monarchy was heriditary and absolute, and the purity of the royal blood was maintained by means of intermarriages with other royal houses. These kingdoms contained cities, towns and villages. The Nága capitals were fortified towns. In the building of forts and in providing them with weapons and missiles, both of offence and of defence, the Nágas had arrived at a very considerable degree of perfection. Kadiramalai as well as Mántai (Mátoṭa) were fortified, and Mántai had, according to tradition, an iron fort, which is confirmed by another tradition that there was in that city a settlement of expert artisans (Pañcha Kammáḷar). The forts were surrounded by impregnable ramparts from which, at times of war and seige, sharp arrows were discharged from machines. They were further strengthened by high walls difficult to scale and by deep moats.* The fort was also surrounded by thick and impenetrable thorny jungle. The traces of the ancient moat at Mátoṭa are still visible. The iron fort at Mátoṭa was so high, and it had such a high tower that the Tamil poets called it a 'hanging fort.'† The cities had wide streets well laid

---

* " அருங்குழுமிளைக் குண்டுகிடங்கி
னுயர்ந்தோங்கிய நிரைப்புதவி
னெடுமதினிரைஞாயி
லம்புமிழயிலருப்பம் ".

Mad : Káñ : ll : 64—67.

Fortifications surrounded by impenetrable jungle and deep moat and provided with gates under high turrets, encircling walls and bastions from which sharp arrows are discharged (by machines).

† See supra, chap. i, p. 19, note ¶.

out; * there were houses and mansions built of stone and wood and surrounded by walls containing gateways. They were guarded by armed warders and even by foreign soldiers. † The palaces and mansions were several storeys high containing terraces and balconies; ‡ the superstructure having been of wood no ruins have remained to testify to us of their ancient splendour. The royal palaces had banqueting halls large enough to entertain 500 to 1000 guests, state rooms which were supported by pillars covered with gold, wide balconies and windows opening

---

* a. "மாடமோங்கிய மல்லன்மூதூர்
ஆறுகிடந்தன்ன வகல்நெடுந்தெருவில்."

Neḍ : Váḍ : ll : 29-30.

In the broad main-street which like a river lies in the prosperous old city of lofty mansions.

b. " நன்னகர்
விண்தோய் மாடத்து விளங்குசுவருடுத்த."

Perumpáṇ : ll : 368-369.

In the good cities where there are sky-scraping mansions be-girt with shining walls.

† "கடவுண் மால்வரைகண் விடுத்தன்ன
அடையாவாயில வனருங்கடைகுறுகி."

Ciṛupáṇ : ll : 205-206.

Having approached his towered city-gateway, which though unclosed (to minstrels, sages and brahmans), yet affords no entrance (to others) and which would resemble the great Méru, the seat of the gods, when it opens but one of its eyes.

‡ a. "சாத்திய வணிஏற்றருஞ் சென்னிமாடம்."

Perumpáṇ ; l : 347.

Mansions with such towering tops that even with the help of the ladders placed against them it is difficult to climb them up.

b "நிரைநிலைமாடத்தரமியந்தோறும்."

Mad : Káñ : l : 451,

In the upper terraces of well-set storyed mansions.

"வேயாமாடம்."

Cilap ; Canto, v. l : 7.

Upper terraces (lit : uncovered mansions).

upon the public streets.* The existence of cities like Laṇkápura of '400,000 streets' of the Yakkhas and Maṇipuram of the Nágas, with parks and flower gardens, not to speak of other cities and towns mentioned in the ancient Epics,—the Rámáyaṇa and the Mahábhárata,—is sufficient proof that at that remote period there must have been, as the centric source of this magnificent city-life, a government sufficiently wise to promulgate noble laws and sufficiently strong to enforce them. Even as early as the Rámáyaṇa period (supposed to be about 2000 B.C.) Bhógavati the capital of the Nága kingdom in the Deccan, is described as follows:—

"Near, Bhógavati stands, the place
Where dwell the hosts of serpent race;
A broad-wayed city, walled and barred,
Which watchful legions keep and guard.
The fiercest of the serpent youth,
Each awful for his venomed tooth;
And throned in his imperial hall
Is Vásuki who rules them all,
Explore the serpent city well,
Search town and tower and citadel
And scan each field and wood that lies
Around it, with your watchful eyes "†.

---

* a. "மான்கட்காலதர் மாளிகை."

Cilap : Canto, v, l : 8.

Palatial buildings with windows like the eyes of a deer.

b. "மழைதோயுமுயர் மாடத்து
....
வளிநுழையும்வாய் பொருந்தி."

Paṭṭina : ll : 145 & 151.

Drawing close to the windows for the admission of the (south) wind, in lofty mansions touching the clouds.

† Rámáyaṇa, G. vol. iv, p. 205.

The splendour of the Nága towns can well be imagined from the descriptíon given—in the Cilappadikáram,—of the city of Kavéripúmpaṭṭínam, which is there stated to be the equal and the rival of the city of the Nágas, * the implication being that the latter was in those days the supreme example of wealth and magnificence.

The kings had large armies composed of elephants trained to war, chariots, cavalry and foot soldiers armed with bows and arrows, swords and shields, spears and javelins, axes and slings. Their cities were protected by garrisons of soldiers. The kings were upholders of *dharma* and were helped in the administration of the country by the five kinds of ministers and the eight assemblies.† The king was the last court of appeal, and justice was meted out to everybody alike, without distinction of class, caste or creed ; the names of some of these kings have been handed down to posterity as paragons of virtue and justice. When they engaged in wars against their neighbours, they took special precautions to protect not only their own priests, women and cattle, but also

---

* "நாகநீணகரொடு நாகநாடதனொடு
போகநீள்புகழ் மன்னும்புகார் நகர்."

Cilap. Canto, i. ll: 21-22.

The city of Puhár where lasting fame —a characteristic of the celestial world, and enjoyment of pleasure—a characteristic of the Nága country, find permanent abode.

† "ஐம்பெருங்குழு வெண் பேராயமும்."

Cilap. Canto. v, l ; 157.

(The king's) Great Council of five and Great Assembly of eight.

" அமைச்சர், புரோகிதர், சேனாபதியர்
தவாத்தொழிற்றூதுவர், சாரணரென்றிவர்
பார்த்திபர்க்கைம் பெருங்குழுவெனப்படுமே."

Tivákaram, 163.

[Contd.]

those of their enemies. * The fame of their heroes was perpetuated on inscribed stones raised as monuments. †

Ministers, Priestly Astrologers, Generals, Ambassadors of unerring diplomacy and Spies; these form the great council of five to the kings.

"கரணத்தியலவர் கருமவிதிகள்
கனகச்சுற்றங் கடைகாப்பாளர்
நகரமாந்தர் நளிபடைத்தலைவர்
யானைவீரரிவுளி மறவரினையரெண் பேராயமென்ப"

Tivákaram, 163.

Administrators, Accountants, Royal dependants (confidential kinsmen, priests, confectioners, physicians and soothsayers), Chiefs of the gate, Urban representatives, Captains of Infantry, Captains of the Elephant squadrons and Captains of the Cavalry regiments; these form the great assembly of eight.

* "ஆவுமானியற்பார்ப்பன மாக்களும்
பெண்டிரும் பிணியுடையீரும் பேணித்
தென்புலவாழ் நர்க்கருங்கடனிறுக்கும்
பொன்போற் புதல்வர்ப்பெறாஅதீரு
மெம்மம்புகடிவிடுது நும்மரண்சேர்மின்."

Puram. v. 9.

Black cattle, Brahmans who are as sacred as the cow, women, the sick and such of you as have not begotten those precious children who have to perform important (religious) rites to the departed spirits (of ancestors), seek ye a safe refuge. I shall discharge my arrows forthwith.

† a. "வில்லேர்வாழ்க்கைவிழுத்தொடைமறவர்
வல்லாண்பதுக்கைக் கடவுட்பேண்மார்
நடுகற்பீலி சூட்ம த்துடிப்படுத்துத்
தொப்பிக்கள்ளொடு துரூஉப்பலிகொடுக்கும்."

Akam. v, 35, ll: 6—9.

For the worship of the deified hero from among the Marava (soldiers) who live by the bow and wear garlands, a stone (with inscription) is planted (in his honour), and decorated with peacock feathers and with the sounding of the (tudi) drum, toddy brewed from rice is offered and lambs sacrificed.

b. "விழுத்தொடை மறவர் வில்லிட வீழ்ந்தோ
ரெழுத்துடை நடுகலின்னிழல்."

Akam, v, 53.

The shade of inscribed stones planted as memorials to wreath wearing heroic Marava soldiers fallen in battle.

Chivalry towards their enemies was considered a virtue, and to receive wounds on the back a disgrace.* While raising the standard of victory after the defeat of an enemy, a ball and doll were invariably attached to it in contemptuous representation of the effeminate nature of the enemy.† Contempt was further expressed by razing the enemy's capital to the ground, by ploughing the site with donkeys yoked to the plough and by sowing castor

---

* "நரம்பெழுந்துலறிய நிரம்பாமென்றோள்
முளரிமருங்கின் முதியோள் சிறுவன்
படையழிந்து மாறினனென்று பலர்கூற
மண்டமர்க்குடைந்தனனாயினுண்டவென்
முலையறுத்திடுவென் யானெனச் சினைஇக்
கொண்டவாளொடு படுபிணம் பெயராச்
செங்களந்துளவுவோள் சிதைந்துவேறாகிய
படுமகன் கிடக்கை காணூஉ
வீன்றஞான்றினும் பெரிதுவந்தனளே."

Puṛam, v, 278

The old woman of lean and lanky shoulders and of slender waist, on hearing from the lips of several persons that her son had turned his back on the field of battle, became enraged and saying that, if her son had shown cowardice while fighting, she would cut off the very breasts which gave him suck, picked up a sword, went to the gory field, turned over the corpses and on finding the body of her son cut in twain was more delighted than on the occasion of his birth.

† "செருப்புகன்றெடுத்த சேணுயர் நெடுங்கொடி
வரிப்புனைபந்தொடு பாவைதூங்க."

Tirumu : II : 67-68.

By the side of the high standard of victory raised on the battle-field, a ball and a doll were hung up.

and cotton or cereals, * in order to make the place overgrown with jungle as speedily as possible. Kings leading their armies to battle had their camps in the battlefield as luxuriously furnished as their palaces. Mutes guarded their bed rooms; † women attended at their meals; dancing girls and musicians amused them through the night hours. ‡

There is ample evidence in the works of Tamil as well as of Greek authors that trade, both by sea and land, was

---

* a. " கடுந்தேர் குழித்தஞெள்ளலாங்கண்
வெள்வாய்க் கழுதைப் புல்லினம் பூட்டிப்
பான்செய்தனையவர் நனந்தலைநல்லெயில்."

Puṛam, v. 15, ll: 1—3.

You destroyed their broad fortifications and turned the streets, over which chariots had run, with plough to which a number of white mouthed donkeys were yoked.

b. " அணங்குடை மரபினிருங்களந்தோறும்
வெள்வாய்க் கழுதைப் புல்லினம் பூட்டி
வெள்ளை வரகுங்கொள்ளும் வித்தும்
வைகலுழவ."

Puṛam, v 392, ll: 8—11.

You, at the dawn of day, ploughed even the places presided over by the gods with ploughs to which white mouthed donkeys were yoked and sowed white millet (varagu) and gram (koḷḷu).

† " உடம்பினுரைக்கு முரையாநாவிற்
படம்புகு மிலேச்சர் உழையராக."

Mullai. ll : 65 & 66.

Coated Mlechchas (foreign mutes) who use the language of signs and not the language of the tongue, serving as guards.

‡ a. " மண்ணமைமுழவின் பண்ணமை சிறியா
ழொண்ணுதல் விறலியர் பாணிதூங்க."

Porunar : ll : 109-110.

The Páṇa women with shining foreheads bearing small well-tuned lyres in their hands, dancing and singing to the measure of drums smeared with resin.

b. " விளங்கிழைமகளிர் பொலங்கலத்தேந்திய
மணங்கமழ்தேறல்."

Mad : Káñ : ll : 779-780.

Fragrant wine in golden cups held by bright bangled women.

extensively practised by the Tamils and the Nágas. Masted ships set with sails ploughed the seas. * They were loaded with articles of merchandise; pearls and muslins, sandalwood and aghil, cinnamon, pepper and other spices, salt and salted fish.† North Ceylon, and especially Jaffna, contained the most important marts and emporia for the distribution of trade to the different ports of India and Ceylon and to countries further West and further East. Merchants from Arabia, Egypt and Rome, India, China and Java frequented these marts. According to the Periplus everything made in Tamilakam and the greatest part of what was brought from Egypt came to the ports of North Ceylon, and were distributed from there. ‡ A similar reference to the imports at Kavérip-púm-paṭṭinam, the Chóḷa capital of the first and second century A.D., can be seen in the Tamil work Paṭṭina

---

* a. See supra, chap. iii, p. 100, note * (c).

b. "பொலந்தரு நாவாயோட்டி."

Puṛam. v. 126, 1 : 15.

Sailing (over seas) in ships for (commercial) prosperity.

† "முழங்கு கடறந்த விளங்குகதிர்முத்த
மரம்போழ்ந்தறுத்த கண்ணேரிலங்குவளைப்
பாதர்தந்த பல்வேறுகூல
மிருங்கழிச் செறுவிற்றீம்புளிவெள்ளுப்புப்
பரந்தோங்குவரைப்பின்வன்கைத்திமிலர்
கொழுமீன் குறைஇயதுடிக்கட்டுணியல்
விழுமியநாவாய்."

Mad. Káñ : ll : 315—123.

Well-built ships loaded with bright and lustrous pearls taken from the roaring seas, broad and shining chank bangles neatly cut with saws, different kinds of grain consigned to merchants, white salt manufactured on clayey beds, sweetened tamarind and fish cut into round pieces by strong-armed Timila fishers and salted and dried on sand dunes.

‡ See supra, chap. iii, p. 97.

pálai. * Large ships intended for this ocean trade were built in some of the northern ports; and the industry, though in a dying state, is still being continued at Kayts and Valveṭṭituṛai. On account of this extensive sea faring trade, the necessity to indicate the ports and harbours at night would naturally have arisen, and light-houses constructed out of stone and mortar or of high tree stumps, with lights placed on them, acted as guides to mariners.† The merchandise was stored in large warehouses in packages, on which the seal of the king was stamped to indicate the payment of customs duty.‡ Trade was carried into the inner country with merchan-

---

* See supra, chap. iv, p. 133, note. *

† a. " வானமூன்றிய மதலைபோல
வேணிசாத்தியவேற்ற ருஞ்சென்னி
விண்பொரநிவந்த வேயாமாடத்
திரவின் மாட்டிய விலங்குசுடர்."

Perumpáṇ : ll : 346—349.

Bright light lit at night in the dome of a tower touching the sky and presenting the appearance of a column supporting it ,the top of which it is difficult to climb even with the aid of the ladder placed against it.

b. "கங்குன் மாட்டிய கனைகதிரொண்சுடர்."

Naṛṛiṇai, v. 219.

Bright light put up at nights (as a signal for sailing vessels).

c. " இலங்குநீர்வரைப்பிற் கலங்கரை விளக்கமும்."

Cilap. Canto .vi, l: 141.

Lights (on light houses, put up) to direct the course of vessels from foreign countries.

‡ " நீரினின்று நிலத்தேறவும்
நிலத்தினின்று நீர்ப்பரப்பவும்
* * * * * *
புலிபொறித்துப்புறம்போக்கி
மதிநிறைந்த மலிபண்டம்

Paṭṭiṇa : ll ; 129-130, 135-136.

Well-estimated goods in abundance being imported and exported with the tiger mark impressed thereon, for the purpose of recovering customs duty.
[Tiger mark was affixed in Chóḷa ports.]

dise loaded in carts and távaḷams.* For fear of robbers the tradesmen, dressed in coats and sandals, went about with swords hanging from their shoulders; † they were also otherwise armed. Important junctions of trade were guarded by soldiers. ‡ In the towns and cities, separate streets were allotted to the different articles of com-

---

* a. "நோன்பகட்டுமணர் ஒழுகை."

Ciṛupáṇ : 1: 55.

The salt sellers' row of carts drawn by strong bullocks.

b. "சிறுதுளைக் கொடுநுக நெறிபட நிரைத்த
பெருங்கயிற்றொழுகை மருங்கிற் காப்பச்
சில்பத உணவின் கொள்ளைசாற்றிப்
பல்லெருத்துமணர் பதிபோகு நெடுநெறி."

Perumpáṇ; ll: 62—65.

The long highway by which the salt-sellers with many (relief) bulls enter villages crying out the price of salt, their row of carts which are drawn by several bulls tied side by side to a yoke with small holes, by means of strong rope, being guarded on both sides by able-bodied men.

† "நோன்றா
ளடிபுதையரண மெய்திப்படம் புக்குப்
பொருகணை தொலைச்சிய புண்டீர்மார்பின்
விரவுவரிக்கச்சின் வெண்கையொள்வாள்
வரையூர் பாம்பிற் பூண்டு......வம்பலர்."

Perumpáṇ : ll; 68—72.

The merchants on whose chests appear scars of wounds caused by warriors' arrows, wearing coats (on their bodies) and sandals on their (well-exercised) strong feet, while from a striped band resembling a rock-snake thrown over the shoulder and across the breast, there hung on one side glittering swords with white (carved ivory) handles.

‡ a. "உல்குடைப் பெருவழிக்கவலைகாக்கும்
வில்லுடைவைப்பின்."

Perumpáṇ. ll : 81-82.

In towns where there are garrisons of bowmen who guard the (toll-recovering) junctions of roads branching from the main highway.

b. "கல்லாமழவர் வில்லிடைவிலங்கிய
துன்னருங்கவலை."

Naṛṛiṇai, v. 387.

Unapproachable junctions where illiterate soldiers rain arrows from their bows.

merce. * Commodities generally changed hands under the system of barter, † but money, both of foreign and Indian coinage, was also a recognised medium of exchange in important centres of trade. Roman as well as Indian coins, as also other unidentified coins—which were possibly coins of local currency—have been picked up in several of the spots where the ancient marts once were.

The caste system, which was introduced by the northern Áryans, had not, during the early centuries of the Christian era, taken a strong foothold in the country. The people were in those days classified according to the nature of the land in which they lived. There were five divisions of land,—kuriñci (hill country), mullai (forest and pasture land), marutam (arable land), neytal (sea

---

* a. "வளர்ந்தலை மயங்கிய நனந்தலைமறுகு."

Paṭṭina, l: 193.

Broad streets teeming everywhere with the wealth of precious goods, which baffle any attempt at estimation.

b. See Cilap. canto, v, ll: 9—56.

† a. "உப்பைமாறிவெண்ணெற்றரீஇய
உப்புவிளை கழனிசென்றனள்."

Kuṛun. v. 269.

To exchange salt for white rice, she did seek the salt-pans.

b. "அளைவிலையுணவிற் கிளையுடனருத்தி
நெய்விலைக் கட்டிப் பசும்பொன் கொள்ளாள்
எருமை நல்லான்கருநாகு பெறூஉம்."

Perumpán. ll; .163—165.

(Herdsman's wife) feeds all her relations with the rice received in exchange of butter milk ; for ghee supplied she accepts not a piece of fine gold, but obtains a she-buffalo, a cow or a black heifer worth its value.

coast), and pálai (dry and arid land). * In kuriñci lived the Kuṛavar and Véḍar or hill tribes; in mullai, the Iḍaiyar or herdsmen; in marutam the cultivators; in neytal the Paratavar or fishers; and in pálai the Maṛavar or robbers and Véḍar or hunters. * The people were more or less tribal or were divided into clans according to the land they dwelt in. Each tribe or clan had its own chieftain under a king who ruled over them all. Priests, ascetics or holy men came from all the tribes; they were called Andanar on account of the compassion shown by them to living creatures or Párpár (seers). † These Andaṇar and Párpár were respected and honoured by the people as beings superior to all the rest.

In the matter of locomotion and conveyances, those early times were not far behind the present day. Royalty rode on elephants, horse chariots including a coach and four were not uncommon; and mechanical contrivances

---

* " குறிஞ்சிபாலை முல்லைமருதம்
நெய்தலெனத் திணைக்கெய்திய பெயரே."

Iṛa. Akap., i, 6.

The five divisions of land are named Kuṛiñci (hill tracts), Pálai (arid lands), Mullai (sylvan tracts), Marutam (agricultural lands) and Neytal (maritime tracts).

There are 14 objects peculiar to each division as originally found there, and they are termed Karupporul (originating objects). They are:- 1. Deity, 2. Chiefs, 3. Subjects, 4. Bird, 5. Beast, 6. Town or Village, 7. Water, 8. Flower, 9. Tree, 10. Food, 11. Drum, 12. Lyre, 13. Tune and 14. Occupation.

† " அந்தணரென்போர் அறவோர் மற்றெவ்வுயிர்க்குஞ்
செந்தண்மை பூண்டொழுகலால்."

Kuṛaḷ, 30.

Towards all that breathe, with seemly graciousness adorned they live;
And thus to virtue's sons the name of 'andanar' men give.

similar to the motor car and the aeroplane appear to have been in use.*

The food of the people consisted chiefly of rice, dry grains, vegetables, milk and curds, meat of goats, fowls, etc., and fish and crabs according to the surroundings and conditions in which they lived. Different kinds of sweet meats and even string hoppers were not unknown.† The Andaṇar, some of whom were family and temple priests, lived in houses the roofs of which were neatly thatched and the floors of which were daintily glossed over with the dung of the cow. They had their household gods, and used as food rice cooked in a variety of ways, vegetables

---

* a. We learn from the Rámáyaṇa, composed about six centuries before Christ, that Rávaṇa, the Yakkha king of Ceylon, abducted Síta, the wife of Rámá, from Central India and carried her off to Ceylon on an aerial car, that his uncle Kubèra had a similar machine and that Indrajit, the son of Rávaṇa, while fighting against the armies of Rámá, dropped bombs containing poisonous gas on the enemy from an aeroplane and rendered them insensible.

b. "புலவர் பாடும் புகழுடையோர் விசும்பின்
வலவனே வாவான வூர்தி
யெய்துப வென்ப"

Puṛam, v. p. 27.

(The learned) say that those who enjoy the fame of being praised by the poets are like unto a car flying through the air undirected by a driver.

c. A car driven by mechanism without the aid of animals attached to it (பூணியின்றிப் பொறியினியங்கும் எந்திரவூர்தி) and a long journey made on an aeroplane are described in Peruṅkadai, a Tamil poetical work of the 4th century A. D. Peruṅkadai, pp : 209, 426, 483.

d. A contrivance in the form of a peacock made to fly through the air with the aid of mechanism, is mentioned in the Jívaka Cintámaṇi of the 9th century A. D.

Cintámaṇi, pp. 76, 86, 95, 755.

† a. "சுவைய, வேறுபல்லுருவின் விரகு."

Porunar, l : 108.

Savoury sweetmeats of shapes many and different.

b. "இழைசூழ் வட்டம்."

Perumpāṇ, l: 377.

Thread like hoppers.

fried in ghee, curds, pickles and preserves.* These Andaṇar eschewed meat of all kinds; so clean were they that they permitted neither dogs nor fowls to enter their houses. The Áryan brahmans who emigrated into the Tamil country from North India imitated their habits

---

* "செழுங்கன்றியாத்த சிறுதாட் பந்தர்ப்
பைஞ்சேறுமெழுகிய படிவ நன்னகர்
மனையுறுகோழியொடு ஞமலிதுன்னாது
வளைவாய்க்கிள்ளை மறைவிளிபயிற்று
மறைகாப்பாளர் உறைபதிச்சேப்பிற்
பெருநல்வானத்து வடவயின் விளங்குஞ்
சிறுமீன்புரையுங் கற்பினறுநுதல்
வளைக்கைமகடூஉ வயினறிந்தட்ட
சுடர்க்கடைப்பறவைப் பெயர்ப்படுவத்தஞ்
சேதாநறுமோர் வெண்ணெயின் மாதுளத்
துருப்புறுபசுங்காய்ப் போழொடுகறிகலந்து
கஞ்சகநறு முறியளைஇப் பைந்துணர்
நெடுமரக்கொக்கினறு வடிவிதிர்த்த
தகைமாண் காடியின் வகைபடப்பெறுகுவிர்."

Perumpáṇ, ll : 297—310.

If you stop in the village of the guardians of the Vedas—who teach the bow-billed parrots the vedic tune—their dwellings which have porticoes with short posts to which sleek calves are tied, their good houses with floor besmeared with cow-dung and with images of gods installed therein, and which the domestic fowl and dog do not defile by their presence, you will at sunset be served with what the bracelet wearing (Brahman) house-wife who has a shining forehead and whose chastity is like that of (aruntadi) the small constellation in the beautiful great northern sky, has methodically prepared out of the rice which bears a bird's name (viz., Rájánnam), with chips of the green fruit of the *Kommatti-matula* shrub peppered and spiced with curry leaf and fried in the fresh butter obtained from the curdled milk of the red cow, and with the excellent pickle of the sliced tender fruit which the mango produces in beautiful bunches.

and raised themselves in the estimation of the people as men of the highest caste. The caste system introduced by them would not have obtained a stronghold, had the brahmans not lived the life of those who were considered, on account of their habits and customs, the best in the country. The Veḷḷaḷa priests (kurukkaḷs), who are the remnants of the ancient Andaṇar, are still strict vegetarians; in their habits they are similar to the brahmans to whom only the terms Andaṇar and Párpár are now applied. The fact that the vegetarians of a caste are, on account of their conservatism, considered higher than their meat-eating brethren is sufficient confirmation of the above statement. In palaces and royal households, although the general diet consisted of rice and vegetables, yet meat and drink were not despised. The guests were entertained according to their inclinations; food and drink were served in golden vessels.* The ever-hungry poets and ministrels of the Páṇa tribe, who frequented the Courts of kings, were first entertained beyond satiation with large quantities of toddy and fried meat; then they were fed with white rice, vegetable curries, milk and

---

* "நுண்பொருட

பனுவலின்வழாஅப் பல்வேறடிசில்

வாணிறவிசும்பிற் கோண்மீன் சூழ்ந்த

விளங்கதிர் ஞாயிறெள்ளுந் தோற்றத்து

விளங்கு பொற்கலத்தில் விரும்புவனபேணி ."

Ciṛupán, ll; 240—244.

Serving different preparations of rice made strictly in accordance with the fine science of cookery, in plates of gold which in splendour excel the rising sun surrounded by bright stars in the firmament.

curds.* Toddy was brewed from paddy or drawn from the palmyra tree, † and meat was either fried in oil or

---

* "மகிழ்ப்பதம் பன்னாட் கழிப்பியொருநாள்
அவிழ்ப்பதங்கொள் கென்றிரப்ப முகிழ்த்தகை
முரவை போகிய முரியாவரிசி
விரலென நிமிர்ந்த நிரலமை புழுக்கல்
பால்வறைக்கருனை காடியின் மிதப்ப
அயின்றகாலை."

Porunar, ll : 111—116.

Many days having been spent in imbibing the exhilarating toddy, one day, while at the earnest request (of the king) to partake of rice, we were having well-cleaned and unbroken rice which looked like Jasmine buds, and the grains of which had become elongated like fingers and did not adhere to one another—along with a dish of vegetables fried in milk, so heartily as to fill up to our very throats.

a. "பூம்புறநெல்லடையளை இத்தேம்பட
வெல்லையுமிரவு மிருமுறைகழிப்பி
வல்வாய்ச்சாடியின் வழைச்சறவிளைந்த
வெந்நீரரியல் விரலலை நறுபிழி."

Perumpáṇ, ll : 278—281.

High flavoured wine which the fingers stir and help to strain and in the brewing of which (pounded) germinating paddy is mixed (with a porridge of rice) and allowed to remain two days and two nights in a strong-mouthed jar, in order to help fermentation.

b. "பிணர்ப்பெண்ணைப்பிழி."

Paṭṭina, l : 89.

Toddy drawn from the palmyra palm of rough exterior.

c. "இல்லடுகள்ளின் தொப்பிபருகி."

Perumpán, l : 142.

Drinking the toddy brewed at home from paddy.

d. "துளங்குதசும்புவாக்கிய பசும் பொதித்தேறல்."

Malai, K. l : 463.

Toddy brewed from germinated paddy in pots.

roasted on spits.* The cultivators—who were much later called the Veḷḷaḷas—lived in houses thatched with cadjans or in high mansions which had cultivated gardens and spacious flower gardens all round. Their diet consisted of well-cooked rice, vegetables and fruits.† The herdsmen's houses were straw-thatched and raised on short pillars. Their doors were low and made of tats. In their yards slept

---

* a. "காழிற்சுட்ட கோழூன்கொழுங்குறை."

Porunar, l: 105.

Fine large pieces of fat meat roasted on iron spikes.

b. "கோழூன் குறைக்கொழுவல்சி."

Mad. Káñ, l: 141.

Beautiful rice cooked with fatted meat.

† "வண்டோட்டுத்தெங்கின் வாடுமடல்வேய்ந்த
மஞ்சண்முன்றின் மணநாறுபடப்பைத்
தண்டலையுழவர் தனி மனைச்சேப்பிற்
றாழ்கோட்பலவின் சூழ்சுளைப்பெரும்பழம்
....
....
குலைமுதிர்வாழைக் கூனிவெண்பழந்
திரளரைப்பெண்ணை நுங்கொடுபிறவுந்
தீம்பலிறுரா முனையிற் சேம்பின்
முளைப்புறமுதிர் கிளங்கார்குவிர்."

Perumpáṇ, ll: 353—356, 359—362,

If you stop in the grove-dwelling cultivators' houses thatched with the strong withered leaves of the cocoanut palm (woven into cadjans), the front yard of which is planted with turmeric and provided with a fragrant garden, and if you have no relish for the big pulpy jak fruit hanging in cluster, the ripe whitish banana the bunches of which hang down through their weight, the tender fruit of the round stemmed palmyra palm and many other sweet things, you will eat ripe yams with the leaves of the chémbu (Caladium nymphœi-folium.)

cattle, goats and sheep.* Their women, who wore their hair in graceful waves, churned butter and carried the butter-milk in pots for sale.† The men bartered ghee

---

* "குரம்பைச்
செற்றைவாயிற் செறிகழிக் கதவிற்
கற்றைவேய்ந்த கழித்தலைச்சாம்பி
னதளோன் றுஞ்சுங்காப்பினுதள
நெடுந்தாம்பு தொடுத்த குறுந்தறிமுன்றிற்
கொடுமுகத் துருவையொடு வெள்ளைசேக்கு
யிடுமுள்வேலி யெருப்படுவரைப்பு."

Perumpáṇ, ll: 148—154.

The hamlet where there are huts with thicket-fringed entrances, rope-made doors and cord-worked bedsteads, covered with varagu straw, and with watch and ward kept by him who sleeps on the hide of the he-goat,—where in the front yard are driven short stakes to which are attached long tethering ropes—where under the fences fastened with thorny twigs lie drooping headed sheep and white goats—and where there is an abundance of dung.

"புலிக்குரன் மத்த மொலிப்பவாங்கி
யாம்பிவான் முகிழன்ன கூம்புமுகை
யுறையமை தீந்தயிர் கலக்கி நுரைதெரிந்து
புகர்வாய்க்குழிசி பூஞ்சுமட்டிரீஇ
நாண்மோர் மாறு நன்மாமேனிச்
சிறுகுழைதுயல்வருங் காதிற்பணைத்தோட்
குறுநெறிக்கொண்ட கூந்தலாய் மகள்."

Perumpáṇ, ll: 156—162.

The cow-herdess, with beautiful dark body, earlobes dangling through the weight of the ear rings, shoulders smooth like the bamboo stem and short wavy hair, who, pulling the strings of the churner which creates a sound resembling the growl of a leopard, stirring the sweet curds the creamy surface of which is marked with air globules like the white crests of the mushroom, skimming the foamy cream and setting the (butter milk) pot which has a speckled mouth on a pad of flowers on the head. sells fresh butter milk.

for paddy and cattle, and amused themselves by playing on the flute. * Their food consisted chiefly of *tinai* rice and milk. † The Kuṛavas or hillmen lived in houses thatched with straw which had porticoes supported by large pillars. Cart wheels and ploughs were placed against the walls. ‡ Around their houses would be seen flour grinding and aval-making mill stones, sugar cane presses, paddy

---

* See supra, chap. iv, p. 149, note † b.

† "மடிவாய்க்கோவலர் குடிவயிற்சேப்பி
னிருங்கிளைஞெண்டின் சிறுபார்ப்பன்ன
பசுந்தினைமூரல் பாலொடும் பெறுகுவிர்."

Perumpāṇ : ll; 166—168.

If your stop in the village of herdsmen whose lips are contorted (by habitual whistling) you will receive with milk, cooked tinai grain, like unto a swarm of the tiny young of the crabs.

"பிடிக்கணத்தன்ன குதிருடைமுன்றிற்
களிற்றுத்தாள் புரையுந்திரிமரப்பந்தர்க்
குறுஞ்சாட்டுருளை யொடு கலப்பைசார்த்தி
நெடுஞ்சுவர் பறைந்த புகைசூழ் கொட்டிற்
பருவ வானத்துப் பாமழை கடுப்பக்
கருவை வேய்ந்த கவின்குடிச் சீறூர்."

Ibid, ll: 186—191.

In the hillmen's hamlets, there are beautiful habitations thatched with (varagu) straw, which in effect look like clouds outspread in the winter sky, each habitation being provided with a front yard where stand clay made granaries like unto a herd of she-elephants, with porticoes where there are grinding stones which resemble the feet of the elephant and with a smoke coloured shed of which the surrounding wall is wasted by stout cart wheels and ploughs leaning against it.

granaries and children's push-carts. * Their chief diet consisted of rice, boiled pulses and cooked fowl.† The

---

* a. "புதுவைவேய்ந்த கவிகுடின்முன்றி
லவலெறி யுலக்கைப்பாடு."

Perumpáṇ : ll; 225—226.

The sound of the pestle pounding aval rice in the front yard of the round roofed shed thatched with new straw.

b. "ஏணியெய்தா நீணெடுமார்பின்
முகடு துமித் தடுக்கிய பழம்பல் லுணவிற்
குமரிமூத்த கூடோங்கு நல்லிற்
றச்சச் சிறாஅர் நச்சப்புனைந்த
ஊரா நற்றேர்."

Ibid, ll : 245—249.

In (those) rich dwellings where large grain chests which are too high to be reached by long ladders, which contain several kinds of old paddy put in there through lidded openings on the top and which, being made of undecaying wood, have lasted long, do tower, and where children's push carts made by young carpenters (are found).

c. "எந்திரஞ் சிலைக்குந் துஞ்சாக்கம்பலை
விசய மடூஉம்புகை சூழாலை ."

Ibid, ll : 260-261.

Smoke roofed sugar-houses where the juice of the sugar cane (is pressed) by ever noisy cane-mills and evaporated and crystallised into sugar.

d. Kuṛun., v. 61.

† a. "குறுந்தாள்வரகின் குறளவிழ்ச்சொன்றி
....
அவரைவான் புழுக்கட்டிப் பயில்வுற்
றின்சுவை மூரற்பெறுகுவிர் ."

Ibid, ll : 193—196.

You will have sweet savoury food being an ad-mixture of the small boiled grains of the short-stalked varagu and of good boiled pulses.

b. "மடியா
வினைஞர்தந்த வெண்ணெல்வல்சி
மனைவாழளகின் வாட்டொடும் பெறுகுவிர்."

Ibid, ll : 254—256.

You will have white rice earned by industrious labourers together with fried meat of the domestic hen.

fishers lived in low huts made of jungle sticks and thatched with grass, over which pumpkin and gourd creepers were made to grow.* Their yards were strewn with nets and fish baskets. Their diet was generally rice gruel, which they drank out of cups made of palmyra leaves (piḻá).† They freely indulged in toddy which they drank with burnt fish.‡ The Véḍar or huntsmen lived in grass

---

* "வேழ நிரைத்து வெண்கோடு விரைஇத்
தாழை முடித்துத் தருப்பை வேய்ந்த
குறியிறைக் குரம்பைப் பறியுடை முன்றில்."

Perumpáṇ, ll: 263–265.

The nest-like hut with low eaves, built with jungle posts planted promiscuously (under the rafters), with bamboo laths spread over in rows and fastened with the fibre of of the screw pine and thatched with kúsa (mána) grass.

"...............வலைஞர் குடிவயிற் சேப்பி
னவையா வரிசி யங்களித் துழவை
மலர்வாய்ப் பிழாவிற் புலரவாற்றிப்
....
....
பெறுகுவிர்."

Ibid, ll: 274–283.

If you stop in the hamlet of the men who work with the fishing net, you will have toddy (brewed) from the beautiful gruelly porridge of uncleaned rice, cooled in an open vessel of palmyra leaf.

b. "இருங்காழுலக்கை யிருப்பு முகந்தேய்த்த
வவைப்பு மாணரிசியமலை வெண்சோறு
கவைத்தாளலவன் கலவையொடு."

Cirupáṇ, ll; 193—195.

White rice well cleaned with pounders set with iron rings, cooked and served with curried crabs and vegetables.

‡ a. "...............நறம்பிழி
தண்மீன் சூட்டொடு தளர்தலும் பெறுகுவிர்.'

Perumpáṇ, ll: 281-282.

When tired, you will have flavoured toddy with half dried fish roasted.

b. "பழம்படு தேறல்............
வறற்குழற் சூட் (டொடு)."

Cirupáṇ, ll: 159—163.

Well fermented toddy with roasted tank fish.

thatched houses in which were stored bows, arrows in quivers and other weapons. Their houses were fenced round with sharp and thorny sticks and were guarded by fierce dogs attached to iron chains.* Their diet consisted of red-coloured rice, beef and other kinds of meat. The flesh of the iguana was considered a delicacy.† They had a strong inclination for toddy which they often obtained in exchange for stolen cattle. ‡ The women of

---

* "சாபஞ்சாத்திய கணைதுஞ்சுவியனகர்
ஊகம்வேய்ந்த உயர் நிலைவரைப்பின்
வரைத்தேன் புரையுங் கவைக்கடைப்புதையொடு
கடுந்துடிதூங்குங் கணைக்காற் பந்தர்த்
தொடர் நாயாத்ததுன்னருங் கடிநகர்
வாழ்முள் வேலிச் சூழ்மிளைப்படப்பை."

Perumpáṇ, ll: 121—126.

(The huntsmen's stronghold has) spacious houses where bows and arows lie about, high ramparts covered with *uka* grass, porticoes on round pillars on which hang quivers with arrows—the notched ends of which resemble the honeycombs found on the hills—and the *tudi* drum, houses unapproachably guarded by chained dogs and having a courtyard or garden surrounded by a live thorny fence and a defensive jungle.

"சுவல் விளைநெல்லின் செவ்வவிழ்ச்சொன்றி
ஞமலிதந்த மனவுச் சூலுடும்பின்
வறைகால் யாத்ததுவயின் றொறும்பெறுகுவிர்."

Perumpáṇ, ll: 130—133.

You will have in every house the red coloured boiled grains of rice grown in high lands, together with a dish of the red meat 'cf the iguana big with ova like unto chank beads—which was the game of dogs.

"கேளாமன்னர் கடிபுலம்புக்கு
நாளாதந்து நறவுகொடை தொலைச்சி
பில்லடுகள்ளின் றொப்பிபருகி
மல்லன் மன்றத்து மதவிடைகெண்டி."

Perumpáṇ, ll: 140—143.

Entering the guarded realms of unfriendly kings, driving their cattle in the morning, exchanging them for toddy, drinking what of home-brewed liquor (is prepared from paddy) and goes by the name of *toppi* and slaughtering in the open a fat bull.

the Véḍar class also used as diet a grain called grass rice which they dug up from the ground, and salted meat.* Even in the present day during times of scarcity, the poor people of Delft dig up grass roots called *musirai arisi* and eat them boiled or roasted.

The people, to whatever class or tribe they belonged, were very hospitable and guests were entertained with honour and respect.† That hospitality was considered one of the chiefest of the virtues can be inferred from the fact that the poet Tiruvaḷḷuvar allotted one chapter of his Kuṛaḷ in praise of it.‡

Men and women wore their hair long, applied oil and combed it smooth. Women either wore it in plaits

---

* "இரும்பு தலையாத்ததிருந்துகணை விழுக்கோ
லுளிவாய்ச் சுரையின் மிளிரமிண்டி
யிருநிலக்கரம்பைப் படுநீறாடி
நுண்புல்லடக்கிய வெண்பல்லெயிற்றியர்
வாராதட்டவாடூன் புழுக்கல்."

Perumpāṇ, ll: 91—94 & 100.

Grass seeds without separating the sand and stones in them are cooked (and eaten) with salted meat by the white teethed Eyina women, who, with crow-bars having chisel-like lips and faultlessly round and strong handles begirt with iron bands on their heads, dig up ant-hills and in turning up clods of earth are be-smeared with the dust of the black-soiled *Karampai* (hard and sterile land) and gather grass seeds from the ant-chambers.

† a. "அல்லிலாயினும் விருந்துவரினுவக்கும்."

Naṟṟiṇai, v. 142.

She is delighted at the coming of a guest though it be at night.

b. "விருந்து விருப்புறூஉம் பெருந்தோட்குறுமகள்."

Naṟṟiṇai, v. 221.

My big shouldered lass who is delighted on entertaining guests.

‡ Kuṛaḷ, chap. ix,

(single or five) which they allowed to hang on their backs, or in tufts (koṇḍe), in the shape of a plantain bud.*

---

* a. "எண்ணெய் நீவிய சுரிவளர் நறுங்காழ்த்
தண்ணறுந் தகரங்கமழுமண்ணி
....
காழகிலம்புகைகொளீஇ.........
....
மணிநிறங்கொண்ட மாயிருங் குஞ்சியின்."

Kuṛiñci, ll: 107, 108, 110, 112.

In the regularly oiled copious curly black hair redolent, of the cooling fragrant pomade applied, and of the excellent perfume of the aromatic dark core of the aloes-wood (aghil) burnt for smoke-drying the tresses.

b, "பிடிக்கையன்ன பின்னுவீழ் சிறுபுறத்துத்
தொடிக்கை மகடூஉ."

Ciṛupáṇ, ll: 191-192.

The bracelet wearing woman whose plaited hair like unto the proboscis of a she-elephant, falls on her slender back.

c. "ஐம்பாலாய் கவினேத்தி."

Kuṛiñci, l: 139.

Praising the choice beauty of us who wear the hair in five different modes.

d. "உமர் இயல், ஐம்பாலுமட்டியர்."

Ciṛupáṇ, l: 60.

Salt selling-women who move about wearing their hair in five different modes.

e, "ஐவகைவகுத்த கூந்தலாய்."

Akam., v. 48.

You (maiden) whose hair is divided into five different modes (plaits).

f. "வாழையீன்றவை யேந்துகொழுமுகை
மெல்லியன் மகளிரோதியன்ன."

Naṛṛiṇai, v. 225.

The plump and pointed bud of the flower produced by the plantain tree resembling the hair knot of a slender maiden,

g. "பெரும்பின்னிட்ட வானரைக் கூந்தலர்
தொன்முது பெண்டிர்."

Mad. Káñ., ll: 408-409.

Ripe old ladies who had their white grey hair tied behind in a tuft.

After a bath the hair was dried with the fragrant smoke of the *aghil*,* which became an important article of commerce, other nations as far as Egypt and Rome, having adopted its use. Jasmine and other sweet-smelling flowers were daily tied round the hair. † Indeed

---

* a. " தண்ணறுந் தகரங்கமழ மண்ணி
ஈரம்புலர விரலுளர்ப் பவிழாக்
காழகிலம்புகை கொளீஇ."

Kuṟiñci, ll: 108—110.

Applying the cooling fragrant pomade and separating the hair with the fingers to remove its wetness and smoke-drying it with the excellent fumes of the aromatic dark-coloured core of the aloes-wood (aghil).

b. " அகிலுண விரித்தவம்மென் கூந்தல்."

Ciṟupāṇ, l: 263.

The beautiful soft hair spread out to be fumigated by the smoke of the aloes-wood (aghil).

† a. " வியல் விசும்புகமழ
நீர்திரண்டன்ன கோதை பிறக்கிட்டு

Mad. Kāñ., ll: 561-562.

Tying round the hair-knots wreaths of white flowers looking like bands, as it were, of frozen water, with the result that the expanse of heaven was redolent of their perfume.

b. " பல்வேறுருவின் வனப்பமை கோதையெம்
மெல்லிரு முச்சிக்கவின் பெறக்கட்டி."

Kuṟiñci, ll: 103-104.

Round our slim dark tufts of hair on the top of our heads gracefully winding several beautiful flower-wreaths of different colours.

c. " சிறுவீ முல்லைப் பெரிதுகமழலரி
தானுஞ் சூடினனிளைஞரு மலைந்தனர்."

Naṟṟiṇai, v. 361.

(The chief) wore the fragrant jasmine flowers of minute petals; and the young men (soldiers, who acccompanied him) also wore them.

d. " ஒலிபல் கூந்தனலம் பெறப் புனைந்த
முகையவிழ் கோதை."

Naṟṟiṇai, v. 260.

Wreath of open flowers artistically worn to adorn the well-grown hair.

flowers played an important part in the social and the religious life of the rich as well as of the poor. Flowers were offered to the gods and adorned their places of worship. Flower garlands were worn by men and women round their necks; flowers in vases decorated their homes; different and vari-coloured flowers represented the different actvities of the soldiers and also feelings of love and hatred. * Even the elephants,

---

* a. "விரையுறுநறு மலரேந்தி."

Tirumu, 1: 188.

Offering good and strongly fragrant flowers.

b. "உருவப் பல்பூத்தூஉய்."

Ibid, 1: 241.

Strewing many red-coloured flowers,

c. "பெருந்தண்கணவீர நறுந்தண்மாலை
துணையறவறுத்துத் தூங்க நாற்றி."

Ibid, ll: 236–237.

Cutting big fresh oleander garlands and others of good fresh flowers, into equal lengths, and hanging them out to swing and to present an incomparable sight.

d. "இல்வளர் முல்லை மல்லிகை மயிலை
தாழிக்குவளை சூழ் செங்கழு நீர்
பயில் பூங்கோதைப் பிணையவிற்பொலிந்து."

Cilap. Canto, v, ll: 191—193.

Beamy with the garlands made of the flowers of home-grown mullai (Jasminum tricho-tomum), Arabian Jasmine (Jasminum Sambac) and Iruvádchi Jasmine, the water lily grown in pots and the sweet-smelling red water-lily (nymphaea ororata), of which beetles are fond.

e. The following flowers were worn by soldiers :—

1. Those who successfully removed the enemy's cattle wore the wreaths of the vedchi flower (வெட்சி—ixora coccinea).
2. Those who recovered the cattle removed by the enemy wore karandai (கரந்தை—ocimum basilicum).
3. Those who prosecuted war wore vañci (வஞ்சி).
4. The defenders wore káñci (காஞ்சி—holoptelea integrifolia).
5. The defenders of a fort wore nocci (நொச்சி—vitex trifolia).
6. Those who seized the enemy's fort wore uḷiñai (உழிஞை —Illecebrum lanatum.)
7. The warriors wore tumbai (தும்பை—phlomus Indica).
8. The conquerors wore vágai (வாகை—albizzia lebbele).

[Contd.]

chariots and horses which went to war were decorated with flowers and garlands.

Sandal, black paste and *kunkumam* were the substances with which the forehead mark was made, and these continue to be so used to the present day. The women of 1800 years ago were no whit behind those of their sex of the present day both in the art of adorning their person as well as in the use of scents and cosmetics. * Betel chewing was a common habit even in

---

f. The following flowers represent the different feelings of love :—

a. Union—vénkai (kino, pterocarpus bilobus), kuriñci (calophyllum inophyllum) and kántaḷ (gloriosa superba).

b. Separation—kurá (webera corymbosa), mará (eugenia racemosa).

c. Waiting—kullai (tulasi, ocymum sanctum), mullai (Jasminum trichotomum), tónṛi (gloriosa superba) and piḍavam.

d. Discord,—lotus, water lily (nymphœa rubra) and kuvaḷai (pontedaria).

e. Commiseration—neytal (nymphœa alba), táḻai (pandana oderatissima), muṇḍakam (lotus) and aḍampam.

* a. "மகளிர்
மணங்கமழ் நாற்றந் தெருவுடன் கமழ."

Mad. Káñ, ll : 446-447.

The perfume of the scents used by the women diffusing as far as the street.

b. "நன்னெடுங் கூந்தனறுவிரைகுடைய
நரந்தமரைப்ப நறுஞ்சாந்து மறுக
மென்னூற்கலிங்கங் கமழ் புகைமடுப்ப."

Mad. Káñ, ll ; 552—554.

To make the perfume of the fragrant ointment applied to work into the beautiful long tresses, to pulverize and prepare musk and sandalwood (for cosmetics) and to fumigate clothes of fine thread with fragrant smoke.

those early days. Arecanut in several forms, chunam and spices were added as condiments.*

Men and women wore garments only from below the waist ; the upper part of the body was bare, except on festive occasions when they covered themselves with transparent silks and muslins. Cloth woven from cotton yarn, dyed and undyed, in different patterns, as well as silk and wool raiments, † were in use. Cotton cloths

---

* "பலர்தொகு பிடித்ததாதுகு சுண்ணத்தர்
தகைசெய் தீஞ்சேற்றின்னீர்ப் பசுங்காய்
நீடுகொடியிலையினர் கோடுசுடுநூற்றினர்."

Mad. Káñ , ll : 399—401.

The sellers of aromatic powder, so fine as to be easily wafted by the wind like the filaments of flowers, and the pounding of which is done by a band of experienced hands, those who sell both the sweet, moist, tender green arecanut prepared with the inspissated esence of ebony—a preparation which helps to beautify the body—and the leaves of the long and mature betel-creeper, and the sellers of lime obtained by calcining shells.

† a. "நேர்கரை
நுண்ணூற் கலிங்கமுடீஇ."

Puram., v. 392, ll : 14 & 15.

Clad in cloth woven of fine thread and with border marked straight.

b. "பட்டினும் மயிரினும் பருத்திநூலினும்
கட்டுநுண்வினைக் காருகர்."

Cilap. Canto, v, ll : 16 & 17.

Silk weavers who do exquisitely fine work (with the needle) in the manufacture of cloths out of silk thread, the hair of rats and cotton yarn.

with silk borders, and muslins interwoven with pearls were not unknown.* The women painted the upper part of their bodies with sandalwood paste or *kunkumam*; they then drew upon their persons devices of leaves an l flowers called *toyil* (தொயில்), or they strewed the pollen of the véṅgai flower (pterocarpus bilobus) on the paste before it became dry.† Both sexes adorned their persons with

---

* See Supra, chap. iv, p. 134, note *f & p. 135.

† a, "திருந்திழைத் தொய்யில் வனமுலை."

Naṟṟiṇai, v. 225, ll: 6-7.

The beautiful toyyil-painted (= streaked with perfumed unguents) breasts of her who wears faultless jewels.

b. "திண்காழ்
நறுங்குறடுரிஞ்சிய பூங் கேழ்த்தேய்வை
தேங்கமழ் மருதினர் கடுப்பக் கோங்கின்
குவிமுகிழிளமுலைக் கொட்டி விரிமலர்
வேங்கைநுண்டாதப்பி."

Tirumu., ll: 32—36.

To the young breasts like unto the globular flower-bud of the silk cotton tree (Bombax gossypinum) applying the fine coloured sandalwood paste, which is prepared by the triturition of a block of its fragrant hard core, with the result that the application appeared as it were one done with the sweet smelling flowers of the maruta tree (Terminalia alata) and strewing over this (while yet moist) the filaments of the flower of the kino tree (Pterocarpus bilobus).

c. "கரும்பும் வல்லியும் பெருந்தோளெழுதி."

Cilap. Canto ii, l: 29.

Drawing designs of sugar canes and cre pers on the broad shoulders (with sandal-unguent).

ornaments made of gold and silver, of beads, corals and chanks and of pearls and precious stones.* Large quantities of beads made of glass, coral, cornelian and agate, with holes pierced for stringing, and broken pieces of glass and chank bangles found at Kantaroḍai and other places,† go to prove the great popularity of these trinkets among the common people. Necklaces made of gold and rings set with stones were worn by the

---

* a. "பூங்குழை ஊசற்பொறைசால்காது."

Porunar. 1: 30.

Ear-lobes swinging with the weight of the beautiful ear-rings.

b. "நூலின் வலவா நுணங்கரின் மாலை
வாலொளிமுத்தமொடு பாடினிபணிய."

Ibid, ll: 161-162.

A gold necklet of delicate workmanship the parts of which are not strung on a thread but linked together—for the dame with the lyre, to be worn with lustrous pearls.

c. "தமனியம்வளை இயதாவில் விளங்கிழை."

Mad. Kāñ. 1; 704.

Glittering Jewels of unalloyed gold set with precious stones.

d. "முன்கை வலம்புரிவளையொடு."

Neḍ. Vāḍ., 1: 142.

With bangles made of right whorled chanks on the forearm.

e. "கோடீரிலங்குவளை."

Kuṛun., vv: 11 & 31.

Bright bracelets made by cutting chanks.

f. "செவ்விரற்கொளீஇய செங்கேழ்விளக்கம்."

Neḍ, Vāḍ., 1: 144.

Red coloured (coral) rings worn on fair fingers.

† Nāgadīpa, J. C. B. R. A. S., vol. xxvi.

opulent;* the breasts of princesses were profusely covered with jewellery from the throat to the waist. The earlobes were weighted with such heavy jewellery that hanging and elongated lobes were greatly esteemed as assets of beauty.†

The Tamil names *kulai* and *todu,* now applied for ear ornaments made of gold or even of precious stones, suggest the very ancient and prehistoric times when leaves and flowers were worn. The habit of small girls wearing a leaf shaped pendant made of silver or gold and of women wearing an ornament called *mekalai* round their waists,‡ is reminiscent of the times when they wore only leaves to cover their nakedness. Some of the kings of Ceylon beginning with Sanga Tissa i, were of such mixed Nága and Tamil origin that they were called

---

* "பொலஞ்செயப்பொலிந்த நலம்பெறு விளக்கம்."

Mad. Káñ. 1: 719.

Beautiful rings (set with stones) which are full of glitter in being made of gold.

† "நெடுநீர்வார் குழைகளைந்தெனக்குறுங்கண்
வாயுறை யழுத்திய வறிதுவீழ் காது."

Ned. Vád., ll: 139-140.

Earlobes somewhat elongated by the weight of the ear studs shedding abundant lustre, but which fit well in the small ear holes.

‡ a. "இன்னகைப்பருமம்."

Tirumu., ll: 145-146.

Girdle (mékalai) of delectable brightness.

b. "வண்டிருப்பன்ன பல்காழ்."

Porunar, l: 39.

Girdle composed of several strings of precious stones like unto a swarm of (diverse coloured) beetles.

Lambakaṇṇas, on account of the heavy jewellery they wore in their ears. The statue of a king, which is carved on a rock at Weligama and called by the people Kushṭa Rája, must be that of one of these Lambakaṇṇas, as would be seen from the elongated earlobes and the heavy ear ornaments that are made to rest on his shoulders. Just as the Tamils had the head of a fish (மகரக்குழை —Makarakkuḻai) represented in their jewellery, the Nágas had the hood of a cobra represented in theirs. Among the Nágas, the symbol of the cobra was in common use as a favourite ornament. It formed the drop of an earring, the clasp of a necklace and bracelet, the decoration of a lady's belt, the support of a lamp, the royal crest, and the emblem emblazoned on the royal standard and on the soldier's scabbard. An ear ornament in the form of the hood of a cobra can be seen on the statue of Vaṭṭagámini in the rock temple at Dambulla. A similar ornament, but smaller in size called 'nágapaḍam' is still worn by Tamil women along the Western coast. A head dress resembling the hood of the cobra is even now worn by the novitiates for the *Upasampada* ceremony, a fact which proves that the earliest Buddhist monks were recruited from among the Nágas.

Women enjoyed great freedom and liberty. Young men and women met each other freely in pleasure gardens, in groves and in the fields where the girls were engaged in guarding the crop. They fell in love and later married with the consent of the parents.* This form of marriage, known among the Áryans as *Gandharva*

---

* See Tolkáppiyam, Poruḷatikáram; Iṛayanár Akapporuḷ; Akapporuḷ Viḷakkam and other Tamil works on Akapporuḷ.

Vaṭṭagámini
from the Rock Temple at Dambulla
(Insert Head enlarged)

To face page 170.] [Photo by John & Co., Kandy.

was called *kalavu*, and appears to have been widely adopted among the Tamils. The secret meetings of the lovers, their feelings when they became separated from each other and even the degrading and contumelious artifices adopted by disappointed lovers are vividly portrayed in most of the ancient Tamil classics. The theme of love, (*akapporul*), formed a part of the earliest Tamil grammars. Arjuna, the Páṇḍava hero, met the Nága princess, Chitrángadai, walking about in her pleasure-garden unattended;—a circumstance which received special mention in the hands of the Áryan author of the Mahábhárata. Women received as much encouragement as men in the matter of education. Some of the best poems—mostly heroic—found scattered among the several anthologies of the third Saṅgam are by Tamil poetesses. The women of the Páṇa tribe, known as *oraliyar*, used to dance in the presence of, and compose extempore verses in praise of, their munificent patrons. Ouvaiyár, the authoress of the collection of moral aphorisms, which still forms one of the subjects of instruction in every Tamil school, was a woman of the Páṇa tribe. Out of the 200 names of poets mentioned as those who composed the verses collected in Kuṛuntogai, thirty at least appear to be those of women. Peruṇkópeṇḍu was the wife of a reigning Páṇḍya, Ádi mantaiyár was a Chóḷa princess, Nannágaiyár, Kuṛamagaḷ Iḷa veyini, Míncṛi Túṇḍalár and Kíran Eyiṭṭiyanár appear to be names of women belonging to the Nága, Kuṛava, Paratava and Véḍa tribes respectively,

The kings, princes and chiefs were patrons of literature and music; poets and minstrels flocked to their Courts for the purpose of singing their praises and receiving presents, which included elephants and chariots.* Most of the Tamil works now extant, of the period of the third Saṅgam, are poems composed in praise of royal and wealthy patrons. Ciṛupáṇáṛṛupaḍai one of the ten Idylls, is a work of that nature composed in praise of one Nalliyakóḍan, a Nága king of North Ceylon. In the anthological work, Puranánúru, there are several poems sung in praise of one Kumaṇan a munificent Chief of Kudiraimalai.† Tamil poetry was of three kinds, Iyal, Isai and Náḍagam (Classical, lyric and dramatic). Lyrical and dramatic poetry were sung to music. The tunes were called paṇ (பண்) and were known by different names. It is said that there were

---

* a. "துடியடியன்ன தூங்கு நடைக்குழவியொடு
பிடிபுணர்வேழம் பெட்டவை கொள்கெனத்
தன்னவை யளவையிற்றரத்தர."

Porunar, ll: 125—127.

Saying "you had better have male and female elephants and baby elephants of shambling gait and having legs like unto a tuḍi drum;" and presenting one after another whatever he had a mind to give such as chariots, raiment, jewellery, etc., according to his estimate of my wants.

b. "மால்கடல்
வளைகண்டன்ன வாலுளைப் புரவி
...............நால்குடன் பூட்டி
யரித்தேர்நல்கி."

Perumpáṇ ll: 487—490.

Presenting a golden chariot to which are attached four (black) horses with white manes, looking like chanks in a dark blue ocean.

c. "ஆடுநடைப் புரவியுங் களிறுந்தேரும்
வாடாயாணர் நாடுமூரும்
பாடுநர்க்கருகா வாஅயண்டிரன்."

Puṛam., v. 240.

Aay Anḍiran who gave without stinting horses trained to war, elephants and chariots with profitable lands and villages to poets.

† Puṛam., vv: 158—165.

103 different paṇs or tunes of which 61 were in vogue during the time of Saint Sambhandar.* His dévárams sung to 23 different paṇs, are still extant. With the introduction into Tamil land of North Indian or Áryan tunes, during the time of the later Pallavas and the Chóḻas, the practice of the Tamil paṇs began to disappear; they would have been altogether forgotten but for the 'Dévárams.' But the times have so changed that even dévárams, which were originally composed to the tune of Tamil paṇs, are now sung to north Indian or hybrid tunes. It is the duty of some Tamil musician to conserve the few remaining pure Tamil paṇs by setting them to music and by publishing their notes for the edification of future generations and for the glorification of ancient Tamil music. Music was produced from stringed instruments akin to the lyre and the violin (called 'Yáḻ') of which there were four varieties;† they were played to the accompaniment of different sized drums.‡ For some reason, now unknown, the 'Yáḻ' has disappeared. Descriptions of these instruments can

---

* "ஏழே ஏழே நாலேமூன்று இயலிசையிசையியல்பாய்."

Dévâram, Sambhandar's, Tirukaḷumalam, v. 11.

To the 61 tunes (paṇs) of the lyrical Tamil.

† a. The four kinds of stringed instruments were :—

1. Périyáḻ (பேரியாழ்) of 21 strings
2. Makara Yáḻ (மகரயாழ்) of 17 strings
3. Sakóḍa Yáḻ (சகோடயாழ்) of 16 strings
4. Seṅkóṭṭi Yáḻ (செங்கோட்டியாழ்) of 7 strings.

Flutes or pipes were made of bamboo, sandalwood, brass, redwood and ebony.

‡ b. Drums were of 30 different varieties and size and were known by different names.

For a fuller description of these musical instruments, See Cilap. Canto, iii, pp. 81—87.

be found in some of the ancient Tamil Classics. * The Nágasuram or pipe now used by the Tamil musicians appears from its name to have been borrowed from the Nágas. A similar instrument, but in a less developed state is also used by the Sinhalese musicians. In the 9th century A.D., a part of Jaffna was colonised by the musical Páṇa tribe, but with the disappearance of their musical instrument the 'Yáḷ,' their music too has disappeared. The only indigenous musical instrument now available in Jaffna is the 'uḍukku,' which can be seen in the hands of mendicant paṇḍárams; but this too is fast vanishing through non-usage. Dancing was indulged in by the people for their own enjoyment; † there were professional dancers among the people of the Páṇa tribe who performed for the amusement of kings, chiefs and wealthy patrons. † Dancing was also indulged in by certain classes of people in praise and in propitiation of the deities. † The degree of perfection to which music and

---

* Tirumuru., ll 140—142; Porunar, ll : 5-20, 63; Ciṛupáṇ, ll : 34—36; Cilap; Canto, iii, Arangéṛṛu Kádai.

† a. " நுண்வினை
யிழையணி அல்குல் விழவாடு மகளிர்
முழங்குதிரையின் சீர்தூங்கு
மழுங்கன்மூதூர்

Naṛṛinai, v. 138.

The ancient village in which the noise made by dancing women wearing gold girdles of delicate workmanship, is like unto the sound of dashing billows.

b. " முழவிமுழு மகலாங் கண்
விழவுநின்ற வியன் மறுகிற்
துணங்கை யந்தழூஉவின்."

Mad. Káñ., ll : 327—529.

The extensive village which has broad streets resonant with the music of drums through constant performance of festivals, in which are performed dances known by the names of Tuṇaṅkai and Kuravai. [Contd.]

dancing had attained during the early centuries of the Christian era can easily be inferred from a careful perusal of the Tamil Epic, Cilappadikáram, and of its commentary.

How far the people of Ceylon had, in the early centuries of the Christian era, advanced in the allied sciences of Astronomy and Astrology can be gauged from the fact that the sciences have made no progress since. This knowledge was confined to a class of people called astrologers and the development of the science has long been stationary for want of munificent patrons. The astrologers in those days cast their own calendars marking the auspicious times for the benefit of their patrons who consulted them as occasion demanded; no work of any kind was commenced or a journey started except at an auspicious moment. These calendars are now computed by a few, printed and sold; the village astrologer has therefore lost his custom. But horoscopists still flourish and the number of persons who pin their faith on horoscopes increases with the prosperity of the country. There were in use appliances and devices to measure time. A *naligai vattil*, a cup which sank in water exactly in a naḻigai (24 minutes) was in common use among the

c. " என்றியாங்
கோத்தகுரவை யுளேத்திய தெய்வநம்
மாத்தலைப்பட்டதுயர் தீர்க்க."

Cilap. Canto, xvii, p. 401.

Let the god, whom we worshipped by thus dancing the Kuravai dance, remove all ills from our cattle.

(For a description of dancing in ancient times and for the names of the many dances, see Cilap. pp. 63—81.)

medical practitioners.* The ordinary people computed time by the length of the shadows. In cities and palaces men were engaged to proclaim the hours of day and night.†

What was the earliest language spoken by the people of Ceylon? A language is invariably known from the name of the country in which it is spoken or from the name of the people who inhabit it, and thus a knowledge of the country is necessarily indispensable to form a conception of its language. However, there are exceptions to this rule, as there are certain instances where a country and its people are primarily known by the language, and there are some languages which have no connection at all with the names of the people who speak

---

* a. "நின்குறுநீர்க்கன்னலினைத் தென்றிசைப்ப."

Mullai., l. 58.

Telling the hour by means of horological cups kept in cauldrons of water.

b. "காலமறிவுற்றுணர்தல் கன்னலளவல்லால்
மாலைபகலுற்றதென வோர்வரிது மாதோ."

Kamban, Kārkālapaḍalam, v. 63.

(The day was so dark that) it was impossible to distinguish morning from evening, except with the aid of horological cups (used for measuring time.)

† a. "குறுநீர்க்கன்னலெண்ணுநர்."

Akam. v. 43.

Those who count hours by horological cups.

b. "கோமகன்கோயிற்குறு நீர்க்கன்னலின்
யாமங்கொள்பவர்."

Maṇi, Canto, vii. ll: 64—65.

Those who proclaim the hours in the palace of the king, by measuring time with cups in water.

c. "பொழுதளந்தறியும் பொய்யாமாக்கள்."

Mullai., l. 55.

Those who correctly compute the time by the sun.

them or of their countries. The name Laṇká, applied to Ceylon, had not the remotest connection with its people or with the language spoken by them. The name Íl̤am which was also given to Ceylon, has some affinity with its earlier language El̤u. The Island must have been called Íl̤am because El̤u was spoken there; or perhaps the language was called El̤u because it was spoken in Íl̤am. The name Íl̤am was undoubtedly given to Ceylon by the Tamils, her neighbours. Was it because El̤u was spoken there or was it because Ceylon was famous for the production of gold and toddy, which in Tamil are synonyms for Íl̤am? El̤u was the language of the common people and therefore the name 'Íl̤am' must have been given to Ceylon by the Indians As Ceylon afterwards became famous for its gold and its toddy, the word 'Íl̤am' later became a Tamil word (an ஆகு பெயர்) to designate gold or toddy metonymically Íl̤am has no root in the Tamil language which can mean either gold or toddy. El̤u was only a spoken dialect and had not reached a state of development sufficient to produce any literature in that language. Tamil was, therefore, the Court language. The poets, kings and pandits cultivated it for literary purposes. Tamil continued to be the Court language of Ceylon kings for several centuries. Even after the adoption of Siṅhalese in Court, Tamil was not despised as Tamil poets and pandits often flocked to the court of a learned Siṅhalese king. It appears that Sarajóti Málai, a Tamil work on astrology received the imprimatur of a Siṅhalese king even so late as the time of Paṇḍita Parákrama Báhu IV. The Nága kings, as well as the Nága people appear to have excelled in Tamil literature. One Muḍi Nágaráyar of Muriñciyúr (perhaps a place engulfed by the sea) was a poet of the Second Tamil Saṅgam established at Kaváḍapuram and lived during the time of the Mahábhárata War. Several Nága poets graced the third Saṅgam, and the excellent Tamil verses composed by them are still extant, and may be found scattered among the anthologies of the poems of the period.* One Púdaṉ Dévaṉ of Íḻam enjoys the honour of having some of his compositions included in the anthologies.† Ciṟupáṇáṟṟupaḍai was composed by a poet called Nattattanár in praise of the Nága king, Nalliyakóḍaṉ of Mántai (Mátoṭa), who was also known as Óymáṉ Nalliyakóḍaṉ.‡

Eḻu, in its imperfect state, could not stand the onslaught of Tamil, Pali and Sanskrit. The first of these languages was introduced into Ceylon at various times by invaders and immigrants. The latter two came in through the introduction of Buddhism. Vijaya and his followers could not have introduced into the Island a new language and imposed it upon the people. They and their descendants would have adopted the language previously spoken in the Island. There would have been an amalgamation of the original language with Tamil and the language of the few Kaliṅga immigrants who arrived in the Island, by the time Buddhism was introduced.

---

* The following are some of the Nága poets, whose names are mentioned as the authors of several poems included in the anthological collections:—

1. Attaṉ veṉ Náganár. 2. Veṅ Náganár, the goldsmith, 3. Pútaṉ Iḻa Náganár, and 4. Marudaṉ Iḻa Náganár, all of Madura, 5. Naṉ Náganár of Vrichiyúr, 6. Náganár of Veḷḷaikuḍi, 7. Tínmati Nágaṉ and 8. Poṉ Nágaṉ.

† Kuṟun: v. 348; Akam vv, 88 and 337.

‡ a Ōymáṉ (ஓய்மான்) is the shortened form of Ōviyar maṉ (ஓவியர்மன்), the king of the Ōviyar.

An Upasampada Candidate

To face page 179.] [Photo by John & Co., Kandy.

Upon the introduction of copious Pali and Sanskrit works, a new language came into existence, with a ground work of Eḷu and Tamil and a superstructure of Pali and Sanskrit. Pali and Sanskrit were dead languages; they, therefore, could not furnish the foundation of a living language, but were only instrumental in furnishing a voluminous vocabulary to the new language. In a similar manner were formed Malayalam and Telugu; from their copious vocabulary of Sanskritic words it is now almost impossible to trace their origin to Dravidian dialects. While the process of forming the Siṅhalese nation was going on by the continual mixture of the Yakkhas, the Nágas, the Tamils and the Kaliṅgas, the Siṅhalese language too was growing and expanding. That the earliest Siṅhalese and the earliest converts to Buddhism were the Nágas can be seen from the dress worn even at the present day by a candidate for the Upasampada ceremony. Although several centuries have passed since the introduction of Buddhism to Ceylon, yet the dress worn by the ancient Nágas is still continued to be worn at the ordination ceremony, thus proving, as if from within, the nationality of the persons who first became Buddhist Monks. The Siṅhalese language, which was in an infantile stage in the 3rd century B.C., as will be seen from the undeveloped phraseology used in the Cave inscriptions of that period, took about 1500 years to reach that degree of development which is necessary for the composition of literary works in that language, for the first work was composed in the reign of Lílávati. Thus it will be seen that the mixed population from Point-Pedro to Dondra Head known by the name of Siṅhalam, with the exception of those living in the maritime districts must have, during the early centuries of the Christian Era, spoken one language. This proposition is further supported by most of the place names in Jaffna which have an Eḷu or semi-Siṅhalese origin. * They became divided only when the Vannias came in and intervened between them. From that time the people in the North became estranged from their brethren in the Centre and the South and progressed altogether on Tamil lines, whereas the Siṅhalese grew into a new nation absorbing into themselves even the millions of pure Tamils who remained in Central and Southern Ceylon after the Chóḷa power had declined,—a process which can be witnessed even today in the Western coast. The difference must have become accentuated after the downfall of Buddhism in Southern India, and after a large number of new Tamil colonists began to settle down in North Ceylon, for we find that even from the 10th to the 15th century A.D. the Siṅhalese element was so strong in the North that there were constant troubles between the Siṅhalese and the Tamils in Jaffna.† It was about that period that the Tamils in the North began to grow so powerful as to challenge the right of the Siṅhalese for dominion over the whole Island.

It is supposed that there are no writings extant in India earlier than the Asoka inscriptions and none in Ceylon earlier than the Cave inscriptions and that the people of India and Ceylon were not acquainted with writing of any nature, because they did not leave any rock inscriptions behind. The argument is also often advanced that the Indians were ignorant of painting and

* Place Names.

† Y. V. M. pp: 13, 19, 25, & 33.

sculpture before the Greek invasions, because examples of such painting or sculpture are not now extant. Negative evidence such as the absence of rock inscriptions, prove little or nothing.

Tolkáppiyam, one of the earliest Tamil grammars which is considered by learned authorities to be anterior to Páṇini's Sanskrit grammar, contains a chapter on letters and their forms. The sound form (olivaḍivu) and the written form (varivaḍivu) are treated in that chapter.* This grammar is said to have been composed about the end of the first Saṅgam or at the beginning of the second, and was the authority specially followed by the poets of the second and the third Saṅgams. The first Saṅgam was at Southern Madurai, the earliest capital of the Páṇḍyas, which was destroyed by the sea about 2400 years before Christ. † There is not the slightest doubt that writing was in vogue in India and Ceylon for centuries before the advent of Vijaya to Ceylon, but as that writing was committed to palm-leaves they were not preserved for any length of time. That is how the Tamil works of the first and second Saṅgams have been altogether lost.‡ This is not in the least surprising when

* Tolkáppiyam. Eḻuttu adikáram.

† See supra, chap: i, p: 42.

‡ "ஏரணமுருவம் யோகமிசைகணக்கிரதஞ்சாலந்
தாரணமறமே சந்தந் தம்பநீர் நிலமுலோக
மாரணம் பொருளென்றின்ன மானநூல்யாவும்வாரி
வாரணங்கொண்டதந்தோவழி வழிப்பெயருமாள." பழங்கவி

Treatises on logic, painting and sculpture, yóga (philosophy), music, mathematics, alchemy, magic, architecture, virtue, poetry, overcoming the nature of the elements, water, soils, metals, (causing of) death, (acquiring of) wealth and many other subjects have been, alas! swept away and swallowed up by the sea, so completely that even their very traditional names have disappeared.

we consider that some of the works that were extant in the 13th and 14th centuries are not now forthcoming. The Nágas who were living in Ceylon must also have committed their language to writing, but the absence of any of their ancient inscriptions does not at all prove that writing was unknown to them. Their language, as well as that of their neighbours the Yakkhas, was Eḻu, a Dravidian dialect intermixed with Tamil introduced by the Tamilian settlers from South India. The earliest characters known to us as used by them are those found in the Tóṇigala and other similar inscriptions. Mr. Parker discovered similar characters on pottery unearthed from the ruins of Tissamaharama and on bricks used in the building of the Mahárama and Yattala dágobas which were erected by Mahá Nága about 240 B.C. Some of them were written with the finger, a few traced with a pointed stick and several others were deeply and beautifully stamped in intaglio with excellent dies apparently made of hard wood. "Writing" says Mr. Parker "must have been long practised before the idea of cutting dies with which to print the letters was originated.* These characters written by low caste potters and brick makers are clear indications of the spread of education in those early days; for, knowing as we now do how few of the castes are even able to read and write now-a-days, those inscribed bricks and pottery speak volumes of the knowledge attained by the people.† How far the ancient Nágas had advanced in the art of writing may be surmised from the fact that the Áryans borrowed their characters from the Nágas and called them Déva Nágari,

* J. C. B. R. A. S. vol: viii, No. 27, p. 169.

† Ibid.

and their advancement in civilization is shown by the word 'nágaríka' (state of the Nágas) used by the Áryans as well as the Tamils for the word 'Civilization.'

The art of painting and sculpture was not foreign to the Nágas. The Tamil word *Oviyam* used for a figure painted or sculptured, appears to have been derived from the word *Oviyar*, the tribe of Nágas who were living in North Ceylon. Similarly the word *kalingam* came to be used in Tamil for cloth as the Kalingas were the first to introduce a certain quality of cloth into the Tamil country. The work of the Óviyar would naturally have been called *Oviyam*. The following narrative fully proves how advanced in painting and sculpture the Óviyar artisans living at Mántai (Mátoṭa) in the 2nd century A.D. were. Kumaṇan was a Tamil chieftain ruling at the town of Kudiraimalai (Acá Nagaram). He was a great patron of learning, as many other Tamil chieftains were in South India during the period, and poets and minstrels flocked to his court.* He (Kumaṇan) was deposed by his ambitious brother, and to save his life on which a prize was placed by the usurper, he was hiding in a jungle. A poet named Peruntalai Cátanár met Kumaṇan in his retreat and begged for aid describing his state of extreme poverty. Kumaṇan pleaded that he was himself not above want when the poet replied in verse "are you so extremely poor as not to be able to release me from the clutches of poverty? Rivers may run dry but do they not possess sufficient moisture as to relieve thirst!"†

* Puṛám, vv: 158—165.

† "ஆறுபெருக்கற்றருந்திடர் தான் பட்டாலும்
ஊறலமையாதோ வுலகாற்றத்—தேறின்
வறியையே யானாலும் வன் கலியை மாற்றச்
சிறியையோ சீர்க்கு மனாசெப்பு."

Kumaṇan was, however, equal to the occasion and handed over his sword, (like Sri Saṅga Bó of later times), to the needy poet and requested him to cut off his head and earn the reward set on it by his brother. The poet refused to do such a dastardly act, but went to a sculptor of Mántai (Mátoṭa), who made a head resembling that of Kumaṇan which, on its production, so deceived the usurper that he began to lament the fate of his elder brother. The poet, finding that the usurper had relented, pretended to bring Kumaṇan back to life and reconciled the brothers.* This shows us that in those early days there lived artists at Mátoṭa who could carve and paint a head in so lifelike a manner as to deceive even the eyes of a brother. It was these royal artisans of Mántai who later developed into the great Siṅhalese artists and sculptors, whose handiwork can still be seen at Sigiriya, Galvihára, Dambulla, Degaldoruwa and Laṅkátillaka. Unlike the present-day artists whose decorative art has deteriorated and declined by the contamination of Western ideas—as will be seen from a study of the mural paintings at the Weligama and Dikwella viháras in the Southern Province,—the art of the early artisans improved by the introduction of the Dravidian, North Indian and Roman art. The Siṅhalese art was therefore of a composite nature without, however, losing its own individual characteristic. Dr. Ánanda K. Coomaraswamy, who made a special study of Ceylon art, therefore said: "Siṅhalese decorative art is thus in a sense both freer and wider than that of Northern India in later times, gentler, less grotesque and more akin to Medieval European than Dravidian art of Southern

---

* See supra, chap: i, p. 21, note *; p. 25, note ‡

India".* The walls of temples and palaces were decorated with paintings delineating stories from the Epics or from the Jataka Tales.†

Hinduism was the religion of the people before Buddhism was introduced during the time of Dévánampiya Tissa, and Siva was the chief deity as will be seen from the temples at Munnésvaram, Rámésvaram, Tiru-Kétísvaram, Kónésvaram and Nakulésvaram —temples which came into existence centuries before the advent of Vijaya. According to the Rámáyaṇa, Ráma, during his invasion of Laṅká worshipped at the temple at Munnésvaram. The Rámáyaṇa, in spite of its attempt to describe the ancient Yakkhas as devils and demons, does not fail to paint in glorious colours the religious devotion of Rávaṇa, their king. He is said to have been a devotee of Siva and to have sung his praises to the accompaniment of music in which he was an accomplished artist. It is also said that he worshipped at Kónésvaram and performed the last rites of obsequy to his mother at the hot springs of Kanniya. From its name of Munnésvaram, this temple appears to have been the first of its kind and the other Ísvarams were of a later origin. The earliest one in Jaffna was Nakulésvaram close to the sacred waters of Nákulam, visited by Arjuna. When Vijaya landed in Ceylon in the fifth century B.C., there were

---

* Med : Siṅh : Art. p: 254.

a. "வேறுபட்ட வினை ஒவத்துவெண் கோயில்."

Paṭṭiña, ll. 49-50.

White walled temples with a variety of paintings on them.

b. "புனைசுவர்ப்பாவையன்ன."

Naṟṟinai, V. 252, ll: 6 & 7.

Like unto a figure beautifully painted on wall.

several Saiva shrines in the Island, and Vijaya himself added to their number. "In the East he erected Konésar-kóyil at Thampala-Kámam; in the west he re-built Tiruk kétich-churan-kóyil which had long been then in ruins; in the south he raised Santhira-sekaran-koyil" (later known as Nága-rísa-níla temple) at Dévi Nuvara or Dondra, " and on the north he constructed Thiruth-thamba-lésuran-koyil at Thiruthampálai at the foot of Kírimalai." He also re-built the temple at Kataragama,* but the author of Yaḻpána Vaipava Málai mistook the tradition and stated that he built the Kadira Áṇḍavar kóyil near Kíri malai. Kónésvaram at Trincomalie was rebuilt and enlarged by Kuḷakóṭṭan, an Indian prince, in the fifth century A.D.†

During the early centuries of the Christian era and for centuries before Christ, Gods, representing the five different sections of land, were worshipped as protectors of the countries in which they were respectively worshipped. The forest country was under the special protection of Máyón, who was later equated with Vishnu and Krishna; the hill country under that of Murugaṉ or Kumáravéḷ, the arable lands under that of Indra, the coast territories under Varuṇa and the desert land under the goddess Koṟṟavai who was later equated with Durga.‡ Siva, the three eyed deity, was the supreme god of all. Indra and Varuṇa appear to be Áryan introductions, and it is not now possible to discover by what names the gods worshipped in those tracts were previously known, as the

* Y. V. M. p: 3.

† Ibid. p: 6.

‡ Akapporuḷ, Sûtras: 20-24.

literature earlier than Tolkáppiyam is lost. There were temples in South India dedicated to Báladéva too, but the worship of Indra, Varuṇa and Báladéva, the Áryan deities, was never popular, and there are now no temples for their worship. It is not now known whether Siva was at any time considered a protector of any special tract of country. Except that of Indra and Báladéva the worship of the other gods was popular in Ceylon. The oldest temples in Jaffna, dedicated to Rámá and Krishna, were at Vallipuram and Punnálai respectively, and they are mentioned in the Kókila Sandésa. * Lakshmaṇa, the brother of Rámá, and—curiously—not Rámá himself appears to have been worshipped in the Siṅhalese districts under the name of Saman Deviyo.

In addition to the worship of the Hindu gods, demonology too was practised to a very great extent by all classes of people. Although Buddhism became the prevailing religion of the Island in the third century B.C., it did not at any time prevent the people from worshipping some of the Hindu gods and other local deities or from practising demonology. The God of Kataragàma, who was known by the name of Vélaṉ, Murugaṉ, Kandaṉ, Kumaraṉ and several other names, was the most popular God. Every village had a shrine consecrated to him, and annual festivals were conducted in his honour when acts of high religious fervour were displayed. The priest or the Kapua became possessed of the god and predicted either good or evil for the following year. After offering sacrifices of boiled rice mixed with the blood of animals, generally of goats, the worshippers indulged in a dance

* Kok: San ; vv. 252-253.

called kuravai kúttu.* The worship of Pattini was introduced by Gaja Báhu in the second century A.D., and her worship too became as popular as that of Murugaṉ. There are many temples in Jaffna consecrated to Pattini (Kaṇṇakai).

The anger of certain demons who were supposed to be the cause of misfortune, diseases and pestilence made the people engage themselves in their propitiation; and ceremonies necessary to please the demons were conducted in every household. The names of some of the demons suggest their having come into existence and vogue both before and after the introduction of Buddhism. Most of

---

* a. "மதவலி நிலைஇய மாத்தாட் கொழுவிடைக்
குருதியொடு விரைஇய தூவெள்ளரிசி
சில்பலிச்செய்து."

Tirumu, ll; 232-234.

Offering pure white rice mixed with the blood of a fat he-goat of strong and sinewy limbs,

b. "நெடுவே
ளணங்குறுமகளிராடுகளங்கடுப்ப."

Kuṛiñci : ll, 174-175.

Like the jerking of blood in the field of sacrifice where goats are decapitated in the ceremonies of exorcisms performed to cure women possessed by the spirit of Murugaṉ.

c. "கணங்கெழுகடவுட் குயர்பலிதூஉய்ப்
பரவினம்."

Naṟṟinai, v. 358.

We worshipped the god attended by dependant celestials by offering great sacrifices.

d. "குன்றகச் சிறுகுடிக்கிளையுடன் மகிழ்ந்து
தொண்டகச்சிறு பறைக்குரவையயர."

Tirumu, ll. 196-197.

Those who live in the small hamlet on the hill side and their relatives clasping each other's hand with joy and dancing the 'Kuravai' dance to the music of the small 'toṇḍaka' drum.

them being local names, this proves their indigenous origin rather than their alien introduction. Dandris de Silva Gunaratne Mudaliyár, in his "Demonology and Witchcraft in Ceylon," says "Many fresh additions were made to demonism, both in the number of demons, and especially in the introduction of a large number of charms or spells recited at every demon ceremony now; so much, indeed, does this appear to have been the case that more than seven-eighths of the charms, belonging to Sinhalese necromancy, are in the Tamil language, a circumstance which has led many to believe, that demonism is altogether an importation from the continent."*

The Tamil charms and incantations are chiefly used in Húniyam and Billi ceremonies, in the exorcism of devils and añjanam eliya or clairvoyance,—branches of the black art—to which the Sinhalese are indebted to the Tamils. and which appear to have been introduced into Ceylon in very early times. But the Bali ceremonies, which seem to have no analogy in the Tamil land are altogether indigenous. The equation of the word 'Yakkha' with 'devil' or 'demon' was due to the extensive practice of demonology which existed among the ancient Yakkhas.

With the introduction of Buddhism Jaffna rose into eminence and importance as a place of Buddhist pilgrimage, for it attracted a large number of pilgrims from all parts of the Buddhist world on account of the existence of the shrine of the gem set seat—which is referred to in the Maṇimékalai as one worthy of disclosing to the worshipper his or her previous births—and of the impres-

* J. C. B. R. A. S., vol. iv, no.13, p: 1-117.

sions of the feet of Buddha. Fa Hien, the Chinese pilgrim who visited Ceylon in the year 413 A.D., remarks briefly "By the strength of his divine foot he (Foe, i.e., Buddha) left the print of one of his feet to the north of the royal city (Anurádhapura) and the print of the other on the summit of a mountain."* Of these two foot prints the one on the mountain was no doubt the same as the one on Adam's Peak; but the other was the one in Jaffna, (referred to in Maṇimékalai as an object of pilgrim worship), the site of which is still called Tiruvaḍi Nilai (position of the sacred feet) at the beach near Chuḷipuram.† The place where the shrine was is now covered by the sea, but the villagers assure that the foot prints can still be seen on a rock in the sea in a fathom of water some distance away from the shore. A large number of Buddhist vihárạs and dágobas arose not only in the Peninsula but also in the adjacent islands, and Kantaróḍai on account of its importance as the place of Buddha's second advent to Laṅká and as the capital of the North, received special marks of royal favour, as is evidenced by the number of Buddhist remains that are found scattered over the village.

In the early days when Buddhism flourished in North Ceylon, the outlying islands off the coast of Jaffna contained important monasteries and viháras. The Mahávaṅsa-Tika, while commenting on the story of Sáli Kumáraya, the son of Dutugámini, and his romantic love towards a Chaṇḍaḷa woman says that they were husband and wife in a previous existence and when they desired to

---

* J. C. B. R. A. S., vol. v, p: 63.

† Nágadipa. : J. C. B. R. A. S., vol. xxvi.

feed eight prominent *theras* with the flesh of a pig which they had prepared, it was the *thera* Dhammadinna of Piyaṅgudípa who divined the wish and went to the village with some of his companions.* Piyaṅgudípa was the present Puṅguḍutíve and was called Puvaṅgu divina in the Siṅhalese Nampota. It is said in the Abitta Jataka (Buddha's Birth Stories) that the brahmin sage Akitta (Agastya?), desiring isolation, went from Benares to Kavéripaṭṭinam and then flew over to the island of Kára set over the island of the Nágas. He dwelt in a rock cell in this island of Káradípa and subsisted on the leaves of the Kára shrub (wehera tetrandra) which he used to boil and eat without salt or spices.† This island of Káradípa set over against the island of the Nágas (Nágadípa) was Káratívu or Kárainagar lying to the west of Jaffna the ancient Nágadípa. These islands, which are mentioned in the ancient books, must assuredly have been well known, enjoying fame as places of Buddhist worship. Since the downfall of Buddhism in India,—mainly through the aggressive influence of the Saiva Saints—Sambandar, Appar and Sundarar, the Dévāram hymners, and Máṇikkavásagar—in whose time it is alleged that the Buddhist monks who went from Ceylon were defeated in a controversy with him,—Hinduism began to gain ground in Ceylon. Although the prevailing religion was Buddhism, yet the worship of Hindu gods was practically admitted in Buddhist temples, and when the rule of the Kaliṅga kings became predominant in the North, Hinduism once again became the prevailing religion there.

---

* Dip: and Mah: p. 37.

† Contributions, p. 49.

CHAPTER V

Foreign Trade and Intercourse—*(Continued)*

A GREAT deal of information regarding the Kingdom of Jaffna, and the important part it played between the ninth and the fourteenth centuries, can be gathered from the writings of early Muhammedan travellers and from medieval European writers. These works, which are only found in the British Museum or in continental libraries, have been consulted in the original by writers like Col. Yule and others, and the conclusions given here are based solely on quotations given by them. Sir Emerson Tennent, who drew largely from those works, has given us only his conclusions; unfortunately he has overlooked those passages which indicate conclusively the identity and location of the Northern Kingdom.

The Arabian traders—not merely did they preserve the Greek traditions but they also made considerable additions to them by personal study and travel. Men like Suleyman (851 A.D.), Abu Zaid (916 A.D.), Mas'udi (956 A.D.), El Edirisi (11th century) and El Kazwani (1275 A.D.) who have left records of their travels, had a fuller and more adequate conception of India and Ceylon than any Christian writer before the fifteenth century.

'The Accounts of India and China' by the two Muhammedan travellers Suleyman and Abu Zaid* are

---

* The first part of this book was written in 851 and the second part in 916 A. D. (See Cathay and the Way Thither, p : cii).

among the earliest and the most descriptive. According to them, the Island of Ceylon was then subject to two kings,* one of whom—presumably the king of Jaffna,—was ruling over an Island called 'Zapage' or 'Zabage,' a name which was employed to include some other Islands dependent on the principal one.† We are also informed by the same writers that the 'Province of Zapage' is opposite to China, and a month's sail distant therefrom by sea, or less if the wind be fair. The king of this country was called *Mehrage*, and "they say it is 900 leagues in circumference and that this king is master of many Islands which lie round about. Among those Islands there is one called Serbeza which is said to be 400 leagues in circuit, and that also of Rahmi."‡ The same writer informs us in another place that, among the Islands of the sea of Harkend towards Serendib, one "is called Ramni and is under several Princes, being 800 or 900 leagues in dimension." "In this Kingdom," it is continued, "is the Island of Cala which is in the mid-passage between China and the country of the Arabs. This Island, they say, is four score leagues in circumference, and hither they bring all sorts of merchandise, wood aloes of several sorts, camphor, sandal wood, ivory, the lead called cabahi, ebony, red wood, every kind of spice and many other things too tedious to enumerate. At present the commerce is most usually carried on from Oman to this Island and from this Island to Oman."¶

* Tennent. vol. i, pt. v, chap. ii, p. 584.

† 'Nights. Vol : iii note 12 of chap. xx.

‡ Ibid

¶ Ibid

Mas'udi, in his "Meadows of Gold," written in the 10th century A.D., says that "the Maharaja of Zabedj or king of the isles possessed Zanig, Kalah, Sarendib and other Islands lying opposite to the Kingdom of Komara."* He mentions Zabedj as one of the countries he visited and adds that the Kingdom of Rahma extends both inland and on sea.†

Col. Yule identifies the Island of Rahmi or Ramni as Sumatra and Cala or Kalah-bar (called elsewhere a dependence of Zabaj), as some part of Malacca, perhaps Kadah, commonly spelt Queddah, Zabaj, representing some great monarchy then existing on the Malay Island, probably in Java, the king of which was known to the Arabs by the Hindu title of Maharaj.‡

An Officer of the Ceylon Rifles, in his book on 'Ceylon,' discusses at length the location of Kalah, but leaves the question in as nebulous a state as the previous writers on the subject, although he disagrees with the identification of Sir E. Tennent and seems to uphold the views of Col. Yule. The Island of Rahmi or Ramni or Rahma in the sea of Harkend, a name applied by the Arabs to a portion of the Arabian Sea and of the Bay of Bengal, "towards Serendeeb" (Ceylon) must be the Island of Rámésvaram (cf. Rahmancor of the Portuguese). And

* "Haec terra regno Mahraj regis insularum, quæ sunt Zanig Kalah Taprobana et aliæ, opposita jacet regnum igitur Kumarense." Mas'udi in Gild: Scrip: Arab: p. 150, quoted by Rifles, Vol. i, p. 225, note.

† Cathay, Intro: p. cx, §. 83.

‡ ibid p. ciii, § 79.

this Island, being one of the many over which the Mehrage (Maharája) of Zapage was master, Zapage must have been Yápáṇam or Yáḷpáṇam. The incredible exaggerations as to their size and dimensions, a common failing of all travellers of that age, appear to have led Col. Yule to think that they referred to the Islands of the Malay Archipelago. For obvious reasons, all students of such writers as these would agree that their impressions as to the distances, the measurements and the relative sizes of countries and their natural features cannot be accepted as accurate or made the sole, or even the main, basis of conclusions regarding the location or identification of countries. The Island being under several princes, such as those of Rámésvaram and Mátoṭa, discloses the fact that the petty chiefs under the Maharája arrogated to themselves kingly powers in different parts of the kingdom. As Cala was said to be one of the Islands in the same kingdom, and in the mid-passage between China and the country of the Arabs, it must have been an important harbour and port of distribution and should be sought for in the Kingdom of Jaffna. The description of the commercial articles brought to this port is similar to the one given by Cosmas four or five centuries earlier, clearly showing that this port served as an emporium of exchange for the merchants of the East and the West. Cala, which was also known as Kalah and as Kalah-bar, represented Kalam, now called Kaḷa Bhúmi, a part of the Island of Káraitíve opposite to the port of Kayts. The place must have received its appellation 'Kala Bhúmi' (land of ships) after the advent of the Kaliṅga kings to Jaffna, as names ending in 'bhúmi' were peculiar to the Kaliṅga country; and there are, in that land, towns called Singhbhum,

Manbhum, etc., to the present day. Kalabhúmi was shortened to Kalah or Calah by foreign merchants and was later changed to Kaḷabhúmi. The harbour was also variously called Koillam, Coulam and Coulon by later European writers and it can be safely conjectured to be a corruption of Kóḷam, a shortened form of Kóvaḷam, which is the point on the North-Western corner of the Island of Káraitíve, where the light house stands at present right opposite to the Port of Kayts. The three points on the Northern Coast of Jaffna are called Kóvaḷam, Jambu Kóvaḷam and Kal Kóvaḷam respectively. The Arabian, Persian, Indian and Chinese ships sought this safe anchorage after trade with Rome had declined and after the Eastern entrance to the Elephant Pass lagoon had become blocked up by a sand bank. The mound of ruins lying at Kaḷabhúmi, close to the shore, may, if investigated disclose proof of the period of its commercial greatness.

El Edirisi, another Arab traveller of the 11th century, describes this Island of Cala in the same manner as the authors of 'The Accounts of India and China,' and adds that in the neighbourhood of this Island are situated those of Jabeh, Selahit and Heraj; each about two leagues from the others; he further states that they all obey the same king named Jabeh. Here, we are told, the Arabs, on their voyage to China, took in water; then they entered the sea of El-Harkend and, having sailed across it, they touched at Lajabulus or Najabulus.*

As Lajabulus (or Najabulus) has been identified by Col: Yule as the Nicobars, there is no room to doubt

* Nights, vol. iii, note 12 of chap. xx.

that Jabeh was the Island of Yál̤pāṇam, close to the Island of Káraitíve, on which was Cala, or Kalam, where the Arab navigators took in water before proceeding to the Bay of Bengal. It is also noticeable that the king was also called Jabeh, after the Island over which he ruled, from the fact that the land was named after Yal̤páṇan, the minstrel to whom it was given as a gift. Selahit was probably Eḷuvaitíve and Heraj must have stood for Karamban, the Tamil name of the Island of Kayts, or Saravanai.

Many a European writer was led astray in the identification of these places by taking for truth the exaggerated accounts of the size of these Islands as given by the Muhammedan writers. Although Renaudot placed the kingdom of Zapage near the point of Malabar, Langles, Col.: Yule and others thought that it was extremely improbable, and conjectured that either Borneo or Sumatara was the Island referred to.* But Sir E. Tennent, having persuaded himself that Cala was Pt. de Galle, thought that there was a Kingdom in the South of Ceylon under a Maharájáh whose sway extended as far as the Malay Peninsula, Sumatra and Borneo.† The Muhammedan writers themselves were to some extent responsible for this confusion, for it is clear from the vagueness of their accounts that their knowledge of the countries from India to China was not only meagre but also wanting even in a correct conception of relative magnitudes. Their works consisting largely of notes of their own experiences and also of information collected from other

---

* Cathay, Intro. p. ciii, § 79.

† Tennent, vol. i, p. 589.

travellers, naturally produced a confusion of place names, and a mingling of the, commercial products of the various countries was only to be expected.

It is said, in the Garshasp Namah, a Persian poem written in the tenth or the eleventh century A. D. by one Asedi, that Zobak—or Dhobak—a king of Persia, (alleged to have been a contemporary of Solomon, but he was in fact a Monarch of the tenth century,) sent his general, Garshasp, with a numerous fleet and an army to help a Maharájah of India, in order to chastise a rebellious prince on whom he (the Maharájah) had bestowed the government of Ceylon. "Hasten to India," said the Persian Monarch to his General, "and avenge his (the Maharájah's) wrongs on the Shah of Serendib, the king of Ceylon. Seize Bahu, drag him thence in bonds to the court of the Maharájah and there let him be hanged"* Garshasp landed at Kalah, so it is alleged, attacked 16,000 war elephants and two million soldiers, whom Bahu had assembled at a distance of two days march from Kalah, and inflicted a severe defeat on Báhu. Whatever might have been the actual cause of this expedition, it appears that Zobak, a king of Persia of the tenth century, sent a fleet to punish one Báhu, a king of Ceylon, for some insult real or imaginary offered by him either to the king of Persia or to an Indian king who was a friend and ally of the Persian Monarch. During that period there was no king of Ceylon with a name ending in Báhu, and the king referred to must therefore have been one of the kings of the Kaliṅga dynasty holding sway over Jaffna; moreover the Kaliṅga kings were

* Ousley, pp. 48:—52 and notes.

the earliest of the Ceylon kings with names ending with the suffix 'Báhu.' If the surmise that the king defeated by Garshasp was a king of Jaffna be correct, the distance from Kalah to the place at which Báhu awaited with his army gives us the clue for the identification of the Port of Kalah as Kayts or Kalabhúmi. The exaggerated account of the numerical strength of Báhu's army whether he was a king of Ceylon or of Jaffna, can safely be dismissed from consideration.

El-Edirisi, while describing the seas of India and China, says :—"From Serendib to the Island of Lankalous is ten journeys, and from Lankalous to the Island of Kalah six journeys. Kalah is a very large Island, situated in the neighbourhood of Selahat and contains an abundant mine of tin. The king is called Jabah or the Indian Prince."* In this passage, if Serendib and Lankalous be taken to refer to the same Island of Lańká (Ceylon),—perhaps to different parts of it—then the position of Kalah under the king of Jabah (Jaffna) is quite clear. By Serendib a port near Mannar was meant and by Lankalous another port, probably Dondra in the South. As Edirisi has called Nicobars Lajabulus or Najabulus,† he would not have used the name Lankalous also to mean the same Island. The mention of tin mines is, of course, an error. It is no wonder that Edirisi, who never visited

* "De Serendib á l'île de Lankalous 10 journies, de Lankalous á l'île de Kalah 6 journies xxxxxx qui est tres grande et ou demeure un Roi quôn nomme Djaba, ou prince Indien. Il y a dans cette île une mine abondante d'étain." Edirisi, trad; Jaubert, i, 77, 80; quoted by Rifles, vol. i, .p. 221, note.

† See supra p. 196, note *.

India or Ceylon thought that Serendib, Laṅká aud Kalah were three different Islands in the sea of Harkend.

Kazwani (1275 A.D.) mentions two Ceylons, one as Sarandib and the other as Sailon. In one place he says, "Sarandib is an Island in the sea of Harkend, at the extremity of India, 80 parasangs in extent, producing all kinds of aromatics and perfumes, agallochum (aghil), nux indica (cocoanuts), musk from deer, and several kinds of hyacinths. It has gold and silver mines, and pearl fishery."* In another place he says, "Sailan, is an extensive Island. situated between China and India, 80 parasangs in circumference. Sarandib is a part of it. It contains many towns and villages and has several kings who obey none. In the ocean around it there is a sea called Salahat. From it are brought sandal wood, spikenard, cinnamon, cloves, brazil wood and various aromatics. It has also gem mines and abound in every luxury."† From these passages it is evident that some of the Arabian writers thought that the northern part of Ceylon, which contained the important ports, was called Sarandib and the Southern part Ceylon or Laṅká.

---

* Rifles, vol. i, p. 247.

† "Sailan ampla insula est Sinas inter et Indiani, ambilis octoginta parasangarum. Sarandib in ea interiore est. Multos vicos et urbes habet et reges plures, nemini obedientes. Mari circa eam nomen maris Salahath est. Veniunt inde res mirae, etiam Santalem, spicanardi, cinnamomum, caryophyllum, bresillum, et alia aromata, quibus prae esteris terris excellit, etiam jemmarum fodinas habere dicitur, et omnibus bonis abundare." Kazwani, opera Gild: Script: Arab: p. 208 quoted by Rifles, vol, i, p. 247, Tennent, vol. i. p. 599.

Ibn-el-wardee, a writer of the fourteenth century, calls the Island of Kalah 'Kulleh,' and adds "it is a great Island; in it are trees rivers and fruits. A king of the sons of Jabah, the Indian, dwelleth in it; in it are mines of tin and camphor trees, one tree of which shadeth a hundred men and more, in it also is the Indian cane; and among its wonders are such things that the describer of them would incur disbelief".* It is clear that the writer has here made a mistake between two places of the name of Calah, (Kalah or Kulleh as he calls it), one being that in which the king of the sons of Jabah dwelt, the other being that in which tin mines were found. Similarly he has confused the tree which produces camphor with the banyan tree which provided shade to hundred men and more. 'The king of the sons of Jabah' is a clear allusion to the gift made to Yáḻpáṇan.

It appears that in the Malay Peninsula there was a place called Qualah (Queddah), which was also known as Calah or Kalah, and this place was often confused by some of the Muhammedan writers with the port in Jaffna. The result was the production of very misleading information, as will be seen from the following quotation from Dulif Misar Ibn Mohalhal, an Arab traveller of the tenth century. He says "leaving Sindabil (the Capital of China) the traveller proceeded to the sea coast and halted at Kalah,† the first city of India (from the East) and the extreme point made by ships going in that direction. If they go past it they are lost. This is a great city with high walls,

* Nights. vol, iii, note 12, chap. xx.

† Ibn Mohalhal visited China in 941 A.D. (see Cathay, Intro: p. ci, § 84).

gardens and canals. Here are the mines of lead called *Qalai* which is found in no part of the world except Qàlah. Here also are made the swords of Qalah, the best in India. The inhabitants rebel against their king or obey him just as they please. Like the Chinese they do not slaughter animals. The Chinese frontier is about 300 parasangs from the territory. Their money is of silver worth three dirhems and is called *fahri*. Their king is under the king of the Chinese and they pray for him and have a temple dedicated to him". From Kalah, Ibn Mohalhal proceeded to 'the pepper country' an appellation by which Malabar is often described.*

Col. Yule disagreed with Renaudot, who thought that it was the Kalliyana of Cosmas, and surmised that it was the modern Singapore, or Malacca, and very possibly Kadah (Queddah).† It is, however, clear that the traveller has mixed up more than one place in his description, possibly Queddah in the Malay Peninsula and Cala. Kalam or Kovaḷam in Jaffna, from which he proceeded to 'the pepper country'. The place where the best swords were made and where the silver coin called *Fahri* was used may probaly refer to a third. Whether the king of Jaffna was ever under the Chinese king is doubtful, but the fact that the Chinese professed to have exacted homage from several foreign kings is confirmed by Marco Polo who says, "China's intercourse in the form of homage succeeded in 1286 with the kingdoms of Mapaeul, Sumantala, Sumenna, Sengkili, Malantan, Laïlai. Navang and Zinghoeul".‡ Mapaeul was probably

---

* Cathay, Intro ; p. ci.

† Ibid.

‡ Ibid, Intro : § 55, quoted from Marco Polo.

Yá̤lpáṇam, and Sumantala Ceylon, from Samanala and Sumanta, native names for Adam's Peak. Sumenna and Sengkili were kingdoms in India, and the rest were probably places in the Malay Peninsula, although the last sounds very much like Siṅhalam and might have referred to Ceylon too. M. Pauthier says that "Ceylon is named in the list of ten kingdoms that paid tribute to Kubali Khan in 1286 A.D."*

There is a great deal of confusion in one of the passages in the 'Accounts of India and China.' It is said that, contiguous to India, was a king of Ruhmi, Rahma or Rahman by name, who was at war with the Jurz and the Balhana. He was not a monarch of great consideration, though he had the largest army and was accompanied by some 50,000 elephants and 15,000 washermen! Muslins that could pass through a ring were made in his country. Gold, silver, aloes wood and cowries were also found in it. Cowries were the money used; and in the forest was the rhinoceros, which is particularly described under the name of *Karkodan*.

Commenting on this Reinaud says, "this seems to me to answer to the ancient kingdom of Visiapur." Lassen, on the other hand, is quite sure that it fits none but the kingdom of the Chalukyas of Kaliyani (in the Dekkan). And Yule thinks that this place was Rahmaniya (Burma).† But the kingdom of Vijayanagar had not then come into existence. Though the Chalukyas of Kaliyani were then very powerful and possessed a large army at the time,

---

* Rifles, vol. i, p. 231.

† Cathay, prelim: essay, p. clxxxv.

there was no reason to call the king Ruhmi or Rahman. Rahmaniya (Burma) too does not fit in with all the details of the description and it is evident that the statement contains confused and exaggerated allusions to several kingdoms. It may more reasonbly be suggested that the kingdom of Rahma or Rahman was that of Rámésvaram, which was then under the overlordship of the king of Jaffna. Muslins that could pass through a ring were made there, and gold, aloes wood and cowries (chanks) were articles of commerce found there. Cowries might have been the currency then in common use, there as elsewhere. Of course an army as large as the one mentioned in the passage was not possessed by any king of India at the time, but these numbers are always a matter of imaginative license. Besides, *Karkodan* was the name of a fabulous serpent, never of the rhinoceros. It is, therefore, not surprising that a country could not be found to fit in perfectly with the description.

The Island of Mihiraj is described in the 'Accounts of India and China' as "extremely fertile, and so very populous that the towns almost crowded one upon the other." It is also said that the palace of a former Mihiraj was "still to be seen" in the time of the author "on a river as broad as the Tigris at Bagdad or at El-Basrah." And it is added "the sea intercepts the course of its waters and sends them back again with the tide of flood; and during the tide of ebb it streams out fresh water a good way into the sea."* It is easy to identify the palace of the former Mihiraj with that at Kantarọ́dai (Kadiramalai) which had, only a short time

* Nights, vol. iii, note 12, chap. xx.

previously, been abandoned by the Jaffna king Ugrasingan, who transferred his capital to Singai Nagar. The river, which was exaggeratedly compared to the Tigris, was no other than the small streamlet Vaḷukkai Āṛu, the course of whose waters is intercepted by the sea and sent 'back again by the tide of flood'; and although 'during the tide of ebb' it does not 'stream out fresh water a good way into the sea,' it was about the tenth century much broader and deeper than it is at present and navigable for boats as far as Kadiramalai (Kantaróḍai).

"This river" it is further said in the 'Accounts of India and China,' "is led into a small pond close to the king's palace". Into this pond gold was thrown by an officer of state every morning right through the reign of the king and on his death it was all taken out and distributed among the members of his household and among the poor.* This was perhaps a custom then prevailing; it is referred to by several writers,† and the description

* Nights, vol. iii, note 12, chap. xx.

† (a) Mas'udi in his 'Meadows of Gold' gives a story similar to that in the 'Accounts of India and China' regarding the Maharaja of the Isles. His palace was over a tank which communicated with the sea. Every morning the Treasurer threw in a gold ingot. At the king's death the accummulation was taken out and divided among the dependents and the poor. (Cathay, p. 82, note 2).

(b). But Friar Odoric attributes the practice to a temple in South India. After describing the realm of Mobar (Coromandel) in which is laid the body of St. Thomas the Apostle, he proceeds to describe a temple, its worshippers and its festivals and continues to state that "hard by the Church of this idol there is a lake, made by hand, into which the pilgrims who come thither cast gold or silver or precious stones in honour of the idol and towards the maintenance

(Contd.)

that the palace overlooked a pond is true as regards the palace at Kadiramalai ; also that the pond was connected with the sea by Vaḻukkai Āṟu.

Marco Polo, the great Venetian traveller who visited Ceylon in 1284 A. D., on his way from China to the West, appears to have landed at a port in the North, for, he says:—" But the North wind there blows with such strength that it has caused the sea to submerge a large part of the Island, and that is the reason why it is not so big now as it used to be. For, you must know that on the side the North wind strikes, the Island is very low and flat, in so much that on approaching on board ship from the high seas you do not see the land till you are right upon it."* This description of the Northern part of Ceylon, coupled with the fact that Brazil wood or aghil is mentioned as a special article of merchandise, confirms

---

of the church, so that much gold and silver and many precious stones have been accumulated therein. And thus when it is desired to do any work upon the Church, they make search in the lake and find all that has been cast into it." (Cathay, p. 82, § 19.) He, however, calls the place where the temple and tank are situated an Island. (Ibid, para. i. § 20 as rearranged.)

(c). Odoric's story is corroborated by the Masalak-al-Absar, which says that among the towns in the South of India conquered by Mahomed Taghlak (a few years after Odoric's visit) was once standing by a lake in the middle of which was an idol temple which enjoyed a great reputation in that country and into which the people used continually to cast their offerings. After the capture of the city the Sultan caused the lake to be drained and the wealth which he found accumulated in it sufficed to load two hundred elephants and several thousand oxen." (Ibid, p. 82, note 2; p. ccxliii.)

* Marco, vol. ii, p. 295.

the theory that he landed at the Northern Port. In describing the people of the Island, he says, "they have a king there whom they call Sandamain and are tributary to nobody. The people are idolators and go quite naked except that they cover the middle. They have no wheat but have rice and sesamum of which they make their oil. They live on flesh and milk and have tree wine such as I have told you of and they have brazil wood much the best in the world."* The king he mentioned was evidently the king of Jaffna and the fact that he was independent without paying tribute to any other king is particularly to be noted. Sesamum is gingely, which is still an important produce of Jaffna and the palm wine is palmyrah toddy. He further says that a great deal of brazil wood is got there which is called *Brazil Koilumin* from the country which produces it and that it is of very fine quality.† The mention of a place called Coilum, from which the brazil wood is exported, leaves one rightly to conjecture that the port of Coulom or Coilum which he describes as lying five hundred miles south-west of Mabar (Coromandel) before reaching Komari (Cape Comorin) and where the merchants from Manzi (China), Arabia and the Levant called with their ships and their merchandise‡ was no doubt Kóvaḷam, the Kalah of the Muhammedan travellers and not Quilon on the Malabar coast.

A Missionary Friar, John of Montecorvino, speaking of vessels passing through the Northern passage in his time (1292 A. D.) says that a large number of them must

* Marco, vol. ii, p. 296.

† Ibid p. 363.

‡ Ibid p. 364.

have availed themselves of this channel, for, as many as sixty of them were wrecked annually on those coasts.* The places where these vessels were probably wrecked were on the coasts of Nainatíve and Neduntíve (Delft). These casualties must have been so frequent that Parákrama Báhu in the 12th century A.D., promulgated an edict concerning their disposal and had it engraved on stone, as will be seen from the inscription found at Nainative.†

---

* Cathay and the Way Thither, vol.

† The following fragmentary inscription was found in a stone slab lying opposite to the temple at Nainatíve. The lower portion of the slab is broken off and has been built into the wall of the shrine. The first portion of the inscription is atogether obliterated by the artisans who built the temple by sharpening their tools on it. The inscription on the reverse side which lay against the ground has escaped mutilation. It is engraved in archaic characters of the 11th or 12th century A.D. The edict appears to have been promulgated by one Parakrama Bhuja who is taken to be Parakrama Báhu the Great.

ஊராத்துறையிற் பரதேசிகள் வந்து இருக்கவேணுமென்றும் இவர்கள் ரக்ஷிப்படவேணுமென்றும் பு(து)த்துறைகளில் பரதேசிகள் வந்த(ாலித்) துறையிலே (ல) சந்திக்க (வே) வணுமென்றும் நா (வாய) ஆனை குதிரையொடு (ம்) பண்டார சேவைக்கு ஆனை குதிரை கொடுவந்த மரக்கலங் கெட்டதுண் டாகில் நாலத்தொன்று பண்ட (ா) ரத்துக்கு கொண்டுமூன்று கூறும் (உ)டை யவனுக்கு விடக்கடவதாகவும் - வாணிய மரக்கலங் கெட்டதுண்டாகில் செம பாகம் பண்டாரத்துக்குக்கொண்டு செமபாகம் உடையவனுக்கு விடக்கடவதா கவும் இவ்வ்யவஸதை * * * தித்து * * * தனையுங் கல்லிலுஞ் செம்பிலும் எழுத்து வெட்டுவித்து இவ்வ்யஸதை செய்து கொடுத்து தேவ பராக்கறம பூஜோ. * * * * * * * *

Foreigners must land and remain at Uraturai (Kayts), and they must be protected. If foreigners land at new ports, they should meet

[Contd.]

There is some confusion also in the version published by Col. Yule in his "Cathay and the Way Thither," of the manuscripts of Friar Odoric, who visited Ceylon in 1322 A. D. The para: of § 24 which refers to the immolation of a wife at the funeral pyre of her husband, must go as the last para: of § 19, and the last para: of § 24 as the first of § 25 which must be numbered 20.* Then it will be seen that § 19 in which the temple and tank are described refers to a rich well-endowed temple in South India, presumably that at Sidambaram. And § 20 which evidently refers to Jaffna will read as follows:—

"§ 20. But the king of this Island or Province is passing rich in gold and silver, and precious stones. And in this Island are found as great store of good pearls as in any part of the world".

"And the king of that country weareth round his neck a string of three hundred very big pearls, for that he maketh to his gods daily 300 prayers. He carrieth also in his hands a certain precious stone called a ruby, a good span in length and breadth, so that when he hath

at this port. If ships laden with elephants and horses, carry elephants and horses for the service of the Treasury, and are wrecked, a fourth share should be taken by the Treasury and the (other) three parts should be left to the owner. If merchant vessels are wrecked a half share should be taken by the Treasury and the other half left to the owner. These edicts are inscribed on stone and copper. These edicts are promulgated by Déva Parakrama Bhújó.

Parákrama Bahu i, is called Srimat Parakrama Bhujá in the Pandawewa inscription (Muller's, No. 142).

* Cathay, p. 84, et seq.

this stone in his hands it shows like a flame of fire. And this, it is said, is the most noble and valuable gem that existeth at this day in the world, and the great Emperor of the Tartars of Cathay hath never been able to get it into his possession either by force or by money, or by any device whatever. This king attends to justice and maintains it and throughout his realm all may fare safely. And there be many other things in this kingdom that I care not write of."

The possession of pearls and of the pearl necklace stamps the owner as the King of Jaffna. The ruby said to have been of 'a good span in length and breadth' was perhaps the same as described by Ibn Batuta to have been in the possession of Árya Chakravarti. According to the latter writer it was a saucer made of ruby as large as the palm of the hand in which he kept oil of aloes.* This gem was also mentioned by Marco Polo as having been in the possession of Sandemain and described to be a 'palm long.' He too spoke of the attempt made by the 'great Khan of China' who sent an embassy to purchase it, and of the excuse given by the king that it belonged to his ancestors and that he could not therefore part with it.† This ruby related by Marco Polo, Friar Odoric, and Ibn Batuta to have been in the hands of the king of Jaffna was perhaps the very one referred to by Hiouen Thsang and Cosmas as the gem which glowed like fire on the top of the dágoba at Anurádhapura when the sun shone on it. It might have found its way to Jaffna as one of the spoils after the sack of Yápáhu and ultimately fell into the hands

---

* Batuta, p. 187.

† Marco, vol. ii, pp. 295-296.

of the Portuguese when Jaffna was plundered by Braganza in 1560, but the Portuguese historians do not make any mention of it.

Ibn Batuta, the Moor traveller from Tangiers, while returning from the Maladives in 1344 A.D., had, on account of the inclemency of the weather, to seek a port in the kingdom of Jaffna which he called 'Battala'* wrongly identified as Puttalam. Battala was equated with Puttalam only on the similarity of sound. Neither the fact that between this city and the Malabar (Coromandel) districts there was a voyage of one day and night nor the itinerary given by Ibn Batuta while travelling from Battala to Adam's Peak was taken into account. If he proceeded from Puttalam there was no necessity to cross a river by boat, to enter the city of Manar Mandali or to pass 'the port of Salavat' modern names easily recognisable as Mannar (Maṇḍalam)and Salávaturai. When we compare such mutilated names like Zapage, Zabedj and Jabeh given by other Muhammedan travellers, Saba by Marignolli and Nepáḻam by Telugu poets, to Yáḻpáṇam, the name Battala given by Ibn Batuta is not surprising. Battala might have stood for paṭṭinam. From the time Yáḻpáṇan and his followers settled at Pásaiyúr and Karaiyúr, the place would have been naturally called Yáḻpáṇa paṭṭinam† like all other villages on the sea coast (neytal tracts); it was a port for foreign vessels and would have been known as Paṭṭinaturai. The great navy of the Árya Chakravartis would have been collected at this safe anchorage as they

* Batuta, pp. 187—191.

† See infra, chap. vi.

were manned and officered by men of the Karáva community, the descendants of the Páṇa settlers. It was there that Ibn Batuta appears to have landed and seen the fleet of ships belonging to Árya Chakravarti. When the Portuguese conquered Jaffna, they built their city close to the Páṇa settlement and called it by the same name as the settlement was previously known viz., Yáḻpáṇa paṭṭinam or according to their parlance Jafana Patao. It was at this port of Patanao (ao in Portuguese is pronounced aṅ), that the Portuguese army under Braganza landed on the 20th October, 1559, to fight against the forces of Saṅkili.* This port must have been close to the present Jaffna Customs and quite distinct from Paṇṇaituṛai and Colomboturai lying at a distance of one and two miles respectively to the west and east of it. It was due to the existence of this port that Yáḻpáṇa paṭṭinam or Yápápaṭuna was more known to the outside world than Singai Nagar, the capital of the Árya Chakravartis. It is also curious that some of the Portuguese writers too have called the place Jafana Putalao† (Jafana patalaṅ) (changing n into l) in the manner Ibn Batuta did. Ibn Batuta called the king of

---

* Queiroz, p. 283.

† "Antes de tratar do Reyno de Candea falarey no de Jafanapatao q.'taobem foy todo da Coroa de Portugal e todo Christao; sua cabeca fica, em forma de penisala, na ponta boreal da ilha de Ceylao, em 10 graos, a dous tercos de elevacao; cujo nome. sem corupcao, dizem ser Jafana-en-putalao, q.' val tanto como; Povoacao do Senhor Jafana, e he o nome do sen pro. povoador. Outros querem fosse o nome Jafana-Patanao-ture q.' qr. dizer porto comprido. Donde parece q.' pr. zombaria ilhe chamassem Napunay-Patanao, q.' vestido diz: Terra de ruym gente."

Queiroz—p. 37.

[Contd.]

Ceylon 'Áriya Chakravati' the *Biruda* borne by the kings of Jaffna, and described his city of Battala as small and surrounded by two wooden fences. According to him the king had "considerable forces by sea", a statement which confirms the story of the strength of his navy—a navy that carried the forces that fought later before the walls of Kóṭṭe. The sea-shore abounded in cinnaman wood, bakum and Kalanji aloe, articles of merchandise distributed from this centre to the other parts of the world. The king treated him as his honoured guest and furnished him with an escort of four yogis, four brahmins, palanquin bearers and provision carriers to accompany him to Adam's Peak. On the first day he crossed a river on a boat made of reeds. This river was no doubt the Jaffna lagoon which he had to cross near Púnakari in order to reach the mainland. He passed through Mannár and Salávaturai, and reached the city of Kankár the seat of the Emperor of Ceylon built in a valley between two hills upon an estuary called the estuary of rubies, and the Emperor was called Kónár. The city was no doubt Kónagar (the city of Kón) not Kurunegala as wrongly surmised by some and the name of the person

---

"Before dealing with the kingdom of Kandy I shall speak of that of Jafanapatam which also entirely belonged to the Portuguese Crown and which was all Christian: its capital is in the form of a peninsula, on the northern point of the Island of Ceylon at ten degrees and two-thirds of elevation; whose name, in its uncorrupted form, they say, is Jafana-en-putalao (Yáḷpáṇan paṭṭanam) which is equivalent to the city of the Lord Jafana, which is the name of its first peopler. Others would have the name as Jafanapatanamturai which means Long port. Hence it seems that it was in derision that they called it Naypunaypatanam which being translated means Land of bad people.

who was in charge of the city supposed by him to be the Emperor was Alagakónár whose name was mutilated to Konár by the traveller. Kónagar was the Fort Kóṭṭe built by Alagakónár, the bold and adventurous henchman of the king of Ceylon reigning then at Gampola, and was referred to as Kotte by Marignolli who visited Ceylon in 1348 A. D.* Col. Yule says that it was first mentioned as a royal residence in 1314 A. D., and it became the capital of the Island in 1410 A. D.† It appears in Fra Mauro's map as Kotte Civitas. Ibn Batuta gives a minute description of the route taken by him to reach Adam's Peak and of his return journey via Devinuvara, Galle and Colombo From the description given it is evident that he climbed the peak by the steep ascent on the Ratnapura side. Of Devinuvara, the present Deundra or Dondra, he gives the information that the town was large and inhabited by merchants, that there was an idol made of gold and as large as a man placed in a very large temple in which there were "about a thousand Brahmins and Jogues and five hundred young women, daughters of the nobility of India who sing and dance all night before the image."

In 1348 or 1349 A. D., John de Marignolli, the Papal delegate to the Court of the Great Khan, on his return from China landed at Columbam. He remained with the Christians there for one year and four months, and after erecting a stone memorial 'in the corner of the world over against Paradise' (supposed to be at Cape Comorin) he went to see the famous queen of Saba

---

* Cathay, p. 369.

† Ibid , note 4.

Naga-risa Nila Temple at Devinuvara
from a Portuguese drawing.

To face page 214.] With permission of C.B.R A.S.

by whom he "was honourably treated" and then "proceeded by sea to Seyllan" (Ceylon.)* His reference to Saba and its queen are widely dispersed throughout his writings and his repeated mention of her whenever opportunity offered testifies to the great respect in which he held her. According to him Saba "was the finest Island in the world",† in it there was a lofty mountain called Gyheit or the Blessed with which legends of Elias and of the Magi were connected, and at the foot of which there was a spring the water of which he tasted.‡ He frequently saw the queen, gave her his benediction, was present at one of her magnificent banquets and was cured of an attack of dysentry he was suffering from for eleven months, by a female physician of the queen, with only the aid of a few herbs. The queen owned chariots and elephants and he himself rode on one of her elephants. The queen bestowed on him a golden girdle such as she was wont to bestow upon those who were created princes and also bestowed 150 whole pieces of very delicate and costly stuff and other raiments.¶ When he left the country of Mynibar on his way to the shrine of St. Thomas the Apostle, he was caught in a storm and driven to a Port in Seyllan called Pervilis over against Paradise,§ where he was robbed of everything he possessed, including the girdle presented to him by the queen of Saba, by a Pirate called Coya Juan. He also speaks of his visit to

---

* Cathay, p. 346.

† Ibid 389.

‡ Ibid 391-392

¶ Ibid 392.

§ Ibid 357

Kóṭṭe and gives a vivid description of Adam's Peak and its neighbourhood which he called Paradise.* Marignolli appears to have thought that the Queen of Sheba who visited the Court of King Solomon was a queen from the country of Saba and stated that the Island was generally ruled by women.† Col. Yule says that Saba and its queen offer the most difficult problem in all the disjointed story of Marignolli's wanderings, as it is difficult to locate the place.‡ Now Marignolli visited the queen once on his way from Columbum and again on his way back from Mayilapore where stood the Church of St. Thomas the Apostle. Saba ought therefore to be on the Southern extremity of the Indian Peninsula. The Queen has been surmised to be either the Queen Kadija of the Maldives visited by Ibn Batúta a few years earlier ¶ or Rudramba the daughter of the Kakatiya King Ganapati of Warangal.§ If she had belonged to the Maldives, Marignolli would not have called the Island the finest in the world. Nor could the queen of the Maldives, who possessed only a single horse during the time of Ibn Batuta,|| have become possessed of elephants and chariots in a few years. Rudramba too could not have lived during the time of Marignolli as her reign extended from 1260 to 1290 A.D., quite half a century earlier.** The

* Cathay, p 354, et seq.

† Ibid 389.

‡ Ibid 321.

¶ Ibid 322.

§ Ibid

|| Batuta, p- 182.

** M. E. R. 1907.

Port Columbum seems to be confounded with two places, with Quilon in Malabar, the pepper country, and with Kóḷam, Koulam or Kóvaḷam in Mynibar. If Columbum the port at which Marignolli landed first be taken as the one in the country of Mynibar, it would have been only too easy for him to visit the Queen of Yáḻpáṇam. Now, Muhammedan travellers two or three centuries earlier called Yaḻpáṇam, Zapage, Zabaj or Jabeh; and 'Saba' is a better phonetic transcription of Yaḻpáṇam or Yápáṇam than any of the earlier names given by the Muhammedan travellers, including Battala the name given by Ibn Batuta. Jaffna too was at the time of Marignolli's visit a flourishing kingdom. It is therefore probable that Marignolli visited Jaffna which was then ruled by a queen whom he for some reason called 'famous."

The Catalan map of 1375 A.D., in which Ceylon is called by the name of "Illa Iana," a corruption of the native name of Íḻam, represents a female sovereign as ruling part of the Island. An Officer of the Ceylon Rifles in his work on "Ceylon" thought that that was "an allusion to the Queen of Wanney, a district of Ceylon at one time ruled by women."* He, relying on Turnour, committed an anachronism by confounding this queen with the later Vannichchis who ruled over different parts of the Vannis later than the Portuguese times. The statement of Marignolli that Saba (Jaffna) was ruled by a queen during his visit has, strangely enough, received confirmation from a totally independent authority like the Catalan map.

---

* Rifles, vol. i, p. 21.

It is, however, strange that the Yáḻpáṇa Vaipava Málai which gives a list of the rulers of Jaffna from perhaps the 13th to the end of the 16th century does not mention a queen as one of the reigning sovereigns. In 1344 A.D., the year in which Ibn Batuta visited Jaffna, the country was governed by a king, and from the statement made by Marignolli, it can be surmised that the king died soon after the visit of Ibn Batuta and was succeeded on the throne perhaps by his minor son for whom the mother acted as regent. If she was the rightful heir to the throne and there was no objection to female succession, her name would have appeared in the dynastic list. The 'lofty mountain of Gyheit' referred to as 'Blessed,' with which Marignolli connected the legends of Elias and the Magi was evidently the unpretentious hill Kírimalai sacred to the Hindus, and supposed to be the residence of holy ascetics in ancient times. The spring at the foot of the hill, the water of which Marignolli professed to have tasted, was, no doubt the sacred *tirta* of Kírimalai which was and still is an attraction to thousands of pilgrims. Marignolli after twisting Yáḻpáṇam into Saba applied it to the country of Saba referred to in the following prophecy in the Bible :—"The kings of Tharsis and the Islands shall offer presents, the kings of the Arabians and of Saba shall bring gifts."* He therefore thought that one of the three Magi who went to Bethlehem to adore the child Christ was from Jaffna. The Yogis and ascetics haunting Kírimalai which Marignolli calls Gyheit must have lent additional confirmation to his theory. This account was perhaps the original of the later garbled version of

---

* Psalm, lxxi, v. 10 (Douay version)

the Portuguese historian de Barros who said that a king of Ceilam named Perimal on being warned by a Sybil at Coulam (Kóvaḷam) of the birth of Christ set sail in a ship and joined two other kings on their way to Bethlehem.*

In one of the maps of Bernard Sylvanus (1511 A. D.) Ceylon is called "Insula Caphane", which name also occurs in the itinerary of John of Hese who says "Insula Caphane vel Taprobane."‡ Insula Caphane no doubt represents the Island of Jaffna. The mistake made by these European writers in styling the whole of Ceylon as "Jaffna" was perhaps due to the necessity of their touching at one of the ports of Jaffna on their voyages. This is perhaps the earliest record in which Yáḻpáṇam was called Jaffna (Caphane) by the European writers.

In the "Thousand and One Nights," commonly known as the 'Arabian Nights Entertainments,' which possesses a world wide reputation and which was written about the 15th century A.D., is given a description of the wonderful voyages made by Es-Sindibad of the sea.† The accounts of these voyages were evidently founded upon the exaggerated reports of various Arabian and other Muhammedan travellers of the period, and disclose the author's intimate knowledge of those writings. In the first voyage, a graphic description is given of Sindibad's escape from being drowned by an immense tortoise, the back of which the sailors mistook for an Island. Sindibad was washed ashore on the coast of an Island governed by El-Mihiraj,

* de Barros, dec. iii, bk. vii, chap. ix.

† Rifles, vol. i, p. 22.

‡ Nights, vol. iii.

where he was met by the grooms of the king's horses and taken before the Mihiraj. The latter received him kindly, treated him "with beneficence and honour" and appointed him "Superintendent of the Sea-port and Registrar of every vessel that came to the coast". In the Court of the said Mihiraj he met a party of Indians who told him that "among them there were Shakireeyeh (Kshatriyas) the most noble of their races, and Brahmins, a people who never drank wine". He also saw an Island called Kasil in the dominions of the Mihiraj in which was heard the beating of tambourines and of drums during the night, and also saw in the sea of that Island a fish 200 cubits long and another whose face was like that of an owl.

We may take it that the coast where Sindibad was said to have been washed ashore was close to Kudiraimalai, that the Mihiraj was the Mahárája of Jaffna and that the sea-port to which he was attached was Kalah or Kóvaḷam. The Island of Kasil, the beating of drums and the meeting with fish of enormous size are all matters copied from the Muhammedan writers. The people still believe that strange noises are heard on certain nights near Kudiraimalai and in the Island of Iranaitíve. Kazwani (13th century) and Ibn-el-Wardee (14th century) relate that in the sea of El Kulzam is a fish in the form of a cow which bringeth forth its young and suckleth like a cow.* The fish here referred to is the dugong which is found in the gulf of Mannar and in the Jaffna seas, and gave rise to many an exaggeration among the early writers regarding its form and size. The Greeks, it is

* Nights, vol. iii, chap. xx, note 49.

believed, received their idea of the mermaid from this fish, and even so late as the time of the Portuguese, it is mentioned in a work called 'Histoire De La Compagnie de Jesus' that in 1560 A.D., seven mermaids were caught in the neighbourhood of Mannar by the fishermen, were taken to Goa and there dissected by a physician on instructions from the Viceroy.* Kulzam was no doubt Kaḷam or Kóvaḷam.

In the fourth voyage, Sindibad, after his escape from the cavern in which he had been buried alive with the body of his wife, pursued his course until he arrived at the Island of the Bell whence he proceeded to the Island of Kela in six days. Then he came to the kingdom of Kela which is adjacent to India, and in it are a mine of lead and places where the Indian cane groweth a d excellent camphor; and its king is a king of great dignity, whose dominion extended over the Island of the Bell. In it is a city called the city of the Bell which is two days' journey in extent. The word which the translator has rendered into 'Bell' is 'Nakoos'† which evidently stands for 'Nágas.' The Island of the Bell and the city of the Bell would therefore represent the Island and the city of the Nágas (Mátoṭa) and 'the king of great dignity whose dominion extended to the Island of the Bell' was the king of Jaffna. Kela was the port of Kalah. The lead mine, the Indian cane and the commercial product found there are taken from the confused writings of the other Muhammedan writers.

---

* Pridham, vol. ii, p. 500.

† Nights, vol. ii, chap. xx, note 59.

In his 5th voyage, it is said that Sindibad passed by an Island in which was cinnamon and pepper, a large quantity of which he took in exchange for cocoanuts. He then passed by the Island of El-Asirat where was the Kamaree aloes wood. After that he passed by 'another Island the extent of which was five days' journey' and in it was the Sanfu aloes wood which was superior to the Kamaree, but the inhabitants of the Island were "worse in condition and religion than the inhabitants of the Island of the Kamaree aloes wood; for they loved depravity and the drinking of wines and knew not the call to prayer nor the act of prayer". He went "after that to the pearl fisheries."* These disconnected statements show that the voyage was made round about the island of Ceylon and that places in it were also called islands. Aloes wood (Aghil)† was in those days obtained from the eastern coast of Ceylon. Most of the aloes wood and cinnamon appear to have been exported to the Jaffna ports from Komari which was situated to the South of Batticaloa. Cinnamon then grew wild in

---

* Nights, vol. ii, chap. xx, note 60.

† Aghil was the hard core of the tree cactus (square stemmed) the fragrant smoke of which was used for perfuming the hair.

"கள்ளிவயிற்றினகில் பிறக்கு மான் வயிற்றின்
ஒள்ளரிதாரம் பிறக்கும் பெருங்கடலுட்
பல்விலையமுத்தம் பிறக்கு மறிவார்யார்
நல்லாள் பிறக்குங் குடி"

Nánmaṇi : v. 6.

The fragrant Aghil is formed in the core of the Cactus (Kaḷḷi) tree, the shining orpiment in the stomach of the deer. and the priceless pearl in the womb of the deep ocean, but does any one know in which family will the good and chaste woman be born.

the forests of Uva and the Eastern Province and was removed for export to Komari which, though now possessing a rugged coast, had probably in those days a harbour at which sailing vessels appear to have called. The author of Kamoos says that the Sanfu aloes wood was inferior to that of Komaree* In the 'Accounts of India and China' which mentions the Komaree aloes wood, the Island of Kamar (or Komar) is said to be divided from the kingdom of the Mihiraj "by a passage of ten or twenty days sail with a very easy gale."† El-Edirisi says that Kamaree is near Sanf separated only by three miles.‡ Ibn Batuta describing the kingdom of the Árya Chakravarti of Jaffna says that "the sea shore abounded in cinnamon wood, bakum and Kalanji aloe which however was not equal to the Komari or the Kakuli in scent."¶ From these scattered writings it is apparent that *Aghil* was brought to Jaffna from Komaree, Sanfu, Kakuli and Kalanji for distribution to other countries. As regards the depravity of the people referred to by Sindibad, it was perhaps what Mas'udi said that there was a race of Indians descended from Cain in the country of Kumar where the aloes wood came from.§ The bay of the pearl fishery was no doubt the gulf of Mannar, the one described by Marco polo as the "bay that lies between Malabar and the Island of Zeilan." ||

---

* Nights, chap. xx, note 12.

† Ibid.

‡ Ibid.

¶ Batuta, p. 184.

§ Cathay, prelim: essay, p ccxlvi

|| Marco, vol. ii. p. 313

In the sixth voyage, Sindibad came upon Ceylon in a miraculous manner by drifting on a raft down stream on a river which passed through a mountain, and then met people who "were of the sown lands and the fields" and who accidentally came upon him when they went to irrigate their fields. A short but a very correct description of Ceylon and of the Adam's Peak is given, and no better description than "the lands of fields and sown lands" for the Northern part of Ceylon (as it then was), could have been thought of.

These scattered references to the Kingdom of Jaffna and to the port of Kalah, not only in the writings of the Muhammedan travellers but also in the Arabian Nights, clearly indicate the route taken by sailing vessels in those early days, and how the port of Kalah or Kóvaḷam was used as an emporium for the commerce between the East and the West. Sir E. Tennent overlooking the fact that Kalah was mentioned as an important port and emporium of Ceylon by the Muhammedan as well as the European writers after the 9th century A.D., proceeded to show the errors into which he thought Bertolacci and other writers on Ceylon had fallen and to adduce reasons which to him appeared plausible, to prove that the ancient Kalah was the modern harbour of Galle. His enthusiasm at his supposed successful identification based as it was on a mere similarity of sound, made him assert that Galle was not only the ancient Kalah but also the Tarshish of Solomon's fleets and the rendezvous of Arabs, Greeks, Romans, Egyptians and Chinese in still more ancient times.*

---

* Tennent, vol. i. p. 560, et seq.

Col. Yule was not at all satisfied with the supposed identification and Mr. Hugh Neville too did not agree with him. "The cramped and rocky creek known as the Galle harbour" thought Mr. Neville, could not be indentified "with the capacious limen or lagoon and tranquil inland harbour often spoken of in connection with the emporium of Kalah" and "the numerous Islands lining the shore which formed such a striking description of the coast by the earlier writers" could not be found in or near Galle which "owed its civilization to comparatively recent times" and "possessed few ancient historical traditions and no historical remains", and that the purely Tamil district of Kalah which "owned the sway of the Maharajas of Zabedj, the Sultans of the Isles" could not be traced to any part of the Southern Province. He also rightly thought that the North Western coast of Ceylon extending from Kalpitiya to Jaffna contained the port which was a great centre of trade from 500 B.C., to a comparatively recent time, and "that it was separated from the capital of the Sinhalese by jealousies that account for the silence of the Sinhalese chroniclers". He was, however, not sure of the location of Kalah, and was inclined to hold, perhaps on account of the similarity of sound, "that the coast around and opposite to Kalpitiya formed the centre of trade and that the emporium was not one defined spot, but a cluster of pretty ports, all bartering the luxuries of the Far East for silver, and the wares af Europe, Persia and Ethiopia; while the site of Tammanna Nuvara with the adjacent ruins of Mahatabawa was the capital of the ruler who governed under the Sultans of Zabedj."*

* J. C. B.R.A.S., vol. vii, pt. ii, pp. 57, et seq.

Professor Q. Muller Hess of Bern in the "Perigrinations of Indian Buddhists in Burma and in the Sunda Islands," while speaking on the situation of Kalah said that he would substitute the North-West coast of the Island of Ceylon for Point de Galle.*

Thus it will be seen that "the central emporium of commerce, which in turn enriched every country of Western Asia, elevated the merchants of Tyre to the ranks of princes, fostered the renown of the Ptolemies, rendered the wealth and the precious products of Arabia a gorgeous mystery, freighted the Tigris with 'barbaric pearl and gold,' and identified the merchants of Bagdad and the mariners of Bassora with associations of adventure and romance" was neither Point de Galle nor Kalpitiya, but Mátoṭa, Kadiramalai and Kayts in the kingdom of Jaffna.†

---

* Ind. Anti.. vol. xlii, p. 41.

† Tennent vol. i, p 392

CHAPTER VI

Sources and Synchronisms.

FROM the fourth to the ninth century A.D., very little can be gathered about the history of the Northern Kingdom. The Mahávaṅsa mentions only a few stray events and Tamil literature is almost blank during this period. Whatever can be pieced together should be taken from the Mahávaṅsa and the Yáḷpáṇa Vaipava Málai and tested in the light of South Indian inscriptions. As the Vaipava Málai is a work written independently of the Siṅhalese Chronicles, it will not be out of place to look into some of the chronological puzzles raised by it as we proceed.

The Vaipava Málai, like the Mahávaṅsa, says that Vijaya died a short time after his marriage with a 'woman from Páṇḍi', that he left no issue, that his minister took charge of the kingdom for a year, that his brother's son Páṇḍuvása came from Láḍa and that he "was the founder of an illustrious dynasty which continued to reign over Laṅká for numerous generations."*

The events concerning the Northern kingdom as far as the fourth century A.D., have been already narrated in Chapter II, and the events here related are those after that period.

It is said that in Saka 358 or 436 A.D., Kuḷakkóṭṭu Mahá Rájá, a Chóḷa king, came to Trincomalie and began

* Y. V. M., p. 4.

to make extensive repairs to the temple Tirukóṇésar Kóvil at Tambalagámam, while Páṇḍu Mahá Rájá was ruling Laṅká from Anurádhapura, and that the latter expelled the Mukkuvas who were helping the Siṅhalese 'traders who supplied dry fish to foreign markets,' from Kírimalai in Jaffna.* Being a Tamil and perhaps a Hindu, it is no wonder that Páṇḍu was instrumental in driving away the Mukkuvas who were desecrating such a holy place as Kírimalai, and thereby were a source of great annoyance to the Hindus. The Chiefs of these Mukkuvas, who afterwards settled at Batticaloa, are still remembered locally by the application of their names to Usmán Tuṛai and Séntánkaḷam, places close to Kírimalai from which they were expelled. The year of Kuḷakkóṭṭan's arrival at Trincomalie falls within the reign of Páṇḍu who, according to the Mahávaṅsa, held Anurádhapura from 434 to 439 A.D.†

The Vaipava Málai closely follows the description given in Tirukóṇésala Puráṇam regarding the building of Tirukóṇésar Kóvil, the appointment of the Vanniyas to manage the temple and its temporalities and the attempted interference of King Páṇḍu's queen during the absence of Páṇḍu at Jaffna. But it does not mention the construction of the Kantalái tank by Kuḷakkóṭṭan with the help of the Siṅhalese minister of king Páṇḍu, as described in the Puráṇam.‡ From an inscription found near the Kantalái Tank it is supposed that Mahá Séna who reigned between 275 and 301 A.D.

* Y. V. M., pp. 4 & 5.

† Mah., chap. xxxviii.

‡ Tiruk. P., Tirukulam Kanḍa Paḍalam.

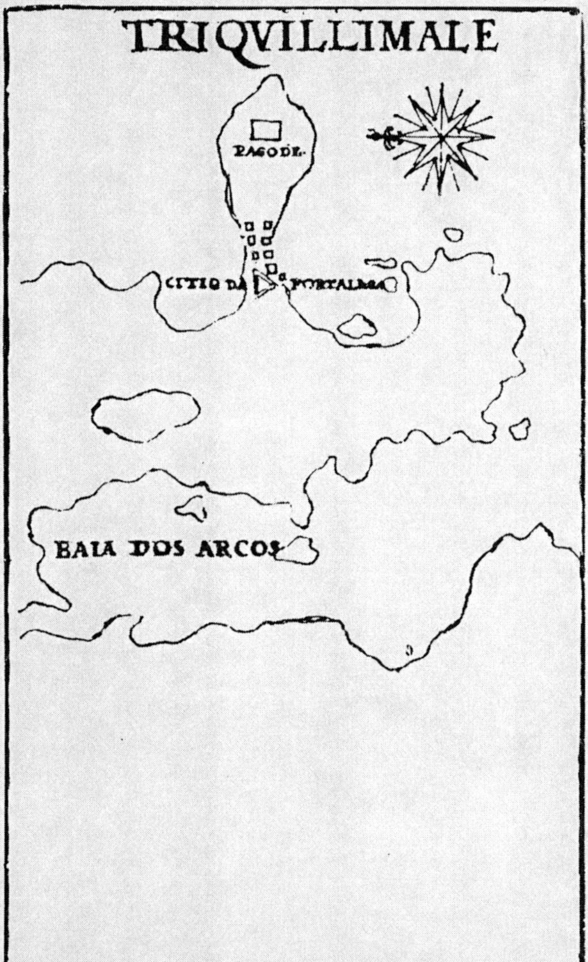

Sketch showing the position of the Temple of Tirukónésvaram from a Portuguese drawing.

face page 228.] [With permission of C.B.R.A.S.]

built that tank. But it is not included in the list of the sixteen tanks mentioned in the Maháyaṅsa as those that were built by him.* As Mahá Séna is chronologically placed about 150 years earlier than Kuḷakkóṭṭan, it is but reasonable to suppose that the tank was built by Mahá Séna and that Kuḷakkóṭṭan repaired and enlarged it for the purpose of irrigating the lands at Tambalagámam which he specially reserved for the maintenance of the temple.

According to the Kónesar Kalveṭṭu and the Tirukóṇésala Puráṇam, Kuḷakkóṭṭan first introduced the Vanniyas into Ceylon as managers of the temple at Trincomalie. It does not appear why the Vanniyas should have been imported as temple managers in preference to all others. Evidently the Vanniyas, who belonged to a fighting caste in India, accompanied the several Tamil invaders who came over from India, for the purpose of conquest, and remained behind. Later they set themselves up as petty Chiefs in different parts of the Island and usurped the management of the Trincomalie temple which possessed a considerable revenue. The two solitary Vanniya Chiefs said to have been brought here in 436 A.D., could not possibly have multiplied so fast and so effectively within a period of 150 years as to occupy all the important places in the Vannis and to make it necessary for Aggrabódhi I, the king of Anurádhapura, to take very elaborate steps in 593 A.D., to put them down. These Vanniyas, who became the petty Chiefs of the tract of land lying between Trincomalie and Mannar, served for a

* Mah. chap. xxxvii.

long time as a buffer state between the Siṅhalese of the South and the Tamils of the North, being at times independent and at times submissive to the one or the other as occasion demanded.

A copper plate grant of the Western Chaḷukya king Pulikésin I of Saka 411 (489-490 A.D) mentions the Simhala king as having paid tribute to him.* This must have been during the time of Kassapa I or Kumára Dása. This is perhaps the earliest mention of the word 'Siṅhala' in an authoritative Indian record.

The new dynasty of kings beginning with Mahá Nága, though said in the Mahávaṅsa† to be of the Móriya or of the Okáka race, appears in reality to be a blend of the Nága and the Tamil. There is no mention either of the Móriya dynasty or of the Okáka (Ikshváku) before the time of Mahánága whose name belies such a supposition. This portion of the Mahávaṅsa was written in the twelfth century A.D., and it is no wonder that a high-sounding title was given to these kings who rose suddenly like mushrooms. Their Nága origin and their Tamil connections are clearly seen from the Nága name of the first king and from the several Tamil armies raised by them to wage war. The statue on the side of a rock at Weligama in the Southern Province commonly known as Kushṭa Rájá is probably that of Aggrabódhi I, as the vihára close to the rock is known as Aggrabódhi vihára. The pendent earlobes loaded with heavy ear ornaments including that of the head of a snake stamps him as a Nága or a Tamil.

---

* Ind. Ant., vol. vii, p. 215.

† Mah., chap. xli.

In the year Saka 515 (593 A.D.,) Aggrabódhi Mahá Rájá perceived that the then reigning Vanniyas were elated with pride and fancied themselves independent kings. He therefore reduced them to their true position, namely that of *Adikaris*, with which they had ever afterwards to remain content.* This king must have been Aggrabódhi I who reigned from 564 to 598 A.D., according to the Editors of the Mahávaṅsa, and from 583 to 617 A.D., as calculated from the date of accession given in the Rájaratnácari to Ambaherana Salaméwan †

Aggrabódhi II built the Relic house Rajayaṭana in Nágadípa.‡ During the reign of Síla Méghavanna (614-623 A.D.,) Sri Nága the Chief, the uncle of Jeṭṭha Tissa—and probably the ruler of the Northern dominion—proceeded to India, gathered together a great number of Tamils, returned to 'the northern part of the country' and tried to take it. But the king having heard of it went up with an army, gave battle at the village called Raja Mittaka, killed Sri Nága, captured a great number of his followers and after he had treated them most cruelly gave them away as slaves to different viháras in the Island.¶

The Pallava king Simha Vishnu, who, according to Professor Jouveau Dubreuil, reigned from 590 to 618 A.D.,§ says in one of his inscriptions that he vanquished "the Siṅhala king who was proud of the strength of his

---

* Y. V. M., p. 7.

† Mah., Editor's List of Kings; Rajarat., p. 77.

‡ Ibid chap. xliii, v. 62.

¶ Ibid xliv, vv. 70—73.

§ Pallavas, p. 73.

arms,"* but no mention of such an invasion is made in the Sinhalese Chronicles. The army of Tamils brought by Sri Nága for the purpose of invading the northern part of Ceylon, might have been very probably a Pallava army given by Simha Vishnu and hence his boast of a victory in spite of a defeat.

Aggrabódhi III who was defeated and driven away by Jeṭṭha Tissa came back with a large army of Tamils and defeated Jeṭṭha Tissa who committed suicide on the battle field.† In the 15th year of the reign of Aggrabódhi III, Dáṭhásiva the general of Jeṭṭha Tissa, who was sent by the latter to collect an army before he took the battle field, returned with an army of Tamils and defeated the king who fled to India.‡ During the reigns of Aggrabódhi III and Dáṭhópatissa I, all the viháras and public buildings were despoiled of their wealth to keep up the Tamil armies of both parties.¶

Dáṭhópatissa, who was defeated by Kassapa II, returned with an army from India, fought against Kassapa and was killed.§ During these reigns the Tamil influence had become so great that they held all high offices and supreme power.‖ The Tamil armies brought

---

* S. I. I., vol. ii, p. 356.

The Kasakudi plates state that Simha Vishnu vanquished the Malaya, Kalabra, Maḷava, Chóḷa and Pāṇḍya (kings), the Simhala (king) who was proud of the strength of his arms and the Kéralas.

† Mah., chap. xliv, vv. 105—112.

‡ Ibid 125—128.

¶ Ibid 131—135.

§ Ibid 153.

‖ Ibid xlv, v. 12.

to Ceylon during this period must have been obtained from the Pallava kings of Káñci, for the Páṇḍya and the Chóḷa Powers were in their wane and were not heard of during the few centuries of Pallava supremacy.

On the death of Kassapa II, his nephew Dappula I took charge of the kingdom and attempted to rid the country of the Tamil officers of influence but Hattha-dáṭha, the nephew of Dáṭhópatissa, who fled to India on the death of the latter, on receiving a message hastened to the Island with an army of Tamils. Whereupon all the Tamils who dwelt in the Island deserted the king (Dappula I) and joined Hattha-dáṭha. He having won over the great men of the Tamil party seized the royal city and proclaimed himself king under the name of Dáṭhópatissa II.*

The continuous influence and authority of the Tamils during this period is further indicated in the reign of Aggrabódhi IV who succeeded Dáṭhópatissa II, by the tradition that a wealthy Tamil named Potha-Kuṭṭha built a house of devotion called Máṭambiya, the commander of the king's army named Potthasáta built a parivéṇa at the Jetavana Vihára, a Tamil named Mahakanda built a parivéṇa and called it by his own name and another built the Cullapantha parivéṇa. This king Aggrabódhi IV was the first to take his abode at the town of Pulathi or Polonnaruwa.† After his (Aggrabódhi's) death the wealthy Tamil Potha-kuṭṭha took over the control of affairs into his own hands leaving his creatures Datta and

* Mah., chap: xiv, vv. 18—22.

† Ibid xlvi.

Hattha-dáṭha to bear the name of kings one after the other.*

Máṇavamma, the son of Kassapa II, who succeeded Hattha-dáṭha II, after his marriage with Saṅgha the daughter of the Rája of Malaya, remained in concealment with her in the Northern country until it came to the ears of Hattha-dáṭha I. Then he went over to India and entered the service of Narasiṁha who must have been the Pallava king Narasimhavarman I. He, by his feats of valour, so pleased the Pallava king as to win his support and the gift of an army to go and fight for his kingdom. He was, however, defeated by Dáṭhópatissa (Hathadáṭha I?) and had to return to his patron for further help. Returning to the attack with another army given to him by Narasimha, he appears to have landed at a port in Jaffna, for it is said that after resting for three days at the place where he disembarked he began to fight, took the northern country and subdued the inhabitants thereof. He then marched towards the city of Anurádhapura, met Potha kuṭṭha and Hattha dáṭha II in battle, defeated them and raised the imperial banner of sovereignty over all Laṅká.† As Máṇavamma escaped to India during the time of Dáṭhópatissa II and came on his second expedition at the end of the reign of Hatthadáṭha II, he must have remained with Narasimha for 25 years.

According to the Kasakudi plates‡ of the Pallava king Nandivarman II (717—779 A.D.,) one of his pre-

* Mah., chap : xlvi.

† Ibid xlvii.

‡ S. I. I., vol. ii, p. 343.

decessors on the throne, Narasimhavarman I, who defeated the Chaḷukya king Pulikesin II at the battle of Vátápi, where the Saiva Saint Siru Toṇḍar is alleged to have fought on the side of the Pallavas,* is said to have surpassed "the glory of the valour of Ráma by his conquest of Lanka". The help rendered by Máṇavamma to Narasimhavarman I in defeating Pulikesin II who was otherwise known as Chaḷukya Vallabha, perhaps at the battle of Vátápi, is described in the Mahávaṅsa.† The reign of Narasimhavarman I is said to have lasted from 630 to 668 A.D., a period of 38 years.‡ The second expedition of Máṇavamma to Ceylon was therefore in 668 A. D., or sometime earlier. But according to the editor of the Mahávaṅsa Máṇavamma began to reign in 691 A.D.,¶ which shows a discrepancy of 23 years. The mistake committed by Mudr: Wijesiṅha in marking out the reigns of the kings of Ceylon can easily be tested in this instance.

The earliest historical date of absolute certainty connected with the chronology of Ceylon kings is that of

---

* "மன்னவர்க் குத்தண்டுபோய் வடபுலத்துவாதாவித்
தொன்னகரந் துகளாகத்துளை நெடுங்கை வரையுகைத்துப்
பன்மணியு நிதிக்குவையும் பகட்டினமும் பரித்தொகையு
மின்னனவெண்ணிலகவர்ந்தே யிகலரசன் முன் கொணர்ந்தார்"

Periya P., Siṛutoṇḍarpuráṇam.

He (Siṛutoṇḍar) led the (Pallava) king's army, destroyed the ancient city of Vátápi (Badami) in the Northern country and brought before the king gems and treasure, crowds of horses and elephants and other countless spoils of viotory.

† Mah., chap. xlvii, vv. 15—27.

‡ Dekkan, p. 70.

¶ Mah., Table of Ceylon Kings, No. 90.

the coronation of Sáhasa Malla, which is given in one of his Polonnaruwa inscriptions, as Tuesday the 12th in the bright half of Binera, 1743 years, 3 months and 27 days after the death of Buddha.* Dr. Fleet has examined this date and has found it to agree with the 23rd day of August 1200 A.D.† Taking this date as the basis and calculating backwards, allotting the traditional regnal years as given in the Mahávaṅsa to each sovereign, the following table of the dates of accession of 45 sovereigns from Máṇavamma to Sáhasa Malla, has been prepared. The only difference is that 48 years as stated in the Maháváṅsa ‡ and not 36 as incorrectly given by the editor, are assigned to Mahinda V, on the suggestion made by Dr. E. Hultzsch.¶ According to this list it will be seen that the date of accession of Parákrama Báhu I (1153 A.D.) agrees with that given by Nikáya Saṅgrahawa (1696 A.B.),§ but there is a difference of four years between the date of accession of Séna I (823 A.D.) as found in this table and that given by Nikáya Saṅgrahawa (1362 A.B.). ‖ The dates of accession of the kings who ruled before Séna, I. calculated from the date found in the Nikáya Saṅgrahawa are therefore included in the table for comparison.

---

* Muller, No. 156.

† J. R. A. S. 1909, pp. 327, 331.

‡ Mah., chap. lv, v. 33.

¶ J. R. A. S. 1913, p. 523.

§ Nik. San., p. 20.

‖ Ibid p. 18.

No.	Names of kings.	Amended date.	Date as per Nik. Sang.	Duration of reign.
90	Mánavamma ...	668 A.D.	664 A.D.	35
91	Aggrabódhi v ...	703	699	6
92	Kassapa iii ...	709	705	6
93	Mahinda i ...	715	711	3
94	Aggrabódhi vi ...	718	714	40
95	Aggrabódhi vii ...	758	754	6
96	Mahinda ii ...	764	760	20
97	Dappula ii ...	784	780	5
98	Mahinda iii ...	789	785	4
99	Aggrabódhi viii ...	793	789	11
100	Dappula iii ...	804	800	16
101	Aggrabódhi ix ...	820	816	3
102	Séna i ...	823	819	20
103	Séna ii ...	843	...	35
104	Udaya i ...	878	...	11
105	Kassapa iv ...	889	...	17
106	Kassapa v ...	906	...	10
107	Dappula iv ...	916	...	—.7.
108	Dappula v ...	917	...	12
109	Udaya ii ...	929	...	3
110	Séna iii ...	932	...	9
111	Udaya iii ...	941	...	8
112	Séna iv ...	949	...	3
113	Mahinda iv ...	952	...	16
114	Séna v ...	968	...	10
115	Mahinda v ...	978	...	48
116	Interregnum Vikrama Báhu ...	1026	...	12
117	Kitti the General ...	1038	...	—.—.8
118	Mahálána Kitti ...	1038	...	3
119	Vikkama Páṇḍu ...	1041	...	1
120	Jagatipala ...	1042	...	4
121	Parákkama ...	1046	...	2
122	Lokessara ...	1048	...	6
123	Vijaya Báhu i ...	1054	...	55
124	Jayabáhu ...	1109	...	1
125	Vikkrama Báhu i ...	1110	...	21
126	Gaja Báhu ii ...	1131	...	22
127	Parákkrama Báhu i ...	1153	...	33
128	Vijaya Báhu ii ...	1186	...	1
129	Mahinda vi ...	1187	...	0-0-5
130	Kitti Nissanka ...	1187	...	9
131	Vikkrama Báhu ii ...	1196	...	0-3
132	Códaganga ...	1196	...	0-9
133	Lilavati ...	1197	...	3
134	Sáhasa Malla ...	1200	...	2

If 668 A. D. be taken as the correct year of Máṇavamma's victory in Ceylon and therefore of his accession, he could not have been present at the battle of Vátápi which took place in 642 A. D.,* as his stay in Narasimhavarman's Court did not exceed 25 years. He must have reached Káñci at least three years before the battle of Vátápi, i.e., in 639 A.D. Twenty five years from that date would be 664 A. D, the date calculated according to Nikáya Saṅgrahawa. Therefore 664 A. D. is more likely to have been the date of Máṇavamma's accession than 668 A.D., and the synchronism between the events in South Indian history and of the Mahávaṅsa is thus established. The reigns of the kings of Ceylon referred to hereafter are according to the above table.

The archaic Tamil inscription found at the village of Sendalai and inscribed by one Perumbiḍugu Muttaraiyaṉ Svaraṉ Máṟaṉ, supposed to be a feudatory and general of the Pallava kings, in which his conquest of Maṇalúr (Jaffna) is mentioned,† may presumably refer to the conquest of Jaffna by Máṇavamma with the help of the Pallava general. The conjecture of Mr: Gopinath Row that Svaraṉ Máṟaṉ was a contemporary of Paramésvaravarman II ‡ cannot therefore be correct.

---

* Dekkan, p. 111.

† "பேய்—புண்ணார்ந்து கையூம்பப் போர்மணலூர் வென்றதே
மண்ணார்ந்தசீர் மாறன்வாள்."

S. Tamil, vol. vi, p. 11.

The sword of noble Máran who enjoyed his possessions, conquered the warlike Mánalúr (Jaffna) so that ghouls feasted (on the dead bodies left on the battle field).

‡ S. Tamil, vol. vi, pp. 9 & 10.

It also appears from Chaḷukya and Pallava inscriptions that Máṇavamma helped the Southern confederacy to which the Pallavas belonged, with an army in 674 A. D. when the Chaḷukya king Vikramáditya was defeated at Uragapuram (Uṛaiyúr) on the southern banks of the Kávéri.* The Chaḷukya king had to contend against the Páṇḍya, the Chóḷa—the king of the Kávérí,—the Siṅhala and other kings. It is therefore not unlikely that Máṇavamma who was the friend of Narasimha was also attached to Paramésvaravarman I, the then king of the Pallavas. So when the latter "was in danger it was his duty to act according to the dictates of the simplest feeling of gratefulness."

In the Vakkaléri plates of the Chaḷukya king Kírtivarman II, of 757 A.D., it is said that Vinayaditya Satyasraya one of his predecessors levied tribute from the "rulers of Kávéra, Parasika, Simhala and other islands."† By the words 'other islands' were meant 'Jaffna and its dependent islands', and it can be inferred that a separate king was ruling over them. Thirty years after the date of this grant, according to Wilson, the Buddhists were expelled from the neighbourhood of Káñci to Ceylon. In 788 A.D., Ahalanka, a Jain teacher from Sravana Belgola, who had been partly educated in the Buddha college at Ponataya (near Trivalúr, south of Káñci) had a discus-

---

* Kuram plates (S. I. I., vol. i, p. 154.)
Udayendiram plates (S. I. I., vol. ii, p. 371.)
Gadval plates (Ep. Ind., vol. x, No. 22.)
Kendur plates (Ep. Ind., vol. ix, No. 29.)

† Ind. Ant., vol. viii, p. 28.

sion with them in the presence of the last Bauddha prince, Hémasítala, and on his overcoming them, the prince became a Jain and the Buddhists were banished to Ceylon.*

Mahinda II (764-784 A.D.) the son of Aggrabódhi VI (718-758 A.D.) was at the time of the death of Aggrabódhi VII (758-764 A. D) living at Mahathitha (Mátoṭa) having gone to the sea-board on some business of the king. When he heard of the king's death, he hastened back to the capital. " Meanwhile the chieftains and land-lords of the Northern districts took possession of the country by force and withheld its revenues and when he came to hear of this he proceeded to the Northern country with a large force and subdued all the chieftains together with their servants."† Dappula, a cousin of Mahinda, was possessed of great wealth and influence and took up arms against him. During this civil war the Northern country was greatly neglected although it is said in the Mahávaṅsa that after the defeat of Dappula, Mahinda had again to take an army to the Northern country to suddue the rebellious chieftains.‡

As stated at the beginning of this chapter very little is known of the doings of the kings of Jaffna from the fourth to the end of the eighth century A. D. The authority wielded by the later kings of Anurádhapura was spasmodic and if a kingdom actually existed in the North, it is not now known if the Nágavamsa kings

* Mackenzie, vol i, p. lxv.

† Mah., chap. xlviii, vv. 80, 83, 84.

‡ Ibid 95, 96.

continued to rule or the country was under chieftains whose power was ephemeral. The last authoritative account of the existence of a separate king in Jaffna was that of the Greek writer Cosmas in the fifth century A. D.

Simhavishnu, a Pallava king, has left epigraphical records that he conquered Ceylon about the end of the sixth century* and a Pallava army helped Máṇavamma to conquer Ceylon about 664 A. D. During these invasions the Pallava armies must have landed at Jaffna and occupied that country first and there is evidence that there was continual intercourse between Ceylon and the Pallava country during this period. As Káñcipuram was the centre of Buddhistic culture such intercourse would have been natural enough. Buddhagosha of Ceylon fame was a native of Káñcipuram. Vatsyáyana the author of Nyaya Báshya was a Tamil of Káñci and lived about 400 A.D. He was known by the name of Pak ḻḷa Swámi, a name which designates his Ceylon origin. Dig Nága of 500 A.D., Dharmapála of 600 A.D. and other Buddhist logicians lived and flourished at Káñcipuram.† In 640 A.D., when Hiouen Thsang the Chinese traveller was at Káñci and intended to go to Ceylon, 300 monks came from there and said that the king had died and there was famine and disorder in the country. His intended visit was therefore abandoned.‡ This must have been on the death of Dáṭhópatissa II and when Potha Kuṭṭha, the Tamil, had taken the Government into his own hands.

* S. I. I., vol. ii, p. 356; Anc. Ind., p. 425.

† Ind. Ant., vol. xliv, p. 87.

‡ Anc. Ind.; Pallavas.

Traces of Pallava occupation are found in Jaffna even now. Pallvaráyankaṭṭu a division in the Púnakari district, the worship of Pótharáyer, a title by which Pallava kings were known and the existence of such families as Nolambaráyar and of the name Nanni (asylum of truth), a *biruda* of the Nolambas of Dharmapuri, a Pallava offshoot, clearly testify to some sort of Pallava occupation. The surmise that Jaffna was during this period under the authority of the Pallavas will therefore not be far wrong.

About the ninth century the Pallava supremacy in South India began to wane overshadowed by the rising power of the Chaḷukyas and about the end of that century the Chóḷas began to reassert their supremacy. Among the Sinhalese, internal dissensions were rife. Tamil influence was gaining ground in the Sinhalese capital. Tamil nobles held all positions of rank and power in Court and Sinhalese princes were fighting against each other with the aid of Tamil armies. It is therefore not surprising that Ugra Singaṉ found an opportunity amidst these factions and party-struggles to seize the throne of Kadiramalai and to establish himself as an independent sovereign.

"In 717 Sáliváhana" (795 A.D.) it is said, that "Ugra Singaṉ, a prince of the dynasty founded by king Vijaya's brother made a descent upon Lanká with a numerous force from *Vadathesam* (India) and after a severe struggle possessed himself of one half of Lanká which had been lost to his dynasty for a long time. He reigned at Kadiramalai while another king reigned over the Southern territories."* The fact that he was mentioned as a prince belonging to the dynasty of Páṇḍuvasa, Vijaya's nephew, by mistake called brother, and that later on he transferred his capital from Kadiramalai to Siṅgai Nagar as related below, stamps him as a descendant of one of those Kaliṅga colonists who emigrated with Vijaya and settled down at Siṅgai Nagar or Siṅhapura.† Conjecture has identified him with Kaliṅga Magha‡ who according to the Mahávaṅsa conquered the North of Ceylon in 1215 A.D.; for he too "after a severe struggle possessed himself of one half of Laṅká." The later doings ascribed to Ugra Siṅgaṉ in the Vaipava Málai, if true, will not admit of such an identification; and on the other hand Kaliṅga Magha reigned at Polonnaruwa and not at Kadira Malai. The statement that Ugra Siṅgaṉ reigned over the Northern portion of Laṅká with his capital at Kadiramalai while another king reigned over the Southern territories clearly defines the position of Kadira Malai, and refutes the idea that it is identical with Kataragama in the South, as stated in the Kailáya Málai and believed by the author of the Vaipava Málai. Ugra Siṅgaṉ was probably the progenitor of that virile dynasty that supplied Kaliṅga Chakravarties to the throne of Polonnaruwa and Árya Chakravarties to the throne of Jaffna.

We may safely pass over the legends that have gathered round the name of Ugra Siṅgaṉ and his son

---

* Y. V. M., p. 8.

† Vide supra, chap. ii, p. 54.

‡ A theory propounded by the Hon'ble. Mr. H. W. Codrington and Rev. S. Gnanapragásar.

borrowed perhaps from similar legends connected with Vijaya and admit only such facts as are of historical worth: that he belonged to the Kaliṅga Chakravarti race, that he conquered North Ceylon and reigned at Kadira Malai; and that he fell in love with Márutappiravíkavalli, a Chóḷa princess who came on a pilgrimage to Kírimalai, carried her off forcibly and married her*—a political move intended perhaps to raise himself in the estimation of his people by making sure that his consort at least had royal blood in her veins.

Ugra Siṅgaṉ passed through the Vannis, received the voluntary submission of the seven Vanniyas and imposed a tribute upon them,† perhaps the incident referred to in the Mahávaṅsa as the insubordination of the chieftains of the Northern countries and their subjugation by Mahinda II.‡

Ugra Siṅgaṉ assisted his wife to complete the building of the Kandaswamy temple at Máviṭṭapuram which she had begun before her marriage. At her request her father the Chóḷá (?) king sent a Brahman family to officiate at the temple together with the necessary images. They landed at the place which is now known as Káṅkésanturai.¶ This port which was previously known as Gáyáturai, or the place of embarkation for Buddhist pilgrims to Gáyá, and afterwards corrupted to Kásáturai, was from this date called Káṅkésanturai the harbour or port at which the image of Káṅgéyan (Kandaswamy) was landed.

* Y. V. M. pp. 9—11.

† Ibid 9.

‡ Mah., chap. xlviii.

¶ Y. V. M., pp. 10-11.

After some time Ugra Siṅgaṉ transferred his capital from Kadira Malai to Siṅgai Nagar, either because the latter was his birth place or at any rate in order to live among people of his own country and race. The statement in the Vaipava Málai that he removed to Seṅgadaga Nagar* (another name for Kandy) is certainly incorrect. It must have been a clerical error of a later copyist, or perhaps of Mailvágana Pulavar himself, who being ignorant of the existence of Siṅgai Nagar, in spite of the fact that the name appears in almost all the Tamil works composed during the time of the Jaffna kings, deliberately changed it to Seṅgadaka Nagar, in order to make it fit in with the mistaken view that Kadira Malai was the present Kataragama. The etymological difference between the two names is indeed very little.

While reigning at Siṅgai Nagar, Ugra Siṅgaṉ had two children—a son and a daughter—who, according to the Vaipava Málai, were united in incestuous marriage and the son succeeded his father under the name of Jeyatuṅga Vara Rája Siṅgaṉ.† The legend of a brother marrying a sister belongs really to a much earlier age and the author of the Mahávaṅsa too made a similar use of it in the case of Vijaya's parents.‡ Whatever the truth of this tradition may be, it is safe to assume that it was during the reign of this Jeyatuṅga that a minstrel, a Páṇaṉ by caste, as all minstrels of that time were, came to his Court and was presented with a sandy uninhabited portion of Jaffna as a

* Y. V. M. p. 12.

† Ibid 12 & 13.

‡ Mah., chap. vi.

reward for his music and his songs.* That he was presented with a region called *Manattidal* in the northern part of Lanká, that he was made the sovereign thereof by the king of Kandy, and that the place was occupied by the colonists brought over from India by the minstrel are no doubt vague statements made by the author of the Vaipava Málai† without understanding the purport of the existing tradition. He was unaware of the mischief that was to be caused by such ignorance and recklessness on his part. Sengadaka Nagar was not in existence then; no Jeyatunga ever reigned at Kandy; and never within historical times was Jaffna a sandy desert fit only to be presented to a Páṇaṉ. The improbability of the story induced one of the later writers of Jaffna history to alter "Sengadaka Nagar" to "Anurádhapura" and to change the name of Jeyatunga into Eléla, who had lived and died a thousand years earlier. He even went so far as to mutilate the Tamil verse ascribed to Víra Rágavaṉ to fit in with his theory.‡ It

---

* Y. V. M., p. 13.

† Ibid.

‡ The verse ascribed to Kavi Vira Rághavaṉ is—

நரைகோட் டிளங்கன்று நல்வளநாடு நயந்தளிப்பான்
விரைபூட்டுதார்ப்புய வெற்பீழ மன்னனென்றே விரும்பிக்
கரையோட்ட மீதின் மரக்கலம் போட்டுன்னைக் காணவந்தால்
திரைபோட்டு நீயிருந்தாய் சிங்கைபூப சிரோன்மணியே.

Tani Páḍal, vol. ii, p, 21.

I came sailing along the coast on a vessel with the idea that the king of Iḷam will graciously grant me a grey young tusker and fertile lands, but you the crest Jewel of Singai sat behind a curtain (to receive me).

[The words 'சிங்கைபூப' in the above verse were altered to 'ஏலேலசிங்க' by the author of the Tamil History of Jaffna.]

did not, however, strike him that a man of the Páṇa caste and a blind one to boot as supposed by him, would never have been invested with sovereignty even by a foreign potentate ignorant of all ideas of caste. The original mistake of changing Siṅgai Nagar into Seṅgaḋaka Nagar had to be followed up with these other mistakes and misconceptions in order to make a plausible story out of the tradition.

The author of the Vaipava Málai has fallen into another error in calling the Páṇa minstrel 'the blind poet Víra Rághavaṉ.'* He has mixed up Andaka Kavi Víra Rághava Mudaliyár, a blind Veḷḷáḷa poet, who visited the Court of Pararájasékaraṉ at Jaffna at a much later period,† with the Páṇa minstrel who was honoured by Jeyatuṅga. The legend of the minstrel appears in Kailáya Málai, Vaiyápáḋal, Trincomalie Kalveṭṭu and Dakshiṇa Kailása Puráṇam. In none of these is the name of the man given; nor is he anywhere described as blind. The legend in the Dakshiṇa Kailása Puráṇam takes the lutist to the time of Vibíshaṇa and is clearly a later interpolation.‡

---

* Kailáya Málai does not state that Yaḷpáṇaṉ was blind or that his name was Víra Rághavaṉ.

"—மங்காத

பாவலர்கள்வேந்தன் பகருமியாழ்ப்பாணன்

காவலன்றன்மீது கவிதைசொல்லி—நாவலர்முன்

ஆனகவியாழினமை வுறவாசித்திடலும்."

K. M., p. 4,

† Vide infra, chap viii

‡ There are two printed versions of the Puráṇam, in one of which the verses regarding the lutist are omitted as interpolations.

The Páṇaṉ returned to India and probably induced some members of his tribe as impecunious as himself to accompany him to this land of promise, and it is surmised that their place of settlement was that part of the city of Jaffna which is known at present as Pásaiyúr and Karaiyúr. As some Páṇar were also fishers by profession, in Jaffna too they probably took to fishing for want of a better occupation.* The settlement would have been in honour of the lutist ordinarily called 'Yáḻpáṇam' and coming to be so known to the mariners and traders who called at the ports which were close by, it would have lent its name in course of time, particularly among such strangers, to the chief town and ultimately to the district itself. But the name did not become popular among the inhabitants of Jaffna until the Portuguese built the town close to the Páṇa settlement and called it Jaffna, and although the name is now used in a wider sense to include the whole district, yet to the people of Jaffna the town only is still known as Yáḻpáṇam.

The earliest mention of the word 'Yáḻpáṇam' in Tamil literature is found in the Tirupugaḻ of Aruṇagiri Nátar, in which it is called Yáḻpáṇa Náyanár Paṭṭinam.† The author mistook the lutist of the Jaffna legend to be

---

* This theory was first propounded by Rev. S. Gnanapragásar, O. M. I.

† "ஏத்தாதாளுந் தர்ப்பண செபமொடு
நீத்தார் ஞானம் பற்றிய குருபர
யாப்பாராயுஞ் சொற்றமிழருட்கு ... ... முருகோனே
ஏற்போர் தாம்வந் திச்சையின் மகிழ்வோடு
வாய்ப்பாய் வாழும் பொற்பீசபை நெடுமெதில்
யாழ்ப்பாணயன் பட்டினமருவிய ... பெருமானே"

Tirup.

the Yáḻpáṉa Náyanár who accompanied the Saint Sampanda Múrti and set his Dévárams to music. Aruṇagiri was a contemporary of Villiputtúrar who was the Court poet of Áḻkoṇḍáṉ, the Koṅgu king, at whose request he is said to have composed the Mahábhárata in Tamil. Áḻkoṇḍáṉ reigned about the middle of the 15th century, A.D.* Yaḻpáṇam is mentioned in several inscriptions of the Sétupatis in the first quarter of the 17th century,† and it is referred to in the mutilated form Népáḻam in some Telugu works also of the 17th century.‡ The Kókila Sandésaya, a Siṅhalese work of the middle of

---

* S. Tamil, vol. vii, p. 405.

† (a) In a copper plate grant of Saka 1526, Mutu Vijaya Raghunátha Sétupati is said to have destroyed Īḻam, Kambalam and Yáḻpáṇa town and had an elephant hunt ("ஈளமுகம்பளமும்யாழ்பாணமும்பட்டணமும்அளித்துகெசவேட்டைகொண்டருளிய").

(b) In a copper plate grant of Saka 1607 granted by Hiranya Garbhayaji Ragunátha Sétupati Kaṭṭa Tévar the following words occur :—

"ஈளமுங்கொங்கும் யாப்பாணப் பட்டணமும் இம்மண்டலமுமளித்து கெச வேட்டைகொண்டருளிய"

Arch. S. S. I., vol. iv.

[Similar eulogies appear in several inscriptions of other Sétupatis extending even as far as Saka 1706, an empty boast which had not the slightest foundation of truth, as by the time the Sétupatis were made Chieftains of Ramnad (1604) A.D.) Jaffna had come under the influence of the Portuguese.]

‡ Raghunáthabhyudáyam of Vijayarághava Nayáka
Sáhitya Súdha of Góvinda Dikshita
Sáhitya Ratnákara of Yagña Naráyana Díkshita
Raghunáthabhyudáyam of Rámabadramba

Sources

32

the 15th century calls the capital Yápápaṭuna.* Some therefore seem to think that the name is a contraction of Yápápaṭṭina or Yahápat paṭṭina, a Siṅhalese translation of Nallúr,† as Nallúr was the capital at the time the Siṅhalese work was composed. Now, Nallúr was not built before the Siṅgai Árya kings reached the zenith of their power. But the name 'Yáḻpáṇam' was certainly known to the Muhammedan travellers of the tenth and eleventh centuries though in the mutilated form of Zapage, Zabaj or Jabeh. Some others are of the opinion that 'Yáḻpáṇam' is the Tamil adaptation of the Siṅhalese name 'Yápaṇe'‡ which like many other Siṅhalese names of places in the district existed prior to the Tamil occupation. The Tamils are alleged to have tamilized it into Yápáṇam and Yáḻpáṇam and to have invented a fanciful derivation for the word by weaving the impro-

---

* "Ran dada kikini del bendi pá peleti rendu
Tentena sadá minimuttu digaṭa aluvidu
Nan siri sapiri niti kindu rinduge purabandu
Santósa venuṅ gos Yápápaṭun vadu."

Kók. San., v. 243.

Yápapaṭuna—which consists of rows of stately buildings decorated with golden flags, and which sheds an extraordinary brilliance on account of its valuable gems and stones glinting everywhere and which in point of splendour and charm can be compared only to the city of Alakamanda of god Vaisrávana—enter this city and worship it.

† This derivation was first suggested by Mr. S. W. Coomaraswamy, the author of "Jaffna Place Names."

‡ Yápane may be a name of pure Siṅhalese origin like Habarane, Tumpane, Balane, Ranne, etc.

bable legend of the lutist.* The surmise which is based on phonetic similarity only holds good for a similar derivation vice versa, and will have to remain a surmise until the town or village which was previously known as Yápaṉe is located. Was Yápaṉe different from Yápápaṭun or did both the names represent one and the same place? The present town of Yáḻpáṇam could not have been the Siṅhalese village of Yápaṉe as it was a jungle before the Portuguese conquest, and there are no grounds to believe that the fisher folk inhabiting Pásaiyúr and Karaiyúr which form a part of the town were Siṅhalese at one time. On the other hand, even the Siṅhalese fishers occupying the coast towns of Ceylon were at one time Tamils and the process of metamorphosis can still be seen at Negombo, Maravila and Chilaw. Yápaṉe or Jápáṉe as the Siṅhalese now call it must certainly be taken to be the Siṅhalese form of Yápáṇam or Yáḻpáṇam and not vice versa. It is not at all surprising to see the name appearing in Siṅhalese and Indian works earlier than in Tamil writings of Jaffna, for it appears that the application of the name for the whole district did not become popular among the inhabitants until the Portuguese period.

Owing to the confusion created by including Yáḻpáṇaṉ among the rulers of Jaffna, there is nothing in the Vaipava Málai to indicate that the descendents of Jeyatuṅga ruled over Jaffna until the time of Vijaya Kúḷaṅkai Siṅgai Árya Chakravarti. From the time of Kúḷaṅkai to the conquest of Seṇpakap Perumáḷ or Sapumal Kumaraya, the kings of Jaffna ruled indepen-

* The Hon'ble Mr. Horsburgh in the Ceylon Antiquary, vol. ii, pt. i, pp. 57 & 58.

dently without a break and it is therefore reasonable to think that the time of Kúḷaṅkai who was in fact the first to secure the throne of Jaffna on a sound basis should be placed somewhere in the 13th century, although the Vaipava Málai places him soon after Jeyatuṅga and Yáḻpáṇaṉ.* Three centuries passed between the time of Jeyatuṅga and that of Kúḷaṅkai and during this long interval, although the kings of the Kaliṅga dynasty of Ugra Siṅgaṉ passed through many vicissitudes and lost their independence several times over, yet they continued to reign even as feudatories and were slowly emerging into prominence as powerful rulers.

During the reign of Séna I (823-843 A.D.) the Páṇḍyaṉ king very probably Varaguṇa invaded Ceylon and soon made himself master of the northern part. He defeated Séna who fled from the capital and took refuge in the Malaya country. Prince Mahinda the king's brother committed suicide and Kassapa another brother fled. Polonnaruwa was sacked and the Páṇḍya carried away as spoils the sacred ornaments of the temple, the golden images, the *jayabera* and the bowl of Buddha. After plundering the capital he recovered a suitable ransom from Séna for the permanent retention of the Island and left the country.† A record in North Arcot mentions a victory of the Páṇḍyas over the Gaṅgas (who were about this time feudatories of the Gaṅga-Pallavas) which occurred about the middle of the ninth century at Tiruppirambiyam near Kumbakóṇam.‡ According to the

---

* Y. V. M., p. 14.

† Mah., chap. L; Puja., p. 31.

‡ S. I. I., vol. ii, p. 381.

Udayéndiram plates of the Báṇa king Prithivipathi II the Páṇḍya referred to was Varaguṇa as he it was that fought at Tiruppirambiyam.* So the Páṇḍyaṉ who made "an unprovoked assault" on Ceylon during the reign of Sèna I must have been Varaguṇa, mentioned in the Sinnamanúr plates as the successor of Rájasimman. The confusion in the traditional history of Jaffna which omitted to mention the successor of Jeyatuṅga and placed a crown on the brow of the low born Yáḻpánaṉ was perhaps due to the invasion of Varaguṇa. The conquest of Manaṟṟi referred to in a Kóvai verse quoted in Iṟayanár Akapporuḷ † was that of Jaffna by Varaguṇa during this period.

Mr. K. S. Srinivasa Pillai of Tanjore in his able work called 'Tamil Varaláṟu' while discussing the age of Máṇikkavásagar, one of the Tamil Saiva Saints,‡ gives several reasons, of which the mention of the Páṇḍya king Varaguṇa in his Tirukóvaiyár is one,¶ to prove that

---

* S. I. I., vol. ii, pt. ii, No. 76.

(†) மின்னேரொளி முத்தவெண் மணன்மேல் விரைநாறுபுன்னைப்
பொன்னேர் புதுமலர்த்தாய்ப் பொறிவண்டு முரன்றுபுல்லா
மன்னேரழிய மணற்றி வென்றான் கன்னிவார்துறைவாய்த்
தன்னேரிலாத தகைத்தின்றியான் கண்ட தாழ்பொழிலே.

Ira. Akap., p. 52.

‡ Tamil Varaláru, pt. ii.

¶ The words "the Lord of Siṭṭambalam praised by the Páṇḍyan king Varaguṇa" found in the following verse :—

"மன்னவன் றெம்முனை மேற்செல்லுமாயினு மாலரியே
றன்னவன் றேர்புறத்தல்கல் செல்லாது வரகுணனாந்
தென்னவனேத்து சிற்றம் பலத்தான் மற்றைத்தேவர்க்கெல்லா
முன்னவன் மூவலன்னாளுமற்றோர் தெய்வ முன்னலனே."

Tirukóvaiyár, v. 306.

Máṇikkavásagar was a contemporary of Varaguṇa. His theory receives confirmation by the fact that Séṇa I of Ceylon was according to the Siṅhalese chronicles converted to Hinduism by 'an ascetic clad in the robes of a priest.'* Although the Tamil puráṇam which treats on the life of Máṇikkavásagar† does not mention that he ever visited Ceylon, it is said that the Ceylon king went with his dumb daughter to Sidambaram to witness the religious controversy between the Buddhist priests of Ceylon and Máṇikkavásagar and that on the latter performing the miracle of making the dumb princess to speak, the king and his retinue including the defeated priests of Buddha became Hindus.

Perunturai (great harbour) to which Máṇikkavásagar went to purchase horses for the Páṇḍyaṉ and of which mention is repeatedly made in his Tiruvásagam, was very probably Mátoṭa. Mátoṭa was frequented by Arabian and Persian traders and horses were imported for the benefit of Eastern potentates. The god of Perunturai to whom the spiritual enlightenment of Máṇikkavásagar is specially attributed was the Lord of Tirukkétísvaram whose praise was sung by the Dévάram hymners. The Perunturai of Máṇikkavásagar and Periaturai of De Couto appear to be the Tamil equivalents of Mátoṭa.

In the reign of Séṇa II (843-878 A.D.) "a prince of the royal family of Páṇḍu having formed a design to

---

* Nik. San. p. 18.
Rajarat., pp. 81 & 82.

† Tirup. V. A. P. (புத்தரைவாதில் வென்ற சருக்கம்.)
Tiru. V..P. P., p. 247

overthrow that kingdom, because he was illtreated by his king" took refuge in Ceylon and sought the aid of the king. Séṇa saw an opportunity for avenging the Páṇḍyaṉ invasion of the Island during the reign of his grand-father Séṇa I, and despatched an army from Ceylon. Madura was taken by seige and the Páṇḍyaṉ "fled from the field of battle on the back of an elephant and gave up his life in the wrong place and his queen also died at the same time".* The account of this invasion is corroborated by the Nikaya Saṅgrahawa which says "After the death of king Matvalasen (Séṇa I) the Maháraja Mungayinsen (Séṇa II), who succeeded to the throne of Laṅká set out with a Siṅhalese army and invaded the kingdom of Páṇḍi, and having slain and routed the Tamils he recovered the drums of victory and the gem set bowl which had been captured in the days of king Matvalasen and then returned to Laṅká."† As according to South Indian epigraphy the Páṇḍya Varaguṇa varmaṉ, the grandson of Varaguṇa who fought at Tiruppirambiyam came to the throne in 862 A.D.,‡ the prince who sought the assistance of the Siṅhalese king was probably Varaguṇavarmaṉ and the Páṇḍyaṉ who was killed by the Siṅhalese army was Srimara Parachakra Kolahala, the son of Varaguṇa who invaded Ceylon during the time of Séna I. The Sinnamanúr plates on the contrary state that Srimara vanquished Máya Páṇḍya, the Kérala, the king of Siṅhala, the Pallava and the Vallabha.¶ The

* Mah. chap. Li, v. 38.

† Nik. San., p. 18; Rajavali. p. 31.

‡ M. E. R., 1906, p. 71, § 25.

¶ Ibid 1907, p. 68, § 23.

mention of Máya Páṇḍya as an enemy of the reigning king implies the existence of factions and parties in the reigning family of Madura, and the mention of the Siṅhalese along with Máya Páṇḍya confirms the theory that the king against whom the Siṅhalese army fought was Srimara. Séna II in an inscription left at Medirigiriya called himself Madhuradunu (conqueror of Madura).*

In the time of Kassapa V (906-916 A.D.), it is said, king Páṇḍu who had warred with the king of Chóḻa and suffered defeat, sent many presents to Kassapa V and solicited his help. An army which was despatched under Sakka Sénapáti, the son of the king, was defeated by the Chóḻas and the Sénapati died of some epidemic disease† there. This account would naturally be taken to refer to the encounter between the Chóḻa king and Rajasimha Páṇḍya mentioned in verses 10 and 11 of the Udayéndiram plates of the Gaṅga Bána king Hastimalla,‡ where the defeat of the Siṅhalese troops is recorded in the following terms. "Having slain in an instant at the head of a battle an immense army despatched by the Lord of Laṅká which teemed with brave soldiers and was interspersed with troops of elephants and horses he bears in the world the pregnant name of Samgraha Rághava (Rámá in battle)". An inscription of the 12th year of Parántaka I, found at Tirupáṭkaḍal in the North Arcot district refers to a defeat of the Páṇḍyaṉ and the king of

* Ceylon Ant., vol. x. pt. ii,

† Mah., chap. lii, vv. 70—78.

‡ S. I. I., vol. ii, p. 387.

ḷḷam at the battle of Vélúr.* As the 12th year of Parántaka I falls in 919 A.D. and the last year of Kassapa V in 916 A.D., the battle of Vélur must have taken place before 916 A.D. When Parántaka in the inscriptions of the third year of his reign called himself Madurantaka or Madurakoṇḍa,† the allusion probably was to his earlier conquest of Madura referred to in the Mahávaṅsa in the words "King Páṇḍu who had warred with the king of Chóḷa and was routed",‡ and in verse 8 of the Udayéndiram plates. The defeat of the Siṅhalese army must therefore have taken place between 910 and 916 A.D. There are two inscriptions in Ceylon one at Elawaewa Pánsala and another at Aetaviragolleva, of Abha Salamévan Dappula (V) in which it is stated that his father Sri Saṅga Bo (Kassapa V) "in the ninth year after he had raised the royal umbrella, ransacked the kingdom of Páṇḍi and having won victory and glory, enjoyed his splendour".¶ Although this statement is not in agreement with the result of the expedition as recorded in the Mahávaṅsa and in Parántaka's inscriptions, yet it confirms the truth of the expedition and helps to fix the date of the battle of Vélúr with some degree of exactitude. As the kingdom of Páṇḍi was said to have been ransacked in the ninth year of Kassapa V, the battle of Vélúr must have taken place in 915 A D.

During the reign of Dappula V (917—929 A.D) "King Páṇḍu because he feared the Chóḷians left his country"

---

* S. I. I. vol: ii. No. 98; M. E. R. No. 693 of 1904.

† M. E. R. of 1906-1907, No. 29 of 1907.

‡ Mah., chap. lii, vv. 70 et seq.

¶ Muller, Nos. 116 & 117.

and came to Ceylon to obtain help against the Chóḻa. While the king was preparing an expedition, internal dissensions arose in the Island and the Páṇḍya had to go away leaving his crown and royal apparel behind.* And during the time of Udaya III (941-949 A.D.) who was a drunkard and a sluggard, the Chóḻas attempted to obtain possession of the crown and apparel but though successful at first were eventually defeated.† It was probably after this invasion that Parántaka called himself the conqueror of Madura and Íḻam, for in an inscription of his 37th year‡ (944 A.D.), he is referred to as the conqueror of Madura and Íḻam, whereas in one of his 36th year¶ he is called the conqueror of Madura only. A record of his 40th year (947 A.D.) mentions Parántaka's invasion of Ceylon.§ Consequently Parántaka's claim to have invaded Ceylon cannot be altogether unfounded and even if he failed to defeat the Siṅhalese king he must have at least subdued the Northern kingdom. His invasion of Ceylon is described in the Tiruvalangáḍu plates of Rájéndra Chóḻa I as follows:—"(All) the waters of the sea were not (enough) to quench the fire of his (the Chóḻa king's) anger which consumed the enemies and which was put out (only) by the tears of the wives of the (king) of Simhala cut and killed by the king's weapons."‖ Udaya III during whose reign this invasion by Parántaka took place was not killed, and the king who was 'cut and killed by the

* Mah., chap. liii, vv. 5—9.

† Ibid 41—45.

‡ M. E. R., 1903-1904, Insc. No. 375 of 1903.

¶ S. I. I., vol. iii, No. 109.

§ Ep. Ind., vol. vii, p. 1.

‖ M. E. R. 1906, p. 67, § 16.

(Chóḻa) king's weapons' must have been therefore the king of Jaffna through whose territories the Chóḻa army had to pass before reaching the dominions of Udaya.

The crown and the robes of state left behind by the Páṇḍya were, however, seized at a later date by the Chóḻa king Rájarája I when he invaded Ceylon, for in an inscription of his tenth year (995 A.D.), he claims to have taken "the crown of the king of Íḻam who came to close quarters in fighting, the exceedingly beautiful crown of the queen of that country, the crown of Sundara and the pearl necklace of Indra which the king of the South had previously given up to that (king of Íḻam); the whole Íḻamaṇḍalam on the transparent sea."* It is however curious that Rájéndra Chóḻa I too in an inscription of his sixth year (1018 A.D.) claims to have taken the jewels of the same description as those taken by Rájarája I, from the Ceylon king.†

The conquest of Ceylon by Rájarája I and Rajéndra Déva I is corroborated by the Mahávaṅsa, for in it, it is said, that in the 36th year of Mahinda V "they (the Chóḻas) took the queen with all the jewels and ornaments and the crown that was the inheritance of the kings and priceless diamond bracelet that was the gift of the gods, and the sword that could not be broken and the sacred forehead-band; and having made a false show of peace, they took the king prisoner in the fastnesses of the forest where he had taken refuge through fear."‡ This

* S. I. I., vol. ii, No. 54.

† S. I. I., vol. iii, No. 205.

‡ Mah., chap. lvi, vv. 16—19.

description of the spoils removed by the Chóḻas is very much like that of the panegyric in the Chóḻa inscriptions. The 36th year of Mahinda V who came to the throne in 978 A.D. falls in the year 1014 A.D. which corresponds to the second year of Rájéndra Chóḻa I. The Chóḻa invasion evidently therefore began about 995 A.D during the time of Rájarája I and continued till the second year of Rájéndradéva I, when the Ceylon king (Mahinda) was ultimately captured.

The Rashtrakúṭa king Krishna III, known as Sri Vallabha and Kannaradéva Vallabha, in his Karhad plates of 958 A.D,* says that he exterminated Káñci and Tañjai, made the Céra, Páṇḍya and Simhala his tributaries and erected a high column at Rámésvaram. In an inscription of his found at Kaḷḷangaṭṭai near Sóḻapuram and in his Átakúr inscription, it is said that he killed Chóḻa Rájáditya at Takkóḷam and entered Toṇḍaimaṇḍalam in 949 A.D.† If he did invade Ceylon it must have been about that time, very probably in 950 A.D. He is supposed to be the Vallabha who invaded Nágadípa during the time of Mahinda IV‡ (952-968 A.D). If Krishna III invaded Ceylon during the time of Mahinda IV, it must have been later than 952 A.D., the year of Mahinda's accession, which is doubtful. The word 'Vallabha' found in the Mahávaṅsa might in all probability be the Tamil word 'Vaḻavan' ,which is the same as Vallabha, an epithet applied to the Chóḻa kings, for it

---

* Ep. Ind., vol, iv, No. 40.

† Ep. Ind., vol. vii, p. 194.

‡ Mah., chap. liv, v. 12; Ceylon Ant., vol. iv, pp : 34 & 35.

appears that a Chóḻa invasion of Ceylon took place during the time of Mahinda IV. It is stated in an inscription of Rájarája I, that one Siriya Véḷar, a Chóḻa officer died in a battle field in Ceylon in the 9th year of Sundara Chóḻa Parántaka II*. This must have been about 966 A.D, in the reign of Mahinda IV. It is very likely that Vaḻavarkónpaḷḷam near Máviṭṭapuram in Jaffna was the scene of this battle and was so named after the event. As the Chóḻa was called 'Vaḻavan' his palace came to be known as 'Vaḻavu' (Walawwa). The term was later applied to the residences of Chiefs and is still used in the Siṅhalese countries for the same purpose, but its application in Jaffna has deteriorated and every compound is known by that name.

There is an inscription at Tiruvoṭṭiyúr temple dated the fifth year (954 A.D.,) of Gandaráditya,† the son of Parántaka I, who ascended the Chóḷa throne in 949 A.D, on the death of Rájáditya who was killed by the Rashtrakúṭa king Krishna III. According to it one Kaḍuttalai Nágamaiyaṉ son of Siṅgamaiyaṉ one of the Nobles (Perundaram) of Uḍaiyár Sri Uttama Choḻa Déva accompanied the latter to the temple at Tiruvoṭṭiyúr and donated 90 sheep for burning lamps and an Íḻaviḷakku (a lamp stand made in Ceylon), to the temple. A reasonable doubt may arise why Uttama Chóḻa was given the title of a reigning king while Gandaráditya was the king. Uttama Chóḻa was actually the Chóḻa Viceroy of Ceylon at the time and the donor in the

* M. E. R., 1896, Insc. No. 116 of 1896.

† M. E. R. 1912, Insc. No. 246 of 1912; S. I. I., vol. iii, No. 115.

inscription accompanied him from Ceylon and hence the donation of an Īḻa viḷakku. This Uttama Chóḻa was the paternal uncle of Rájarája I, and succeeded Parántaka II, to the Chóḻa throne. As Polonnaruwa had not then fallen into the hands of the Chóḻas, the Chóḻa viceregal capital must have been either at Mátoṭa or Padaviya where Chóḻa inscriptions have been found. Thus it will be seen that, in 954 A.D., Ceylon or a portion of it was under the Chóḻa rule, and Uttama Chóḻa was reigning there as the Viceroy of Gandaráditya.

Rájarája I (985-1012 A. D.,) extended his rule throughout the Madras Presidency and in some directions even beyond it. On the west his sway extended as far as Quilon and Coorg, on the north-east to the borders of Orissa, and his conquests included Ceylon and 'the 12,000 ancient islands of the sea'. As parts of Burma and the Malay Archipelago were added to these dominions by his immediate successors, 'the ancient islands of the sea' included Jaffna and its dependent islands, the Maladives and the Laccadives. 'Many ancient islands whose old great guard was the ocean, which makes the conches resound,* an expression invariably found in the Chóḻa inscriptions must indubitably refer to the Jaffna islands surrounded by seas in which chanks abound.

Rájarája's and Rájéndra Chóḻa's conquest of Ceylon seems to have been complete enough to bring the whole of the island under the dominion of the Chóḻas. Ceylon was made a province of the Chóḻa Empire and named

* "சங்கதிர்வேலைத் தொல்பெருங்காவற் பல் பழந்தீவும்."

Mummuḍi Chóḷa Manḍalam, after one of the well known birudas of Rájarája. Polonnaruwa the capital was called Jananátapuram or Jananáta Maṅgaḷam. Mátoṭa was renamed Rájarája puram and the Sivan temple there Rájarája Ísvaram.* They built several Hindu temples at Polonnaruwa, Mátoṭa and Padaviya; the bronze images of Naḍarája and the Saiva Saints, now placed in the Colombo Museum, were found in a ruined Chóḷa temple at Polonnaruwa. A Sivan temple in honour of Rájéndra Chóḷa's wife was built there and called Vánavaṉ Mádévi Ísvaram.† Several inscriptions of Parakésarivarman Rájéndra Chóḷa I, were found not only at Polonnaruwa but also in other parts of the Island. The village of Chembiyanpattu, perhaps a name originally given to a district, is at present the only reminder in Jaffna of the ancient Chóḷa occupation of the Peninsula.

Rajádhi Rájá I (1018-1052 A.D,) says in his inscriptions that he inherited the kingdom of his father (Rájéndra Chóḷa I) "who had captured Gaṅga in the North, Laṅká in the South, Mahadaya (Cranganore) on the West and Kiḍáram (Lower Burma) in the East."‡ After Rájádhi Rájá I, Ceylon was under three Chóḷa kings, Rájéndra Déva II, Víra Rájéndra and Adhi Rájéndra. Adhi Rájéndra who was the brother-in-law of the Chaḷukya

* From a Tamil inscription of the time of Rájéndra Chóḷa I, found at Mátoṭa and now at the Colombo Museum.

† From two Tamil inscriptions found on the walls of Siva temple No. 2 at Polonnaruwa.

‡ M. E. R. Insc. No. 75 of 1895 at Tirumalaivádi, and No. 96 of 1896 at Cape Comorin.

king Vikramaditya II, was, in spite of the assistance rendered by the latter, killed by Kulóttunga I, before he could have secured the Chóḷa crown. Adhi Rájéndra was the Chóḷa Viceroy at Polonnaruwa during the time Víra Rájéndra was the Choḷa Emperor, and has left two inscriptions there.*

The northern part of Ceylon came under the Chóḷa dominion during the time of Parántaka I about 944 A.D., and the whole island of Ceylon in 1012 A. D., when Mahinda V was captured by Rájéndra Choḷa I, and continued till 1070 A.D. the year of accession of Kulótunga I, a period of 126 years. But Nikáya Sangrahawa and Pújavaliya state that Ceylon was under the Chóḷa yoke for only 86 years,† a mistake calculated perhaps from the accession of Rájarája I. According to the Mahávansa the Chóḷas were driven out of Ceylon in the 15th year of Vijaya Báhu I‡ which agrees with the year of Kulóttunga's accession. On account of the internal dissensions between two rival claimants to the Chóḷa throne, Kulóttunga and Adhi Rájéndra, who had to leave Ceylon on the death of Víra Rájéndra, the power of the Chóḷas in Ceylon was weakened, their affairs in the Island were neglected and they were ultimately obliged to leave the country. The fact of the Véḷaikkara army taking service under Vijaya Báhu and of their insurrection when Vijaya Báhu proposed to lead an expedition to the Chóḷa country testifies rather to the voluntary evacuation of Ceylon by the Chóḷas than

---

* On the walls of Siva temple at Polonnaruwa; vide supra p. 263. note †

† Nik. San. p. 19; Puja., p. 33.

‡ Mah., chap. lviii, v. 59.

to their forcible expulsion as claimed by Vijaya Báhu* and as elaborately described in the Mahávaṅsa.

During the Chóḷa supremacy it was not likely that there was an independent kingdom in the North. The Jaffna kings must have been Chóḷa feudatories. There is no reason to doubt their existence. As for the Ceylon kings during that time, the Maháváṅsa gives a list of those who are alleged to have reigned in unbroken succession except for a short interregnum of 12 years from 1012 to 1024 A.D.‡ It must, however, be taken that after the capture of Mahinda V, in 1012 A.D., to the accession of Vijaya Báhu in 1054 A.D., these kings exercised an ephemeral authority off and on for a period of about 16 years somewhere in the South of the Island.

Kulóttuṅga I, made several conquests as far north as Kaliṅgam and as far south as Ceylon, and his conquest of Ceylon is mentioned in his inscriptions. Kulóttuṅga's reign extended to 1118 A.D., and Vijaya Báhu died, in 1109 A.D. The Maháváṅsa says that Vijaya Báhu made preparations to lead an expedition against the Chóḷas in his 30th year (1084 A.D.) and again in his 45th year (1099 A.D.,) both of which, however, did not come to pass.‡ A Chóḷa invasion of Ceylon either during the latter part of Vijaya Báhu's reign or after his death is not mentioned in the Maháváṅsa. If Kulóttuṅga ever led an expedition to Ceylon it must have been between 1109

---

* In his Maṇipravāḷa (Tamil and Grantha) inscription at Polonnaruwa; J.C.B.R.A.S, vol: xxix, pp: 266 et seq:

† Mah, Nos. 116 to 122 in Mudr. Wijesiṇha's list.

‡ Mah, chap. lx, vv. 36 & 46.

and 1118 A.D., after Vijaya Báhu's death. According to one of his inscriptions found at Srinivasa Nallúr in the Trichinapoly district inscribed in his 42nd year (1112 A.D.,) the conquest of Kaliṅga mentioned in it should have taken place in 1111 A.D.* His conquest of Ceylon was before that event as will be seen by an allusion in Kaliṅgattu Paraṇi, a Tamil poem composed in praise of his famous general Karuṇákara Toṇḍaimaṉ.† It was this Karuṇákara Toṇḍaimáṉ who opened Toṇḍaimáṉ Áṟu for the purpose of removing salt from the salterns of Kaṟanavay and Veḷḷaipparavai in the North of Jaffna, and it was this expedition in search of salt which was perhaps magnified into a conquest in the inscriptions. The author of the Vaipava Málai has erroneously placed this event in the reign of Ugra Siṅgaṉ.‡ Karuṇákaraṉ while being engaged in collecting salt lived at Iṇuvil and built there a temple for the worship of Piḷḷaiyár which is still called Karuṇákara Piḷḷaiyár temple. It now lies

---

* M. E. R., 1900-1901, p. 9.

M. E. R. of 1905, p. 51, § 13; Insc. No. 608 of 1904.

† (a) இலங்கை யெறிந்த கருணாகரன்ற
னிகல் வெஞ்சிலையின் வலிகேட்பீர்
கலிங்கமெறிந்த கருணாகரன்றன்
களப்போர் பாடத்திறமினோ

You who have heard of the prowess of Karunákara's bow when he conquered Ceylon, open (your doors) to hear the poetic praises of Karunákara's war in which he conquered Kaliṅgam.

(b) ஒதஞ் சூழிலங்கைப்போர்க்
கொட்டிரட்டி கலிங்கப்போர்।

Kaling., Péymuraipáḍu, v. 20.

The Kaliṅga war was as doubly fierce as the Ceylon war

‡ Y. V, M,, p. 8.

within the village of Urumparay. There is a stone inscription in the temple of the year 1567 A.D., in which the temple is mentioned as Karunákara Piḷḷaiyár temple.

Within a century of the departure of the Chóḷas, Ceylon was able to take the offensive against them. The great Parákrama Báhu whose reign of 33 years stands out as a glorious record of able administration in greatly improving the resources of the country, was perhaps the only king of Ceylon who believed in an imperial policy. He was as ambitious as Alexander the Great and his invasions into the Chóḷa territories seem to have been only the preliminaries of a greater and more formidable scheme for bringing the greater part of India under his sway.

During his reign two rival candidates began to fight for the Páṇḍya crown and one of them Kulasékara was assisted by the Chóḷas, and the other Parákrama Páṇḍya sought the aid of Parákrama Báhu who sent a powerful army under Laṅkápuri Danḍanayaka. The expedition of Laṅkápuri is described in two long chapters of the Mahávaṅsa,* and it is said that after devastating the Páṇḍya and Chóḷa dominions and defeating Kulasékara and the Chóḷa armies, Laṅkápuri crowned Víra Páṇḍya the son of Parákrama Páṇḍya at Madura and returned to Ceylon covered with glory. He is even said to have built a town in South India by the name of Parákrama puram and struck coins to commemmorate his victory. But there is a stone inscription on the south wall of the Tiruvatisvara temple at Árpakkam,† a village 8 miles from

* Mah., chap. lxxvi and lxxvii.

† M. E. R., 1899-1900, Insc. No. 20 of 1899.

Káñcipuram, dated the fifth year (1168 A. D.,) of Parakésari Rájádhi Rája II which also speaks of the invasion of the Siṅhalese army sent by Parákrama, but flatly contradicts the Mahávaṅsa as regards the result of the invasion. The inscription, after dealing with the devastation and havoc committed by the Siṅhalese army, goes on to state that at the earnest request of one Edirili-Sóḻa-Sambuvaráyer whose son was leading the Chóḻa army, one Umapathi Sivam was pleased to worship Siva for 28 days continually praying for the defeat of the Siṅhalese army, and that Laṅkápuri and the other generals had to run away. The Madras Epigraphist commenting on the statement of the Mahávaṅsa that the Siṅhalese army went back to Ceylon of its own accord after placing Víra Páṇḍya on the throne of Madura, states that "unlike the Mahávaṅsa which does not record even a single victory gained by the Chóḻa king, the inscription though referring to the Siṅhalese in words expressive of contempt and abhorrence does not fail to acknowledge the victories gained by them," and that "this circumstance alone apart from being a record of contemporary events, entitles the inscription to greater credence than the chronicle."* It was therefore he thought that the Siṅhalese army was actually defeated and compelled to leave India.

A stone inscription of the 8th year of Rájádhi Rájá II (1170 A. D.) has since been found at a temple at Pallavaréyanpéṭṭai in the Tanjore Taluq, according to which a Chóḻa minister named Tiruchiṭṭambala Muḍaiyaṉ Perumanambi alias Pallavaráyar went to the aid of Kula-

* M. E. R. 1899-1900. p. 13, Insc: No. 36.

sékhara Páṇḍya on the command of the Chóḻa King and defeated the invading army of Ceylon. Laṅkápuri Daṇḍanayaka and his generals were put to death, and their heads were nailed on to the gateway of Madura. Necessary precautions were taken against the future annexation of the Páṇḍyaṉ territory to Īḻam, and Kulasékhara was reinstated on the throne of Madura. After all this was done, the minister Pallavaráyar died of some disease. In recognition and in appreciation of the faithful services rendered by him to the State, gift of lands was made to his relations, and this inscription contains a record of such gift.*

The early success of the Siṅhalese army and the defeat of the Chóḻas is attributed to the part played in the war by a traitor named Sri Vallabha, in another of Rájádhi Rájá's inscriptions found at Tiruvalaṅgáḍu.† The title "who was pleased to take Madura and Ceylon" found in another Tiruvalaṅgáḍu inscription‡ was evidently assumed by Rájádhi Rájá after the victories achieved by the Chóḻa armies sent to assist one of the claimants to the Páṇḍyaṉ throne.¶ There are other inscriptions, one of his 13th year (1176 A. D.) at the Kailasanátha temple at Aṭṭampákkam and another of his 14th year at Máyavaram, § in which he is described as one "who was pleased to take Īḻam and Madura." The earliest record in which this

---

* A. R. S. I. E., 1923-1924, p. 104, Insc. No. 433 of 1924.

† M. E. R., 1905-1906, Insc. No. 465 of 1905.

‡ Ibid p. 70.

¶ M. E. R., 1909-1910, Insc. No. 731 of 1909 at Kailásanáta temple at Aṭṭampákkam.

§ M. E. R., 1911-1912, Insc. No. 300 of 1911 at Máyavaram.

epithet appears is dated the 13th year (1175 A. D.,) and he must have assumed it after the war of the Páṇḍyaṉ succession and after the defeat of the Siṅhalese army. He never led an invasion to Ceylon and hence the above surmise.

It appears from other South Indian inscriptions that the assistance given by the Siṅhalese to the Páṇḍyaṉ in his prolonged struggle with his opponent did not end with the death of Laṅkápuri. Kulasékhara died soon after the events described in the Mahávaṅsa and his son Vikrama Páṇḍya continued the war with Víra Páṇḍya's son and his Siṅhalese allies. Some of the details of this campaign are recorded in an inscription at Tirukkaḷambudúr of the fourth year of Kulóttuṅga III (1182 A.D.)* According to it the son of Víra Páṇḍya was defeated and the Siṅhalese soldiers had their noses cut off and they rushed into the sea to escape from the Chóḻa troops. According to another inscription of his ninth year (1187 A. D.) found at Sidambaram, Parakésari Kulottuṅga III assisted Vikrama Páṇḍya against the son of Víra Páṇḍya drove the Siṅhalese army into the sea, took Madura from Víra Páṇḍya's son and bestowed it on Vikrama Páṇḍya.†

It will thus be seen that notwithstanding the glorious account of success detailed in the Mahávaṅsa during the time of Parákrama Báhu the Great, the Siṅhalese troops were twice defeated, once in 1175 and again in 1182 A. D. It is, however, difficult to say

---

* M. E. R., 1899-1900, Insc. No. 1 of 1899.
Ibid p. 14 § 38.

† Ep. Ind., vol. vii, p. 169.

now on which account more reliance can be placed as it can never be imagined that the Chóḷa kings would have admitted in their inscriptions their defeat at the hands of the Siṅhalese. This of course is not the only instance where each of the contending parties has claimed the victory for itself. On the other hand, had Parákrama Báhu succeeded, the author of the Mahávaṅsa would have developed the idea of imperial policy more clearly. The discovery of the inscription at Pallavaráyanpéttai in 1924 in which the death of Laṅkápuri is specially mentioned clears all doubt as to the issue of the earlier campaign and to the unreliability of the Mahávaṅsa as a historical narrative.

CHAPTER VII

The Origin of the Kings of Jaffna

THE prevailing belief that Ugra Siṅgaṉ reigned in a town beyond the limits of the Jaffna Peninsula, and that a Yáḻpáṇaṉ to whom Jaffna was presented as a sandy district, colonised it and reigned over it, a belief founded on the quasi-historical writings of a later period, has been refuted in the last chapter. The events which are recorded as the natural consequences of such misconceptions have also to be tested and verified. According to the Kailáya Málai there was an interregnum after the death of Yáḻpáṇaṉ. Then a chieftain named Páṇḍi Maḻavaṉ of Ponpaṟṟiyúr, a colonist, went over to South India and fetched a prince described as the son of a Páṇḍyaṉ in the Kailáya Málai* and as a Chóḻa prince in the Vaipava Málai.† This

---

கோலநகர்ச்

* செல்வமதுரைச்செழிய சேகரன் செய்மாதவங்கள்
மல்கவியன் மகவாய் வந்தபிரான்—கல்விநிறை
தென்ன னிகரான செகராசன் தென்னிலங்கை
மன்னவனாகுஞ் சிங்கையாரியமால்"

K. M., p. 5.

Siṅgai Áryaṉ, the king of Laṅká, Segarájaṉ (Segarájasékaraṉ) full of learning like unto Yama (the god of death), the son of Cheḻiyaṉ (Páṇḍyaṉ) of the beautiful and wealthy Madura, born as the result of his (Páṇḍyaṉ's) religious austerities.

[Segarájasékaraṉ was contracted to Segarájaṉ in order to suit versification.]

† Y. V. M., p. 14.

prince who was known as Segarásaṉ and Siṅgai Áryaṉ was afterwards called Vijaya-Kúḷaṅkai-Chakravarti on account of a defect in one of his arms. He is said to have built the town of Nallúr and his successors were called Árya Chakravartis.* It has already been stated that most of the fictions found in the Kailáya Málai were unconsciously taken over by the author of the Vaipava Málai. As the later kings of Jaffna claimed no relationship with the lowborn lutist, the pious author of the Kailáya Málai was obliged to state that the Páṇaṉ died without issue, and as the real origin of the Árya Chakravartis was not known to him, his fertile imagination invented the story of Páṇḍi Maḻavaṉ, the crown-giver. In spite of the fact mentioned in the Kailáya Málai that the first king was the son of a Páṇḍyaṉ, Mailvágana Pulavar described him as the son of a Siṅgha Kéthu, a son of Tisai Ugra Chóḻaṉ the father of Márutapiravíkavalli.† Had he any authority for that statement? Having naturally taken the list of kings either from Pararájasékaraṉ Ulá or Rájamuṟai, he must have woven the story in such a manner that Vijaya Kúḷaṅkai, the first named king in the list, fitted in with the prince alleged to have been brought by Páṇḍi Maḻavaṉ. He found that the statement made in the Kailáya Málai that the prince was the son of a Páṇḍyaṉ did not agree with tradition. The later kings of Jaffna claimed no affinity with the Páṇḍyaṉs; they called themselves 'Áryas' a name which a Páṇḍyaṉ would have scorned to adopt. The poet therefore made him out to be a scion of the Chóḻas whom he thought to be of Áryaṉ

---

* Y. V. M., p. 14.

† Ibid.

origin. It was perhaps this idea which led even later writers like Casie Chetty to think that the Chóḻas were of Áryaṉ origin. The present day scholars engaged in historical research have taken the list of kings given in the Vaipava Málai as correct, and having found from other sources that Jaffna was conquered by Sapumal Kumáraya about 1450 A.D.,* during the reign of Kula-sékara Siṅgai Áryaṉ, have allotted an average reign of 25 years to each king before him, and have arrived at the conclusion that Vijaya Kúḷaṅkai must have come to the throne about 1250 A.D. This conclusion coupled with the peculiar interpretation of a stray verse regarding the year in which the town of Nallúr was built† has led an erudite scholar like Mr. V. Coomaraswamy to identify Vijaya Kúḷaṅkai with a prince of the Telugu Chóḻas of Nellore or Wickrama-Siṅghapuram, who were about 1257 A.D., conquered by Jaṭávarman Sundara Páṇḍya I. (1251—1271 A.D.). To him, Tika Wikrama became Tisai Ugra, Tika's son Kéta became Siṅgha Kétu, Vikrama Siṅha Puram became Siṅhapuram or Siṅgai Nagar and Nellore became Nallúr.‡ These plausible inferences led him so

---

* Rajavali, p. 269.

† "இலகிய சகாப்தமெண்ணூற்றெழுபதா மாண்டதெல்லை"

About the Saka year 870.

[In translating a similar verse "எண்ணிய சகாப்த மெண்ணூற் றேழின்மேல்" relating to the date of the imprimatur of Kamban's Rámáyaṇam, a writer to the Sen Tamil (vol. iii, p. 178-179) has interpreted the words "எண்ணூற்றேழு" to Saka 1107, taking the word "எண்" to mean a special number 1000. In the same manner the year referred to in the Jaffna stray stanza was also construed to mean Saka 1170.]

‡ In a paper read before the Jaffna Historical Society and afterwards published in the Hindu Organ.

far as to surmise that the prince lost his arm in the war with Sundara Páṇḍya. This theory of the presentation of a captured Chóḻa prince by the Páṇḍyaṉ does in a way explain the contradictory statements made in the Kailáya Málai and the Vaipava Málai. But if the assertion in the Vaipava Málai that Vijaya Kúḷaṅkai was the grandson of Tissai Ugra Chóḻa be taken as correct, the earlier statement that Máruthapiravíka Valli was the daughter of Tisai Ugra Chóḻa should also be taken as correct. She married Ugra Siṅgaṉ about 800 A.D. A nephew to be 450 years younger than his aunt appears incredible. This theory can be partially maintained if Ugra Siṅgaṉ can be identified with Kaliṅga Magha. But there are several difficulties in the way of such identification as research will disclose that kings of the Kaliṅga dynasty calling themselves 'Áryas' reigned at Jaffna earlier than the 13th century.

The Mahávaṅsa says that Mahinda IV (952—968 A.D.) married a princess of the Kaliṅga Chakravarti race and made her his chief queen.* What was the Kaliṅga Chakravarti race if it did not refer to the Kaliṅga dynasty ruling in Jaffna? Did it refer to a dynasty ruling in Kaliṅgam (Orissa)? The Eastern Gaṅgas had not by this time established their power at Kaliṅgam, and Mahinda could not have found a wife among them; he must therefore have married a princess of Jaffna. He appears to have been married before he came to the throne for he made his sons Governors within his reign of 16 years. This fact points to the probability of his alliance rather

* Mah., chap. liv, vv. 7—16.

with a royal dynasty in Ceylon than with one in a far off country. His concern in sending his Chief Captain Ṣéna with an army to fight against the hosts of Vallabha who were trying to subdue Nágadípa* points to the same inference. No doubt that at the time Mahinda contracted his marriage, the Jaffna kings were not known as Chakravartis, but at the time this portion of the Mahávaṅsa was composed they were so known and hence the designation.

When Séna V, the son of Mahinda IV by the Kaliṅga queen, killed the son of his Chief Captain and fled from the capital fearing the wrath of the latter, the queen and her younger son the sub-king did not fly with him, but she sent for the chief Captain to whom she did not show any anger. Being thus favoured by her, the Chief Captain assembled together the Tamils and made over the country to them.† The favour shown to the Chief Captain by the queen clearly verifies the Tamil origin not only of the Queen but also of the Chief Captain.

The reference in the Persian work called Garshasp Namah of an expedition sent by a Persian Monarch to chastise a king of Ceylon called Báhu, in the tenth or the eleventh century A.D., has been already mentioned.‡ This Báhu was probably the king of Jaffna. Some of the later kings of Jaffna and the Kaliṅga kings of Polonnaruwa were known by such names as Jaya Báhu, Parákrama Báhu, Vijaya Báhu, etc., and the existence of a Kaliṅga king iu Jaffna with his name ending in Báhu cannot therefore be doubted.

---

* Mah: chap. liv, vv. 12—16.
† Ibid vv. 63—68.
‡ Ousley, pp. 48—52 and notes. See supra, chap. v. p: 198

Vijaya Báhu (1054—1109 A.D.) being "desirous to prolong and establish his race sent forth and brought a princess of exceeding beauty and delicate form born of the race of the kings of Kaliṅga whose name was Tilakasundari and anointed her as his queen."* Three princes her kinsfolk, Madhukaṇṇava, Bhímarája and Balakkára by name also came from Siṅhapura and were favoured by the king.† The princess and her kinsmen might have come from Siṅhapura, the Siṅgai Nagar of Jaffna. Although the names of the princes appear very much like the Kaliṅga names of the Eastern Gaṅgas, the Siṅhapura they came from could not have been that of Orissa as it had by that time sunk into insignificance.

King Vijaya Báhu built the Jambukóla Vihára and Jumbukóla Lénaka‡ which must have been at Jambukóla (Sambutturai) in Jaffna, and also Ballataka Vihára probably at Valveṭṭyturai,¶ an instance of his interest in Jaffna perhaps due to his marriage with a Jaffna princess. In the 19th year of his reign, Vijaya Báhu, in order to put down certain rebels in the Rohana and Malaya countries "sent into the field an Officer born of his wife's brother's race."§ If the translation in the Mahávaṅsa is correct, it clearly shows that his wife's brother was a ruling prince and if our surmise is correct he must have been the king of Jaffna. Vikrama Báhu, the son of Vijaya Báhu, appears to have been a follower of Hinduism, his mother's religion, for he

* Mah., chap. lix, vv. 29—30.

† Ibid vv. 46—49.

‡ Ibid lx, v. 62.

¶ Vide supra, chap ii, p: 76.

§ Mah., chap. lix, vv. 18—21.

despoiled the viháras and allowed his Tamil soldiers to dwell in them. The priests therefore removed the Tooth Relic and went to Rohana.*

An inscription of the 29th year (1046 A.D.) of the Chóḻa King Rájádhirája I, found at Maṇimaṅgaḷam,† records that "of the three allied kings of the South, the king

---

* Mah., chap. lxi, vv. 54—61

† "திங்களேர் தருதன்றொங் கல்வெண் குடைக்கீழ்
நிலமகணிலவ மலர்மகடபுனர்ந்து
செங்கோலோசசிக் கருஙகலி கடிநதுதன
சிறியதாதையு நதிருத தமையனுங்
குறிகொள தனனிளங கோககளையும
நெறியுணர் தனறிருப்புதலவாதமமையும
துன்றிய தெறசிலவானவ னமலலன
மீனவன கஙகனிலஙகையாக கிறைவன
புலஙகழற பல்லவன கனனகுசசியா காவலனெனப
பொனனணிசசுடாமணி மகுடஞ சூட்டிப
படாபுகழாஙகவாக கவா னாடளித்து
பாஙகுறு தெனனா மூவருள
மானாபரணன பொனமுடி ஆனாப்
பருமணிப பசுநதலை பொருகளததரிநது
வாரளவிய கழல வீரகேரளனை
முனைவயிறபிடித்து தனததிவாரணக
கதககளிறறுனுதைப பிததருளி
அநதமில பெரும புகளச சுந்தர பாணடியன
கொறறைவெண குடையுங கறறைவெண கவரியும
சிஙகாதனமும் வெஙகளத திழநதுதன
முடிவிழததலை விரிததடி தளாநதோடத
தொலலையமுலலை யூரததுரத்தி ஒலகவில
வேணாடடரசை சேணாடடொதுககி
மேவுபுகழிராம மகுடமூவா கெடமுனிந்து
விலைகெழு விலலவன குடாமடிக கொணடு

* * * * *

ஒருதனித தணடாறபொரு கடலிலஙகையா
கோமான் விக்கிரம வொாஹுவினமகுடமு
முனறனக குடைந்து தெணடமிழ மணடல
முழுவது மிழநதேழகட

[Contd.]

வீழமபுககவிலங கேசுரனாகிய
விககிரம பாணடியன பருமணிமகுடமும்
காணடகு தனனதாகிய கனனகுசசியினு
மாாகவியீழஞ சீரிதெனறெணணி
உளஙகொளதனனுடு தனனுறவொடும புகுந்து
விளங்கு முடிகவித்த வீரசலா மேகன
பொருகளத்தஞ சிதனகராக களிறிழந்து
சவவையிறரேூடக் காதலியொடுநதன
றவவையைபபிடித்து தாயை மூக்கரிய
ஆஙகவமானம நீஙகுதறகாக
மீட்டுமவந்து விடடொழில புரிந்து
வெங்களத்துலாநத வசசிங்கள வரைசன
பொன்னணி முடியுங் கன்னரனவழிவங்
துரைகொளீழத்தரைச நாகிய சீர
வல்லவ மதனராஜன மெலலொளித
தடமணி முடியுங் கொண்டு"

S. I. I., vol. iii. pt. i, p. 54.

"While the goddess of earth was flourishing under his fringed white parasol, which resembled the moon (in coolness) (he the king) wedded the goddess of fortune, wielded the sceptre and destroyed the dark Kali (age).

(He) bestowed crowns of gold adorned with brilliant gems on his father's younger brother, his elder brother, his distinguished younger brothers and his sons who knew the right path, as the following rulers, Vánavan (Chéra), Mallan (Chalukya), Mínavan (Páṇḍya), Gangan, the king of the people of Lanka, Pallavan of wide ankle rings and protector of the people of Kannakuchchi (Kanyakubja ?) and granted to these relatives of great renown the dominions of these (hostile kings).

Among the three allied kings of the South (he) cut off the beautiful head of Manábharaṇan wearing a golden crown set with large jewels on the battlefield, seized in battle Víra Kéraḷan (Chéra) of wide ankle rings and was pleased to have him kicked by his furious elephant Athivárana and drove to the Mullayúr Sundara Páṇḍyan of endless great fame, who lost in battle his royal white parasol, his fly whisks of white yak's hair and his throne and ran away dropping his crown with dishevelled hair and wearied foot. (He) sent the undaunted king of Véṇáḍu to heaven and destroyed

[Contd.]

cut off on the battle field the beautiful head of Mánábharaṇa adorned with great gems and a golden crown; captured in fight Víra-Kéraḷan of the wide ankle rings and was pleased to have him trampled to death by his furious elephant Attivāraṇa, and drove to the ancient river Mullaiyár, Sundara Páṇḍya of great and undying fame who lost in the stress of battle his royal white parasol, his fly-whisks of white yak's hair and his throne and fled leaving his crown behind him with dishevelled locks and weary feet." Of the three kings of the South who allied themselves to fight against the Chóḷa sovereign, the

---

in anger the three (princes) of the famous Irámaguḍam. While the strong Villavan fled from his country with bowels protruding and hid himself in the jungle, (the Chóḷa king) wearing a new wreath of vanji flowers destroyed his fleet at Kandalúr Sálai.

* * * * *

By despatching a single army (he) took the crown of Vikrama Báhu the king of the people of Lanka on the tempestuous ocean, the crown of large jewels of the Lord of Lanka, Vikrama Páṇdyan who having been previously defeated by him (the Chóḷa king) and having lost the whole of the Tamil country, had entered Īḻam (surrounded), by the seven oceans; the beautiful golden crown of the king of Siṅhala Víra Salámêghan, who believing that Īḻam (surrounded) by the ocean was superior to the beautiful Kannakuchchi (Kanyakubja) which belonged to him, had entered (the Island) with his relatives and his countrymen, and had put on the brilliant crown; who had fled ignominiously from the battlefield having lost his black elephant; and who, when (the Chóḷa king) seized his wife and his elder sister and cut off the nose of his mother, had returned in order to remove the disgrace (caused) thereby, and having fought with his bow dropped his crown in the battle field; and the extremely brilliant crown of large jewels of the king of Īḻam, Sri Vallavan (Sri Vallabha) Madana Raja who had come from Kannara and settled here."

Páṇḍya and the Céra are mentioned in the inscription separately and the third king Mánábharaṇa cannot therefore be a Páṇḍyaṉ as surmised by Dr. Hultszch. The Ceylon Chronicles do not mention a Mánábharaṇa as a king ruling in Ceylon during the period but another Maṇimaṅgaḷam inscription of the 4th year (1055 A.D.) of the Chóḷa King Rájéndra Déva* calls Mánábharaṇa the King of Ceylon. He was therefore in all probability the King of Jaffna. The former inscription further states that Rájádhi Rája deprived of their crowns four Ceylon kings, viz.:—Vikrama Báhu, Vikrama Páṇḍya, Víra Sálamégha and Sri Vallabha Madana Rája. The first two of these Ceylon Kings can be identified with Vikrama Báhu and Vikrama Páṇḍu being Nos. 116 and 119 respectively of Mudlr: Wijesiṅha's table in the Mahávaṅsa. The former died in 1038 A. D., and the latter in 1042 A.D., eight and four years respectively before the date of the inscription. But who were Vírasalá Mégha and Sri Vallabha Madana Rája? Víra Salá Mégha is described in the inscription as the

---

* "தென்றிசை வயிற் [போர்ப்படை நடாத்திக
கார்க் கடலிலங்கையில் [விறற்படைக் கலிங்கா மன
வீரசலா மேகனைக் [கடறகளிற றொருமெகப்படக்
கதிர்முடிகடிவித்
திலங்கையிற் றிறைவன மாணபரணன்
காதல விருவரைக் களத்திடைப் பிடித்து"

Ep: Ind; vol. vi, pp. 24—38.
S. I. I., vol. iii pt. i, p. 61.

(The Chóḷa king) led a warlike army to the Southern region captured in Laṇká (surrounded) by the dark ocean, the Kaliṅga king Víra Salámégaṉ who had a powerful army with his oceanlike elephants and cut off his head with the brilliant crown, and seized on the battlefield the two sons of Mánábharaṇa the king of Laṅká.

King of Siṅhala (Ceylon) who came from his country Kannakuchchi,* (which Dr. Hultzsch thought was Kanyakubja) " to Íḻam with his relations and countrymen " and had put on the crown. Kannakuchchi is here used to represent the country of Kannakuchchiyar, a word employed earlier in the inscription to denote a certain type of people. 'Kannakuchchiyar' appears to have been a derisive term used for the Malabar immigrants in Jaffna who had their hair tied in a knot on the side of the head and who perhaps formed the majority of the population, by the other Tamil and Siṅhalese inhabitants who had their knots tied on the back of the head. Till very recent times most of the Tamils of Jaffna had their hair knots tied like those of the modern Siṅhalese and even now some may be seen in villages further away from the town wearing their hair in a similar manner. When Sapumal Kumáraya invaded Jaffna one of the Tamil regiments that opposed him was composed of " Conta Cara Demalis " (கொண்டைக்காறத் தமிழர் — Tamils with knots on the back of the head) according to Valentyn.† The relic of the Malabar custom of wearing the side knot also continued in Jaffna till about 40 or 50 years ago. The Malabar immigration having taken place perhaps a short time before the Chóḻa invasion referred to in the inscription, and the Kaliṅga kings too having usurped the kingdom of Jaffna only about two centuries earlier, the King Víra

* The important passages in the inscriptions are fully quoted (notes in pp. 278—281, 283) with the translations given by Dr E. Hultzsch so that our rendering of the word 'Kannakuchchiyar' may be correctly appreciated.

† J.C.B.R.A.S., vol. xxii, p. 38: quotation from Valentyn.

Salá Méghan was also supposed to have come from the same place as the immigrants. Kannakuchchi did not therefore represent Kanyakubja but the country of the Malabar immigrants of Jaffna. The people having been called Kannakuchchiyar, the country from which they emigrated and the country in which they settled were also called Kannakuchchi as would be seen in another inscription of Rájéndra Chóḷa.* Víra Salá Mégha who was deprived of his crown by Rájádhi Rája was very probably therefore the King of Jaffna and his proper designation 'Kalinga King' is given to him in an inscription of Rájéndra Chóḷa.* Sri Vallabha Madana Rája is also stated in the inscription to be one descended from Kannara, a term wrongly employed for the Kaliṅgas. He too was probably a prince of the Kaliṅga dynasty of Jaffna and was perhaps a brother of Víra Salá Mégha.

The other Maṇimaṅgaḷam inscription already referred to, of the fourth year (1055 A. D.) of the Chóḷa king Rájéndra Déva, reports that he despatched an army to Ceylon and the Kaliṅga King Víra Salá Mégha was

---

* " * * * * * *
அன்பொடுகெருது காதலருள்
* * * * * *
செந்தமிழ்ப் பிடிகவிரட்டபாடிகொண்ட சோழனை
தொல்புவியாளுடைச் சோழகன்னகுச்சிய ராஜனென்று
* * * * * *
பருமணிசுடாமணி மகுடஞ் சூட்டிப்
படிமிசைந்திகழு நாளினில்"

S. I. I., vol. iii, p. 61.

(He) bestowed high crown resplendent with large gems on Iraṭṭapáḍi Konda Chóḷan who was the rock of support to pure Tamil, one of his affectionate sons (with the title) Chóḷa-Kannakuchchiya Raján, the lord of the ancient earth.

decapitated and the two sons of the Ceylon king Mánábharaṇa were taken prisoners. This Víra Salá Mégha was probably the same king who was deprived of his crown by Rájádhi Rája, and Mánábharaṇa, whose sons were captured by Rajéndra Déva, was the King whose head was cut off by Rájádhi Rája as mentioned in the previous inscription of 1046 A. D. Mánábharaṇa who went over to India to assist the Céra and the Páṇḍya was killed perhaps sometime earlier than 1038 A. D. In 1038 A.D., Víra Salá Mégha was deprived of his crown by Rájadhi Rája when Vikrama Báhu was killed, and Sri Vallabha Madana Rája was killed in 1042 A.D., with Vikrama Páṇḍu. Víra Salá Mégha appears to have seized the throne of Jaffna after he was deprived of his crown in 1038 A.D., and he would have been killed by Rájéndra Déva sometime before 1055 A. D., when the two sons of Mánábharaṇa were captured. When Mánábharaṇa was killed the heir to the throne was very likely a minor and hence the necessity for Víra Salá Mégha and Sri Vallabha who were perhaps the heir's uncles, to rule successively in Jaffna during the minority of the heir. The Maṅimaṇgaḷam inscriptions do, therefore, make it plain that three kings of Jaffna were killed during the Chóḻa invasion, one before 1038 A.D., another in 1042 A.D., and a third in 1054 A.D.

From a compendium of Tamil poems called 'Tamil Návalar Saridai' it appears that a Tamil poet named Pughaléndi visited the Court of one Árya Ségaraṉ of Siṅgai who presented him with thousand pieces of gold and an elephant which the poet removed to Madura. A verse which he uttered when the Páṇḍyaṉ went to his house in order to secure the elephant,* and another when he heard of the death of the Árya King† are extant. The poet also visited Kataragama travelling via Colombo where he composed a verse in praise of a ferry boatman.‡

---

* "பாவலன் வாசலில் வந்திபம் வாங்கப்படி புரக்குங்
காவலர் நிற்கும்படி வைத்த வாகண்டி யொன்பதினும்
மேவலர் மார்பினுந் திண்டோளினுஞ் செம்பொன் மேருவினுஞ்
சேவெழுதும் பெருமான் சிங்கையாரிய சேகரனே."

Tam. Náv. S., p. 146.

He who made crowned heads to attend at the door of the poet and to beg for his elephant was Siṅgai Ārya Sékaraṉ who inscribes (his emblem) 'the Bull' on the nine kandies (continents), on the breasts and broad shoulders of his enemies and on the golden Méru.

[Here the word Segarájasékaraṉ or Pararájasékaraṉ is contracted to Sékaraṉ.]

† "அஆ விதியோ வடலாரியர் கோமான்
எ.எ வலராவிழந்த நாள்—ஒஓ
தருக்கண்ணிலுங் குளிர்ந்த தண்ணளி தந்தாண்ட
திருக்கண்ணினுஞ் சுடுமோ தீ."

Tam. Náv. S., p. 144.

Oh, is it fate ? (Curse) the day in which the great Ārya king was carried away by the messengers of Death! Will fire burn his sacred eyes which were beaming with grace and were even cooler than the eyes of the young fruit of the palmyrah?

‡ "கயக்காவி நாறுங் கொழும்பிற் பிரசண்டா
சாரோர்கொடைச் செங்கை யாரோ தன் மைந்தா
இயக்காநின்மார்பிற் செழும் புன்னையந்தார்
இப்போது நீ நல்கிலென் பேதை தன்மேற்
சயங்காமவேளம் புதையாது முத்தின்
தாமஞ் சுடாசந்தனம் பூசினாலுந்
தியக்காதுவேயுஞ் செவிக்கும் பொறுக்குந்
தீயென்றுழலாது திங்கட்கொழுந்தே."

Tam Náv. S., p. 146.

Oh! Prasandá (strong and brave man) of Colombo ever smelling of fish! Oh Yákka! the son of Āródan with the hand of beneficence similar to the dark cloud! If you hand over at once the garland of Punnai flowers you are wearing on your breast, the arrows of Cupid will not wound her etc.

Pughaḷéndi is well known as the earlier contemporary of the famous poet Oṭṭakúttaṉ who was the Court poet of three Chóḷa kings, viz., Vikrama Chóḷa, Kumara Kulótuṅga II and Rája Rája II, as will be seen from Saṅgara Chóḷaṉ Ulá.* Vikrama was the son of Kulótuṅga I and reigned from 1118 to 1143, Kulótunga II from 1143 to 1146, and Rájarája II from 1146 to 1163 A.D. Pughaḷéndi lived during the time of Vikrama and Kulótuṅga II.† From the above, it will be seen that kings calling themselves Árya Sékaraṉ (Parարájasékaraṉ or Segarájasékaraṉ) were reigning at Siṅgai Nagar in Jaffna during the early part of the 12th century. It was with the help of this king that the poet made his pilgrimage to Kataragama as did Ibn Batuta to Adam's Peak with the help of another in the 14th century.

The earliest mention of the Áryas is made in the Mahávaṅsa Chapter LXI. During the time of Vikrama Báhu (1121—1142 A.D.) the son of Vijaya Báhu I, it is

---

* "கூடலா
ரும்பரணிகொள்ளக் கொள்வித் தொருகலிங்க
வெம்பரணி கொண்ட விறலோனுஞ்—செம்பதத்துக்
கூடிய 'சீர்தந்த' வென்றெடுத்த கூத்தனுலாச்
சூடிய விக்ரம சோழனும்—பாடிய
வெள்ளைக்கலியுலா மாலையொடு மீண்டுமவன்
பிள்ளைத்தமிழ் மாலை பெற்றோனுந்—தெள்ளித்தம்
முன்னாயகரினவன் மூதுலாக் கண்ணிதொறும்
பொன்னாயிரஞ் சொரிந்த பூபதியும்"

S. Ch. Ulá.

Kalingattuparaṇi was composed in honour of Kulótunga I.		
Vikrama Chóḷan Ulá	„	Vikrama Chóḷa.
Ulá and Piḷḷai Tamil	„	Kumara Kulótunga II
An Ulá for every verse of which Kúttan was paid 1000 gold coins.	„	Rájarája II

† S. Tamil, vol. ii, p. 393 et seq.

said, that " a certain valiant and furious man named Víra Déva who was born in the country of the Áryas and was the Chief of Pálandípa landed at Mahatittha with mighty men," invaded Ceylon and defeated Vikrama Báhu who fled for security to the fastnesses of the mountains in the centre of the Island.* By the country of the Áryas, no doubt, was meant the kingdom of Jaffna For, Pálandípa of which Víra Déva was the Chieftain must be the insignificant island Pálaidívu which at that time might have been populated and possessed a chieftain strong enough to invade Ceylon. It is not possible to conceive of any other island or of any country in India which the author of the Mahávansa would have called by that name.

It appears from an allusion in the Tamil work Chóḻa Manḍala Sadagam† that at a time of great famine in Ceylon, a thousand boatloads of paddy were sent by Saḍayaṉ or Saḍayappa Mudali of Puduvai (Pondicheri) to Pararájasingaṉ, the King of Kandy, to relieve the distress. Saḍayappa Mudali was a wealthy Veḷḷáḷa Chief who had his residence both at Puduvai and at Tiruveṇṇai

---

* Mah.. chap. lxi, vv. 36 –45.

† "தேனார் தொடையார் பரராசசிங்கப் பெருமான் செழுந்தமிழ்க்குக்
கானார் நெல்லின்மலைகோடி கண்டிநாடு கரைசேரக்
கூனார் கப்பலாயிரத்திற் கொடுபோயளித்த கொடைத்தடக்கை
மானாகரன் சங்கரன் சடையன் வளஞ்சேர் சோழமண்டலமே."

Ch. Maṇ. S., v.

Saṅgaran Saḍayan of the liberal hand, who sent mountain loads of paddy in thousand ships to the country of Kandy for a Tamil verse (in his praise) composed by the king Pararájasingaṉ wearing the honey dripping garland, was of Chóḻa Manḍalam.

Nallúr and was the patron and benefactor of Kamban, the author of the Rámáyaṇam in Tamil. As Kamban was the later contemporary of Oṭṭakúttan and appears to have survived him and his patron, and as the Chóḻa power declined after his death as the result of a curse uttered by him at his death, he must have been killed by the Chóḻa king Kulótuṅga III (1178—1216 A.D.). Kamban, when he fell out with the Chóḻa king sought the patronage of Rudra I the King of Waraṅgal, who came to the throne about 1162 A. D. He would not have done so, if Saḍayaṉ had been alive at the time. Saḍayaṉ must have died soon after the Rámáyaṇam had received its imprimatur in the reign of Rája Rája II. Parakrama Báhu came to the throne of Ceylon in 1154 A.D., and it must have been some famine such as this immediately before his accession that made him undertake the construction and restoration of several large tanks in the Island, in order to prevent the recurrence of the famine. It was actually during this period that Saḍayappa Mudali lived and his munificent donation to relieve distress in Ceylon would not have been an exaggeration. About the middle part of the 12th century there was no king reigning at Kandy and the Tamil Chóḻa Maṇḍala Sadagam which contains a reference to the event, being a recent composition composed at a time when Kandy was well known as the Capital of Ceylon, the author mistook Pararájasingaṉ who received the bounty for one ruling at Kandy. This Pararájasingaṉ was, therefore, a King of Jaffna and a descendant of Jayatuṅga who was himself known as Pararájasiṅgaṉ or Vararájasiṅgaṉ as stated in the Vaipava Málai. A beautiful Tamil verse in which the thanks of the King were couched and sent to Saḍayappa Mudali is also extant.*

According to the historical introduction of a Tamil inscription of the 20th year (1236 A.D.) of Máravarmaṉ Sundara Páṇḍya I (1216—1244 A.D.) found at Tirukólúr, he conquered the Chóḻa king, drove him into the forest, set fire to Tanjore and Uraiyúr, anointed himself as a hero, cut off the head of one Pararája and went to Sidambaram. While there, the Chóḻa king came to him and begged for his crown and he (Sundara) accordingly granted him back his crown and the kingdom.† The Pararája whom the

---

* "இரவு நண்பகலாகிலென் பகலிருளறு விரவாகிலெ [லென்
னிரவியெண்டிசை மாறிலென் கடலேழு மேறிலென்வற்றி
மாபுதங் கியமுறைமைபேணிய மன்னர் போகிலெஞுகிலென்
வன்மையின்புறு சோழமண்டலவாழ்க்கை காரணமாகவே
கருது செம்பொனி னம்பலத்திலோர் கடவுணின்று நடிக்குமே
காவிரித் திருநதியிலே யொருகருணை மாமுகிறுயிலுமே
தருவுயர்ந்திடு புதுவையம் பதிதங்கு மன்னிய சேகரன்
சங்கரன்றருசடைய னென்றொருதரு மதேவதைவாளவே."

S. Tamil, vol. iii, p. 6.

" * * * * * *
தஞ்சையு முறந்தையுஞ் செந்தழல் கொழுத்தி
* * * * * *
செம்பியனைச் சினமிரியப் பொருதுசுரம் புகவோட்டி
* * * * * *
சோழவளவ னபிஷேக மண்டபத்து
வீராபிஷேகஞ் செய்து புகழ்விரித்து
நாடும்பாராச னாமத்தலை பிடுங்கி
மூடுந்தறுகண் மதயானைமேல் கொண்டு
* * * * * *
தெய்வப் புலியூர் தெருவெல்லையிற்புக்கு"

S. Tamil, vol. xii, pp. 346—350.

He (Sundara Pàṇḍya) set fire to Tanjore and Uṛaiyúr, fought the Chòḻa, defeated him and drove him into the forest, spread his fame by annointing himself as a hero in the coronation hall of the Chòḻas, severed the head of the *Pararaja* and riding on an elephant entered the streets of the holy city of Sidambaram.

Páṇḍyaṉ killed was no doubt a Pararájasiṅgaṉ or Pararájasékaraṉ of Jaffna. The word 'Pararája' is used in the inscription in the sense of a specific king and does not admit the interpretation of 'an enemy king.' The Jaffna king must have gone to the help of the Chóḷa sovereign in the prosecution of the war against the Páṇḍyaṉ as the itinerary described in the historical introduction precludes the possibility of the Páṇḍyaṉ army landing in Ceylon. The event must have taken place before 1224 A.D., for in an inscription of the same Páṇḍyaṉ of his 8th year found at Áḻvár Tirunagari, he is described as the Sri Sundara Páṇḍya Dévar who was pleased to return the Choḷa country (to its ruler).*

From an inscription found at Tiruvandipuram, of the time of the Chóḷa King Rájarája III, it appears that in the 14th year of his reign (1231—1232 A.D.), Hoysala Narasinha II went to the help of the Chóḷa king who was captured by one of his chieftains Kópperuñjiṅga of Séndamaṅgaḷam.† In the early part of the 13th century, the Chóḷa power in South India had become so weak as to bring about the disintegration of the Empire. Several chiefs who were once the vassals of the Chóḷa kings and who had helped in the expansion of that great and powerful Empire, fortified their own towns and citadels and began to set themselves up as independent lords of their own little principalities. The foremost among them was Kópperuñjiṅga Déva the Pallava chieftain of Séndamaṅgaḷam. Narasiṅha II of the newly risen Hoysala Ballala

---

* "சோணாடு வழங்கியருளிய ஸ்ரீ சுந்தர பாண்டியதேவர்

S. Tamil, vol. xii, p. 498.

† Ep. Ind., vol. vii, p. 163; M. E. R., 1902. § 9 p. 15; Insc. [142 of 1902

dynasty of Halebid, who was related to Rájarája III by alliance, having heard of the misfortune that befell his relative, led an expedition, defeated Peruñjiṅga and his allies, released Rájarája from his captivity and replaced him on the Chóḻa throne. The inscription also adds that among the partisans of Peruñjiṅga, were Parákrama Báhu the King of Ceylon and three of his Officers, and that Parákrama Báhu lost his life in the course of the war. Who was this Parákrama Báhu? He was evidently the King of Jaffna. Kaliṅga Magha or Vijaya Báhu was, from 1215 A.D., reigning at Polonnaruwa and he was also the King of Jaffna, as his forts extended from Úratoṭa to Colombo, and from Colombo to Coṭṭiár. Parákrama Báhu who is betrayed by his Kaliṅga name as well as the Pararájasiṅgaṉ who was killed by Máravarmaṉ Sundara Páṇḍya I in 1224 A.D., were probably the viceroys or sub-kings ruling in Jaffna. Parákrama Báhu having thrown his lot with the other Chóḻa chieftains fought on the side of Kópperuñjiṅga and was killed in battle. It was perhaps the part played by Parákrama Báhu, which is alluded to in the historical introduction of the astrological work 'Segarájasékaram' where an ancestor of the Jaffna kings is said to have fought the Poysala (Hoysala) king * The earlier portion of the verse

* "சென்றுகருநாடகரை யந்தரவல்லியிற் பொருது செயித்த [வேந்தும்
கன்றிவருமத வேழக்கரந்துணித்துப் போசலனைக் கடிந்தவேந் [தும்

Sega. A., Sirappupayiram, v. 6.

The king who went, fought and conquered the Canarese at Antaravalli, and the king who punished the Poysala (Hoysala) by cutting off the trunk of (his) enraged elephant (that came against him.)

states that a king fought the Kannaṭas at Antaravilli. Hoysala Narasiṅha is called a Karunaḍa (Kannáḍa) king in an inscription of Jaṭávarmaṉ Sundara Páṇḍya I.* The two events mentioned in the verse might refer to the part played by the same king at the same time. Was Antaravilli another name for Séndamaṅgaḷam?

It was perhaps to avenge the act of the abovenamed Parákrama Báhu which was not forgotten by the Chóḻa kings, that a Chóḻa army invaded Jaffna during the reign of Rájendra Chóḻa III, the successor of Rájarája III, as will be seen by his Srirangam inscription of the 7th year (1253 A.D.) and by the one at Lépaka in the Cuddapah District,† which described him as a great hero "a very Rama (in destroying) the northern Lanka which was renowned as the abode of Vírarákshasas." The heroism displayed by the Jaffna army is acknowledged in the epithet "Vírarákshasas." It is perhaps a battle field of this invasion which is alluded to in a verse in Angádipátam (anatomy), a portion of the Tamil medical treatise "Ségarájasékaram" as the one where the bodies of the Vaḍakkar (northerners) were rolled over.‡

---

* See infra chap. viii. p.

† M. E. R. of 1912, § 32. p. 69; insc no. 64 of 1892 & no. 42 [of 1911.

‡ "இயம்பிய வுடலுமூனு மென்பு நாடிகளுமற்றும்
செயம்பெறுசிங்கை நாடன் செகராச சேகரன்மா
லுயர்ந்தவாழ் வடக்காரக முருட்டிய கழத்தின்மீதே
அயஞ்சிறிதுளதுதீர வழந்தழந் தறிந்த தாமே."

Sega. M. Aṇkádipátam.

(The information aş regards) body, blood, bones, arteries and veins above described was, to dispel whatever little doubt that remained, obtained by repeated measurements on the bodies of the Northerners, which the great sword of the victorious Segarájasékaraṇ of Siṅgai had rolled on the battle-field.

From the foregoing allusions found in the Mahávaṅsa, Tamil literature and Indian inscriptions, it can be gathered that Kaliṅga kings calling themselves Áryas were reigning in the 10th, 11th and 12th centuries and in the early part of the 13th century in Jaffna. They were probably the descendants of Ugra Siṅgaṉ who pounced upon the throne of Jaffna in 795 A.D, as stated in the Vaipava Málai. The mention made by the Mohammedan travellers of the 10th and 11th centuries of "a Mihiraj of Zapage" adds confirmation to this inference.

Why the Kaliṅga kings of Jaffna called themselves Árya Chakravartis is a matter worthy of further investigation. The kings who reigned at Jaffna up to the 17th century until the kingdom fell ultimately, in 1618 A.D., into the hands of the Portuguese, claimed that they were descended from two Brahman kings who were appointed by Ráma himself, after his conquest of Ceylon and the establishment of the Rám´svaram temple, to rule over the Northern District of Ceylon including Rámésvaram.* It

---

* 1. "எழில்வாய்ந்தமணி மௌலித்துளவணி மாறசாதன்சேயென [வந்தெய்தித்
தொழில்வாய்ந்த விளவலொடு சென்று முனிவோனினருள் [சுரந்துகாத்துப்
பொழில்வாயந் தமிதிலைநகர்வில்லிறுத் து;த்திருவை மணம் [புரிந்து வெண்சங்
குழிவாய்ந்த மணிகொழிக்குந் தன்னகர் வந்தன்னை தரு முறை [யைவேண்டி

2. மின்னுடனெடிய கானகம் புகுந்து விராதனை மாய மாரீசன்
றன்னை வாலியை யேழ்மராமரங்களை வெஞ்சாயக மொன்றினுற் [றடிந்து
மன்னு நீர் வேலை யடைத் தடலிலங்கை வளநகர் புகுந்தெழிற் [கும்ப
கன்னனையரக்கர் கோவினைச்செயித்துக் கமலநாயகி சிறைகடிந்து

[Contd.]

3. கருங்கடற்சேனை வெள்ள முந்தானுங் கந்தமால்வரைப் புறத்
[தணுக
விருங்கதத்தரக்கன் சாயைவிட்டகன்றவியல் பினைத்திருவுளத்
[தெண்ணி
வருங்கலைப்பொதிய மாமுனிக் குரைப்பவ னுமத்தலத்தின
[தியலைப்
பெருங்கதைப்படுத்த வதிசயத்தந்தப் பெருங் கதையாதாம்
[பிணிப்ப

4. அந்தமாதலத்தி லான்றனைத் தாபித்தருச்சனை புரிந்து தன்
[னு மஞ்
சிந்தையாலருளியப்பதி தனக்குத் திருப்பெயரன்னதேயாக்கி
நந்தலில் பஞ்சக்கிராம வேதியராய் நான்மறைப் பொருளுளம்
[பிரியாப்
பைந்தொடைப் பாசுபதர்களைஞ்ஞூற்றுப் பன்னிருவரை வர
[வழைத்து

5. பூசனைசெயுமினீரெனக் கருணைபுரிந்தவர் தங்களிலிருவர்
காசினிதாங்கும்படி வரங்கொடுத்துக் கமழ் செழுந்துளப மாலி
[கையு
மாசறு சுருதியாரியவேந்தென்றணி மணிப்பட்டமும் சொடுத்
[துத்
தேசறுகுடையு மொற்றையும் வெற்றித்திகழ்'விடைத்து வசமு
[நல்க"

Sega. A., Siṛappupáyiram, vv. 1- 5

1. The *tulasi* wreathed Vishnu having incarnated as (Ráma) the son of Dasarata of the beautiful gem set crown. he (Ráma) with his valiant younger brother went and guarded (the sacrifice of) the Rishi (Viswámitra) whose grace he received. He bent the bow at the green groved Mitilai and married Lakshmi (Síta). On his return to the city where the dust of white chanks are washed on to the river banks, obedient to the wishes of his mother,

2. he repaired with his wife to the impentrable forest where he killed Biráda, the wily Marisa and Báli and shot through seven gigantic trees with a single arrow. He dammed the sea of broad waters, entered the beautiful city of forest clad Lanká, conquered the mighty Kumbakarna and the king of the Yakkhas (Rávana), and rescued his lotus faced wife from captivity.

3. When he with his vast army like unto a dark ocean approached the Kandamádanam hill, the shadow (the stain of the guilt of killing) of the Rákshasa of great iniquity (Rávana) which haunted him, vanished from his presence. Having noted this peculiar occurrence he related the same to the learned rishi (Agastya) of the Potiya hill. The latter revealed to him the (sacred)

[Contd.]

is also said that Ráma gave them the title of Árya kings and granted to them the parasol, the single conch, the bull standard and the emblem of Sétu.* It cannot be now denied that they were called Árya kings. That name appears not only in the literature of the period but also

importance of the place which roused his wonder and being impressed with the (Puranic) sacredness of the story,

4. he established the worship of Siva at the place, and involuntarily gave the God and the sacred place his own name, and having sent for 512 brahmans of the Pásupata sect whose minds were full of the knowledge of the four Vedas,

5. he gracefully directed them to officiate (at the temple) and invested two of them with the authority of sovereignty, granting to them the wreath of the sweet smelling Tulasi, the title of the spotless vedic Ārya king, the beautiful parasol, the single (conch) and the victorious bull flag.

[That 512 brahmans first came from Benares and settled at Rámésvaram is confirmed by the following lines from a Tamil work called Dévai Ulá composed by Palapaṭṭaḍai Chokkanáta Pulaver.

"மெய்நூற்றுறையின் விதிவழியே பூசிக்கும்
ஐந்நூற்றுப் பன்னிருவர் ஆரியரும்—இந்நிலத்திற்
றேற்றுமலையத்தனையுஞ் சேதுபந்த மீதுகுடி
யேற்றுலக நாதமுனி யென்போனும்"

The use of the word Ārya for brahmans in the above lines is noticeable.]

* a. Sega. A., Siṛappupáyiram, v. 5.

b. "அடற்கரிமூவாயிரத்தோடெழுநூறு பாவருலக் களித்தகோவும்
விடைக்கொடியுஞ்சேதுவு நீள் கண்டிகளொன்பதிற் பொறித்து
[மிகைத்த கோவும்
வடக்கெழுவாடைக்கு மிளந்தென்றலுக்குந் தன்குலப்பேர்
[வழங்குகோவுங்
கடக்கலுழியத்திதனை யிரவலர் தங்கட்களித்த கருணைக்கோவும்
Ibid. v. 7.

And the king who presented 3700 wild elephants to poets, and the one who inscribed the bull flag and (the emblem) Sétu in profusion on the nine continents, and the king who gave the name of his dynasty to the north wind and the south wind and the ruler who presented elephants to the beggars.

["நீள் கண்டிகளொன்பதும் பொறித்து" is in the printed version but we have corrected it to "நீள் கண்டிகளொன்பதிற் பொறித்து"; vide Pughaléndi's verse; supra, p. 285, note.*]

in several later works and inscriptions.* The fact that they called themselves Áryas must have been due either to a Brahman origin or to Brahman connections. The Brahman origin is certainly mythical and appears to have been one adopted by the later kings after they attained power and eminence, in the same manner as most of the Indian royal dynasties manufactured a Puranic geneology in order to trace their origin back either to the Sun or to the Moon. That the Kings of Jaffna wore a sacred thread over their shoulders,† an emblem not worn

---

* (a.) "கந்தமலையாரியர்கோன் செகராச சேகரமன் கங்கைநாடன்"
Sega. A., Siṛappupáyiram v. 11.
Segarâjasêkaraṉ the Ârya king of Kandamâdaṉam and of the [Gaṅgakula.

(b.) "வென்றிசேராரிய வாரியர் குலாதிபன்"
Sega., A., p. 69, v. 9
The king of the victorious Ārya dynasty.

(c.) "மன்னர்மன்னு செகராச சேகரன் மணவையாரிய வரோதயன்
ibid p. 69, v. 10
Segarâjasêkaraṉ the king of kings, the Ârya king of Maṇavai.

(d.) "சிங்கை நகராரியனைச் சேராவனுரேசர்"
Kotagama insc.; Bell
The lords of Anurai who did not join the Ârya king of Siṅgai

(e.) "கங்கையாரின் பதுமத்தாள்" Ragu. Pad. x. v. 223.
The lotus like feet of the Ārya of Gaṅga (vamsa)
"கங்கையாரின் விடையினவாணி" Raghu. Pad. xiii. v. 107.
The Bull banner of the Ārya of the Gaṅga (vamsa)
"சிரியசெயற் பரராச சேகர
வாரியன் றடம்புகள்" Raghu. Pad. vii. v. 63.
The wide fame of Pararâjasekara the Âryan.

† "முத்தமிழ்தேர் செகராச சேகர மன்றிருமார்பின் முன்னூ [லென்ன"
Sega., A, p. 53, v. 37.
Like unto the sacred thread worn on the breast of Segarâjasè-karaṉ learned in the three kinds of Tamil (classic, lyric and dramatic.)

by any other kings of South India or Ceylon, is a sure sign of their Áryaṉ origin, whether they wore the thread as brahmans or as kshatriyas. There is no earlier record of any brahmans having reigned in any part of Ceylon either at Rámésvaram or elsewhere. It was perhaps after hearing of these brahman kings that Bertolacci wrote, "The town of Mantota is said to have been the capital of a kingdom founded by the brahmans who had possession of almost all the northern parts of Ceylon including Jaffnapatam."* The earlier kings of Jaffna were Nágas and in the beginning of the 9th century came Ugra Siṅgaṉ the first Kaliṅga king, and it would be seen that after him Kaliṅga kings occupied the throne of Jaffna. The first Árya king was, according to the Vaipava Málai, a Chóḷa prince and, according to the Kailáya Málai, a son of the Páṇḍya king. If he was a Páṇḍyaṉ or a Chóḷa how did he become an Áryaṉ? The clue to this problem is, however, given by the Portuguese historian De Quieroz. He says: "In process of time there came some brahmins natives of Guzerat, called Arus and with the favour of the Nayak of Madura got the temple Ramanacor, whence they came for trade and friendship with the kings of Jaffna and one of them married a daughter of that king and finally his descendants became heirs of that kingdom.†" Simon Casie Chetty, without referring to De Queiroz, says "some accounts represent Singha Áriya as sprung from the stock of Chóḷa by a brahmin female of Mañavy in Ramnad, and hence he is said to have assumed the ambiguous title of

* Bertol, Intro. p. 12.

† Quieroz, liv. i, cap. vii, Translation by Rev. S. Gnanapragasar.

Áriya to signify both sides of his parentage, for the word 'Áriya' is a synonym for the Chóḻa kings as well as for the brahmins."* Whatever might have been the authority of Casie Chetty for the above assertion, he was not correct in stating that a brahman female married a Chóḻa, or that Maṇavai was in Ramnad or that 'the title Árya was ambiguous and was a synonym for the Chóḻa. The Chóḻas never called themselves Áryas and Maṇavai was a contraction of Maṇalúr or Maṇavúr one of the ancient names of Jaffna.† Casie Chetty, taking the statement in the Yáḻpáṇa Vaipava Málai that the first king of Jaffna was a Chóḻa prince as true, and hearing of the brahman marriage, wove out a story from his own imagination. The marriage might have taken place in the manner described by De Queiroz. He too has committed two anachronisms in his statement. He confuses the Indian emigrants from Guzerat to Java in the 7th century‡ and the Sétupatis, the earliest of whom received Rámnad from the Nayak King of Madura in 1604 A.D., with the brahmans of Rámésvaram. That the brahmans went for trade to Jaffna is doubtful, but that one of them married a princess of Jaffna which was then known as Maṇavai is

* J. C. B. R. A. S. vol. i. p. 76, note.

† See supra chap i, pp. 37, 38.

‡ "The Javanese chronicles state that about 603 A. D, a ruler of Guzerat forewarned of the coming destruction of his kingdom, started his son with 5000 followers, among whom were cultivators, artizans, warriors, physicians and writers, in six large and 100 small vessels, for Java where they laid the foundation of a civilization that had given to the world the sculptures of Borobudur."

Ind. Ship., p. 49.

highly probable. When did this marriage take place and who was the first of the Árya kings? We have seen that the name Árya as applied to the kings of Jaffna was first mentioned in the Mahávaṅsa and by the poet Pughaḻéndi about the early part of the 12th century. So the brahman alliance with the royal house of Jaffna must have taken place much earlier than the 12th century and the kings called themselves Árya kings, and when they had grown strong enough to invade the rest of Ceylon they called themselves Árya Chakravartis. One is, however, led to surmise that 948 A.D. as stated in the first line of the stray stanza referred to earlier* denotes the date of accession of the first king of the brahman parentage. Brahman alliances with ruling dynasties were not uncommon in South India. As late as the 14th century A.D., Virupadevi, a daughter of Bukka I of Vijaya Nagar, was married to a brahman named Bommanna Odeya who enjoyed the position of Governor of certain districts which were called Árya Rájya after him, and members of his family became the hereditary governors of that Rájya.†

Either because Rámésvaram was under their sway or because the brahman progenitor of their dynasty came from Rámésvaram, they took the legend 'Sétu' as their emblem and seal. The fact that they called themselves 'Sétukávalan' or 'Sétukávalavan'‡ clearly proves their dominion over Rámésvaram. The Sétupatis became the

* See supra, p. 274, note,*

† Ep. Ind. vol. xv, p. 12.

‡ a. "சேதுக்காவலவன் விஞ்ஞைச்விஞ்சு செகராச சேகரன்'

Seg. A p. 40, v. 5

The learned Segarájasékaraṉ the protector of Sétu.

b. "சிங்கையாரியன் சேது காவலன்"

Dak. K. P., Siṛappupáyiram.

Siṅgai Áryaṉ the protector of Sétu.

Chiefs of Rámnad including Rámésvaram during the reign of Muttu Krishnappa Naik of Madura. Saḍayakka Uḍayáṉ, the obscure chief of Pogalúr, was granted the title of Uḍayáṉ Sétupati and made the Over-lord of all the Maravars for acts of conspicuous bravery and loyalty.* From that time the Sétupatis exercised authority over Rámésvaram. Saḍayakka Uḍayán received his appointment in 1604 A.D, and the inscriptions of the Sétupatis are all subsequent to that date.

The fact that the kings of Jaffna used the legend 'Sétu' as their emblem can be seen from the Kotagama inscription† where it is used as an invocation in place of 'Svasti Sri' found in the Chóḷa and the Siṅhalese inscriptions, and from the coins issued by them. There are several varieties of these coins and about 20 of them are shown in the paper "The forgotten coinage of the Jaffna kings."‡ The Jaffna as well as Polonnaruwa kings imitated the coinage of the Chóḷas; but while the Polonnaruwa coins were the exact replicas of the Rájarája type, the obverse only of the Jaffna coins was of the Chóḷa type. The reverse on the other hand contained the crest and emblem of the Jaffna kings in imitation of the coins issued by the Gaṅga kings of Kaliṅgam. Four gold coins found at Gañjam and described by Dr. E Hultzsch in his paper entitled "Miscellaneous South Indian Coins" published in the Indian Antiquary.¶ had a recumbent

* Ind. Ant. vol. xlv, p. 105.

† Bell; Inscription slab in the Colombo Museum.

‡ We were the first to suggest that the bull coins with the legend 'Sètu' were issued by the kings of Jaffna and it was later confirmed by Rev. S. Gnanapragàsar in his "Forgotten Coinage of the Kings of Jaffna."

¶ Ind. Ant., vol. xxv, p. 322.

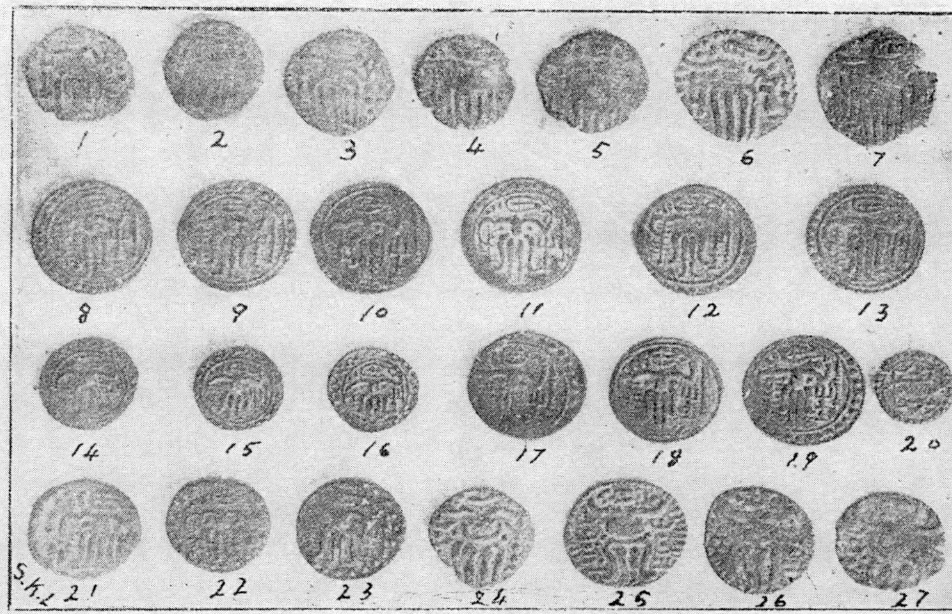

Jaffna Coins (Obverse)

with the kind permission of Rev. S. Gnanapragasar O. M. I.

To face page 300.] Photo by S. K. Lawton.]

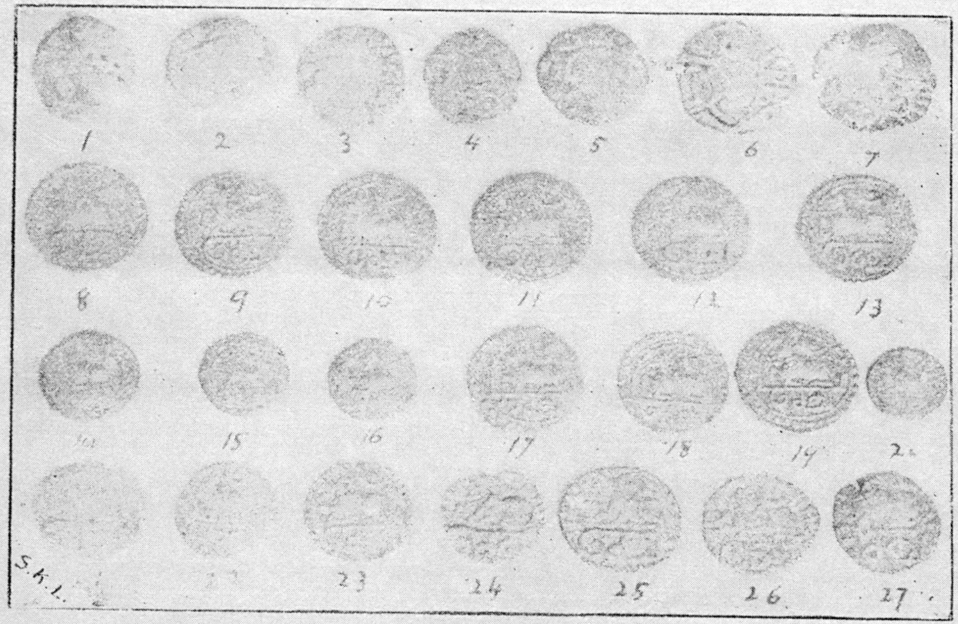

Jaffna Coins (Reverse)

with the kind permission of Rev. S. Gnanapragasar O. M. I.

To face page 301.]

Photo by S. K. Lawton.]

bull facing the left with the Sun, Crescent or Linga in different positions as regards the bull, with the legend on the reverse supposed to be the regnal year of Anantavarman an Eastern Gaṅga king who came to the throne in 1078 A.D. In the list of "Doubtful coins of Southern India" published by Robert Sewell in the Indian Antiquary, * three (Nos; 43 a, 43 b and 43c) which were not identified by him, are coins issued by the kings of Jaffna. In them the legend 'Sétu' is written with the letter 'tu' above the 'sé' with a line between. There is no bull and the obverse is of the debased Chóḷa type. These coins perhaps belong to an issue earlier than the type containing the recumbent bull and to a time in which the Jaffna kings had not adopted the bull as their emblem. Did they then use the lyre for their standard and does the lyre flag referred to in one of the verses of the Kaliṅgattu Paraṇi † as one conquered by the Chóḷa Kings

---

* Ind. Ant., vol. xxxii. p.

† "கேழன்மேழி கலையாழி வீணைசிலை
கெண்டையென்றிணைய பல்கொடி
தாழமேருவிலுயர்த்த செம்பியர்
தனிப்புலிக் கொடிதழைக்கவே."

Kalin., Saptamátar Tuti, v. 18.

Several flags like the boar, the plough, the stag, the lion, the lyre, the bow and the carps went down and the single tiger flag of the Chóḷas which was raised on (Mount) Méru only flourished.

[The boar represented the Chaḷukyas.

,,	plough	,,	Yádavas.
,,	stag	,,	Pálas of Bengal.
,,	lion	,,	Siṅhalese.
,,	bow	,,	Céras.
,	carps	,,	Páṇḍyas.

Did the lyre represent the Jaffnese? Its position in the verse next to to the Siṅhalese and before the Céras and the Pàṇḍyas is evident confirmation of the surmise.]

represent the Jaffna flag of the period? If the lyre flag was ever used by the kings of Jaffna it must have been earlier than the twelfth century, A.D., for the literary works composed in and after the twelfth century speak of the bull flag only.

It is now impossible to say whether the Jaffna coins were earlier than those of Parákrama Báhu, I. It is also not known if Jaffna had any gold issue as no gold coin of the type has yet been found. The scarcity of gold coins may perhaps be due to the fact that they were melted down as soon as they were found.

The recumbent bull with the crescent and the sun was represented not only on their coins but also on their banners and flags. There are several allusions to the bull flag in the literature of this and of later periods.* There were several dynasties in India who had the device of the bull on their flags and coins. The Pallavas had a standing humped bull as well as a couchant bull with the

---

* a Sega. A., Sirappupáyiram, v. 7; supra, p: 295, note * b.

b. "விடலாண்வயமா விளங்கிய கொடியான்"

Dak. K. P., Sirappupáyiram.

He of the bull flag.

c. "அண்டருலக நிமிர்ந்தாடும் பரிசுடைத்தாய்
கொண்டவிடைகாட்டுங் கொடியினன்"

K. M., p. 5.

He who possessed the flag displaying the Bull and waving as high as the region of the gods.

d. "வெற்றிவிடைக்கொடியார் மேலாரிய குலத்தி
னுற்ற மடப்பளியிலுள்ளோரும்"

Kiḷḷai V. T., v. 152.

The Madapaḷḷis who belong to the high Āryakula and who are entitled to the flag of the victorious Bull.

(The Madapaḷḷis, a special class of Veḷḷaḷas nowadays, claim to have descended from the kings of Jaffna.)

crescent, sun and one or more stars on their crest. * The Maitrakas of Valabi who flourished circa 500 A.D., had for their crest a bull couchant facing right with the legend "Sri Bhatakkah" underneath. † The Rashtrakúṭas of Malkhed who reigned from 675 to 1000 A.D. had a bull with the sun above it, and a cow and calf with the moon above them. ‡ The Kalachuris of Kalanjara had the banner of a golden bull. § The kings of the Nimbara dynasty of the North Western Provinces who were powerful in the ninth century A D. had for their seal emblem a couchant bull.¶ The seal of the Buddhist kings of Uttara Tosali in Orissa bore the figure of a bull couchant on a short pedestal.|| Several Gaṅga families reigned at different places in Mysore, in Talakhad, Malkhed, and Kuvaḷálapuram (Kolar). The Gaṅgas of Talakhad had an elephant as their emblem ** and those of Kuvaḷálapuram a couchant bull†† The Eastern Gaṅgas of Kaliṅga who reigned from Kaliṅgapuram (modern Mukhaliṅgam) had for their crest a couchant bull facing left. ‡‡ The Reddi Chiefs of Rájamahéndra who exercised an ephemeral sovereignty for a short time in the 15th century had for their crest a

---

* Ep. Ind., vol. viii, p. 144, Maiḍavólu plates of the 8th century.

Ibid vol. vi, p. 84.

† Ibid vol. viii,

‡ Ibid vol. vi.

§ Ibid vol. v, p. 257, Ablur inscription.

¶ Ind. Ant., vol. xxv.

|| Ep. Ind., vol. xv, p. 1, Neulpur grant of Subhakara.

** Ibid vol. vi.

†† Ibid vol. vi.

‡‡ Ibid vol. iv, p. 243; Naḍagam Plates.

couchant bull and a sun and moon*. The Reddi Chiefs of Kondaivídu who were related to the Chiefs of Ràja-Mahèndra had for their seal a couchant bull with the sun and the crescent moon†.

Did the Kings of Jaffna who used the couchant bull with the sun and the crescent moon as their emblems belong to any of the above families?. Did they borrow their crests from any of them as a matter of right or was it an imitation? It is indeed a very difficult matter to apply the process of elimination unless we enquire into their *vamsa*.

The kings of Jaffna claimed to belong to the *Ganga Vamsa* ‡. There were several Gaṅga chiefs who held high offices of state under the Chóḻas and the Pallavas. Laṅkapuri the General of Parákrama Báhu I, who went to

---

* Ep. Ind., vol. v, No. 9, Konkuduru plates of Alleya Dodda.

† Ibid vol. iv, No. 46, Tottaramudi plates of Kaleya Vima.

‡ a. "கந்தமலையாரியர்கோன் செகராச சேகரமன் கங்கை நாடன்"

Sega. A., Siṛappupáyiram, v. 11.

Segarájasékaraṉ, the Ārya king of Kandamádanam, and of the Gaṅgakula.

b. "கங்கையாரியன் பதுமத்தாள்"

Raghu, Pad, x, v. 223.

The lotus like feet of Gaṅgai Āryan

c. "மன்றுகண்டருளுங் கங்கையாரியன் விடையின்வானி"

Raghu. Pad. xiii. v. 107.

The bull flag of the Āryan of the Gaṅga (vamsa) who dispenses Justice in his Audience Hall.

d. "கங்கைநாடன் கற்றவர்திலகன்"

Dak. K. P., Siṛappupáyiram,

He of the Gaṅga country (vamsa), a forehead mark among learned men.

India with a large army to help one of the claimants to the Páṇḍyaṉ throne and to fight against the Chóḻas "went against the country of Víra Gaṅga and laid waste Kunnappu Nallúr,'* and out of the chiefs taken by Kulasékara to give battle to Laṅkápuri were Gáṅgéyar and Víra Gaṅga.† According to the Tamil work 'Toṇḍai Maṇḍala Sadagam, Karikála the Great brought a number of families from the Gangetic valley (and on that account said to belong to the Gaṅgakula) settled them in the 24 districts (Kóṭṭam) of Toṇḍai Maṇḍalam and bestowed on them rich gifts.‡ These were the progenitors of the Gaṅga Chiefs who later fought on the side of the Pallavas and of the Chóḻas and whose names appear in several of their inscriptions. It is significant that the Telugu Chólas of Vikramasiṁhapuram from whose family, according to Mr. V. Coomaraswamy, came the first of the Árya Chakravartis did not belong to the Gaṅga vamsa. There is no tradition that they belonged to any family of the Gaṅga Chiefs of Toṇḍai Maṇḍalam or Chóḻamaṇḍalam.

In an inscription belonging to the 27th year of the Chóḻa king Kulótunga III (1205 A.D.) found at Káñci,¶

* Mah., chap. lxxvi, vv. 133—134.

† Ibid vv. 139—144.

‡ காவியமாகிய காமீகங்கண்டுங்கங் காகுலத்தோ
றோவிய சூத்திராக விருபத்து நான்குயர்ந்த
மேவிய கோட்டத்திலுங் கரிகால வளவன்மிக்க
வாவியமேன்மை கொடுத்தளித்தான் றொண்டைமண்டலமே.

Ton. M. S., v. 97.

¶ Ep. Ind. vol. viii, p. 293.

Siya Gaṅga is described in the inscription as "ஸ்ரீ மறகுவளால புர பரமேச்வரன் கங்ககுலோற்பவந் சீய்யகங்கன் அமராபரணன்"

Siya Gaṅga Amaràparaṇan born of the Gangavamsa a supreme ruler of Kuvaḷálapuram. cf. நன்னூல் சிறப்புபாயிரம்.

one Síya Gaṅga the patron of Pavaṇandi, the Jain author of the Tamil grammar Nannúl, is mentioned as the ruler at Kuvaḷálapuram (Kólar). Síya Gaṅga was the feudatory of Kulótuṅga III. Was the first king of Jaffna a scion of this family? We shall first try to trace the history of the Gaṅga family and that of its several branches and see which of them has an early mythical history similar to that of the Jaffna kings.

Mr. Hira Lal, B.A of Nagpur says "Orissa is the country where the Ganga vamsa originated. King Indra Varman of Kalinga Nagara is spoken as the 'establisher of this spotless family of the Gangas.' This name was a matronymic and was carried to other places than Orissa. Regarding the tendency, which always existed and still exists to adopt eponymous names under the influences of the gradual brahmanising of castes, it would not be surprising to find a family with a dubious patronymic insinuating a non-brahmanical origin, preferring a matronymic connected with so holy a deity as the Ganges."*

The earliest genuine Gaṅga prince was Satyasraya Dhuruvarája Indravarman of the Goa Grant, according to which he was a viceroy under the Western Chaḷukya kings Kírtivarman I, Mangalésa and Pulikésin II, under an appointment running from 591—592 A.D. He was an ancestor and probably the grandfather of Rájasimha Indravarman I, the first king of the earlier Gaṅga dynasty of Kaliṅga, who adopted the era of 591—592 A. D., as the official reckoning in his dominions. †

* Ep, Ind., vol. ix, p. 43.

† Ibid vol. vi, pp. 591-592.

These early Gaṅga kings of Orissa and Kaliṅga who reigned at Pishtapura and Siṁhapura appear to have been suppressed by the Chaḷukyas about the 7th century A.D. and supplanted by the kings of the Késari dynasty who were feudatories of the Maghadas and the Kósalas and were reigning at Cuttack. Their seal was Lakshmi with an elephant on either side*. They were replaced by the Eastern Gaṅgas who came from the South (Gaṅgaváḍi) about 1038 A. D. Kings of the Gaṅga dynasty were also ruling at Talakhad under the name of Western Gaṅgas and at Kuvaḷálapuram or Kólalapura calling themselves pure Gaṅgas. About the end of the 9th century this dynasty was overthrown by the Chóḻas and not long after, the Hoysala Ballalas of Dwára Samudra rose to power in that country. It thus appears that when the final catastrophe occurred the family dispersed chiefly northwards. Some members of the same line founded the Gaṅga Vamsa dynasty of Orissa, the founder of which was Vajrahasta who was also known as the Lord of Kólahala, but some also went southwards as would be seen from the number of Gaṅga Vamsa chiefs who flourished in the Chóḻa territories in the 12th century.

Vajrahasta I, the first Eastern Gaṅga king, came to the throne in 1038 A. D. and ruled at Kaliṅga Nagaram which has been identified as Mukhaliṅgam. In his Náḍagam plates, it is said, that these kings belonged to the Atréya Gótra and had received their royal insignia, viz:—the unique conch shell, the drum, the five mahásabdhas, the white parasol, the golden chauri and the excellent bull crest by the favour of Gókarnaswamin of

* Ep: Ind; vol. iii, Records of Samavasi kings of Cuttack.

Mount Mahéndra.* In the Vijagapatam copper plates of Anantavarman Chóḍagaṅga who came to the throne in 1077 A.D., the full geneology of the Gaṅga kings in addition to the above information is given. † According to it the earlier Gaṅga kings reigned at Kolahalapur (Kuvaḷálapuram or Kólar) in the Gaṅgaváḍi district, and the fifty-first of the line, a king named Kamarnava I (Indravarman?) 'gave over his own territory to his paternal uncle, and with his brothers set out to conquer the earth and came to the mountain Mahéndra. Having there worshipped the God Gókarnaswamin, through his favour he obtained the excellent crest of a bull; and then decorated with all the insignia of universal sovereignty, he went and conquered King Baladitiya and took possession of the Kaliṅga countries. This was perhaps a reference to the earlier Gaṅga invasion of Kaliṅga.

The description given in the above inscriptions, of the receipt of the insignia of sovereignty by the kings of the Eastern Gaṅgas, appear very much like the one given in Sekarájasékaram. According to these inscriptions one of their kings Vajrahasta is said to have "given away a thousand elephants whose throats were trickling with rut" to mendicants,† a statement which is reproduced with more exaggeration in the Sekarájasékaram and applied to an unnamed ancestor of the Jaffna king. It will be interesting to note the coincidences and parallel passages of geneological and historical interest contained in the inscriptions of the Eastern Gaṅgas and the description given in Sekarájasékaram.

---

* Ep: Ind: vol. iv, p. 243, Nadagam plates.

† Ind. Ant. vol. xxviii, p. 170.

	Eastern Gaṅgas	Jaffna Kings
Vamsa	Gaṅga	Gaṅga
Gótra	Ātréya	Pásupada
Temple at which Insignia were received.	Mahéndra	Kandamádanam or Rámésvaram.
From whom received.	Gókarnaswamin	Ráma
Insignia received	Single conch shell White parasol Bull crest Drum Panjamahasabdhas Golden chamara	Single conch shell White parasol Bull crest The title Ārya king. Tulasi wreath
Presented	1000 elephants to mendicants. Brother decorated with a necklace (Kanthika).	Elephants to mendicants and 3700 elephants to poets. King decorated with tulasi wreath.

These parallel passages clearly indicate that the kings of Jaffna belonged to, claimed connection with or imitated the Eastern Gaṅgas who went from Gaṅgaváḍi and settled at Kaliṅga. If the earliest king of Jaffna came from among them, it must have been Ugra Siṅgaṉ, for it was after his time that the Kings ruling in the North were called Kaliṅgas. Whether Ugra Siṅgaṉ was a member of the Eastern Gaṅgas or not, he came down with a large army of Kaliṅgas to secure the throne of Kadiramalai for himself. As it is said in the Vaipava Málai that he was 'a prince of the dynasty founded by King Vijaya's brother' it may be surmised that he was a member of one of the Kaliṅga families that came with Vijaya and settled at Siṅgai Nagar near Vallipuram.* It is impossible to believe that the colonists at Siṅgai Nagar were totally isolated from their people in Orissa.

* See supra chap. vi, p. 243.

The position of their town was such that commercial intercourse must have been maintained for centuries and Ugra Siṅgaṉ whether he came from Kaliṅga Nagaram or was a local celebrity, seems to have been aware of local conditions before he made a bold bid for the crown of Jaffna. The Pallava authority, if there was any, had dwindled to a mere nothing; and the Siṅhalese kings of Anurádhapura at that time were busy with their own chaotic affairs; so that no great effort was necessary on the part of Ugra Siṅgaṉ to seat himself on the throne of Jaffna. His later alliance with a Chóḷa (?) princess strengthened his claims to Royal rank and it is not unlikely that his descendants continued to occupy the throne of Jaffna, and to adopt the insignia of royalty in imitation of those of the Eastern Gaṅgas with whom they were in constant touch, basing their claims for such adoption on the right of their being Kaliṅgas.

Thus it would be seen that a brahman of Rámésvaram married a princess of the Kaliṅga dynasty of Ugra Siṅgaṉ in Jaffna and his descendants adopted the patronymic of 'Árya' and the 'Sétu' crest but retained their maternal *vamsa* name and the insignia of royalty.

The reason given above for locating the city of Siṅgai Nagar or Siṅhapura at Vallipuram on the east coast of Jaffna has still to be verified. The name Siṅgai Nagar came into prominence only after the Árya Chakravartis, and although its earlier existence may be proved by its identity with one of the ports mentioned by Ptolemy* and with the place to which Ugra

---

* See supra chap. iii, p. 117.

Siṅgaṉ transferred his capital from Kadiramalai,* there are scholars who try to establish that Nallúr was the place known as Siṅgai Nagar.† In the Kotagama inscription, the town is described as Siṅgai Nagar of resounding waters,‡ thus showing that it was on the shore of some boisterous sea, whereas Nallúr is not even on the coast of a lagoon. If the surmise that the town to which Ugra Siṅgaṉ transferred his capital from Kadiramalai was Siṅgai Nagar, be correct Siṅgai Nagar was certainly other than Nallúr. The latter was not built till long afterwards. Its position on the eastern coast of Jaffna with perhaps a harbour, had the advantage of continuing the early commercial relationship with Orissa and other parts of the Coromandel coast. This was the town which gave birth to Parákrama Báhu the Great who rebuilt, enlarged and embellished it, and this was the town where the father of Nissaṅka Malla and Sáhasa Malla lived and reigned.

It will not be out of place here to consider the origin of Parákrama Báhu I, in the light of certain other statements made in the Mahávaṅsa, in order to test the truth of the earlier statement that the husband of Mitta the sister of Vijaya Báhu was a Páṇḍyaṉ prince. The author of the Mahávaṅsa, in his attempt to ignore the importance of the Northern kingdom and the part it played in the history of Ceylon from the 12th to the 15th century, has

---

* See supra chap. vi, p. 245

† Mr. V. Coomaraswamy of Jaffna maintains this theory.

‡ "பொங்கொலிநீர்
சிங்கைநகர்"

Siṇgai Nagar of resounding waters.

in several instances, unconsciously revealed the truth. The suppression of these facts was obviously intentional and he had to turn and twist facts to suit his own purpose. Some of the glaring inconsistencies found in the Mahávaṅsa are given below. Mitta, the sister of Vijaya Báhu I, married a Páṇḍyaṉ prince, says the Mahávaṅsa, thus making Vijaya Báhu prefer a Páṇḍyaṉ prince of the race of the Moon to a reigning Chóḻa king belonging to the dynasty of the Sun, although the latter had entreated him often.* But this appears to have been quite contrary to the practice of the early royal dynasties. The Chóḻa king of the time occupied almost the whole of Ceylon and one in the position of Vijaya Báhu would not have rejected such an alliance, which would have led to the possibility of his sister's son inheriting the crown of Ceylon in the event of his failure to obtain it. This very Vijaya Báhu who, for the purpose of establishing his own race, gave his son in marriage to Sundari, the sister of the three Kaliṅga princes who came to his court,† would not have sent for a Páṇḍyaṉ prince to marry his sister. It is more reasonable to think that the husband of Mitta was a prince of the Kaliṅga royal house of Jaffna as the sequel will show. The author of the Mahávaṅsa made a mis-statement presumably on purpose to conceal the actual origin of the grand-father of Parákrama Báhu, the greatest of the kings of Ceylon. When Sri Vallabha desired to give his son in marriage to the daughter of Mánábharaṇa and Ratnavalli, she (Ratnavalli) is alleged to have said "when the prince Vijaya slew all

---

* Mah., chap. lix, vv. 40-41.

† Ibid v. 49.

the evil spirits and made the Island of Laṅká a habitation for men, from that time forth came the race of Vijaya to be allied to us, and we gave not in marriage save unto those born of the race of Kaliṅga; and so long as there remain princes born of the race of the Moon, how can an alliance take place between us, and this prince who is only known unto us as an Áryan, albeit born of you."* Sri Vallabha was Mánábharaṇa's brother and Ratnavalli was his wife's (Sugala's) aunt. Then where was the difference in rank between them? Ratnavalli said to have been 'an ornament of the race of the Sun' was the daughter of Vijaya Báhu who refused to give his sister to another ornament of the race of the Sun, the Chóḻa king, and yet she glories in alliances with members of the race of the Moon. Her daughter according to the Mahávaṅsa, belonged to the race of the Moon and was therefore not fit to marry the son of Sri Vallabha, the brother of her own husband who also belonged to the race of the Moon. In his anxiety to belittle the royal family of Jaffna, the author of the Mahávaṅsa put such glaring contradictions into the mouth of Ratnavalli. If Sri Vallabha was an Áryan as Ratnavalli calls him, his brother who was her husband must have been an Áryan also, in the sense in which the term was applied to the Jaffna kings. Therefore their father must have been a prince of the dynasty of the kings of Jaffna and his Páṇḍyaṉ connection which the author of the Mahávaṅsa tried to emphasize appears to have had no foundation in fact. How unceremoniously the kings of South Ceylon attached themselves to the Solar race or to the dynasty of

* Mah. Chap. lxiii, vv. 11—15.

some supposed great and divine personage can be seen from many of their inscriptions. Dappula V was the earliest to mention the Ikshváku family.* Mahinda V and Vijaya Báhu I mentioned the same family,† but the family of Mahinda IV the father of Mahinda V was unknown to the author of the Mahávaṅsa.‡ Parákrama Báhu I whose parentage is well known, is described in the inscription found at Padivil kulam, perhaps his earliest, as Parákrama Báhu Chakravarti descended from ancient princes. In other inscriptions he is called Srimat Parákrama Bhúja, Sri Laṅkádinádha Parákrama Báhu and Sri Saṅgabo Parákrama Báhu Laṅkésvara, but in the Galvihára inscription, perhaps his latest, he is said to have descended from the unbroken line of Mahasammata¶ and the others born of the Solar race. From these inscriptions it will be seen how the status of his ancestors rose in proportion to his power and eminence. He was the first to claim a descent from a divine personage mentioned in Buddhistic legendary lore. The General Kírti Séna, the consort of Queen Lílavati, claimed to be not only an Abha Salaméwan but also a descendant of the Ikshváku family.§ Kaliṅga kings Nissaṅka Malla and Sáhasa Malla claimed that they belonged to the Ikshváku dynasty.‖ Parákrama Báhu VI made out that he was of the family of the Sun and descended from Mahasammata;** and Sri Vijaya Báhu V not satisfied with the respect-

---

* Müller, Nos. 116 & 117.

† Ibid No. 121.

‡ Mah., chap. LIV.

¶ Müller, No. 137.

§ Ibid No. 157.

‖ Ibid Nos. 148, 149 & 156.

** Ibid No. 160.

ability of the Sun and Mahásammata proclaimed that he was an illustrious progeny of Vaivasanta Manu!!* These boasts were not a peculiar failing of the Ceylon kings alone. It was quite common among all the royal dynasties of India. Whatever the caste or family of a man, he had only to become a king in order to claim descent from the Sun or the Moon. It was perhaps necessary in those days to impress upon the common people the greatness and the divine right of kings.

To return to the subject under discussion—it is more than probable that Tilakasundari the Kaliṅga princess who was married to Vijaya Báhu I was from the Kaliṅga house of Jaffna, and it must have been her brother, and not a prince from Páṇḍyaṇ lands, that married Mitta, the sister of Vijaya Báhu. Mánábharaṇa, whose two sons were captured by Rájéndra, was the father of the prince who married Mitta, and her son was named Mánáhbaraṇa after the grand-father. Her other sons too were named Kírti Srimégha and Sri Vallabha, perhaps after their father's uncles whose names are mentioned in the Maṇimaṅgaḷam inscriptions. These very names were again given to the sons of Prince Mánábharaṇa by Pabbhavati and Mitta the sisters of Parakrama Báhu I. This Mánábharaṇa was a son of Sri Vallabha, the brother of Parákrama Báhu's father, by Sugala daughter of Víravamma and grand-daughter of Vijaya Báhu I. The following geneological table prepared from information given in the Maṇimaṅgaḷam inscriptions and in the Mahávaṅsa will show how closely connected were the Kaliṅga kings of Polonnaruwa to the dynasty of the Kings of Jaffna.

* Müller. No. 172.

Mánábharana (killed by Rájádhi Rája before 1038 A.D.) | Vira Salá Mégha (killed by Rájendra in 1054 A.D.) | Sri Vallaba Madana Rája (killed by Rájádhi Rája in 1042 A.D.)

Children of Mánábharana:

Vijaya Báhu I = Tilakasundari | A Prince (married to Mitta sister of Vijaya Báhu.) | Two Princes (captured by Rájéndra in 1054 A.D.)

Ratnavalli [daughter of Vijaya Báhu I] = Mánábharana. [son of A Prince] | Kirti Sri Mégha. [son of A Prince] | Sri Vallabha = Sugala. [son of A Prince]

Children of Ratnavalli = Mánábharana:

Parákrama Báhu I. | Mitta = Mánábharana. | Buddhavati = Gajabáhu II. | Pabbhavati = Mánábharana. [son of Sri Vallabha = Sugala]

Sri Vallabha. [son of Mitta = Mánábharana] | Kirti Sri Mégha. [son of Pabbhavati = Mánábharana]

The frequency with which the names Mánábharaṇa, Salámégha or Srimégha and Sri Vallabha appear in the above table is not only striking but also strengthens the conjecture that the earliest Mánábharaṇa, who was a king of Jaffna, was the grandfather of Mánábharaṇa, the father of Parákrama Báhu I and that the latter Mánábharaṇa was not a Páṇḍyaṉ prince.

Mitta, the sister of Vijaya Báhu, had three sons, Mánábharaṇa, Kírti Srimégha and Sri Vallabha. * After Jayabáhu and his confederates were defeated by Vikrama Báhu who occupied Polonnaruwa, the three brothers, his cousins ruled over different parts of the Island independent of Vikrama Báhu. According to the Mahávaṅsa all the three brothers reigned in the southern districts: Kírti Srimégha at Mahanágacula, Sri Vallabha at Uddhanadwára and Mánábharaṇa at Punkhagama.† The location of these places is not known, but when Vikrama Báhu began to fight against them and proceeded northwards, after defeating them at three different places he won a fourth victory over them at Kálavápi and a fifth at Uddhanadwára.‡ The latter place therefore must have been somewhere to the north of Kálavápi. Punkhagama must have been Panangámam in the Tunukai district of the Northern province, which became afterwards the seat of some of the later Vannian chieftains. It will thus be seen that while Kírti Sri Mégha was ruling at Mahánágacula in Rohana, the other two brothers Mánábharaṇa and Sri Vallabha were ruling at Punkha-

* Mah., chap lix, v. 42.

† Ibid chap. lxi, vv. 21-27.

‡ Ibid v. 16.

gama and Uddhanadwara respectively, which places were to the north of Polonnaruwa. When Vikrama Báhu heard of the birth of a son to Mánábharaṇa, he exclaimed that he (the child) would "be a sparkling central gem in the chain of kings beginning with Vijaya."* Is not the Kaliṅga connection here expressed? If Mánábharaṇa's father was a Páṇḍyaṉ prince, how were the links in the Vijayan chain forged?

On the death of Mánábharaṇa, his brothers Kírti Srimégha and Sri Vallabha hastened thither and Kírti Srimégha took possession of his elder brother's country and gave the other two kingdoms to Sri Vallabha who took his abode at Mahánágacula.† Was it the northern kingdom that was ruled by Mánábharaṇa and later taken possession of by Kírti Srimégha?

When Parákrama who was staying with his mother's sister thought of going to the land of his birth, where he expected to be at least a sub-king, he surely must have meant the kingdom of Jaffna where his uncle Kírti Srimégha was reigning.‡ On his way, he went and stayed at Sangathali, which might be Sangattár Vayal near Elephant Pass, where Kírti Srimégha came to meet him and escorted him in great pomp to the city the name of which is advisedly omitted in the Mahávaṅsa. In an inscription found at the Giant's Tank,¶ Parákrama Báhu

* Mah. Chap. lxii, vv. 56-57.
† Ibid lxiii, vv. 1-2.
‡ Ibid v. 43.
¶ "Srimat Sihapuré játa Sri Parákrama Báhu nakaritan visva lokáṭu karyavya páritat maná."

"Made for the benefit of the whole world by the prosperous Sri Parákrama Báhu born at Siṅhapura minded of what was fit to be done."

Parker, p. 250.

claims that he was born at Siṅhapura, which signifies that his father Máṇábharaṇa, notwithstanding the author of the Mahávaṅsa, was ruling at Siṅhapura or Siṅgai Nagar in Jaffna, and was therefore a king of the Kaliṅga royal family of that place. It is, however, curious that the Rajavali should say that the father of Parákrama Báhu was Kit-Sri-Newan-Rajah.* (Kírti Srimégha) who was really his uncle.

Although the tonsure and the Upanayana ceremonies were performed on all the youths of the Brahman, Kshatriya and Vaisya castes, these ceremonies performed on Parákrama Báhu are specially mentioned in the Mahávaṅsa.† This leads one to surmise that Parákrama belonged to the Brahman-Kaliṅga dynasty of Jaffna. The kings of South Ceylon claimed to be Kshatriyas and to belong to the Ikshváku dynasty, but there is no evidence that the Upanayana ceremony was ever performed on any of them or that they wore the sacred thread over the left shoulder. Even the Chóḷas and the Páṇḍyas who claimed descent from the Sun and the Moon respectively did not appear to have worn the sacred thread.

According to the Mahávaṅsa when Parákrama Báhu fled from his uncle's palace and went on collecting an army from place to place, he appears to have travelled from north to south, although the places mentioned cannot be identified.‡ When he was still a Governor and in charge of the kingdom left by his father he enlarged Páṇḍavápi or Paduvilkulam on the borders of the Mullaittívu District

---

* Rajavali, p. 252.

† Mah., chap. lxiii, v. 5; chap. lxiv, v. 13.

‡ Ibid lxvi.

and called it the sea of Parákrama Báhu.* He must have therefore been the Governor, if not the King, of the Northern Kingdom.

The existence of an ancient trunk road along the eastern coast of Jaffna from Siṅgai Nagar perhaps to Polonnaruwa can be inferred from the remains of ruined buildings in the following places:—Kuḍattanai, Poṟṟoḍai, Amban, Nágarcóil, Kuḍárappu, Chempianpaṭṭu, Nelliyán, Dévaduravu, Marudankérni, Turukkitiḍal, Uḍutturai, (Uddanadwara?) Veṭṭilaikérṇi, Kaṭṭaikáḍu, Vaṇṇánkuḷam and Veṭṭukérṇi, along the route. Broken bricks and pieces of ancient flat tiles and pottery indicate vestiges of ancient occupation. This trunk road, the course of which beyond the Peninsula may be traced without difficulty through the Vanni to the centre of the Island, indicates that there was constant communication between Siṅgai Nagar and Polonnaruwa, during the period of the Chóḷa occupation and of the Kaliṅga kings.

After Parákrama Báhu became the sole monarch of Ceylon, he caused three smaller cities to be erected, viz: Rájavési Bhújáṅga, Rájakulantaka and Vijitapura.† It is also said that he built the Kúsinára vihára at the branch city of Siṅhapura.‡ Now Siṅhapura is not mentioned as one of the new cities built by him, and must therefore have been the old one already in existence. In all probability it was the Siṅhapura of Jaffna. Or if Rájakulantaka was a town built close to Polonnaruwa

* Mah. Chap. lxviii, vv. 39-40.

† Ibid lxxiii, vv. 151—153.

‡ Ibid lxxviii, v. 87.

Nissanka Malla
from a wooden Statue in Dambulla Vihara

To face page 321.] [Photo by John & Co., Kandy.

and was also called Siṅhapura, it must have been so named after the town of his birth.

If the traitor Sri Vallabha in the camp of the Chóḻa king, who is referred to in the Tiruválaṅgáḍu inscription of RájádiRája II, was the king of Jaffna,* he would have been the uncle of Parákrama Báhu I, and either succeeded Kírti Srimégha, his brother, to the throne of Jaffna or led his army which went to the help of the Chóḻa king. It appears incredible that the Jaffna king should have gone in person to help the Chóḻas against the troops of Parákrama. The Jaffna kings had always been the allies and for sometime before this, feudatories of the Chóḻa Emperor. Knowing only the feud which previously existed between the kings of North and South Ceylon, and ignorant of the new relationship between them, he (the Chóḻa king) would have ordinarily sought the aid of his old ally. And the Jaffna king, perhaps with the knowledge of Parákrama, might have readily agreed with the ultimate object of betraying his friend. It is impossible to believe that Parákrama was not a party to the treacherous designs of his relative who must have at that time been his viceroy at Jaffna.

The couchant bull, the emblem of the Jaffna kings, carved on several Buddhist shrines built by Parákrama Báhu, especially on the Nága Guard stones in front of Jetawanaráma at Polonnaruwa and of the ruined Vihárasat Vijitapura, and the sacred thread over the shoulders found on his statue carved out of a rock on the bund of Tópawewa † and on the statue of Nissaṅka Malla in the rock temple at Dambulla clearly

* See supra, chap. vi, p. 269.

† See Frontispiece

stamp them as the scions of the royal house of Jaffna. It was perhaps after looking at the statue at Tópawewa and reading about the Upanayana ceremony in the Mahávaṅsa that Farrar, one of the latest writers on Ceylon said that Parákrama Báhu was a brahman of the Hindu religion.* The idea of religious tolerance practised by Parákrama Báhu can well be described in the words of Farrar. "The oriental from the very dawn of history, has always understood that all good men are of one religion; tolerance, to his view, is not even a virtue, it is simply an inevitable result of logic and reason; and intolerance is not so much a sin as folly, amounting almost to imbecility. Parákrama, then, observed a decent kindly line; there is no idea that he ever renounced his Hinduism, as his Hindu buildings at Polonnaruwa are as beautiful as anything there; but, not only, no doubt, from tolerance, but also from policy, he showed the greatest consideration and munificence towards the religion of the land. Perhaps his very position as an alien and an outsider made it easier for him to embark on that thorniest of all paths that of a peace-maker in ecclesiastical quarrels."†

Nissaṅka Malla in his Dambulla inscription derives his descent from the race of King Vijaya of the dynasty of Kaliṅga,‡ and in his Ruanweli inscription describes himself as "having come from the royal line of the Ikshváku family having become like a forehead mark to the royal family of the Kaliṅga emperors born at Siṅhapura."¶ In his Galpota inscription, it is said that

* Farrar, p. 171.
† Ibid
‡ Müller, No. 143.
¶ Ibid No. 145.

he was born of the queen Párvati and King Jayagópa "the glory of the dynasty which reigned in the city of Siṅhapura" and on being "invited by the king (Vijaya Báhu II) landed with a great retinue on Laṅká" and was in the office of Aepa under his 'senior kinsman' Vijaya Báhu II.* His wives were Kaliṅga Subadrádévi and Gaṅgavamsa Kalyáṇamahadévi.

Where was the city of Siṅhapura where Parákrama Báhu and Nissaṅka Malla were born? Was it in the country of Kaliṅga (Orissa) or in the Jaffna peninsula? Nissaṅka himself says that he was the son of Jayagópa who was the reigning king at Siṅhapura. Was there a king reigning at Siṅhapura of Orissa during this period? The earlier dynasty of the Gaṅga kings of Siṅhapura was supplanted by the kings of the Késari dynasty and it was the second line beginning with Vajra Hasta that was reigning from 1038 A.D. at Kaliṅgapuram. Jayagópa the father of Nissaṅka Malla must therefore have reigned at Siṅhapura of Jaffna. But how could Vijaya Báhu, the son of Gaja Báhu and Buddhavati the sister of Parákrama Báhu I, be the 'senior kinsman' of a prince of Orissa. On the other hand, if it was true that he was invited by Vijaya Báhu II, the nephew and successor of Parákrama Báhu I, to be his sub-king, there was no necessity for Vijaya Báhu to go so far as Orissa to get a sub-king. It is doubtful whether within a short reign of one year he could have sent for a prince and made him his sub king. There were Mánábharaṇa and Kírti Srimégha the sons of two sisters of his own mother. This Jayagópa, the father of Nissaṅka Malla, must have been a son and successor of

* Müller, No. 148.

Kírti Srimégha, the uncle of Parákrama Báhu, reigning at Siṅgai Nagar.

Sáhasa Malla too, in his inscription at Polonnaruwa, says that he was born at Siṅhapura to Góparája and his queen Bahidálóka.* He must, therefore, have been a half-brother to Nissaṅka Malla. The inscription goes on to say that he was brought over by the Chief Mallik Arjuna and established in the Chóḻa country at Kahacoṇḍapaṭṭanam. The necessity for this additional information does not appear, wherever Kahacoṇḍapaṭṭanam might have been. It is a story remarkably similar to that of Páṇḍimaḻavaṉ and Kúḷaṅkai.

The author of the Máhavaṅsa who allots several chapters to the reign of Parákrama Báhu disposes of the reigns of Nissaṅka Malla and his successors in a few verses, although the glories of some of them, in spite of all their troubles and strife are well enough indicated in their inscriptions. They seem to have been passed over because of their leanings towards Hinduism, although they really were exceptionally tolerant. Nissaṅka Malla's long inscriptions appear to have been intended to impress upon the people the necessity of selecting one of the Kaliṅga princes as their sovereign and not one of their own men who were described as of the Govi tribe. It is stated in the Daladamandirama inscription that "nobody should take the Crown of Lanka except those descended from the Kaliṅga vamsa—not one of the Govi tribe." † Strangely enough, most of the later kings of Ceylon were of Tamil origin, although the Chronicles attempt to trace

---

* Müller, No. 156.

† Ibid No. 149.

them to the lineage of Sri Sangha Bódhi and the kings speak of themselves in their inscriptions as of the Ikshváku dynasty. "The high estimation," says Casie Chetty, "in which Tamil blood had always been held, became in later times an article of political faith; and it prevailed to the end of Sinhalese sovereignty so much so that no individual of pure Sinhalese extraction could be elevated to the supreme power."* But there is also the less sentimental view of Sir Emerson Tennent who thought that the acquiescence of the Sinhalese to the rule of the Tamils was due, possibly, to the fact that they recognised to some extent the claim of the Tamils, founded as they were on their relationship to the old lawful dynasty that had ruled over the Island. †

---

* Gaz., p. 229.

† Tennent. vol. i, p. 396,

CHAPTER VIII

The Árya Kings of Jaffna.

FROM the ninth century onwards, it has been shown, the Kaliṅga dynasty of Ugra Siṅgan̲ was reigning in the kingdom of Jaffna which included the northern part of Ceylon and the Island of Rámésvaram. In the twelfth century they were known by the name of Árya Kings. During the ninth and tenth centuries and the first half of the eleventh century their fame was not known outside, for during the occupation of Ceylon by the Chóḷas these kings were their feudatories and subservient to them. But when Vijaya Báhu ascended the throne of Ceylon and married a princess of the Jaffna dynasty, many of her relations flocked to the Court of Polonnaruwa. The extent and the nature of this intercourse are shown clearly by the number of ruins found scattered along the Eastern coast of the peninsula from Point Pedro to Elephant Pass.* We have seen that a king called Mánábharaṇa was reigning before 1038 A D., and two others of the name of Víra Salamégha and Sri Vallabha Madana Rája after him. The latter two were killed by the Chóḷas before the accession of Vijaya Báhu, and were succeeded by their nephew, the son of Mánábharaṇa. This was the prince who married Mitta the sister of Vijaya Báhu. He had three sons Mánábharaṇa, Kírti Sri Mégha and Sri Vallabha. After the death of Vijaya

---

* Vide supra, chap. vii. p. 320.

Báhu and an unsuccessful war with Vikrama Báhu, the three brothers ruled over separate districts of Ceylon independently of Vikrama Báhu (but with his knowledge and consent). Of these three divisions, the Northern was ruled by Mánábharaṇa. It was perhaps at his instigation that Víra Déva of Páladívu invaded Ceylon during the time of Vikrama Báhu. Mánábharaṇa died sometime before Vikrama Báhu's death which took place in 1131 A.D., and he was succeeded by Kírti Sri Mégha, his brother, during the minority of his son Parákrama Báhu. Parákrama Báhu, even after he attained the age of discretion, refused to take up the reins of government out of gratitude to the uncle who had brought him up with loving care and tenderness;* and it was not until Kírti Sri Mégha died during the reign of Gaja Báhu II, that Parákrama Báhu succeeded him as the king of the Northern Dominion. This must have been about 1140 A.D. It was probably the Court of Parákrama Báhu or of his uncle that was visited by the Poet Pughaḻéndi. The famine which devastated the north of Ceylon and which necessitated the munificence of Saḍayappa Mudali must also have occurred during the time Parákrama Báhu was reigning in Jaffna. It was perhaps the memory of this famine and a desire to prevent the recurrence of similar disasters that induced Parákrama Báhu to take up the stupendous task of restoring and constructing some of those large tanks that are still the admiration of the world. The public works carried out by him during the 33 years of his wise and beneficent rule are enumerated in detail in the Mahávaṁsa. He became king of Ceylon in

* Mah. chap. lxiv.

1153 A.D., and the king who reigned at Jaffna during the rest of his reign was very likely his viceroy. His choice would naturally have fallen on his uncle Sri Vallabha. And it was Sri Vallabha who was called a traitor in the Árpakkam inscription of Rájádhi Rája II.* Jaya Gópa the father of Nissaṅka Malla and Sáhasa Mallạ and perhaps the son of Kírti Sri Mégha the uncle of Parákrama Báhu, must have been a later king. Vijaya Báhu II perhaps fearing his power and influence sent for one of his sons to be his sub-king in place of Kírti Sri Mégha and Sri Vallabha, kinsmen though they were.

The next king of Jaffna to rise to power and fame was Kaliṅga Magha who overran the whole island of Ceylon and who, according to the Siṅhalese chronicles, destroyed many Buddhist temples in a fine frenzy of fanaticism.† He erected fortresses in different parts of the Island, viz.:—Polonnaruwa, Pulaccéry, Kotasara (Coṭṭiár), Gantala (Kantalai), Kandupulu, Kurundu, Padimana (Padivil or Padaviya), Matugona, Debarapatun (Demalapaṭaṇam—Jaffna), Uratota (Kayts), Gomudu, Mipatota, Mandali and Mannaram.‡ He took Colon Nuwara¶(Colombo) and placed Malabars at Mahagama.§ As he and his men are described as Malabars and Tamils by the chronicles and as he was known as Kaliṅga Vijaya Báhu, it is plain that he was a king of Jaffna. The

* M. E. R. No. 465 of 1905.

† Mah., chap. lxxx, vv. 56—79
Rajavali, pp. 256, 257.

‡ Nik. San, p. 23-

¶ Rajavali, pp. 256, 257.

§ Ibid.

power wielded by him for 21 years as the over-lord of all Ceylon leads one to surmise that he probably was one of the better known of the Segarájasékarans, either the first Árya Chakravarti or perhaps Kúḷaṅkai himself. For, the name of Kúḷaṅkai was Vijaya Kúlaṅkai Chakravarti which bears a remarkable resemblance to Kaliṅga Magha's full name Kaliṅga Vijaya Báhu.* The name Kúḷaṅkai, a sobriquet acquired by the loss of a forearm, first appears in the Yáḻpáṇa Vaipava Málai and not in any of the earlier works like Kailáya Málai or Vaiyápáḍal. It may, therefore, be surmised that it was a misreading for Káliṅga. Káliṅga in Tamil manuscripts can be easily mistaken for Kúḷaṅkai and Vijaya Káliṅga Chakravarti was thus mutilated to Vijaya Kúḷaṅkai Chakravarti † either by Mailvágana Pulavar himself or by some later copyists. It is, however, to be noted that the first king is called Segarájaṉ (Segarájasékaraṉ) in the Kailáya Málai.‡

According to the Editor of the Mahávaṅsa, he (Kaliṅga Magha) reigned from 1215 to 1236 A.D. It has, besides, been shewn that a Pararájasiṅgaṉ was killed by Máravarmaṉ Sundara Páṇḍya I in 1224 A.D., and that a Parákrama Báhu was killed by Hoysala Narasimha II

* Nik. San. p. 22.

† A theory for which we are indebted to Rev. Father S. Gnanapragasar.

‡ "தென்னவனிகரான செகராசன் றென்னிலங்கை
மன்னவனுகுஞ் சிங்கையாரியமால்."

K.M.

Siṅgai Āryan Segarájaṉ (Segarájasékaraṉ) the king of Ceylon like unto the Páṇḍyaṉ.

at Séndamaṅgaḷam in 1231 A.D.* These two were probably the viceroys of Kaliṅga Magha at Jaffna. It is stated in the Vaipava Málai that Kúḷaṅkai built the city of Nallúr and directed his Minister Puvinéya Váku (Bhuvanéka Báhu) to build the Kandaswámy temple at Nallúr which he finished in the year Saka 870 (948 A.D.).† We have seen that most of the Árya Chakravartis reigned at Siṅhapura or Siṅgai Nagar, and that this place was not Nallúr. There can be no doubt that Mailvágana Pulavar borrowed the story of the building of the city of Nallúr from Kailáya Malai and obtained the date of the Kandaswámy temple from the stray stanza which mentions the year.‡ Kúḷaṅkai could not have built Nallúr and made it the Capital because the most eminent of the Árya Chakravartis who succeeded him certainly reigned at Siṅgai Nagar the site of which is found at Vallipuram as already stated in the last chapter. It is true that when the Portuguese invaded Jaffna, the capital was at Nallúr and had been there during the reigns of some of the

---

* Vide supra, chap. vii. p. 290-292.

† Y. V. M., pp. 14, 17.

‡ " இலகியசகாப்தமெண்ணூற்றெழுபதாமாண்டுதன்னி
லலர்பொலிமாலைமார்பனும்புவிநேயவாகு
நலமிகுந்திடு யாழ்ப்பாண நகரிகட்டுவித்து நல்லைக்
குலவிய கந்தவேட்குக் கோயிலும் புரிவித்தானே."

In the year Saka 870, Puvinéya Váku (Bhuvanéka Báhu,) wearing the garland of flowers, caused the city of Yaḻpáṇam to be built and erected a temple for (the worship of) Kandaswámy at Nallúr.

[It should be noted that as the present city of Jaffna did not come into existence before the time of the Portuguese, this verse must have been composed later than that.]

‡ Y. V. M., p. 25.

predecessors of Saṅkili. But a clue to the time of the transfer of the capital from Siṅgai Nagar to Nallúr is found in the Vaipava málai itself. All the kings up to the conquest of Seṇpahap Perumáḷ were called Siṅgai Áryans, an epithet placed after their names, but the son of Kanakasúriya who reconquered the kingdom after the departure of Bhuvanéka Báhu to Cóṭṭe, was called Siṅgaip-Pararájasékaraṉ. It is therefore probable that when Kanakasúriya returned from India on the departure of Bhuvanéka Báhu he must have found that his old capital had been razed to the ground and that a new and beautiful town had risen at Nallúr. He therefore took possession of it and he and his successors resided at Nallúr. It appears therefore that Sapumal Kumaraya alias Seṇpahap-Perumáḷ who ascended the throne under the name of Bhuvanéka Báhu built the town of Nallúr and the author of Kailáya málai took him to be the Tamil minister of the king. It is not unlikely that there was also a Tamil minister of that name. According to the Vaipava málai, he was a Tamil scholar and poet, he extemporised certain Tamil verses in praise of the feast given to him by the Brahman priest of the temple at Máviṭṭapuram.* Seṇpahap-Perumáḷ alias Bhuvanéka Báhu was himself the son of a Tamil † and his knowledge of Tamil may have been such that he was able to compose verses in that language. It may therefore be presumed that Bhuvanéka Báhu the Siṅhalese conqueror was the first to establish the seat of Government at Nallúr and that the Jaffna kings who succeeded him reigned there.

* Y.V.M. p. 17.

‡ Couto, Dec. v, bk. I, chap. v; J.C.B.R.A.S., vol. xx, p. 69.

A Tamil verse, quoted by Mr. Mootootambypillai in his 'History of Jaffna,'* alleged to have been found in an unpublished work called Visvanátha Sástriar Śambavakkurippu (memorandum of notable events by Visvanátha Sástriar) says that Bhuvanéka Báhu who caused the Jaffna Town and the Nallúr temple to be built was known as Sri Saṅghabódhi, a title borne by the Siṅhalese kings. The surmise of Dr. P.E. Pieris that Bhuvanéka Báhu who is daily invoked in the *kattiyam* of Nallúr Kandaswámy temple was Seṉpahap-Perumāḷ † is therefore correct. In the Kaṭṭiyam too he is referred to as Sri Saṅghabódhi Bhuvanéka Báhu.† The year Saka 870 given in one verse ‡ and 874 in the other ¶ are, however, both incorrect. The mistake may have been made either purposely to obscure the Siṅhalese origin of the town and the temple, or honestly and unintentionally

---

* " இலகியசகாத்த மெண்ணூற்றேடெழுபத்து நான்கி
னலர் திரிசங்கபோதியாம் புவனேகவாகு
நலமுறும் யாழ்ப்பாணத்து நகரிகட்டுவித்து நல்லூர்க்
குலவிய கந்தனார்க்குக் கோயிலொன்றமைப்பித்தானே."

In the year Saka 874, Sri Saṅgha Bódhi Puvanéka Váhu (Bhuvanéka Báhu) caused the good city of Yaḷpáṇam to be built and a temple for (the worship of) Kandaswamy erected at Nallúr.

† J.C.B.R.A.S., vol. xxvi, pt. i, p. 16.

[The following is a part of the Kaṭṭiyam daily repeated at the Kandaswámy Temple at Nallúr during festivals :—

"Sriman Mahárájáti rájáya ahaṇḍa Púmaṇḍala pratiyati kandara visvànta kírti Sri Gajavalli mahàvalli saméta Subramaṇya pádára vinda janatirúḍa Sóḍasa mahádána Súryakula vamsótbhava Sri Saṅgabódhi Bhuvanéka Báhu smuhá."]

‡ Vide supra, p. 330, note ‡.

¶ Vide supra, note *.

in the attempt to fix a date regarding which only the cyclic name of the year was known to tradition, or perhaps the years given in these verses may have a confused reference to the time when the descendants of the Rámésvaram Brahman and the Jaffna princess came to the throne of Jaffna, and so started the line of the Árya Chakravartis.

The author of the Kailaya Málai has perpetrated another anachronism in stating that the temple of Kailáya Náthar at Nallúr was built by the first king.* author of the Vaipava Málai has blindly copied this mistake in his work and credited it to Kúḷaṅkai.† The Kailáya Málai calls this temple the third Kailáyam.‡ The first was in India, the second at Trincomalie and the third at Nallúr. The Dakshiṇa Kailása Puráṇam composed during the time of king Segarájasékaraṉ of the great literary period,¶ was in honour of the temple at Trincomalie which was called Dakshiṇa Kailáyam or Tenkaiyilai. If the temple at

---

* K. M.,

† Y. V. M.. p. 18.

"நந்தமிர்தச்
சித்திரகைலாசமொடு தென்கையிலையில்லிரண்டு
நித்தமுளமோர்ந்துறையு நேயபத்தி-யத்துடனே
முக்கையிலையாக நல்லைமூதூரினென்றமைந்த
தக்கைலை மீதினமர்ந்துறைய"

K. M.,

¶ That .there was a Tamil Saṅgam in Jaffna can be found from the following lines in the Kailayamálai.

"புவிதிருத்தியாண்டுவைத்த
சங்கச் சமுகத்தமிழாளன்"

The Tamil king who built the town and established the Saṅgam there.

Nallúr existed then, the Puráṇam would have been of right composed in honour of it. It is also said that the priest to officiate at this temple was obtained from Ramésvaram through the help of Sétupaty, the Rajah of Ramnad.* Raméswaram was under the sway of the Jaffna kings for a long time as is shewn by their title Sétukávalan and the term Sétu on their crests. So if they required a priest from Ramésvaram they need not have asked for the aid of the Rájah of Ramnad for that purpose. On the other hand the first appointment of a Sétupaty was given by Muttu Krishnappa Naik of Madura in 1604 A.D., to Saḍayakka Thévan an obscure chief of Pogalúr for loyal services rendered by him.† If we consider that the Kailáya Málai was composed at the time the Kailásanáta temple was consecrated, we should place the time between 1604 and 1620 A.D., for there was no king of Jaffna after 1620 A.D., and there was no Sétupaty before 1604 A.D. It is impossible to conceive that a big temple such as that described in the work could have been built at a time which was the most troublesome period in the history of the Jaffna kings. They were at that time harassed a great deal by the Portuguese and were busy

---

* "அந்தணருளாய்ந்திங்கனுப்புமெனச்-செந்திருவார்
சேதுபதிக்குச் செழும்பாசுரமனுப்பி
யாதிமறையோர்கள் புகழாசிரியன்-வேதமுணர்
கங்காதரனெனும் பேர்க்காசிநகரோனையினி
இங்கேயவனனுப்ப வெய்தியபின்"

K. M.

When he (the king) sent a letter to Sétupathy asking him to select and send a Brahman, he sent a Brahman of Kasi (Benares) learned in the Védas, and a teacher praised by the ancient Vedic priests, of the nameof Gaṅgadhara.

† Ind. Ant., vol. xlv, p. 105.

devising ways and means to overthrow the power of the invaders begging for aid, for instance, from the Naik of Tanjore and the king of Kandy. It follows therefore that the temple must have been built before 1604 and that the Kailáya Málai was composed after that date. The building of a temple under this name would have become necessary only after the Jaffna kings were deprived of facilities for visiting the shrine at Trincomalie. Such a necessity did not arise till the conquest of Sapumal Kumárayá. The temple must therefore have been built by Kanakasúriya or his successor after the year 1467 A.D., and earlier than 1519 A.D., the probable date of Saṅkili's accession, as it is not at all likely that a tyrant like Saṅkili would have conceived of such an undertaking.

Mailvágana pulavar has also taken over the names of the Veḷḷáḷa colonists from the Kailáya Málai. * It would not have been possible for a prince to collect a number of respectable and influential chieftains from different parts of South India, from Káñci on the East to Vañji on the West, persuade them to leave their ancestral lands and go abroad as colonists with their relations and retainers. Even, a severe famine would not have driven them. Dishonour and loss of prestige and caste to themselves and their women were the only forces which could have made them leave the country of their birth and abandon the fertile lands of their ancestors. This, we may suppose, happened during the 13th and 14th centuries when the Chóḷa and Páṇḍya kingdoms had suffered disintegration and were hard pressed by the Hoysala

* Y. V. M., pp. 15-16; K. M.

Vijayanagar Kings, when Malik Kafur and other Muhammedans invaded and ravaged Southern India and when Visvanatha Naik planted Telugu Polygars all over the Madura and the Tanjore Districts. In times such as these many respectable Veḷḷáḷa families may have emigrated to Ceylon. Some of them settled in Jaffna and others sought refuge under the Siṅhalese kings and having accepted positions of honour and trust became the progenitors of some of the most respectable Veḷḷáḷa families of the South. Such a migration of respectable Veḷḷáḷa chieftains is highly probable; and there are hundreds of families in different parts of the Jaffna Peninsula, who trace their descent from one or other of these early colonists.

While Magha was reigning at Polonnaruwa another prince called Vijaya Báhu, also of Kaliṅga origin, * established his kingdom at Dambadeniya and began to collect together the scattered Siṅhalese forces, to foster Buddhism and to protect its priests. His son, Pandita Parákrama Báhu II, became so powerful that Magha and his satellites had to quit Polonnaruwa and retreat to safer places, perhaps in the Northern kingdom. † Before they were expelled from their strongholds, says the Rajaratnacari, the Siṅhalese army had to fight "twelve pitched battles against the Malabar king, Tambalingama Rajah." ‡ Was this Tamil Kaliṅgam Rájah or another name for Magha?

---

* Rajarat., p. 94.

† Mah., chap. lxxxiii, vv. 21—34; Rajavali, p. 260.

‡ Rajarat., p. 94.

The Mahávaṅsa records that, in the 11th year of Parákrama Báhu's reign, one Candabhanu alleged to be a Malay (Jávaka) prince overran the whole of Laṅká but was defeated by Parákrama Báhu's forces.* A few years later, the said Candabhanu "collected a great number of Tamil strong men from the Páṇḍu and Chóḷa countries, and descended again upon Maháthitha with a host of Malays. After he had subdued the inhabitants of Padi. Kurundi and other countries he proceeded to Subhagiri (Yápáhu) and encamped there."† There Vijaya Báhu the son of Parákrama Báhu surrounded his army, and utterly routed it. Vijaya Báhu after putting Candabhanu to flight "took his chief women and all his horses and elephants, his swords and other weapons many in number, his great treasure, his royal chank and the royal umbrella, the royal drum and the royal banner."‡ Who was Candabhanu? Was he a Malay as stated in the Mahávaṅsa and the Pujavalia? If he was a Malay prince or even a Malay pirate how could he have landed at Mahathitha? How could he have collected a great number of Tamil strong men from the Páṇḍu and the Chóḷa countries? On the other hand the Rajavali says, "a short time afterwards, another Malabar king called Chandra Báhu Rájah made a descent on Ceylon and gave battle to the king Alese, and was opposed by the second king, or Parákrama Báhu's youngest brother, who vanquished the army of Malavas, and extirpated the whole out of the

---

* Mah., chap. lxxxiii, vv. 36—47.

† Ibid chap. lxxxviii, vv. 62—75.

‡ Ibid.

Island."* Thus it will be seen that it was the Tamils who in those days were called Malabars, Malavas and also Malays. It was once supposed on the strength of certain inscriptions of Jaṭávarman Sundara Páṇḍya I (1251—1270 A.D.) found on the walls of the Sidambaram temple, that Candabhanu or Chandra Báhu was an error for Sundara Páṇḍya. One of them records that Sundara Páṇḍya fought the Koṅgus with the elephants he recovered as tribute from the king of Īḻam.† The historical introduction of another inscription states that he went aginst Séndamaṅgaḷam after recovering tribute from the Kannaṭa (Hoysala) king and the Ceylon kings.‡ The

* Rajavali, p. 260.

† "கொங்கருடல் கிழியக்குத்தி யிருகோட்டெடுத்து
வெங்கணழலில் வெதுப்புமே-மங்கையர்கண்
சூழத்தாமம்புனையுஞ் சுந்தரத்தோள் மீனவனுக்
கீழத்தானிட்ட இறை"

S. Tamil, vol. iv, p. 493.

The elephants given as tribure by the king of Īḻam to the Pāṇḍyaṉ of beautiful shoulders wearing the garland of flowers and surrounded by women, pierce the bodies of the Kongús, remove their entrails on their tusks and dry them with the fire flying from their eyes.

‡ "நண்ணுதல் பிறாரெலண்ணுதற்கரிய
கண்ண நூற்கொப்பத்தைக் கைக்கொண்டருளிப்
பொன்னிசூழ் செல்வப்புனனாட்டைக்
கன்னிநாடெனக் காத்தருள் செய்யப்
பெருவரையானிற் பின்னவருக்காக்கிய
கருநடராசனைக் களிறுதிறைகொண்டு
துலங்கொளிமணியுஞ் சூழிவேழமு
மிலங்கைகாவலனை யிறைகொண்டருளி
வருதிறைமறுத்தங் கவனைப்பிடித்துக்
கருமுகில்வேழங்காலிற்சேர்த்து
வேந்தர்கண்டறியாவிற்றிண் புரிசைச்
சேந்தமங்கலச் செழும்பதிமுற்றிப்
பல்லவனடுங்கப் பலபோராடி"

S. Tamil, vol. iv, p. 515.

[Contd.]

Hoysala king was no doubt Someśwara the successor of Narasiṁha II who presented the Chóḷa country to Rája-rája III, and the Ceylon king from whom he recovered tribute of gems and elephants must have been Parákrama Báhu II. But who was the king whom he tied to the leg of his elephant for refusing to give tribute? He was certainly the king of Jaffna. Sundara Páṇḍya fought Kó Peruñjiṅga of Sénda Maṅgaḷam in 1257 A.D. Therefore his invasion of Ceylon must have been a year or two earlier, perhaps in 1256 A.D. Parákrama Báhu came to the throne in 1240 A.D., according to the editor of the Mahávaṅsa, or in 1236 A.D., according to the Dambadeniya Asna and other Siṅhalese records.* If the latter date is accepted as correct, 1247 A.D. is the 11th year of Parákrama Báhu II, when Sundara Páṇḍya had not come to the

---

He (Sundara Páṇḍyan) was pleased to take Kannanúr Koppam inconceivable by anybody else and in order to preserve the fertile country of the Chóḷa surrounded by the Káveri as a land of the Kumari (Páṇḍyan country) recovered tribute of elephants from the Kannaḍa (Hoysala) king who in his bounty returned it (the Chóḷa country) to its ruler (Rájarája III), was pleased to recover tribute of glistening gems and elephants bedecked with jewels from the king of Īḷam, chained him, who refused to pay tribute, to the leg of his elephant similar to a dark cloud, reached the beautiful city of Séndamaṅgaḷam containing a fortress guarded by strong bowmen and fought several battles to make the Pallava (Kó Peruñjinga) tremble.

* "Buddha varshayan ekva dahas aṭa siya sú vissakvu avurudu vap maṅgal karana dineyehi Nambara Kalikala Saṅgita Sáhitya Sarvagñña Paṇḍita Parákrama Báhu nam maharajayaeyi kiya oṭuna pelenda rajjaya karana samayehi".

Damba.

In the year of Buddha 1824, having been crowned on the day of the sowing feast, as Nambara Kalikála Saṅgita Sáhitya Sarvagñña Paṇḍita Parákrama Báhu Maharája, and whilst he was reigning.

[The year 1824 mentioned here is from the year of Buddha's enlightenment and not from his nirvana. The Atanagalavaṅsa too gives the same date for Parákrama Báhu's accession.]

throne. Candabhanu, therefore, might have been a Malay pirate as stated in the Mahávaṅsa and other Siṅhalese records, and having been defeated and driven away by Parákrama Báhu, he perhaps took service under the Páṇḍyaṉ king and accompanied him in the second invasion which took place in the 20th year of Parákrama Báhu's reign or 1256 A.D. This year agrees with the date of the inscriptions. The second invasion was therefore Sundara Páṇḍya's and if as we conjecture Candabhanu came as his general, the second invasion too would naturally be attributed to the Malay. This would account also for the statement that he collected "a great number of Tamil strong men from the Páṇḍu and Chóḷa countries." But in spite of his overthrow in this war, the Jaffna king appears to have gone to the help of Kó Peruñjiṅga during his war with Sundara Páṇḍya, for there are certain other inscriptions in the same temple which describe him as having inflicted a severe defeat on the Teluṅgas at Mudugúr slaughtering them and their allies the Áryas.* The Áryas mentioned here refer probably to the army sent up by the king of Jaffna. In the Tirukaḷukuṉṟam inscription of Sundara Páṇḍya of 1259 A.D., he is described as a second Rama in plundering the Island of Laṅká.† He is said to have penetrated as far as Nellore where he had himself anointed as a hero.

There is an inscription at Kuḍumiyamalai of Jaṭavarman Víra Páṇḍya (1252-1267) which records that "he killed one of the two kings of Ceylon, captured his army, chariots, treasures, throne, crown, necklaces, bracelets,

---

* M.E.R., 1915, Nos. 332, 340 and 361 of 1914.

† Ep. Ind., vol. vii, p. 145.

parasols, chaurie, and other royal possessions, planted the Páṇḍya flag with the double fish on Kóṇamalai and the high peaks of Trikuṭagiri mountain, and received elephants as tribute from the other king of Ceylon."* The two kings mentioned in the above inscription were in all probability Parákrama Báhu II and his contemporary of Jaffna. The king who was killed by Víra Páṇḍya must have been some successor of Kúḷaṅkai. The double fish engraved on the stone pillars now supporting the gates of Fort Frederick at Trincomalie may have been those engraved by Víra Páṇḍya at Kóṇamalai, but the mutilated section of a verse appearing below the carps seem on palæographic evidence to have been the work of a much later period. The second invasion of Candabhanu described in the Mahávaṅsa must have, therefore, been that of Víra Páṇḍya. Directly contradicting the boast of Víra Páṇḍya, the Mahávaṅsa claims the victory for the Siṅhalese. Could it be that the victory was obtained by sacrificing a number of elephants and much treasure to the rapacity of the Páṇḍyaṉ army? It is however, strange that the spoils of Vijayabahu's victory are almost similar to those mentioned in Víra Páṇḍya's inscription. The victory claimed by Sundara Páṇḍya appears to have been the same as that of Víra Páṇḍya, for the former too recovered tribute from one Ceylon king and punished the other by tying him to the leg of his elephant.

Parákrama Báhu II was succeeded by his son Vijaya Báhu but, within 2 years of his reign, he was murdered by his Siṅhalese general Mitta, who with the 'brethren of

* M.E.R., of 1912. No. 366 of 1906.

the Munasiṅha family' and the Siṅhalese soldiers turned traitors to the king. But the army of "Áryan warriors" is said to have stood by his brother Bhuvanéka Báhu. They put Mitta to death and raised Bhuvanéka Bahu to the throne.* Who were these "Áryan warriors" who stood by Bhuvanéka Báhu against the Siṅhalese rebels? Their acts of allegience and loyalty on the one hand and the traitorous dealings of the Siṅhalese on the other clearly show that Bhuvanéka Báhu and these Áryan warriors were alike of Tamil origin. If they were Tamils and were called Áryas, they must have come from north Ceylon. If they were at Dambadeniya during the time of Vijaya Báhu, they must have been there during the time of Parákrama Báhu II too. If that is so, it points to an alliance, or at least a friendship, between Parákrama Báhu and the king of the northern dominion. Surely all the story of the defeat and expulsion of Magha from Polonnaruwa as stated in the Siṅhalese Chronicles cannot be fiction. The description of this event as given in the Rajavali † leads one to surmise that Magha left Polonnaruwa on the understanding that while Parákrama reigned at Dambadeniya, he himself should be satisfied with the Northern Kingdom. Unless peace and friendship existed between these two kings it would be hard to account for the presence of a Tamil army of Áryan warriors at the Court of Dambadeniya.

It is also said that Bhuvanéka Báhu drove away his Tamil foes Káliṅga Ráyer and Cóḍagaṅga‡. Who were

* Mah., chap. xc.

† Rajavali, p. 260.

‡ Mah., chap. xc. v. 32.

they ? There were, no doubt, chiefs so named belonging to the Gaṅgavamsa in the Chóḷa country. Did they come over to fight against the Siṅhalese ? But these were also names borne by the Eastern Gaṅgas to whose family belonged the kings of Jaffna. They may have been princes of the Royal Family of Jaffna attempting to secure the Government of some outlying provinces of Ceylon or Vanni chieftains as surmised by Mr. V. Coomaraswamy of Tellipalai.*

It is doubtful whether the kings whose names are given in the Vaipava málai reigned in the order there given, and it is impossible to state with any degree of certainty whether Vijaya Kúḷaṅkai was the first of the Árya chakravartis or when he began to reign. Mr. Mootootambipillai distributed the 11 kings named in the Vaipava málai between the years 101 B.C. and 1460 A.D., eight from 101 B.C. to 130 A. D. and three from 1260 to 1460 A. D.† A more arbitrary method of distribution could not have been imagined. It has been now surmised that Kaliṅga Magha of the Mahávaṅsa was 'Vijaya Kúḷaṅkai' and it has been noticed that during his reign at Polonnaruwa one Parákrama Báhu probably the sub-king reigning at Jaffna was killed by Hoysala Narasiṅha II at Séndamaṅgaḷam and another king by Jaṭavarman Sundara Páṇḍya I, or by Víra Páṇḍya. We shall now try to find out from other sources if there are any important events which can be made to fit in with the time of any of the kings mentioned in the Vaipava málai.

---

* The Hindu Organ.

† Jaf. Hist. p. 9 et seq.,

The Mahávaṅsa says that after the death of Bhuvanéka Báhu I, during a famine in the country "the five brethren who governed the Páṇḍyan kingdom sent to this island at the head of an army, a great minister of much power who was a chief among the Tamils, known as Árya Chakravarti, albeit he was not an Árya," that "when he landed and laid waste the country on every side, he entered the great and noble fortress, the city of Subhagiri (Yápáhu)," that "he took the venerable Tooth-Relic and all the solid wealth that was there and returned to the Páṇḍyan country" and that "he gave the Tooth-Relic unto the king Kulasékhera."* It also adds that when Parákrama Báhu III, the son of Buvanéka Báhu, "raised the canopy of dominion," finding that the Tooth-Relic was to be obtained by conciliation alone "he proceeded with a certain number of crafty and strong men" to the Páṇḍu country and having pleased the Páṇḍyan by his pleasant conversation, "obtained the Tooth-Relic from the king's hands."† This is corroborated in every detail by the Rajaratnacari. ‡ But the Yáḻpáṇa Vaipava málai relates as follows :—"In the year 1380 of the Salivahana Sakaptam, this celebrated young king (Jeya-Vira-Singai-aryan) had a misunderstanding with Puvinéya-Váku (Bhuvanéka Báhu), king of Kandy, touching the pearl fishery. Both kings rushed to arms, and after severe losses on both sides victory declared herself in favour of Jeya-Vira-Singai-Áryan. The victor became master of the territories of the vanquished and

* Mah., chap. xc., vv. 42—47.

† Ibid 52—54.

‡ Rajarat, pp: 107-108

one flag, the flag of Yalpánam, waved over the whole Laṅká. This state of things continued for twelve years, when the king of Yálpáṇam restored the kingdom of Kandy to Prakkirama Vaku (Parákrama Báhu) on his undertaking to pay a tribute.* The amicable arrangement was brought about by the interference of the Páṇḍyaṉ who personally guaranteed the due payment of the tribute by the king of Kandy and Kandy continued to be a tributary of this Kingdom for a number of successive reigns." * An investigation of this will show that the Jaffna tradition is more probable and that the Siṅhalese chroniclers have attempted to conceal the truth. About the time of the death of Bhuvanéka Báhu (1288 A.D.), there were five kings reigning in the Páṇḍyaṉ country although they were not brothers.† They were—

1.	Máravarman Sri Vallabha		1257—1292 A.D.
2.	Máravarman Kulasékhara I		1268—1310 „
3.	Jaṭavarman Sundara	II	1270—1302 „
4.	Jaṭavarman Sundara	III	1276—1293 „
5.	Jaṭavarman Vikrama		Circa 1280 or
	Máravarman Vikrama		1283—1291 A.D.

This fact is confirmed by Marco Polo who says, "In this province (Maobár) there are five kings who are own brothers................At this end of the Province (he was writing from Kayal) reigns one of those five Royal brothers, who is Crowned King and his name is Sundar Bandy Devar."‡ Wassaf speaking of the same king under the name 'Dewar Sundar Pandi' says he had "three

* Y.V.M., p. 22.

† New Dates; Ind: Ant., vol. xlii.

‡ Cathay, vol. ii, p. 267.

brothers each of whom established himself in some different country." * Had any of them a minister called Árya Chakravarti.?

A mutilated Tamil inscription found at the left entrance of the Gopura of Jagannathaswami temple at Tirupulláṇi and inscribed in the 37th year (1305 A.D.) of Máravarman alias Tribhuvana Chakravarti Kulasékhara Déva 'who conquered every country' records an order of a certain Árya Chakravarti. † It is, therefore, suggested that this Árya Chakravarti must have been the minister mentioned in the Mahávaṅsa as the one who conquered Ceylon during the time of Bhuvanéka Báhu I. The inscription is so mutilated that no further details of this Árya Chakravarti can be gathered from it. It was quite as possible for the king of Jaffna who was a friend, feudatory and ally of the Páṇḍyaṉ to build a portion of the Gopura at Tiruppulláṇi which is close to Rámésvaram, as it was for the Páṇḍyaṉ minister. Rámésvaram was at that time under the sway of the Jaffna kings who may have exercised some kind of influence over that portion of the Ramnad district where Tirupulláṇi is situated. On the other hand, many residents of Ceylon have left records in South India of their charitable acts and donations to the temples of that country. It is again suggested that there was a chieftain called Malawa Chakravarti who fought against Laṅkápuri, the general of Parákrama Báhu I. So there is no improbability in there being a chieftain named Árya Chakravarti as a high officer in the

* Cathay, vol. ii, p. 269.

† M.E.R., of 1904, No. 110 of 1903.

Páṇḍyaṉ Court. There may possibly have been about this time a Páṇḍyaṉ minister named Árya Chakravarti, but there is no further record in India regarding such a minister; the event itself is not mentioned in Kulasékhara's inscriptions. These considerations, coupled with the fact that the Árya Chakravartis of Jaffna had at that time become powerful, support the view that the person who conquered Ceylon, during the time of Bhuvanéka Báhu I, was the king of Jaffna.* The tradition recorded in the Vaípava málai that the Jaffna king defeated Bhuvanéka Báhu, ruled over Ceylon for 12 years and restored the kingdom to Parákrama Báhu, through the mediation of Kulasékhara, on the Siṅhalese king undertaking to pay tribute to him seems to be more reliable. The records of this event in the Mahávaṅsa and the Yáḻpáṇa Vaipava Málai corroborate each other in almost every detail, except that in the Mahávaṅsa a Páṇḍyaṉ minister is substituted for the Jaffna king and that no mention is made of the undertaking given by Parákrama Báhu to pay tribute to the Árya Chakravartis.

The Rájaratnacari calls Árya Chakravarti the ambassador of the five brothers of the coast of Coromandel, and the statement in it that the Tooth-Relic was sent as part of the spoils to Kulasékara, the king of the Carnatic,† confirms the theory that the Árya Chakravarti referred to was the king of Jaffna. There was no necessity to send the spoils to Kulasékara if the victor was the minister or the ambassador. He could have taken them with him. The cause of war between the two kings who had apparently

* Almanac. p. 259.

† Rajarat., pp. 107—108.

been friends previously must have been the dispute regarding the ownership of the pearl fishery as stated in the Vaipava málai.

The ability of the king of Jaffna to send Ibn Batuta from Jaffna to the Adam's Peak in 1344 A.D. with an escort, unchallenged by any other king of Ceylon, and the description by Ibn Batuta himself of the naval supremacy and power wielded by the Árya Chakravarti and the fact that the Sinhalese kings had been driven to seek new kingdoms in the fastnesses of the mountains for reasons the Sinhalese chroniclers are careful not to disclose, clearly prove the overlordship of the Jaffna kings, during the fourteenth century, established after the memorable victory gained at Yápáhu.*

The year of the above invasion is given in the Vaipava Málai as Saka 1380 (1458 A.D.).† But this is a mistake of the poet, due to a wrong calculation of the cyclic year. The name of the cyclic year for Saka 1380 is identical with that of Saka 1200, and rectifying the confusion and calculating on the latter basis we find that the date ought to be 1278 A.D., which is within a pardonable margin of 10 years from the date worked out by the editor of the Mahávansa. South Ceylon, after this memorable conquest, was under the sovereignty of the

* In an able paper entitled "The Overlordship of Ceylon during the 13th, 14th and 15th centuries" read before the C.B.R.A.S., Dr. S. C. Paul M.D. has treated this matter of the conquest of the Ārya Chakravarti most exhaustively, and readers are referred to Journal C.B.R.A.S., vol. xxviii, pp. 83 et seq.

† Y.V.M. p. 22.

Jaffna kings for 12 years, and the Siṅhalese kings were feudatories of the Jaffna kings until the conquest of Jaffna by Sapumal Kumaraya. The Siṅhalese kings, therefore, removed their capitals from place to place, so that only the most powerful of the Jaffna kings were able to recover tribute from them. This tradition of the supremacy of the kings of Jaffna during the latter part of the 13th century and during the 14th century is confirmed by Marco Polo and Ibn Batuta. When Marco Polo visited South India in 1284 A.D., the king of Ceylon, according to him, was *Sandamain.** The name has not been identified but in all probability it was intended to be one of the Kings of Jaffna.

If the surmise that the Sandamain of Marco Polo was a king of Jaffna is correct, and if he was the king of all Ceylon during the visit of Marco Polo, the battle of Yápáhu must have been earlier than 1284 A.D. The year 1278 A.D. as deduced by us from the traditional year given in the Vaipava Málai may therefore be correct. If the date of accession of Parákrama Báhu II be taken as 1236 A.D. as mentioned earlier, Bhuvanéka Báhu I must have come to the throne in (1236 plus 35 plus 2) 1273 A.D. The invasion by the Jaffna king took place in 1278 A.D., the fifth year of Bhuvanéka Báhu's reign and not after his death as stated in the Mahávaṅsa and the Rajaratnácari. It is not stated in the Vaipava Málai that Bhuvanéka Báhu was killed in this campaign. He died perhaps in the 11th year of his reign (1284 A.D.) and there was no king for 12 years after his death. Parákrama Báhu,

* Marco. vol.

his son, sought the aid of Kulasékara, obtained the Tooth Relic and became a feudatory of the king of Jaffna in 1296 A.D., and hence the statements in the Vaipava Málai that the Jaffna flag waved over the whole of Lanká for 12 years.* The dates of accession given to the kings of this period by the editor of the Mahávaṅsa are not quite correct. The date of accession of Parákrama Báhu IV can be fixed from other sources. According to a Tamil astrological work called Sarajóti Málai, it received its imprimatur at the Court of Parákrama Báhu of Dambadeniya in the year Saka 1232 or 1310 A.D.,† the

---

* Y.V.M, p. 22.

[The Jaffna flag was not 'the Gemini and the Lyre,' as stated by Mr. Brito in his translation of the Vaipava Malai but 'the Couchant Bull' as would be seen in the literature of the period.]

† "உரைத்த சகவருடமுழுமாயிரத் திருநூற்
றொருநாலெட்டினிலிலகு வசந்தந்தன்னிற்
றரித்திடுவைகாசி புதன் பனையினுளிற்
றம்பைவளர் பராக்கிரம வாகுபூப
னிருத்தவையிற் சரசோதிமாலை யீரா
றெய்து படலநூற்றொன்பான் முப்பானான்காம்
விருத்தமரங்கேற்றினனாற் போசராச
விஞ்சைமறைவேதியனும் புலவரேறே."

Saraj. Málai.—சிறப்புப்பாயிரம்.

Sarajóti málai containing twelve chapters and 934 verses was composed by the Brahman poet Bhója Raja Pandita, and was exhibited at the Court of King Parákrama Báhu of Damba (deniya) on Wednesday in the month of Vaikási (May-June) in the spring of the Saka year 1232 under the asterism of Anusha.

[The above statement was tested with the help of Mr. Swami-Kannupillai's "Indian Chronology" and it was found that the asterism of Anusha in the month of Vaikasi of Saka 1232 fell on a Wednesday.]

7th year of his reign.* Two Parákrama Báhús, the Second and the Fourth, reigned at Dambadeniya according to a Sinhalese work called Dambadeniya Asna. According to another Sinhalese book called Kurunegala Vistaraya, after the massacre of Vastuhimi, the Muslim usurper, the prince who was at Kalundéwa was installed as king under the title of Paṇḍita Parákrama Báhu and he removed the seat of government to Dambadeniya.† Therefore the patron of the author of Sarajóti Málai was Pandita Parákrama Báhu IV. If to 1236, the year of accession of Parákrama Báhu II, the following periods are added:—

35 the reign of Parákrama Báhu II
2 the reign of Vijaya Báhu III
11 the reign of Bhuvanéka Báhu I
12 years under the Jaffna flag
5 the reign of Parákrama Báhu III
2 the reign of Vathimi Bhuvanéka Báhu II

1303

we get 1303 which is also the year when, according to the Sarajóti Málai, Parákrama Báhu IV came to the throne. That the invasion of Yápáhu took place in 1278 A.D.

---

* "கனகமாமகுடஞ் சூடிக் காசினியனைத்துங்காக்குந்
தனிமதிக்குடைக்கீழ்ச் சிங்காசனத்தின் மேலினிதிருந்து
மனுநெறிநடாத்திவாழு மங்கலவாண்டோரேழி
லினியசோதிட நன்னூலைத் தமிழினாலியம்பென்றோத"

Sara. M. Páyiram, v. 7.

In the auspicious seventh year after his coronation while he was reigning with justice seated on the throne under an umbrella which protects the whole earth and which is as cool as the moon, he (Parákrama Báhu) directed that a work on astrology should be composed in sweet Tamil.

† J. C. B. R. A. S., vol xiii, pp. 45-46.

according to the correct calculation made from the traditional cyclic year given in the Yalpáṇa Vaipava Málai, and that Ceylon was under the sway of the king of Jaffna for 12 years before the accession of Parákrama Báhu III, have thus been proved to be true by the independent evidence of the Sarajóti Málai. The Kurunegala Vistaraya which records the reigns of the kings who ruled at Kurunegala says that Parákrama Báhu IV had to remove his capital from Dambadeniya to Kurunegala, on account of an insurrection of the people of Yápápaṭuna. The insurrection of a people living more than a hundred miles away would certainly not have made any king remove his capital from one place to another. The cause of this change was really the pressure brought to bear on him by the king of Jaffna for the payment of tribute. Otherwise we shall have to imagine a similar insurrection in later times to explain the abandoning of Kurunegala for the mountain fastnesses of Gampola.

In Quatremère's memoir on Egypt and the Mamelouk Sultans translated from Arabian manuscripts, there is an account of an embassy, which arrived at Cairo during the reign of Melek Mansour Qaláyoon one of the Mamelouk Sultans, from a sovereign of Ceylon, named Abu-Nekbah-Lebabah. The object of the mission was to establish commercial relations with the Sultan of Egypt. It says:— "In the year 682 of the Hegira (1283 and not 1304 A.D.) there arrived in the Court of Egypt an embassy from the Prince of Ceylon and the king of India. The Ambassador, named Al-adj-Abou Othman, was accompanied by several persons. According to their statements they embarked in a Ceylon vessel, and after having touched at this island, they arrived at the port of Ormus, proceeding up the Eupharates to Bagdad, and thence to Cairo. A letter from the king was presented to the Sultan, enclosed in a golden box, enveloped in a stuff resembling the bark of a tree. The letter was also written in indigenous characters upon the bark of a tree. As no person in Cairo could read the writing, the ambassador explained its contents verbally, saying that his master possessed prodigious quantity of pearls, for the fishery formed part of his dominions, also precious stones of all sorts, ships, elephants, muslins and other stuffs, bakam wood, cinnamon, and all the commodities of trade which the Sultan obtained from the Banian merchants." The ambassador also stated that his master received an envoy from the Prince of Yemen, proposing an alliance, but he had rejected his overtures on account of the Sultan.

The embassy is stated to have been well received by the Sultan and dismissed with a letter to the king; but nothing appears to have resulted from the mission.*

There appears to be no doubt that the prince of Ceylon and the king of India named Abou Nekbah was Bhuvanéka Ba or Bhuvanéka Báhu and it has been surmised that Lebabah is a misreading for Yápáhu. The alliance desired by the Siṅhalese king Bhuvanéka Báhu I was perhaps intended for the purpose of strengthening his position against the aggresions of Árya Chakravarti, the king of Jaffna, who had defeated him in 1278 A.D. The mention of pearls and of the Pearl Fisheries in his letter appear to be a special inducement offered to elicit

* Rifles, vol. i, pp. 247-248.

the Sultan's sympathy and to arouse his desire with the ultimate object of wresting the fisheries from the hands of the king of Jaffna. Bhuvanéka Báhu I died in 1284 A.D., perhaps before the return of the embassy. The bark of the tree on which the letter was written was clearly a piece of Ola. It is impossible to guess the ambassador's name which has received a thoroughly Muhammedan rendering although 'Othman' sounds very much like 'Uttaman.'

When Ibn Batuta visited Ceylon in 1344 A.D., the Árya Chakravarti was the 'Sultan of Ceylon.' On his way to Adam's Peak he passed Kóṭṭe the city of Alagakónar, but the latter raised no objection as Ibn Batuta was travelling under the protection of the king of Jaffna.*

The Jaffna king to whom the victory at Yápáhu is attributed is alleged to be Jeya Víra, the ninth in the list of kings given in the Vaipava:málai.† If Jeya Víra is taken to have lived in 1278 or 1288 A.D. then the reign of one king only intervenes between him and Kanakasúriya, in whose reign Sapumal invaded Jaffna.‡ It is known from other sources that the invasion of Sapumal took place about the middle of the 15th century.¶ It is therefore clear that Mailvágana Pulavar by fixing the traditional year of the above conquest at Saka 1380 allotted it to one of the later kings in the list or, as conjectured by Dr. Paul, he has fallen into the error of

* Batuta,
† Y. V. M., p. 22.
‡ Ibid 23.
¶ Rajavali, p. 265.

giving the "terminal date Saka 1380 as the year of commencement of the great series of events which started with the establishment of the suzerainity of Jaffna over the rest of Ceylon and ended with the capture of Jaffna."*

The Vaipava Málai says that in the reign of Varótaya Siṅgai Áryaṉ, Santhirasékara Páṇḍyaṉ, king of Madura, driven from his kingdom by foreign invasion wandered into Laṅká in search of an asylum. Varótaya befriended him, brought together his scattered army, added to it numerous forces of his own, crossed the sea, beseiged Madura, took part in many bloody engagements, routed the usurpers and reinstated the Páṇḍyaṉ on his throne.† Who was this Páṇḍyaṉ?

Máravarman Kulasékhara I, who reigned for about 40 years, had two sons Sundara Páṇḍya by his lawful wife and Vira Páṇḍya an illegitimate child. He designated the latter to be his successor. Sundara Páṇḍya enraged at this, slew his father and seized the throne, but Vira Páṇḍya drove him out of Madura. Sundara Páṇḍya sought aid from the Muhammedans, which led to Malik Kafur's raid in 1310 A.D.‡ This raid is perhaps referred to as the 'foreign invasion' in the Vaipava Málai. Malik Kafur who conquered Madura in 1310 A.D. returned immediately, and Madura was invaded by the Céra king in 1313 A.D.¶ The Céra occupation was also transitory; for a Mussalman dynasty was shortly after-

---

* J. C. B. R. A. S., vol. xxviii, No. 74, p. 90.

† Y. V. M., p. 21.

‡ Ep. Ind., vol. x, p. 145.

¶ Ibid vol. iv, p. 146.

wards established at Madura. If the king of Jaffna assisted the Páṇḍyaṉ to regain his kingdom, it must have been soon after Malik Kafur's raid, when the Páṇḍya had the satisfaction of occupying the throne of Madura for three years. The Mussalman dynasty was replaced by Kampanna Uḍaiyár, the viceroy of the king of Vijayanagar, in 1365 A.D. It was Sundara Páṇḍya's name that has been transformed to Sandraségara. As soon as Malik Kafur's back was turned on Madura, Vira Páṇḍya must have again driven away Sundara Páṇḍya and hence the latter's appeal to the king of Jaffna. The assistance rendered to the Páṇḍya king is referred to in the historical introduction to the Astrological work Segarájasékaram, the episode, however, being attributed to the Segarájasékaraṉ the patron of the author.*

During the absence of Varótaya on the continent trying to regain his kingdom for the Páṇḍyaṉ, the Vanniyar appear to have risen in revolt and to have sought the aid of the Siṅhalese. They failed because the Siṅhalese king was unable to help them and they were compelled to submit once more, to Varótaya and appease

---

* "கோமாறன் கரகமல மோடை பட்டக்குளமீது குவியக்கண்டு
மாமாரிமதக்கலுழிக்கிளையானை செம்பொனுடன் வழங்கு
வேந்தன்"

Seg. A., Sirappupayiram, v. 9.

The king (Segarájasékaraṉ) on seeing the lotus like hands of the Páṇḍyaṉ joining together on his forehead (i.e., worshipping him) presented him with gold and a herd of elephants pouring streams of must.

[The words இடை, பட்டம் and குளம் are here used to mean forehead.]

the King's resentment with costly gifts.* If the appointment of a Vanniya Chieftain, as the ruler of a country referred to in Segarájasékaram, refers to the creation of a new chief at Ómantai it must have been on the suppression of this attempted revolt.† Ómantai was for a long time the seat of a Vanniya Chieftain.

Varótaya is the 8th king in the list of the Vaipava málai, and it will be seen that an event of 1310 or 1311 A.D. is attributed to the 8th king and one of 1278 A.D. to the 9th king. It is therefore clear that Mailvágana Pulavar who knew the several events which happened during the period of the Árya kings of Jaffna either from oral tradition or from one of the works mentioned by him as his authorities, has distributed them promiscuously among the several kings mentioned in the list not conscious of the anachronisms he was perpetrating.

If it was the same king who went to help the Páṇḍyaṉ, who appointed the Vanniya chieftain, he was the Segarájasékaraṉ during whose time Jaffna rose to the zenith of its power and fame. He was a patron of learning

---

* Y. V. M., p. 21.

† "பாய்மாவு நிதிக்குலமும் பட்டமு நீடாசுரிமைப்பதியுமிக்க
தேமாலே புனைபுயத்தோமந்தையர் கோன்றனக்களித்த செங்கை
வேந்தன்"

Sega. A., Sirappupayiram, v. 9.

And he (Segarájasékaraṉ) presented the Chief of Ōmantai who wears the honeyed wreath, with prancing horses, heaps of treasure, a title and right to govern a country.

[புயத்தேமத்தையர்கோன் is another reading and the present rendering is on the suggestion of Rev. S. Gnanapragasar.]

and poets and pandits flocked to his Court. He established a college of literati (Tamil Saṅgam)* and several works on astrology and medicine and translations from Sanskrit Puráṇas were composed during his time. The king himself rivalled his pandits in learning. Segarájasékaram, a work on Astrology, from which several quotations are cited in this book, and a work on medicine in all its different branches, Dakshina Kayilása Puráṇam and several other works received the imprimatur of his Court. The fact that Siṅhalese kings paid tribute to him is proved by an allusion made in a verse of Sarpasástram (a work on snake-bite) which is a portion of a treatise on medicine. The plural word 'kings' used in the verse is sufficient confirmation of the fact that at that period there were several kings reigning in different parts of Ceylon,

---

* Vide supra, p. 333. note ¶.

† "பாரிலுள்ள சூத்திரனும் பாம்புபுற்றிற்
பரிந்திருக்குமிரையெடுக்கிற் பலவுந்தின்னு
மேருடனே தானுடிற் பத்மாராக
மிலங்குமணிமுடிபுனையு மிலங்கைவேந்தர்
சீரியபொன் திறையளக்கச் செங்கோலோச்சுஞ்
செகராசசேகரமன் சிங்கைமேவு
மாரியர்கோன் வெண்குடையினிழலேசெய்யு
மவனிதனைப்பார்த்து நின்றேயமர்ந்தாடும்மே."

Sega. M., Sarpa Sastram, No. 8.

The Sudra variety of the cobra lives in ant-hills, feeds on whatever it pleases him, and plays spreading his hood looking at the earth—the earth which is covered by the shade of the white umbrella of Segarájasékaraṉ, the king of the Āryas, residing at Siṅgai, who weilds his sceptre so that the kings of Ceylon wearing crowns resplendent with sapphires measure their tribute in gold.

such as, Kurunegala, Gampola, Péradeniya and Kóṭṭe. The reign of his successor Pararájasékaraṉ was equally illustrious. The encouragement given by the latter to literature resulted in the composition of the very able and learned work called Raghu Vamsam by Arasakésari, afterwards the son-in-law of the king, and of another work on medicine called Pararájasékaram.† The fact that there is at Nallúr a land called Arasakésari Valavu* points to the time when Arasakésari lived and when Nallúr was the capital of Jaffna. It is therefore submitted that Pararájasékaraṉ the father-in-law of Arasakésari was the son and successor of Kanagasúriya who established himself at Nallúr after the town had been abandoned by Seṉpahap-Perumáḷ (Bhuvanéka Báhu VI of Cóṭṭe). As this Pararájasékaraṉ reigned between 1478 and 1519 A.D.,† the Raghu Vamsam was composed about the end of the 15th or at the beginning of the 16th century. Antaka Kavi Víra Rághava Mudaliar, a blind Veḷḷáḷa poet, said to have been a contemporary of Kacciappa Pulavar, the author of the Tamil Kandapuráṇam,‡ visited the Court of a Pararájasékaraṉ, and at the king's request composed a work called Árúr Ulá which received the imprimatur of his Court. After an exhibition of several rare feats of memory by the poet, the king not only

* Sen Tamil, vol. xii. p. 81.
Jaffna Kings—p. 54.

† Vide infra p. 374.

‡ So says the compiler of Tamil Navalar Saridai on the authority of a verse composed by Kachchiapper in praise of Vira Raghavan.

Tam. Nav. S. p. 103, v. 242.

composed a verse in his praise,* but also presented him with a nugget of gold.† As the name "Gaṅgakula Kulasékara" is mentioned in a verse sent to the king apprising him of the intended visit of the poet,‡ the Pararájasékaraṉ in whose Court the poet flourished was Kulasékara Parárájasekaraṉ the immediate successor of Kaliṅga Magha (1246—1256 A.D.). The Tamil Kandapuráṇam, therefore, received its imprimatur at the Court of a Chóḻa sub-king reigning at Káñcipuram about the middle of the 13th century. The supposition of certain scholars that Víra Rághavaṉ visited the Court of the king of Jaffna, during

---

* The following verse was composed by the king when Ārúr Ulá was dedicated to him:—

"புவியோர்பெறுந்திருவாரூ ருலாவைப் புலவர்க்கெல்லாஞ்
செவியேசுவைபெறுமாறு செய்தான் சிவஞானவனு
பவியேயெனு நங்கவி வீரராகவன் பாடியநற்
கவியேகவியவனல்லாதபேர்கவி கற்கவியே"

Tam., Na., S., V. 256.

† "பொங்குமிடியின் பந்தம்போயதே யென்கவிதைக்
கெங்கும் விருதுபந்தமேற்றதே-குங்குமந்தோய்
வெற்பந்தமான புயவீரபா ராசசிங்கம்
பொற்பந்தமின்றளித்தபோது"

Tam. Na, S. v. 243.

My bondage to poverty disappeared, and my poetry raised the banner of victory when Pàrarájasiṅgaṉ whose vermilion smeared shoulders resembling (two) hills, presented me today with a nugget of gold.

‡ எடாயிரங்கோடியெழுதாது தன்மனத்தெழுதிப்படித்தவிரகன்
இமசேதுபரியந்தமெதிரிலாக்கவி வீரராகவன் விடுக்குமோலை
சேடாதிபன் சிரமசைத்திடும்புகள் பெற்றதிரிபதகைகுலசேகரன்
தென்பாலை சேலம்புரந்துதாகந்தீர்த்த செழியனெதிர்கொண்டு
காண்க
பாடாதகந்தருவ மெறியாதகந்துகம்பற்றிக் கொலாதகோணம்
பறவாத கொக்கனற்பண்ணுத கோடைவெம்படையிற்
றொடாதகுந்தம்
சூடாதபாடலம் பூவாதமாத்தொடை தொடுத்துமுடியாத சடிலஞ்
சொன்னசொற்சொல்லாத கிள்ளையொன்றெங்குந்துதிக்க
வரவிடல்வேண்டுமே

Tam. Nav. S. v. 251.

திரிபதகை குலசேகரன் = Gaṅgakula Kulasékara.

the time of Edirmanna Siṅha Pararájasékaraṉ who died in 1614 A.D., cannot. for obvious reasons, be maintained.*

About this period there lived a man called Alaga Kónara or Alakéswara whose actual origin is not known, but of whom various facts are alleged to match the greatness he attained in after-life The Mahávaṅsa says that he was a mighty prince dwelling at Péradeniya; but according to the Rájavali, he was the minister or Adigar of a king called Vijaya Báhu and lived at Raigam Nuwera. The Kìrti Sri Mewan inscription on the other hand describes him as the tenth in succession to Nissaṅka Alaga Kónara, the chief of Vañjipura and a member of the Girivamsa.† His ancestor must have hailed from Vañji the capital of Malayalam (Malabar) and hence the adoption of Giri or Malaivamsa. The Chiefs of Tirukkóvalúr are also said to be of the Malaiyakula,‡ but Alagakóṇár's family could not have been from Tirukkóvalúr because they are specially mentioned as natives of Vañjipura. He was a man of lofty ambitions and low cunning, and, knowing well the weakness of the Siṅhalese kings, and the inability of the Jaffna king to oppose a powerful enemy far away from his capital, he started to fortify the village which was afterwards called Kóṭṭe or Jayawardhanapura, ostensibly for the purpose of befriending his puppet king, but with the ulterior object of becoming the king of the Siṅhalese countries, if not the overlord of the whole of Laṅká.

* Place Names, p. 126.

† Ceylon Ant., vol. i, p. 154.

‡ Ep. Ind., vol. vii, p. 135, Inscription of Krishna iii, No. 362 of 1902.

The Siṅhalese chroniclers are not agreed as to the exact time when he started to fortify Kóṭṭe. According to the Mahávaṅsa it was in the time of Vikrama Báhu* who came to the throne about 1351 A.D., but the Rajavali says that it was after Vijaya Báhu was captured and taken as a prisoner to China.† But according to the Chinese records the Siṅhalese king was captured by the Chinese in 1409 A.D.‡ The statement in the Rajavali cannot therefore be true. Ibn Batuta visited Kóṭṭe in 1344 A.D., when Alagakónár pretended to be the king thereof. As it was not called Kóṭṭe then, he might have just started building the town about that time; but when Marignolli visited it in 1348, it had taken the form of a fort and was called Kóṭṭe. Alagakónáṛ was therefore king de facto from about 1340 A.D. and was fortifying Koṭte with the sole object of overthrowing the power of the Jaffna king. As soon as he had sufficiently fortified the place and made his position secure by getting into the town the necessary provisions and weapons for withstanding a long and strenuous seige, he threw down his challenge by seizing and hanging the emissaries of the Jaffna king who went to collect tribute.¶ The king of Jaffna on hearing of this outrage declared war and despatched his army in two divisions: one by land and the other by sea. On being informed of the arrival of the first division at Matale, the Siṅhalese king fled from Gampola. The division despatched by sea landed at Colombo and Páṇadure.

* Mah., chap. xci, v. 7.

† Rajavali, pp. 263—264.

‡ J.C.B.R.A.S.. vol. xxiv, No. 68, p. 97 and note.

¶ Rajavali. pp. 264—265.

Alakésvara attacked and defeated them at Dematagoda and Gorakavana and burnt the ships at Páṇadure. The people of Udarata joined together and completely routed the division that reached Matale. This is the version of Rajavali.* If a victory of so splendid a nature did actually release the Siṅhalese kings from the position of being feudatories to a small kingdom like that of Jaffna, why has the author of the Mahávaṅsa suppressed it ?. He has also omitted to mention the later and the more glorious victory of Sapumal. Did the saintly author think that even the mention of the kingdom of Jaffna was a shame or a crime, or did he intentionally suppress the fact in order that the payment of tribute by the Siṅhalese to the Tamils for more than a century and a half, might not be known. The Nikáya Saṅgrahawa says that Árya Chakravarti came, "with a mighty host of Tamils at once by sea and land with war-like purpose all clad in armour of various hues, bearing weapons, and with *visapelali*, (poison screens) *nadasala* (dancing girls?) and *marasi*, in support. All these he (Alakésvara) put to flight, and he captured their encampments at Colombo, Wattala, Negombo and Chilaw and defeating the mighty hostile hosts who were swarming (in these places) caused his fame and glory to spread in all directions."† The Nikáya Saṅgrahawa does not mention the division that went to Matale. The half-hearted and improbabale manner in which the story of the invasion and of its result is narrated in the Rajavali and the Nikáya Saṅgrahawa leads one to suspect that the victory was not altogether Alekésvara's, and a Tamil

* Rajavali, pp. 264—265.

† Nik. San., p. 26.

inscription, found by Mr. H. C. P. Bell at Kotagama in the Kegalle district,* confirms the suspicion. It is a record of victory left by the king of Jaffna and it is impossible to believe that in his headlong flight after a crushing defeat he would have stayed at Kotagama to put up this inscription. On palæographic grounds the inscription must be attributed to this or to a later period. The characters are not archaic and are quite similar to the letters in the Jambukésvaram inscription of Akkola Rája of the year 1482 A.D The letter *ra* which retains the archaic form is the same in both the inscriptions.† It continued to be so written till

---

* "சேது
கங்கணம் வேற்கண்ணிணையாற் காட்டினார்காமர்வளைப்
பங்கயக்கைமேற்றிலதம் பாரித்தார்-பொங்கொலிநீற்
சிங்கைநகராரியனைச் சேராவனுரேசர்
தங்கள்மடமாதர்தாம்"

Bell; Adm. Rep. of 1911.

The women folk of the Lords of Anurai who would not submit to the Āryan of Siṅgai Nagar of resounding waters shed tears from their eyes that glinted like spears and performed the rites of pouring water with gingely seed from their be-jewelled lotus like hands.

[The language used in the first two lines of this verse is rather obscure. It contains a figure of speech called (தொடர்பின்மையணி known to Sanskrit grammarians as Asangadi Alankara (அசங்கதியலங்காரம்). The word கங்கணம் means 'a bracelet' as well as 'drops of water' (tears). and திலதம் 'a fore-head mark' stands for திலோதகம் 'libation of water poured on gingely seed placed on the palm of the hand held downwards' as a last rite for departed souls. This rite is never performed by women, but they had to do so in this instance as there were no men relations left. Such is the inference.]

[The Sinhalese Chieftains are here called Anurésar (Anurai-Isar, lords of Anurai or Anuradhapura). An inscription of Parákrama Páṇḍya Arikesari Deva of the 15th century calls the capital of the Siṅhalese 'Anurai' although Anuradhapura had been abandoned centuries earlier. (Travancore Arch. Series, Pt. vi.]

† Ep. Ind., vol. iii, p. 7.

a very late period. Mr. Bell very correctly assigned the inscription to the 15th century, but unless proof of a later invasion and victory by the king of Jaffna is forthcoming, it will not be unsafe, on the strength of the inscription, to consider that the Árya Chakravarti was victorious, that Alakésvara was defeated at least by one section of the Jaffna army and that the Sinhalese kings continued to pay tribute. This invasion according to Dr. S. C. Paul took place in 1391 A.D.*

In the Ariyur plates issued in 1390 A.D. by Virupaksha I, of Vijaya Nagar, he is said to have conquered Ceylon.† In his Sorakkavur plates issued in 1386 the conquest is not mentioned.‡ Virupaksha's invasion of Ceylon must have, therefore, taken place between 1386 and 1390 A.D. This conquest is probably the one referred to in the Rajavali as the Malabar invasion of Maha Désa Rajah, in which Vijaya Báhu the king of Gampola was captured and taken away and four of his brothers killed.¶ The Rajavali, of course, confuses the capture of Vijaya Báhu with that of Alakèsvara by the Chinese in 1409 A.D. As this invasion preceded that of the king of Jaffna, it was Virupaksha that captured Vijaya Báhu and left a viceroy in Kandy who is called Sojawna Sevo Raja in the Rajavali and Jothia Seti or Jothia Stoenum Raja by Valentyne.§ He or his successor was later defeated and driven away from Kandy by Ambulagala Kumara who

---

* Paul; J. C. B. R. A. S., vol. xxviii, No. 74, p 115.

† Ind. Ant., vol. xxxviii, p. 12.

‡ Ep. Ind., vol. viii, p. 398.

¶ Rajavali, p. 263.

§ J. C. B. R. A. S., vol. xxii, No. 63, p. 37; Philalathes, p. 39.

had been sent with an army for the purpose by Parákrama Báhu VI in the 52nd year of his reign (1467 A.D.).* It is also stated that when Vijaya Báhu was captured, his queen Sunetra Dévi fled with her infant son who afterwards became king Parákrama Báhu VI. As he came to the throne in 1415 A.D., and as he was an infant in 1389 A.D., when Virupaksha conquered Ceylon, he must have been more than 26 years of age when he came to the throne and not 16 years as mentioned in the Rajavali. Alakésvara must have declared himself king of Ceylon in 1389 A.D., as soon as Vijaya Báhu had been captured, and he reigned 26 years before he was killed by Parákrama in 1415 A.D. If he started building the town of Kóṭṭe in 1340 A.D as mentioned earlier he must have been a centenarian at the time he was murdered.

It appears that a Pararájasékaraṉ was reigning in Jaffna in 1414 A.D., for there were inscriptions on the base of the chief shrine at Rámésvaram which recorded that the principal shrines there were built by Pararájasékaraṉ in Saka 1336.† The stones were hewn at Trincomalie, numbered on the spot ready to be put together and then transported to Rámêsvaram. Most of these inscriptions, however, were either destroyed or removed, and forged ones inserted during a suit between the priests and the Rájáh of Rámnad about 1866 A.D.

During the reign of Déva Rája II of Vijayanagar (1422—1449) Lakkaṇṇa Daṇḍaṇáyaka, his general, crossed over to Ceylon about 1432 A.D. and evidently compelled

* Rajavali, p. 270

† Arch. S. S. I., vol. iv, pp. 56, 57; Shrines.

the Island to acknowledge the suzerainty of Vjjianagar* The Nayar inscription of the same king of the year Saka 1360 (1438 A.D,) describes him as one who recovered tribute from Ceylon (ஈழந்திறைகொண்ட).† Nuniz says that the king of Ceylon (Ceylao) paid tribute to Dêvaráya II.‡ Was it Parákrama Báhu VI or the king of Jaffna or both who were forced by Lakkaṇṇa to pay tribute? This invasion was probably the one alluded to in Philalates' History of Ceylon as having taken place in 1451 A.D.

The Páṇḍya king Jaṭavarman Parákrama Arikêsari Dêva (1422—1463 A.D) in one of the inscriptions of his 28th year (1450 A.D) on the Visvanátaswámi temple at Tenkási records that he defeated his enemies at Singai and Anurai besides other places in South India ¶ But no mention of any such Páṇḍyaṇ invasion or conquest is made either in the Siṅhalese chronicles or in the Vaipava málai; and the inscription may have been merely an empty boast. It serves to show, however, that the Siṅhalese kings were even then described as kings of Anurádhapura, although this ancient city had ceased to be their capital centuries earlier.

Parákrama Báhu as a preliminary to the conquest of Jaffna appears to have led an expedition into the Vannis, subjugated the Vanniyar who had grown very powerful and very troublesome and exacted tribute from them.§

* Ind. Ant., vol. xliii, p. 10.

† M. E. R. of 1917, No. 144 of 1916.

‡ Arch. S. R., 1907-1908, p. 259, note 10.

¶ Trav. A. S., No. vi, pp. 89, 91.

§ Perak. S. and Para. San.; J. C. B. R. A. S., vol. xxii No. 63, p. 26.

The subjugation of the Vannis and making the Vanniyar submit to him was a skilful move, intended to prevent them from joining forces with the king of Jaffna against whom he intended to proceed. And "accordingly having assembled his forces he placed them under the command" of Seṇpahap-Perumáḷ alias Sappumal Kumaraya* who was the son of an Indian Paṇikkan by a Siṅhalese lady and adopted by Parákrama Báhu as his own son,† and sent them against the kingdom of Jaffna. Sapumal raided the frontiers of the kingdom and returned with a few captives. He was sent out again with a larger force* and proceeding along the Western coast via Chilaw, Puttalam, Mannar, Púṇakari and Chavakachcheri, he entered the city of Jaffna itself and made himself master of the Ports thereof.‡ Mounted on a black steed he "sprang among the enemy like a tiger on his prey" and "made such carnage that the streets of Jaffna ran with blood that day as if it had been a river."* Árya Chakravarti fled the country with his wife and children, * but the Rajavali will have it that Sapumal seized him and put him to death and taking his wife and children to Kóṭṭe presented them to Parákrama Báhu.* The conquest of Sapumal is passed over in the Vaipava málai as a rebellion of the Siṅhalese subjects of the king of Jaffna, assisted by the Vanniyar, on account of the king's unjust rule and weakness.¶ Like the priestly authors of the

* Rajavali, p. 268, 269.

† De Couto, Dec. v, Bk. 1, chap. v; J. C. B. R. A. S., vol. xx, No. 60, p. 69; [According to Kókila Sandesa (v. 258) he was Parákrama Bahu's own son.]

‡ Kók. San.

¶ Y. V. M., p. 23.

Siṅhalese chronicles, the author of the Vaipava Málai too intentionally suppressed an event, which, to him, appeared as a dishonour and a disgrace.

Parákarama Báhu VI came to the throne in 1410 A.D., according to the Mahávaṅsa,* and in 1415 A.D., according to other Siṅhalese works.† Mr. H. C. P. Bell favours the latter view. Parákrama Báhu VI reigned 52 years and died in 1467 A.D. As Sapumal reigned in Jaffna for 17 years ‡ before he was called away by the death of Parákrama Báhu his conquest of Jaffna must have taken place in 1450 A.D. Kanakasúriya was the king reigning in Jaffna at that time. If we allow ten years as the length of his reign prior to Sapumal's invasion, then it follows that his predecessor Gunavíra must have died about 1440 A.D. Magha whom we considered to be Kúḷaṅkai started reign at Polonnaruwa in 1215 A.D. He went back to Jaffna in 1236 A.D. As Magha started to reign at Jaffna earlier than 1215 A.D. he must have reigned for a long time. We may, therefore, assign another ten years for his reign in Jaffna after 1236 A.D. So his successor must have come to the throne about 1246 A.D. It was perhaps his successor who is called Kulasékara in the Vaipava Málai and who was killed by Sundara Páṇḍya in 1256 A.D. Between him and Kanakasúriya there were 8 sovereigns the lengths

* Mah., chap. xci, vv. 15, 16.

† Rajavali, pp. 265, 267. [The year of Paràkrama Bahu's accession is incorrectly stated to be the year of Vijaya Bahu's capture, but note the astrological agreement.]

Muller, No. 160; Pepiliyana Vihara Inscription, Kavya.

‡ Y. V. M., p. 24.

of whose reigns aggregates to 184 years, from 1256—1440 A.D. This gives an average of 23 years for each sovereign which is by no means unreasonable.

From the fact that there had been kings who called themselves Pararájasékaraṉ and Segarájasékaraṉ before the conquest of Sapumal, and that the Portuguese Historians called those after Saṅkili by similar names, it appears that the kings of Jaffna, following the custom which prevailed among the kings of the Chóḷa, Páṇḍya and Siṅhalese dynasties,* called themselves by the alternate names of Pararájasékaraṉ and Segarájasékaraṉ.† The author of the Vaipava Málai who mistook these titles for names thought that there was only one king of the name of Pararájasékaran and that the other was his brother.

The following list of kings who reigned at Siṅgai Nagar from the 13th to the middle of the 15th century is adapted from the Vaipava málai giving the probable dates of accession according to the average :—

Vijaya Kúḷaṇkai (Kaliṅga Magha)	Segarájasékaraṉ	circa 1210 A.D.
Kulasékara	Pararájasékaraṉ	1246 „
Kulóttuṅga	Segarájasékaraṉ	1256 „
Vikrama	Pararájasékaraṉ	1279 „
Varótaya	Segarájasékaraṉ	1302 „
Mártáṇḍa	Pararájasékaraṉ	1325 „

* The Chóḷa kings were called Rájakésarivarman and Parakésarivarman, the Páṇḍyas Máravarman and Jaṭavarman and the Siṅhalese Sri Saṅgha Bódhi and Abe Salamévan, alternately.

† Mr. H. W. Codrington, C.C.S., was the first to propound this theory.

Guṇapúshaṇa	Segarájasékaraṇ	1348 A.D
Virótaya	Pararájasékaraṇ	1371 „
Jayavíra	Segarájasékaraṇ	1394 „
	or more probably	1380 „
Guṇavíra	Pararájasékaraṇ	1417 „
	or more probably	1410 „
Kanagasúriya	Sekarájasékaraṇ	1440 „
Sapumal Kumaraya Bhuvanéka Báhu	(Seṇpahap Perumáḷ)	1450 „

According to the above table it would appear that Kavi-Víra Rághavaṇ visited the court of Kulasékara; that Kulóttunga was responsible for the victory at Yápáhu; that in the reign of Vikrama, Marco Polo visited Jaffna and called him Sandamain and Parákrama Báhu III obtained the tooth relic from him; that Varótaya was the Segarájasékaraṇ who went to the help of Sundara Páṇḍya and established the college of literati; that Mártáṇḍa reigned during the visit of Ibn Batuta and died in 1348; and that his successor Guṇapúshaṇa being then a minor, his queen mother was perhaps acting as regent during the visit of Marignolli to Jaffna. There is a discrepancy as regards Jayavíra and Guṇa Víra, for in 1414 A.D. a Pararájasékaraṇ built the shrine at Rámésvaram. Gúnavíra to whom the Vaipava Málai ascribes a long reign had perhaps ascended the throne before 1414 A.D. As Jayavíra too is said to have reigned so long, the dates of Jayavíra's and Gunavíra's accession may be safely set back to 1380 and 1410 A.D. respectively, thereby reducing to nine years the reign of Virótaya who according to the Vaipava Malai too reigned only a few years and died young. Then it would be Jaya

Víra who fought against Alakésvara and left the inscription at Kotagama.

Sapumal, when he went to Parákrama Báhu with the spoils of victory, was sent back to Jaffna to reign there under the throne-name of Bhuvanéka Báhu. * He was the son of a Tamil and therefore a Hindu but he practised tolerance towards the Buddhists. The Siṅhalese in the district who were still Buddhists continued their worship without any interference and during his reign a large number of Buddhist shrines were built, the ruins of which can still be identified in different parts of the Peninsula. One at Chunnagam and another at Point Pedro excavated by Dr. P. E. Pieris belong to this period. It was Bhuvanéka Báhu in all probability, who built the town of Nallúr and the temple of Kandaswámy in it. The other temples at Nallúr seem to have been built later. Before building Nallúr he destroyed the town of Siṅgai Nagar and razed it to the ground. The Siṅhalese work Kokila Sandésa (the Cuckoo's message) composed by the priest of Irugalkulaprivena at Mulgirigala near Dondra Head in the Southern Province, in order to send his blessings to Sapumal Kumáraya who was then reigning in Jaffna, contains a description of the town which he calls Yápápaṭuna. † It is not clear whether Siṅgai Nagar or Nallúr was meant. According to the itinerary given in the Sandésa the Cuckoo after leaving Mannar passes through Mávatupaṭuna (Mátoṭa) and flying over jungles and forests and passing Jávaka Kóṭṭe (Chávakachchéri)

---

* Rajavali, p. 269.

† Kók. San., vv., 243 254.

and Kalmunai reaches Yápápaṭuna. From this doubtful itinerary of the bird it may be inferred that Sapumal was then reigning at Nallúr but the Shrines of Yápápaṭuna are said to be one dedicated to Ráma and another to Sakra (Indra?) at Punnala. * The temple of Rama was at Vallipuram and the other where Krishna is worshipped is at Punnalai near Moolai. The Siṅhalese author has therefore used Yápápaṭuna to mean the capital as well as the District.

Sapumal Kumaraya alias Bhuvanéka Báhu reigned in Jaffna for 17 years and on hearing of the death of Parákrama Báhu and the accession of his grandson (called Jaya Báhu by the Mahávaṇsa † and Víra Parákrama Báhu by the Rajavali ‡) to the throne of Kóṭṭe, he hastened with an army to Kóṭṭe, murdered the rightful heir and ascended the throne under the name of Bhuvanéka Báhu (VI.) §

On coming to know of the departure of Bhuvanéka Báhu from Jaffna, Kanakasúriya who had been living in South India as a refugee returned to Jaffna with his sons. § He found that one Vijaya Báhu had usurped the throne lately vacated by Bhuvanéka Báhu. Vijaya Báhu was defeated and killed, and Kanakasúriya, after an absence of 17 years, again ascended the throne of his forefathers. §

The Period extending from 1467 to 1620 A.D., when the Portuguese became the sole masters of the kingdom

* Kók. San., vv., 252,253.

† Mah, chap. xcii, v. 1.

‡ Rajavali, pp. 271, 272.

§ Y. V. M.. pp. 23, 24.

of Jaffna, has been exhaustively treated by Rev. S. Gnanaprakasar, O.M.I. of Jaffna in a brochure entitled "The Kings of Jaffna during the Portuguese Period" and published in 1920, and it is unnecessary for us to go over the same ground. We shall, however, deal here with such events and matters as have not been touched upon by him. According to him the following kings reigned at Nallúr from 1467 A.D. :—

1.	Kanagasúriya	Segarájasékaraṇ	1467 A.D.
2.		Pararájasékaraṇ	1478 „
3.	Saṅkili	Segarájasékaraṇ	1519 „
4.	Puvi Rája Paṇḍáram	Pararájasékaraṇ	1561 „
5.	Kachi Nayinar (usurper)	Pararájasékaraṇ	C 1565 „
6.	Periya Pulle	Segarájasékaraṇ	C 1570 „
7.	Puviràja Paṇḍáram	Pararájasékaraṇ	C 1582 „
8.	Hendarmana Cinga (Edirmanna Siṅgha)	Pararájasékaraṇ	1591 „
9.	A minor son under the Regency of—		
	1. Arasakésari		1615 „
	2. Saṅkili Kumára		1617 „
10.	Philip de Oliveira, Portuguese Governor,		1620 „

An important event that took place during the reign of Pararájasékaraṇ (No. 2 above) was the arrival at his Court of a remarkable visitor in the person of one Subhadiṭṭa Muni and his prophecy regarding the future rulers of Jaffna. The prophecy was to the effect that his royal descendants would not inherit his crown and that the kingdom would pass into the hands of strangers. He also foretold that the Parangis (Portuguese) would be the first to seize the kingdom and after a tyrannical reign of 40 years, it would pass into the hands of the Ulanthes (Hollanders) whose cruel reign would last 140 years. Then the Inthirésu (English) would wrest the kingdom and reign with justice for 79 years. In the latter part of his reign the Inthirésan would not reign with the same justice as he did at the commencement. When the Inthirésan had governed his allotted years the Piráñchu Rásá (the French king) and the Ulanthes king would take the kingdom by fraud and reign in Colombo. Then the Government of the whole of Ceylon would be handed over to Valasingan.* This prophecy is contained in four Tamil verses found quoted at the end of a manuscript copy of the Vaipava Málai.† It is, however, difficult to say

---

* Y. V. M., pp. 25 et seq.

† (1) "திருமருவுயாழ்ப்பாண நாட்டையாண்ட
சிங்கையாரியன் குலத்தைத் தீங்குசெய்து
பெருமையுடன் காலயுத்தியானிமாசம்
பிலிப்பனெனும் பறங்கிகிளை யரசையாண்டு
குருநெறியுமனுநெறியு மில்லாதாக்கிக்
கொடுமையுடன் நாற்பஃதாண்டளவும் போக்க
உருமருவு முதயகிரியிரவிபோல
வுலாந்தேசமன்னவன் வந்துதிப்பன்றனே"

After destroying the dynasty of the Singai Árya kings who reigned over the country of Yálpánam, the band of Parangis (Portuguese) of the name of Philip shall from the month of June in the year Kálayutti, rule with pride for a period of forty years with neither rectitude nor justice and committing acts of tyrrany, when the king of the Ulanthes (Hollanders) will rise like the sun over the hill tops on the East.

[The cyclic year Kálayutti agrees with the year 1618—1619 A.D.]

(2) "உதிக்கின்ற விளம்பிதனிலானிமாச
மொன்பதனிலுலகுபுகள் உலாந்தேசண்ணல்
மதிக்கின்றமனப்பறங்கிக் கிளையையெல்லாம்
வாள்வலியாலுயிர் தொலைத்துவாரியள்ளிக்

கொதிக்கின்றதென் கடலிலடையவீசிக்
கோட்டையொப்புக் கொண்டேற்றுக்கொடியுந்தூக்கித்
துதிக்கின்றயாழ்ப்பாண நகரிதன்னிற்
சோதிதிகள்மணி மகுடஞ்சூட்டுவானே''

The Ulanthes king praised on earth, shall, on the 9th day of June in the year Vilambi, put the whole band of the Portuguese to the sword, throw their bodies into the boiling southern sea as so much refuse, seize the fort, raise his flag and be crowned with a crown sparkling with gems, in the town of Jaffna.

[The cyclic year Vilambi agrees with the year 1648—1649 A.D.]

(3) " சூட்டியபின் னூற்றின் மேலையெட்டாண்டு
தொல்வினைபோல் வல்வினைகளெல்லாஞ்செய்து
ஈட்டுபொருளுள்ளதெல்லாங் கவர்ந்துதேடி
யிடர்விழைத்து யாவரையுமிளிகோலாக்கிக்
கூட்டுறுமின்மினி வீழ்ந்தக்கினியின் மாய்ந்த
கொள்கையெனவவன் குலமுநாசமாக
நாட்டுபுகள் யாழ்ப்பாண நாடெங்கெங்கும்
நன்மைபெற நல்லரசு நடக்குந்தானே

After the coronation, his dynasty shall reign for 140 years committing such wicked acts as if they were the results of past sins, avariciously amassing all the wealth that could be made, doing harm and making everybody poverty stricken, and shall be destroyed like a firefly that falls into the fire. Then good and just rule shall obtain throughout the land of Jaffna.

[The duration of the Dutch rule was not 140 years but 148 years (1648—1796 A.D). The reading might be a corruption for "சூட்டியபின் நூற்றின் மேலா றெட்டாண்டு."]

(4) நல்லரசு நடத்திவிட்டானனைவோருக்கும்
நன்றாக யிராக்கதக் கன்னி தொட்டு
வல்லபுகழிங்கிலேசர் எழுபத்தொன்பான்
வருஷமரசாண்டு மனுநீதிதப்பித்
தொல்லைவரிகுடிகளுக்குச் சுமத்துநாளில்
தொன்மைபுகழ் பிராஞ்சு பிறர் துணைவரோடும்
அல்லல்வழுநாடு வவ்விவாலசிங்க
மகிபனுக்குமணிமகுடம் வளங்குவானே.

The English after reigning wisely and righteously for 79 years from the month of September in the year Rákata (1796. A.D.) shall then swerve from the path of justice and burden the subjects with troublesome taxes. Then the French of ancient fame shall with the help of others wrest the country from them and hand over the same to Bálasingam and crown him king.

whether these verses were the source from which Mailvágana Pulavar transferred the details of the prophecy to the lips of Subhadiṭṭa Muni. While the periods assigned in the prophecy to the rule of the Portuguese and the Dutch are correct, the total number of years for each of the other nations is not given. How could Mailvágana Pulavar who wrote during the Dutch times have predicted the rule of the English? There must have been a genuine Prophecy in his time or the passage in question must be an interpolation of later times. It is, however, true that a prophecy of a similar nature, though not in such details existed in the country before the arrival of the Portuguese; for a portion of a verse containing such a prophecy can still be seen inscribed in a stone door jamb removed from the Koṇésar temple and now placed at the entrance to Fort Frederick at Trincomalie.* In a despatch sent to

---

* "முன்னாட்குழக்கோட்டன் மூட்டுந்திருப்பணியைப்
பின்னாட்பறங்கி பிடிப்பனே-பொன்னாரும்
பூனைக்கண்செங்கண் புகைக்கண்ணராண்டபின்பு
தானுந்தமிழாய்விடும்"

The temple built by Kuḻakkóṭṭan in ancient times will be later seized by the Paraṅgi (Portuguese) and after the successive reigns of the catseyed, the red eyed and the smoke eyed (nations) it will voluntarily revert back to the Tamils.

The visible and readable portion of the inscription as it now appears on the door jamb at the entrance to Fort Frederick is as follows ;—

ன னே குள
காட முட டு
ருபபணியை
ன னேபறங்கி
ககவே மனன
னபொன்ற
னையயறற
தேவைத
ற
கள.

 (contd.)

the king of Portugal by Constantine de Sa, between 1624 and 1627 A.D., he describes the temple as follows:—"The land of the Pagoda is 600 fathoms long and 80 feet at its broadest narrowing to thirty feet, which is the place where the Fort stands. The place is impregnable owing to the high cliffs and the village which lies therein could with very few fortifications be made one of the strongest places of the whole of India. When I went there to make this Fort, I found engraved on the Pagoda among many other inscriptions one which ran thus:—"This Pagoda has been built by———. Nevertheless shall the time come that a nation of the Frangis will destroy it and thereafter shall no king of the Island of Ceylon rebuild it."* The existence of the inscription is confirmed by de Queiroz who says that it was afterwards translated by some

---

According to the interpretation given by Constantine de Sa and Queiroz it can be reconstructed as follows:—

(மு) னனேகுள (க்)
(ே) காடன மூடடு (ந்)
(தி) ருப்பணியை (ப்)
(பி) னனே பறஙகி (பி)
(ரி) ககவே-மனன (வ)
(பி) ன பொண்ணா (த)
(த) னையியறற (வழி)
(த்) தேவைத் (து)
(எண்) ணா (ரேபின்)
(னரசர்) கள்

முன்னே குளக்கோடன் மூட்டுந்திருப்பணியைப்
பின்னே பறங்கி பிரிக்கவே - மன்னவபின்
பொண்ணாததனையியற்ற வழித்தேவைத்து
எண்ணாரே பின்னரசர்கள்.

* Found among the Portuguese manuscripts at the Hague by Mr. E. B. Reimers, the Covernment Archivist.

Temple of Tirukónésvaram
from a Portuguese drawing.
with kind permission of the Royai Asiatic Society (Ceylon Branch.)

[To face page 379.

Ceylonese skilled in ancient writings and sent to the king of Portugal. He gives a copy of which the following is a translation. "Manua Raja Emperor of this Lanka erected this temple to the God Vidia Malmanda in the year (equal to 1300 B.C.). There is a nation called Francos who will destroy it, and there will be no king in this island who will rebuild it once more."*

If the ellipsis in De Sa's copy is supplied with the word "Kuḻakkóṭṭaṉ" it will tally with the portion of the verse now extant on the door-post at Fort Frederick. But the Ceylonese 'skilled in ancient writings' appear to have added their own explanation to the words appearing in the verse, in the translation given by de Queiroz. As Kuḻakkóṭṭan was the son of Maṉu-níti-kaṇḍa-Chóḻaṉ or Maṉu Véntaṉ,† he was called Manua Raja, 'ancient times' were supposed to have been about 1300 B.C., and the sacred edifice constituted the car-street and the first hall (வீதியும் மேல்மண்டபமும்). The first two lines of the prophecy therefore were as they are now extant and the other two lines were to the effect that thereafter shall rise no other king of the Island who will rebuild it. The prophecy is after all not a myth. The existence of such a prophecy before the arrival of the Portuguese is proved by the despatch of Constantine de Sa. The last two lines of the verse now extant are probably a later addition in place of the lines obliterated from the stone door-post, for neither de Sa nor Queiroz says

* Queizor, p. 57.

† Dak. K. P. Tirunagara Carukkam, vv. 27, 34, 37.

Y.V.M. pp. 4, 5.

anything about the cat's eyed, red eyed and smoke eyed nations who were to succeed the Parangis. The palæographical appearance of this mutilated inscription will not admit the possibility of placing it before the 15th century and therefore it must have been the echo of the Jaffna prophecy which reached Trincomalie in time to be engraved before the arrival of the Portuguese. If there is any truth in the statement that a Saint named Subhaḍiṭṭa Muni visited the Court of the Jaffna King, it must have been during the time of the Pararájasékaraṉ, son of Kanagasúriya, who began to reign at Nallúr in 1478 A D, and to whose reign points the tradition embodied in the Vaipava Málai. It was probably in the second part of the verse manufactured later that Mailvágana Pulaver discovered the allusion to the Dutch, the English and the French.

During the reign of Vijaya Báhu VII, of Kóṭṭe, his three sons Bhuvanéka Báhu, Raigam Bandára and Máyádunne fearing punishment at the hands of their father fled to Jaffna in 1534 A.D. They are said to have besought the aid of the king of Jaffna against their father, and Máyádunne then went to the hill country to obtain the aid of the king there. With the forces obtained from the kings of Jaffna and Kandy, the three princes went to Kóṭṭe, defeated the forces of their father and murdered him. The eldest of them became king of Kóṭṭe as Bhuvanéka Báhu VII.* The Jaffna king who befriended these princes must have been Saṅkili as he came to the throne about 1519 A.D,† although it is said that

* Rajavali, pp. 281—285.
De Couto, Dec. v, Bk. v, chap. v; J.C.B.R.A.S., vol. xx, p. 72.
† Jaffna kings, p. 6.

he was not crowned.* The author of the Vaipava Málai has evidently confused him with the other Saṅkili who about 1617 A.D. usurped the throne putting out the eyes of the real king who was a minor under his guardianship. It is doubtful whether the former who was known as Segarájasékaraṉ was the illegitimate son of his predecessor, as stated in the Vaipava Málai.

According to the Portuguese historians the Christian converts at Mannar were massacred by Saṅkili in 1544 A.D.,† but according to the Vaipava Málai this event took place in the month of Aḍi (July-August) of the cyclic year Khara‡ which agrees with the year 1531-1532 A.D. The year mentioned in the Jaffna chronicle is therefore incorrect, for Francis Xavier who was responsible for the conversion of the Kadeyas at Mannar did not reach Goa till 1542 A.D.

An interesting fact which came to the knowledge of the Portuguese in the expedition of Martin Affonso de Sousa of 1543 in which the ships of the expedition were driven by the monsoon to Neduntivoe called Ilhas dasVacas (Isle of Cows) was that the largest of the goats that were slaughtered there for the Armada contained bezoar and "it afterwards became a custom for the Bengal ships to call at this Island for these concretions."¶

In 1555 A.D. Vídiye Banḍára, called Tribule Bandar (Teruwe Panḍáram) by the Portuguese historians, on being defeated by Rája Siṅha, the Lion King, fled with

---

* Y. V. M., p. 36.

† Jaffna Kings, p. 9.

‡ Y. V. M., p. 33.

¶ J. C. B. R. A. S., vol. xx, p. 120, Note 4.

his son to Jaffna and sought refuge in the court of Saṅkili. He was encamped near Tárákuḷam.* Soon afterwards at a festival in the temple, presumably that at Nallúr, suspecting the accidental firing of gunpowder to be an attempt made on his life, Vidiye Baṇḍára drew his sword ; a *fracas* ensued and he and his son were killed by Saṅkili's men and all his treasures including the Tooth Relic fell into the hands of Saṅkili.*

When Constantine de Braganza entered the city of Nallúr in 1560 A.D. and destroyed several villages and temples, the Tooth Relic was one of the articles included in the plunder. Braganza chose to destroy it by fire, rather than sell it to the king of Pegu who offered him 800,000 lirves for it.† The author of 'Ceylon during the Portuguese Era' says that the tooth destroyed was a model of the Relic set in gems and gold and carried, perhaps for the purpose of private adoration, on the person of Vidiye Baṇḍára during his flight to Jaffna ‡ But Quieroz who gives a minute description of its capture and destruction will have us believe that the tooth destroyed was the genuine one.¶ The offer of the king of Pegu and the grim determination of the Portuguese to destroy it, both suggest that the Portuguese did then believe it to be the original Danta Dátu.

After the massacre of the Christians Saṅkili's insane fury longed for more victims and he fell upon the

* Pieris. vol. i. pp. 136. 137, 157.

† Rebeiro, chap. xii ; Reb. Ceilao, p. 49, Couto : Dec. vii, Bk. ix, chap. xvii

‡ Pieris. vol. i. p. 136.

¶ Queiroz, pp. 251, 260, 293.

Buddhists of Jaffna who were all Siṅhalese. He expelled them beyond the limits of the country and destroyed their numerous places of worship. Most of them betook themselves to the Vannis and the Kandyan territories,* and those who were unable to do so became the slaves of the Tamil chieftains and are now known as 'Kóvia,' a caste peculiar to Jaffna alone. The term is no doubt a corruption of the Siṅhalese word 'Goviya' or 'Goiya' and that their original status was equal to that of the Veḷḷáḷas can be inferred from certain customs which are still in vogue in Jaffna. The Tanakáras and Naḻavas of Jaffna should also be considered as Siṅhalese remnants in spite of the fanciful derivation of the word 'Naḻava' given by the author of the Vaipava Málai.† The Naḻavas were perhaps originally the Siṅhalese climbers and received the Tamil name on account of their peculiar way of climbing trees. They too became the slaves of the Tamil Chieftains. The Tanakáras were the ancient Elephant keepers and those who supplied the necessary fodder to the stables of the king (Sinh: Tana-grass). They perhaps on account of the service rendered by them were not expelled from the country and later became inseparably mixed with the Tamils among whom they had to remain. The Paḷḷas were the only slaves who accompanied their aristocratic masters from India and were employed in cultivating the fields of their lords.‡ They

---

* Y. V. M., p. 33.

† Ibid 35.

‡ The Tamil Chieftains who emigrated from India came down with their vassals and slaves (kuḍimai and aḍimai). The places where they settled can be traced through Paḷḷa occupation. Those who did not possess Paḷḷa slaves did not belong to the Chieftain class.

took to climbing trees at a much later period when the Kóvia slaves became too numerous. When slavery was abolished the Paḷḷas and Naḷavas retained their tree climbing occupation while the Shánár who were numerically few gave up their original pursuits and took to agriculture. The Kóvias became domestic servants and being attached to the houses of their Veḷḷáḷa masters ousted the Paḷḷas from their customary occupation of cultivating their master's fields. The fact that the Kóvias, Tanakáras and Naḷavas were originally Siṅhalese can be seen from the peculiar dress of their women who wear the inner end of their cloth over the shoulders in a manner quite strange to the genuine Tamils.

That Jaffna was occupied by the Siṅhalese earlier than by the Tamils is seen not only in the place names of Jaffna* but also in some of the habits and customs of the people. The system of branding cattle with the communal brand by which not only the caste but also the position and the family of the owner could be traced, was peculiarly Siṅhalese. The very ancient way of wearing the hair in the form of a koṇḍe behind the head, a habit of the ancient Nágas, was very common among the people of Jaffna till very recent times. The women's fashion of dressing their cloth across their breasts and men's of wearing their tufts of hair on the side of the head, as was the custom in Jaffna, were introduced by the Malabar immigrants.

Several of the kings of Vijayanagar state in their inscriptions that they conquered Ceylon. An inscription

* Place names.

of Krishna Déva Ráya (1509—1530) of the year 1528 found at Piranmalai asserts that he conquered the Island of Ceylon in 1522 A.D.* The inscriptions of Achayuta Ráya (1530—1542) call him conqueror of Ceylon. An inscription in Rájagópála Perumál temple in Tanjore dated 1539 A.D. informs us that Achayuta conquered Ílam (Ceylon). He is said to have planted a pillar of victory at Támraparni and married the daughter of the Páṇḍyaṉ.† If this is true, his conquest of Ceylon cannot absolutely be a piece of fiction. Inscriptions of Sadásiva Ráya (1542—1565) say that he was the conqueror of all countries and of Ceylon.† Was the boast of the these successive kings of Vijayanagar an empty one, or did the Ceylon kings conciliate them by paying tribute as did Parákrama Báhu VI to the kings of Jaffna and of China?

According to a Telugu work called Siṅhaladwipa Katá, Kumára Krishnappá the Naik king who reigned at Madura (1562—1572) conquered Kandy, killed the king, sent his wife and children to Anuradhapura and placed his brother-in-law Vijaya Gopala Naidu as his viceroy in Kandy.¶ Krishnappá's supremacy, if true, must have been short-lived. The king of Kandy about this time was Dom Joao Periapandar alias Don Juan who about the year 1580, on being defeated by Rája Siṅha, fled with his family and attendants in the direction of Jaffna. The

* Ind. Ant., vol: xliii, p. 45; M. E R., of 1904, No. 149 of 1903.

† Ibid p. 186; M. E. R., No. 40 of 1897 and Nos. 49 & 50 of 1900.

‡ Ibid p. 230, Note.

¶ Ibid xlv, p. 18.

Portuguese historians as well as the Rájavali give different versions of this event.* It is just possible that these accounts are confused versions of Krishnappá's invasion.

In a copper plate grant of Tirumalai Uḍaiyán Sétupati of Saka 1530 or 1608 A.D. there appear the words meaning, " he who conquered the army of Pararájasékaraṉ, the Árya Chakravarti."† The king reigning in Jaffna in 1608 A.D. was Edirmanna Siṅga Kumara who was a Pararájasékaraṉ. But the same words also appear in another grant of Raghunátha Sétupati of Saka 1581 or 1659 A.D.,‡ when the Dutch had already wrested the kingdom from the Portuguese. No reliance can therefore be placed on these inscriptions.

Allusions to the help given by the Naiks of Tanjore to the kings of Jaffna during this period are found in certain Telugu works. It is said that during the time of Achayuta Naik, a king of Jaffna, who had been dispossessed of his kingdom by the Portuguese, went to his Court with his family and attendants and begged of him (Achayuta) to render him the necessary help to regain his kingdom. Achayuta took pity on the deplorable condition of the refugees, gave them one of his own palaces to live in and promised to send his army in the following autumn against the Portuguese.¶ The king who went for help must have been Saṅkili Kumara who had murdered Arasakésari, the regent uncle of the minor king,

* De Couto, Supplt. to Dec ix; J. C. B. R. A. S., vol. xx, pp. 258-259; Rajavali, p. 307.

† Arch. S. S. I., vol. iv, No. 2.

‡ Ibid No. 5.

¶ Sah. Rat., Sarga viii; Sources.

and usurped the regency The Portuguese drove him out and he with an army under Kheen Naik of Tanjore returned and defeated the Portuguese army and established himself on the throne. The Portuguese then recognised him as king but ultimately dethroned him and occupied Jaffna.*

Again during the reign of Raghunátha Naik the king of Jaffna went to Tanjore and complained that the Portuguese had stormed his capital during his absence and that he had to flee in a ship and to seek refuge at Tanjore. Raghunátha rode out in state to the sea-coast at the head of an army and crossed over to the Island by means of a bridge of boats. The Portuguese resisted his landing but were defeated and leaving behind them their treasure, arms and ammunitions escaped by sea. Raghunátha then placed his own garrison in the Island and celebrated the coronation of his ally.† From the above details it does not appear who the king was who was so assisted. Whether Sankili went over a second time, obtained the necessary assistance and had himself crowned before Oliveirá's forces came up and captured him or whether the story is a confused account of the help given to the prince of Rámésvaram on whose behalf the people of Jaffna revolted against the Portuguese,‡ it is difficult to say.

When the kingdom ultimately fell into the hands of the Portuguese all the members of the royal household, the nobility and the chiefs became Christians. Some of

---

* Port. Ind., vol. ii, chap. viii.

† Ragunath. R., sargas vii & ix; Sources.

‡ Jaffna Kings, pp. 58, 74.

them were removed to Goa while those who stayed behind were treated respectfully and given high appointments under the Government. According to the Vaipava málai the descendants of the last kings of Jaffna were called Maḍapaḷḷis, a title said to have been created by Saṅkili to please the disappointed heir to the throne. The story runs that seven sons of the prince were given that title and made chiefs of districts and their descendants were called Rája or Kumára Maḍapaḷḷis.* But there were in Jaffna two other sets of Maḍapaḷḷis supposed to be lower than the Rája or Kumára Maḍapaḷḷis. Most of the Kaliṅga colonists in Jaffna must have been emigrants from the village called Maḍapaḷḷi in Orissa (not Mottupalli as conjectured by Mr. V. Coomaraswamy) and called Maḍapaḷḷis after their original home.

The name is by no means unknown. There have been two villages in recent times known as Madappulli, one near Madhina, a station on the Nizam's State Railway, and the other near Ellore. The ancient Maḍapalli was said to have been in the District of Nathaváḍi in the Kaliṅga country. An inscription has been found at Bezwada which records a gift to a temple by one Mahamanḍalésvara Rudradéva Rája of Madapulla in Nataváḍi, the son of Buddha Rája who was the brother-in-law of the Kakatiya king Gaṇapati. The date of the inscription is 19th April 1201. There is another inscription on a pillar at Amaravati of Bayyamamba or Kota Bayyala Mahadévi, the daughter of Mahamanḍalésvara Rudradeva Maha-

* Y. V. M., pp. 37, 47.

Rája who resided at Maḍapalliin the district of Nata-váḍi.*

From these inscriptions it appears that Maḍapaḷḷi was a seat of royalty and the petty kings ruling there were connected with the Kakatiya kings by marriage Names like Sathanapaḷḷi, Chintapaḷḷi, Móṭupaḷḷi, Kéta-paḷḷi, etc ending in paḷḷi are common in the Kaliṅga country.

Márudap-pira vika-valli supposed to be a Chóḷa Princess who came to Kírimalai on piligrimage and who was forcibly carried away by Ugra Siṅgaṉ might have been a princess of this family of petty kings who resided at Maḍapaḷḷi. Siṅgha Ketu and Tissa Ugra mentioned in the Vaipava Málai † and Madhu Kannava, Bhima Rája and Ballakkara mentioned in the Mahávaṅsa‡ appear to be names of princes perhaps of this district. Immigration of relations and dependants would have naturally followed the marriage of Márudap-pira-víka-valli with Ugra Siṅgaṉ. The Vaiyápáḍal says that Maḍapaḷḷis were immigrants and colonists. As the kings of Jaffna were Kaliṅgas, their descendants too were called Maḍapaḷḷis and given the epithet Rája or Kumára in order to distinguish them from the rest. Although the princes of Jaffna took their wives from Veḷḷáḷa families and although their daughters too were often married among the Veḷḷáḷas,¶ the Maḍapaḷḷis perhaps on account of their royal origin considered themselves higher than

* Ep. Ind., vol. v, pp. 156—159.

† Y. V. M., p. 14.

‡ Mah., chap. lix. pp. 46—49.

¶ Y. V. M., p. 47.

the Veḷḷálas. Their struggle for supremacy continued for a very long time and became so troublesome that the Portuguese and after them the Dutch Governments had to secure peace by treating them exactly alike in the matter of honours and offices. The Dutch Governor Van Rhee writing in 1697 had to exclaim, "I think it necessary to state that a bitter and irreconcilable hatred has always existed in Jaffnapatam between the caste of the Bellalas and the Madapallis so that these may not be elevated in rank and the offices of honour one above the other. For these reasons the two writers of the commander are taken from these two castes so that one of them is a Bellala and the other a Madapally."*

---

* J. C. B. R. A. S., vol. vi, p. 12.

INDEX

C

E

F

G

I

J

M

N

T

U

W

ERRATA ET CORRIGENDA.

Page 10, Notes, line 26, *for* Ahapporuḷ *read* Akapporuḷ.
„ 14, „ „ 6, „ prased „ praised.
„ 15, „ „ 1, „ artizans „ artisans.
„ 16, „ „ 16, „ Visva „ Visva : P.
„ 20, line 11, „ with artisans „ with the artisans.
„ 21, Notes, line 19, „ வருஉங் „ வருஉங்.
„ 22, „ „ 28, „ Náḻtukádai „ Váḻtukádai.
„ 23, line 12, „ Mavilaṅgai's „ Mávilaṅgai.
„ 23, line 14, *for* Cirupáuṇáṟṟupaḍai „ Ciṟupáṇáṟṟupaḍai.
„ 23, Notes, line 2, *for* I. A. „ Ind : Ant.
„ 24, line 7, *for* Cirupáṅáṟṟupaḍai „ Ciṟupáṇáṟṟupaḍai.
„ 24, Notes, line 13, *for* fresh „ flesh.
„ 24, „ „ 27, „ such, is „ such is.
„ 25, lines 1 and 3, „ Kudira „ Kudirai.
„ 25, Notes, line 13 „ அகிரா „ அதிரா.
„ 35, „ „ 7 „ நகுலம் „ (நகுலம்).
„ 35, „ „ 7 „ கீரி „ (கீரி).
„ 38, „ „ 6 „ தென்டினை „ தெண்டினா.
„ 39, line 17, „ hence the „ hence.
„ 43, „ 21, „ Ceylon king „ Ceylon kings.
„ 45, „ 11, *for* Kirindi Oya and ; others „ Kirindi Oya — and others.
„ 45, „ 13, „ Trincomalie the „ Trincomalie—the.
„ 49, Notes, line 5, *for* Sinha „ Siṅha.
„ 52, line 14, *delete* comma after the word Guzerat.
„ 55, Notes, line 1, *add* pp. 104-105.
„ 72, line 16, *for* Isnald *read* Island.
„ 76, „ 3, „ well „ wall.
„ 78, „ 8, „ therfore „ therefore.
„ 78, „ 16, „ become „ became.
„ 80, „ 6, „ controlr „ control.

Page 82, line 8, *for* Nevill *read* Neville.
" 83, " 9, " Lanká " Lańká.
" 89, " 17, *delete* the word and' at the end of the line.
" 89, " 19, *for* apes and *read* apes, aghil and.
" 92, " 17, " Báhuvi " Báhu vi
" 94, " 26, " and I the " and the,
" 100, " 8, " town " towns.
" 102, " 4, " as a Ilam " as Ilam.
" 104, " 9, " Lanká " Lańká.
" 177, " 1, " Lanká " Lańká.
" 177, " 26, " a I learned " a learned.
" 178, Notes, line 9, " a Ōymán " Ōymán.
" 247, " " 8, *add* pp. 359–360 after viii.
" 283 line 12, *substitute* † in place of * after the word Chóla.
" 283, Notes, *add* †, vide note * on page 281.
" 292, Note *, *add* 338, note †, after p.
" 293, line 3, *for* Kalinga *read* Kalińga.
" 293, Notes, line 10 *for* மாங்கலை *read* மாங்களை.
" 296, " " 14 & 16 " கங்கையாரின் " கங்கையாரியன்.
" 301, " " 1 *add* 313—325 after p.
2, *for* கலியாழி *read* கலியாலை
" 307, " " 1 *for* Samavasi *read* Sómavási.
" 311, " " 5 " Singai " Sińgai.
" 321, line 27, " Viharasat " Viháras at.
" 331, " 4, " Singai " Sińgai.
" 333, " 11, " author " The author.
" 346, " 17, " Ráméswaram " Rámésvaram.
" 349, Note, line 1. *add* ii, p : 297 after Vol :
" 360, Notes, line 27, *for* வேண்டுகே *read* வேண்டுகேம.
" 364, " " 13, *remove* bracket before தொடர்பின்மை.
" 367, line 1, *for* Vjjianagar *read* Vijaya Nagar.
" 368, " 19, " * *substitute* ¶.
" 369, " 16, " started reign *read* started to reign.
" 373, " 13, " Mahávansa " Mahávańsa.
" 382, " 13, " lirves " livres.